Distinguishing the Views and Philosophies

Distinguishing the Views and Philosophies

Illuminating Emptiness in a Twentieth-Century Tibetan Buddhist Classic

Bötrül

Translated, Annotated, and Introduced by
Douglas Samuel Duckworth

SUNY PRESS

Published by State University of New York Press, Albany

Printed in the United States of America

For information, contact State University of New York Press, Albany, NY
www.sunypress.edu

Production by Kelli W. LeRoux
Marketing by Anne M. Valentine

Library of Congress Cataloging-in-Publication Data

Mdo-snags Bstan-pa'i-ñi-ma, Bod-pa Sprul-sku, 1898–1959.
[Lta grub shan 'byed gnad kyi sgron me yi tshig don rnam bshad 'jam dbyangs dgongs rgyan. English]
Distinguishing the views and philosophies : illuminating emptiness in a twentieth-century Tibetan Buddhist classic / Bötrül ; translated by Douglas Samuel Duckworth.
p. cm.
Includes bibliographical references and index.
ISBN 978-1-4384-3437-7 (hardcover : alk. paper)
ISBN 978-1-4384-3438-4 (paperback : alk. paper)
1. Rñin-ma-pa (Sect)—Doctrines. 2. Mi-pham-rgya-mtsho, 'Jam-mgon 'Ju, 1846-1912. Nes bsad Rin po che'i sgron me. I. Duckworth, Douglas S., 1971– II. Title.

BQ7662.4.M4313 2011
294.3'420423—dc22 2010018520

10 9 8 7 6 5 4 3 2 1

Contents

Bötrül at Dzokchen Monastery

Translator's Introduction

Distinguishing the Views and Philosophies brings to light a number of significant philosophical and doctrinal issues in the Nyingma (*rnying ma*) tradition of Tibetan Buddhism. In this text, Bötrül (*bod sprul mdo sngags bstan pa'i nyi ma,* 1898–1959) lays out a systematic exposition of Mipam's (*'ju mi pham rgya mtsho,* 1846–1912) voluminous writings on the Middle Way. While addressing a number of specific issues of Buddhist philosophy and doctrine, Bötrül situates Mipam's Nyingma views amidst a plurality of positions held by competing sects in Tibet. By juxtaposing opposing traditions, Bötrül's presentation helps his readers navigate the breadth and depth of the intricate world of Buddhist Tibet.

Bötrül considered his *Distinguishing the Views and Philosophies* to be a "meaning-commentary" (*don 'grel*) on Mipam's *Beacon of Certainty.*[1] The *Beacon of Certainty* is a Tibetan classic of philosophical poetry that integrates the view of the Great Perfection (*rdzogs chen*) with the Middle Way. Like the *Beacon of Certainty, Distinguishing the Views and Philosophies* presents a distinctively Nyingma view of the Middle Way, and addresses several key points of Buddhist philosophy—spanning both Sūtra and Mantra.

Bötrül's text offers a remarkable window into the dynamics of Tibetan scholarship by providing a catalogue of a wide range of views that are held within Tibetan traditions. His approach gives a clear picture of issues at stake that otherwise tend to be obscured when only a single tradition's interpretative system is presented. Moreover, looking at different traditions side-by-side reveals the considerable differences between various schools of Buddhist thought in Tibet. Scholarship in English has just begun to uncover the depth and range of competing voices within the different sectarian traditions in Tibet. In particular, the works of José Cabezón, Georges Dreyfus, and Jeffrey Hopkins have furthered our appreciation for the extent to which views differ among Tibetan monastic traditions.[2] From the antirealist epistemological tradition of the Sakya (*sa skya*) to the "semirealist" Geluk (*dge lugs*)—and from the Middle Way of the Geluk to the "other-emptiness" of the Jonang (*jo nang*)—the gulf dividing Buddhist sects seems to be vast.

Although Bötrül highlights the differences between distinct interpretations of Buddhist doctrine, he advocates a position that he calls "nonsectarian." His model for nonsectarianism is certainly not one that compromises distinctions between the traditions. Rather, by contrasting his own views with the claims of several different traditions, he represents his Nyingma tradition within a rich constellation of diverse views. Such a "nonsectarian" work thus involves an explicit intertextuality through which the author defines his own (sectarian) identity by means of explicitly drawing upon others' texts.

We should keep in mind that the term *nonsectarian*—particularly as it applies to a scholarly movement in Tibet that stems from the nineteenth century—is multivalent. It certainly does not refer to a single system of interpretation. Also, it need not mean that all traditions are necessarily taken as equal on all levels. Rather, a general characteristic of what it means to be "nonsectarian" in Tibet is a broad-based approach to Buddhist traditions that contrasts with a more insular model of scholarship that frames the boundaries of discourse within a narrowly delineated tradition of interpretation. Thus, we can understand what came to be known as the "nonsectarian movement" as a broad set of traditions, stemming from eastern Tibet in the nineteenth century, which developed a common interest in preserving a variety of Buddhist traditions as a response to the singular dominance of the Geluk school.

Like the primary target of Mipam's polemics, most of the positions Bötrül argues against are endorsed by followers of the Geluk tradition. Even so, he describes Tsongkhapa (*tsong kha pa blo bzang grags pa,* 1357–1419), known as the founding father of the Geluk tradition, as like a second Buddha. This reveals an intricacy to his agenda that is easily overlooked in the polemical rhetoric. Bötrül also distinguishes his Nyingma tradition's claims from Gorampa (*go rams pa bsod nams seng ge,* 1429–1489) in the Sakya; the Eighth Karmapa Mikyö Dorjé (*mi bskyod rdo rje,* 1507–1554) in the Kagyü (*bka' brgyud*); and Tāranātha (*jo nang rje btsun tā ra nā tha,* 1575–1634) in the Jonang (however, he rarely mentions names). Some of the positions he argues against are also held by followers of the Nyingma tradition. Bötrül aligns himself with the Nyingma tradition of Mipam, which he traces back through Lochen Dharmaśrī (*lo chen dharmaśrī,* 1654–1717), Longchenpa (*klong *chen rab 'byams*, 1308–1364), and Rongzom (*rong zom chos kyi bzang po, ca.* eleventh century).

Bötrül contends that most monastic textbooks of other traditions offer merely a simple sketch of the claims of the Nyingma tradition, "merely the understood meanings of an old grandfather"[3] as he puts it. He cites this as part of what inspired him to write the text. He writes in his autocommentary that he initially had no intention to write a commentary on his text, due to the fact that it might appear to be "perpetuating pointless attachment and aggression."[4] He reportedly composed the root text while traveling in the summer,[5] and later wrote the autocommentary at the request of his disciples while he was on an excursion doing village rituals.[6] Both the root text and his autocommentary are translated below.

These two texts are an important source for understanding the contemporary traditions of scholarship within Tibetan monastic colleges. In his texts we can find a wide range of topics on complex points of Buddhist doctrine, which are clearly presented within a beautifully structured composition in verse and prose. Since Bötrül's root text is an independent composition, not an exegesis on a single scripture, he does not have the constraints of Tibetan commentarial prose, and is thereby free to weave together the views of many texts and traditions. He composed the texts in the period immediately prior to the devastation of Buddhist monasteries in Tibet under Chinese Communism, and thus, his works offer us a window into Buddhism in Tibet at the end of an era. His work represents a golden age of Buddhist scholarship in eastern Tibet in the first half of the twentieth century.

Bötrül's Works

Bötrül's writings should be seen in light of the development of monastic colleges in eastern Tibet in the nineteenth and early twentieth centuries. In a significant way, his texts are an extension of those of Mipam, the most influential figure in the Nyingma tradition of this era. Before Mipam, the Nyingma did not have their own authoritative corpus of commentaries on exoteric texts (i.e, sūtra). Mipam made a robust contribution to his Nyingma tradition by providing commentaries of sūtra topics (e.g., the Middle Way) based on the works of Longchenpa and Rongzom. His texts came to be used in the newly established monastic colleges across eastern Tibet.

It is significant that Bötrül wrote two commentaries on the *Abhisamayālaṃkāra*, an important treatise on the Perfection of Wisdom, given that Mipam did not write a complete commentary on this text. By providing the Nyingma tradition with its own distinctive commentary on this central treatise, Bötrül extended Mipam's project of producing distinctively Nyingma commentaries on important exoteric texts.

Bötrül's biography conveys that he wrote his *Abhisamayālaṃkāra* commentaries inspired by a vision he had in a dream when he beheld Maitreya holding two mirrors, in which he saw the words of the root text and commentary.[7] Here we are reminded that the tradition of revelation is not limited to the tantric tradition of treasure texts (*gter ma*) but is a characteristic of Mahāyāna in general.[8] Unfortunately, it appears that Bötrül's *Ornament of Maitreya's Viewpoint* is no longer extant. His other commentary on the *Abhisamayālaṃkāra*, the *Words of Maitreya*,[9] has been recently republished in his *Collected Works*.

His two commentaries on Candrakīrti's *Madhyamakāvatara*[10] are also currently unavailable, as is his *Key to the Provisional and Definitive*, a text he references in *Distinguishing the Views and Philosophies*. He additionally wrote a commentary on Āryadeva's *Catuḥśataka*[11] (another important Middle Way text for which Mipam wrote no commentary), as well as a commentary on a prayer to be born in the Buddha-field of Sukhāvatī,[12] a short commentary on Mipam's *Lion's Roar: Exposition of Buddha-Nature*[13] (entitled *Notes on the Essential Points of* [*Mipam's*] *Exposition* [*of Buddha-Nature*][14]), and other short texts, including a beautiful devotional text that is a guru yoga for Rigzin Chödrak (*rig 'dzin chos grags*, 1595–1659), a prominent figure in the Drigung (*bri gung*) Kagyü lineage.[15] These texts are included in his *Collected Works*, recently published in Sichuan.[16]

Bötrül had many students in the course of his life who were among the most influential figures in the past generation of the Nyingma tradition. His students include Khenpo Chökhyap (*chos dbyings khyab brdal*, 1920—1997), Khenpo Dazer (*lza ba'i 'od zer*, 1922–1990), Khenpo Petsé (*padma tshe dbang lhun grub*, 1931–2002), Khenpo Jikmé Püntsok (*'jigs med phun tshogs*, 1933–2004), and Tarthang Tulku (*dar thang sprul sku kun dga' dge legs*, 1935–) among several others. Khenpo Chökhyap, who was a prominent teacher in Tibet after the Cultural Revolution, studied with him for over ten years and remained in eastern Tibet. Khenpo Dazer, after fleeing for India in 1959, came to teach at the Ngagyur Nyingma Institute in India, which is the largest Nyingma monastic college in exile. He later returned to teach at the Śrī Singha monastic college at Dzokchen monastery in Tibet.[17] Khenpo Petsé, apparently the first to compose a biography of Bötrül,[18] also taught at the Śrī Singha monastic college and in India and Nepal, too.[19] Khenpo Jikmé Püntsok founded Larung Gar (*bla rung gar*) in Serta (*gser rta*), a thriving Buddhist community in eastern Tibet that is currently the largest monastic college in the world.[20] Tarthang Tulku settled in the United States,[21] and has been instrumental in publishing a number of Buddhist texts in Tibetan and English, including Tibetan editions of the root text and autocommentary of Bötrül's *Distinguishing the Views and Philosophies*.

Distinguishing the Views and Philosophies continues to be widely taught and studied in Nyingma monastic colleges across Tibet and India. In preparing my translation, I have had the fortune to consult an audio recording of a commentary on the text spoken by Bötrül's close student, Khenpo Chökhyap. Having access to Khenpo Chökhyap's commentary has given me a wonderful opportunity to delve deeply into this text, and the recording has been an invaluable source for identifying other traditions that Bötrül frequently cites, but without mentioning names. Before turning to the contents of the text, I will offer an account of Bötrül's life.

Life of Bötrül

Typical of Tibetan biographical accounts, or hagiography (*rnam thar*), the events of Bötrül's life portayed in his biography are embedded within a mythos of Buddhist culture in Tibet.[22] In a land of divine intervention—of miracles, visions, and prophecies—no events are left to mere chance. In light of this, these accounts perhaps tell us more about the context of Bötrül's life than a rigidly "historical" list of names and dates. I will now present some of the important events in Bötrül's life as they are conveyed in his biography.

Bötrül was born in Dakpo[23] in central Tibet in 1898. He was the oldest of four children and had two brothers and a sister. He was a remarkable child; there are even said to be handprints that he left in rocks while playing as a child, like impressions in the mud that can be seen today.[24]

As a boy, Bötrül studied with his father, who was a tantric practitioner, at Benchok hermitage (*ban cog ri khrod*). From his father, he learned to read, and he also received empowerments, reading transmissions, and instructions. His father told him that he should go to Domé (*mdo smad*) to study, but his father did not have provisions to provide for him, such as food or a horse. Instead, his father gave him a skull cup and told him that if he did not lose it, he would not go without food and clothing.[25]

When Bötrül was about fifteen, his father passed away, at which time auspicious signs of rainbow lights are said to have appeared in the sky. When his father was on his deathbed, he told his son that he should go to Kham (*khams*). Based on this—and the fact that from a young age, whenever he heard the name "Kham Dzokchen," he had a special feeling from the awakening of his predispositions—he felt compelled to go to Kham. He asked his mother for permission to go; however, she did not grant it. She told him that he would have to stay because she had a dream that she thought might be a bad sign: some riders (*skya mi*) had carried off a crystal stūpa that she had in her hand.[26]

Around the year 1916, he again asked his mother for permission to leave, this time for permission to go to nearby Lhasa on a pilgrimage. Instead of going to Lhasa, however, he secretly ran off to Kham with some pilgrims from there. At one point on the way to Kham, he stayed at an old woman's house. She told him not to stay long, but to go on quickly. She then gave him a big sack of dried meat to offer for teachings. When he later got to Kham, this offering for teachings turned out to be very beneficial. Later when he was staying in Drigung (*bri gung*), he thought that this old woman was probably a divine emanation.[27]

He arrived at the Śrī Singha monastic college at Dzokchen where he studied with Khenpo Tupten Nyendrak (*mkhan chen thub bstan snyan grags*) and Khenpo Genam (*rto ru mkhan po dge rnam*) beginning with the *Bodhicaryāvatāra*. In his time there studying, he did not even take tea breaks; he just drank cold water mixed with roasted barley flour for both food and drink.[28] Due to the fact that he was very young, and far away from his homeland, he could not provide provisions for his studies. He underwent incredible hardships reminiscent of the life story of Milarepa.[29] Since he had ragged clothes, some shameless monks ridiculed him. However, when they got to the Wisdom Chapter of the *Bodhicaryāvatāra*, he was the most intelligent student, and the harassment stopped.[30]

He took full ordination from Abu Lhagong (*a bu lha dgongs*) and received the name "Tupten Shedrup Tösam Gyatso" (literally, "ocean of study, contemplation, explanation, and practice of the Buddha's teachings"). For his entire life, he upheld the foundation of the Vinaya discipline, such as not eating after noon.[31] The Fifth Dzokchen Rinpoché, Tupten Chökyi Dorjé, recognized him as an incarnation of a sacred being, and henceforth, everyone called him "Bötrül" ("the incarnate lama from [central] Tibet"). He received many empowerments, reading transmissions, and instructions from Dzokchen Rinpoché—foremost of which he received was Longchenpa's compilation called *Heart Essence in Four Parts* (*snying thig ya bzhi*).[32]

He had great confidence in Mipam's tradition, and decided that it was indispensable for him to meet a teacher who upheld Mipam's own tradition.[33] Dzokchen Rinpoché told him that it would be good to go to Dzatö (*rdza stod*), where Khenpo Künpel (*kun bzang dpal ldan,* 1870/2–1943) was staying.[34] Khenpo Künpel, who taught at Gegong (*dge gong*) Monastery, was a direct disciple of both Peltrül (*dpal sprul o rgyan chos kyi dbang po,* 1808–1887) and Mipam.

Bötrül went to meet Khenpo Künpel on a very auspicious occasion. He arrived carrying a sack, and Khenpo Künpel recognized Bötrül as an incarnation of Peltrül. Previously, when Peltrül was about to die, Khenpo Künpel requested him to come back soon. He asked Peltrül how to find his reincarnation, but Peltrül replied that he was not going to have a reincarnation. He then told Khenpo Künpel that he need not look for his reincarnation, but said, "It is certain that a monk carrying a sack will arrive whom you think is me—claim him." This turned out to be Bötrül.[35]

Khenpo Künpel taught Bötrül the texts of Longchenpa, Rongzom, Peltrül, and mainly those of Mipam. When Khenpo Künpel was dying, he told Bötrül to take over the responsibility of teaching at Gegong Monastery, which Bötrül did.[36]

One day at Gegong Monastery, a strange bird perched on the roof of a house and made various sounds. The bird spoke in *ḍākinī* language—telling Bötrül that his teacher from a previous life was in Domé, and that he should go there and "eliminate superimpositions regarding the instructions." He wondered which teacher was in Domé, and then realized that Chöying Rangdröl (*chos dbyings rang grol,* 1872–1952) was teaching the Great Perfection there; so Bötrül prepared to leave for Serta in Domé.[37]

He met Chöying Rangdröl, and they compared experiences and had discussions about the Buddhist vehicles in general, and the Great Perfection in particular. There, Bötrül was able to "eliminate superimpositions regarding the quintessential instructions." Chöying Rangdröl praised Bötrül's knowledge of Mipam's tradition, and Bötrül stayed there for a few months teaching to the monastic community. He taught texts such as Mipam's *Overview: Essential Nature of Luminous Clarity*[38] and *Lion's Roar: Exposition of Buddha-Nature.* Also, it was at this time that he wrote his *Notes on the Essential Points of* [*Mipam's*] *Exposition* [*of Buddha-Nature*]. After he had accomplished the purpose of his visit, he went back to Gegong monastery. On the way back, he cried at the top of the mountain when Chöying Rangdröl's house was no longer in sight.[39]

He continued to teach at Gegong monastery, giving empowerments, reading transmissions, and instructions on the *Kālacakra* and the *Heart Essence in Four Parts,* among others. He came a few times to the hermitage at Padma, at the request of Khenpo Petsé, and also visited

Kaḥtok (*kaḥ thog*) monastery. He also visited Zhechen (*zhe chen*) monastery at the request of Zhechen Kongtrül (*zhe chen kong sprul padma dri med,* 1901–1960), and stayed at Zhechen teaching for some time.[40]

Bötrül also visited monasteries of other sectarian traditions in the direction of Sershül (*ser shul*) monastery. He discussed philosophy with many renowned scholars in other traditions such as Litang Lekden (*li thang legs ldan*). He debated with many scholars about the fine points of scripture and philosophy; in the end, it is said that he left his opponents "with nothing to say."[41]

After spending nearly thirty years in Kham, the Sixth Dzokchen Rinpoché, Jikdral Jangchup Dorjé (*'jigs bral byang chub rdo rje,* 1935–1959), told Bötrül that his mother was sick, and that her doctor wanted to see him. Dzokchen Rinpoché told him that it would be good to go back to central Tibet soon. Since Bötrül's eyes were quite bad, he had previously wanted to go back to central Tibet to seek medical attention. He had asked Khenpo Tupten Nyendrak several times for a divination about his trip, but it had not turned out well. This time he asked again for a divination, and Khenpo Tupten Nyendrak said that this divination showed it to be a good time for him to go.[42]

Around 1957, two years before the Tibetan uprising against the Chinese in Lhasa, he left for central Tibet with many monks and attendants. When he got to Drigung, Khenpo Ayang Tupten (*a yang thub bstan*), a student of the famed Khenpo Zhenga (*mkhan po gzhan dga',* 1871–1927), was teaching at the monastic college there. This Khenpo, along with the head monastic office at Drigung, requested Bötrül to stay there and teach. He declined, saying that he needed to go on to see his mother. However, it then snowed many times, making the road between Drigung and Dakpo treacherous. Seeing it as a sign that he should stay, he thought the snowfall was due to the miraculous power of Achi (*a phyi*), the Drigung protector deity.[43]

He stayed at Drigung for a little over a year teaching at the Nyima Changra (*nyi ma lcang ra*) monastic college. While there, he had a vision of Achi and composed a ritual text for propitiating her.[44] The next year, in 1958, he finally got on his horse and went to Dakpo to see his mother. When he arrived, however, his mother had already passed away. He performed the ritual offerings of the *Peaceful and Wrathful* (*zhi khro*) and gave teachings and empowerments there in his birthplace. He then returned to continue teaching at the monastic college at Drigung.[45]

He had taught at Drigung for nearly three years when the uprising occurred in central Tibet in 1959. Many Tibetan lamas, such as his student Khenpo Dazer, who had accompanied him to central Tibet from Kham, left for India during this violent time. Bötrül fled northwest, toward Nakchu (*nag chu*), and stayed near Begu (*be gu*) monastery.[46]

He died in that year, in the morning of the full-moon day of the ninth lunar month. He passed away sitting in meditative posture, as if he had no sickness. When he died, some local people saw white lights and rainbow lights in the sky, and many other miraculous signs such as the red form of a bird flying toward the west.[47]

When we consider the details of Bötrül's life, we may find ourselves struck by the fact that the philosophical rigor of such a scholar takes place in a world where rational philosophy and magic appear to coexist seamlessly. This is a striking feature of the rich culture of the Tibetans, the "civilized shamans,"[48] where a sophisticated intellectual tradition is embodied within scholars who, along with rigorous rational analyses, participate in a richly mythic dimension of reality. We can see how Bötrül's life is depicted against a backdrop of a divine landscape—a world seen to be alive and pregnant with symbolic meanings. This is not only evident in the way that others viewed him, but also in his own reflections on the events portrayed in his life story. We also find here a moving story of a man who underwent great hardships far from his homeland in order to study Buddhism. In any case, a tangible result of this remarkable individual's life is present in the texts he left behind.

Summary of Important Issues in *Distinguishing the Views and Philosophies*

The bulk of *Distinguishing the Views and Philosophies* is structured into three main sections: the ground, the path, and the fruition. The ground can be said to deal with ontology, what is; the path depicts the (apparent) process of transformation, how one becomes a Buddha; and the fruition concerns eschatology, the end result of a manifest Buddha. Or, as Bötrül states it: the ground is the unity of the two truths (relative and ultimate); the path is the unity of the two accumulations (merit and wisdom); and the fruition is the unity of the two exalted bodies (Form Bodies and Truth Body). I will briefly summarize some of the topics that he addresses in the text.

In one of the first sections of the text, Bötrül distinguishes the Mahāyāna from the Hīnayāna. He makes a distinction between the Mahāyāna and Hīnayāna by means of:

1. the view—whether or not it has perfected the twofold selflessness

2. the meditation—whether or not its method and insight are exceptional
3. the conduct—whether or not it is endowed with the six transcendent perfections, and
4. the fruition—whether or not it accomplishes the great awakening

Throughout his text, Bötrül primarily deals with distinctions in the view. In terms of the view, he distinguishes Mahāyāna from the Hīnayāna by means of the Mahāyāna realizing the view (1) clearly, (2) extensively, and (3) completely. He uses these same three elements to distinguish Sūtra and Mantra: in Mantra, luminous clarity (*'od gsal*) is shown (1) clearly, (2) extensively, and (3) completely. However, in Sūtra, it is merely shown (1) by means of a metaphor, (2) as a brief summary of the possession of Buddha-nature, and (3) as a mere luminous clarity that is the suchness of mind.

Early in the text, an important topic he discusses is valid cognition (*tshad ma, pramāṇa*), the theory of knowledge. He states that different views and philosophies developed in Tibet because of the different presentations of valid cognition. Thus, valid cognition is the key factor by which he distinguishes the different views of Buddhist sects in Tibet.

Following Mipam, he delineates four valid cognitions: two that are ultimate and two that are conventional. The two ultimate valid cognitions are respectively based on (1) the uncategorized, or nonconceptual, ultimate (*rnam grangs ma yin pa'i don dam*) and (2) the categorized, or conceptual, ultimate (*rnam grangs pa'i don dam*). The categorized ultimate is an absence, the lack of true existence; in contrast, the uncategorized ultimate is beyond the mind and so is not even a negation. These two ultimate valid cognitions are particularly important in philosophical discourses pertaining to Sūtra, and are also the primary means of distinguishing Svātantrika and Prāsaṅgika in this Nyingma tradition.

The two conventional valid cognitions are: (1) confined perception (*tshur mthong*) and (2) pure vision (*dag gzigs*). Confined perception is the domain of ordinary modes of being in the world. The domain of pure vision, on the other hand, pertains to an undistorted reality of authentic experience—the culminant experience of postmeditation. The conventional valid cognition of pure vision is particularly important in tantra, as the means to legitimate a divine reality.

In contrast to pure vision, confined perception concerns ordinary experiences of the world, those which are distorted and dualistic. While there is a degree of validity to ordinary experience, like seeing a rope in front of you as a rope and not a snake, in the end even our ordinary perceptions of a rope do not remain valid. That is, an ordinary experience of the world (for example, as a separate self interacting with an external world) is only true as long as we sustain the working assumptions of *saṃsāra*—namely, ignorance. When our ignorant perspective, our "confined perception," gives way to a divine world of pure vision, the ordinary world will no longer be ordinary or valid for us; rather, we will inhabit a world that is divine, a world that is pure. Bötrül describes the conventional valid cognition of confined perception as that which is laid out in the works of Dharmakīrti (600–660), who had articulated a sophisticated system of knowledge in his texts on valid cognition. The conventional valid cognition of pure vision, on the other hand, he says is found in such texts as the *Uttaratantra*, and in tantras such as the *Guhyagarbhatantra*.

The fourfold scheme of valid cognition adds a second tier to each of the Buddhist two truths; thus, there are two tiers of the two truths. The second tier plays an important part in his comprehensive interpretation of Buddhism—an interpretation that integrates valid cognition, the Middle Way, and tantra. Incorporating the discourse of tantra within a comprehensive theory of knowledge is an important part of his exegesis, and is a principal factor that distinguishes the Nyingma view.

We can see how this comprehensive approach to truth plays out in his interpretation of Candrakīrti (600–650), the definitive voice of Prāsaṅgika-Madhyamaka in Tibet. Bötrül points out that Candrakīrti's explicit characterization of the two truths—the ultimate as "the object of authentic seeing" and the relative as "false-seeings"[49]—is incomplete.

Table 1. Two Truths and Four Valid Cognitions

Valid Cognition	*Type*	*Domain of Observation*	*Primary Associations*
Conventional	confined perception	way things appear	Sūtra (Dharmakīrti)
	pure vision		Mantra (*Guhyagarbhatantra*)
Ultimate	uncategorized	way things are	Prāsangika (Candrakīrti)
	categorized		Svātantrika

The dotted line represents that while there is a provisional distinction between the two truths (appearance and emptiness), in fact they are a unity.

He says so because this characterization only encompasses the ordinary way that non-Buddhas understand, not the extraordinary way of the Buddha's wisdom. That is, in contrast to ordinary beings, Buddhas fully know both truths simultaneously, without separating meditative equipoise and postmeditation. For this reason, in the way Bötrül characterizes the ultimate truth, he says that the ultimate is beyond the domain of the distorted mind, but not beyond the domain of undistorted wisdom. Also, he defines the relative truth as the domain of mind in general—undivided into mind and wisdom, because both confused sentient beings and enlightened Buddhas perceive the relative truth (by mind and wisdom respectively).

Here we can see the importance of distinguishing between truth from (1) a *Buddha-centric* presentation, which emphasizes reality as known by a Buddha, and (2) a *sentient being-centric* presentation, which emphasizes reality as seen by benighted sentient beings. Bötrül wants an interpretation that accounts for both, and the two tiers of the two truths provide him with a perspectival means to do so. The integration of different perspectives on truth—the Buddha's, bodhisattvas', and sentient beings'—is a central issue that confronts all commentators who seek to articulate a unified and consistent Buddhist tradition. Significantly, the distinctive ways these perspectives are weighted is a primary factor that distinguishes the different Buddhist sects in Tibet. As such, rather than a radical disparity between traditions, as is often conveyed in the polemics of sectarian rhetoric, the distinctions between the sects in Tibet can be seen as one of *emphasis*—an emphasis on a certain perspective, or a particular aspect, of a Buddhist worldview.

In solely a sentient being-centric discourse, there is a danger of confining reality to mistaken perceptions—as inescapably caught up in a self-spun web of conceptual constructs. An appeal to a Buddha-centric presentation supplements this. However, a presentation that solely describes reality in terms of a Buddha's experience, without reference to a world as perceived by sentient beings, loses grounding in an inconceivable realm without any verifiable criteria for truth. Bötrül, following Mipam, seeks to forge a middle way between these two polarities. An important means for doing this is through a presentation of the two truths, and in this particular case, two models of the two truths. His presentation of the two truths is found in the first major section of the text: the ground.

Ground: The Unity of the Two Truths

Bötrül discusses the two truths in the section on the ground of the Middle Way, which is the longest section of the book comprising nearly one half of the entire text. The central topic of this section is a twofold delineation of the two truths into (1) the two truths as appearance/emptiness (*snang stong bden gnyis*) and (2) the two truths as authentic/inauthentic experience (*gnas snang bden gnyis*). The former scheme delineates ultimate truth in terms of the mode of reality (*gnas tshul*)—the way things are—as known by ultimate valid cognition. The latter scheme delineates ultimate truth in terms of the mode of appearance (*snang tshul*)—the way things appear—as known by conventional valid cognition. This twofold delineation of the two truths, which follows Mipam's presentation, is an important means by which Bötrül offers a unified interpretation of Buddhist doctrine.

Bötrül states that the first two-truth model (appearance/emptiness) is the one found in the middle wheel of sūtra and in Candrakīrti's *Madhyamakāvatāra*—the doctrines that treat *the explicit teaching of emptiness*. The second two-truth model (authentic/inauthentic experience) is the one found in the last wheel of sūtra and in the *Uttaratantra*—the doctrines that deal with *the explicit teaching of the appearing aspect of Buddha-nature*. The harmony between the *Madhyamakāvatāra* and the *Uttaratantra*, as noncontradictory texts, is an important theme in this section on the ground. A central issue at stake here is the relationship between emptiness and Buddha-nature.

Based upon these two models of the two truths, Bötrül argues that there are two criteria for delineating the definitive and provisional meanings. Distinguishing the category of "the definitive meaning," as opposed to "provisional meanings," is a common means for Buddhists to distinguish what is really true from what is merely *provisionally*, or *heuristically* true. According to Bötrül, emptiness alone is the ultimate according to the appearance/emptiness model of the two truths, while anything that appears is a provisional meaning. However, according to the authentic/inauthentic experience model, pure appearances—deities, maṇḍalas, etc.—of authentic experience are the ultimate and thus the definitive meaning. In this way, he says that the middle wheel (emphasizing emptiness) and the last wheel (emphasizing appearance, or clarity) are both the definitive meaning.

Bötrül cites a delineation of the definitive meaning from middle wheel sūtras, such as the *Samādhirājasūtra*, in accord with Candrakīrti's statement in his *Madhyamakāvatāra:*

> Whatever sūtras have a meaning that does not explain thusness,
> Know these to explain the relative, what is provisional.
> Know those that have the meaning of emptiness as the definitive meaning.[50]

Candrakīrti delineates the sūtras that mainly express the topic of emptiness as the definitive meaning, and sūtras that mainly express the topic of the relative truth as provisional meanings. Bötrül accepts this delineation and argues that just because appearances are provisional meanings according to this division, it does not follow that all appearances—pillars, pots, the presence of wisdom, etc.—are necessarily nonexistent conventionally.

In another delineation of the definitive meaning, he cites Buddha-nature Sūtras of the last wheel, such as the *Dhāraṇīśvararāja*. These sūtras treat the sequence of the three wheels of doctrine as a hierarchy, likened to the process of cleansing a jewel using progressively refined means. In this delineation, understanding emptiness in the middle wheel is seen as a step toward understanding the more complete representation of Buddha-nature in the last wheel. In this way, Buddha-nature is positioned as the most comprehensive disclosure of ultimate truth in sūtras.

Although he accepts sūtras of the last wheel as the definitive meaning, he makes a distinction within it. He separates the sūtras of the last wheel into those of (1) Mind-Only and (2) Middle Way. He states that the Mind-Only refers to the four Mind-Only Sūtras,[51] such as the *Saṃdhinirmocana*—the tradition of vast activity—in which the definitive meaning is accepted as:

- sūtras that teach three consummate vehicles, and
- sūtras that mainly teach the three natures in the Mind-Only tradition.

In contrast, the Middle Way in the last wheel refers to the ten Buddha-Nature Sūtras,[52] such as the *Dhāraṇīśvararāja*—the tradition of profound view—in which the definitive meaning is accepted as:

- sūtras that teach a single consummate vehicle, and
- sūtras that mainly teach Buddha-nature.

In the Middle Way Sūtras of the last wheel, Buddha-nature—the unity of appearance and emptiness—is the definitive meaning.

Bötrül cites the *Uttaratantra*, which is a commentary on the Buddha-Nature Sūtras of the last wheel, to support that ultimate truth is not only a mere emptiness:

> The basic element (*khams*) is empty of those adventitious
> [phenomena] that have the character of separability,

> But not empty of the unexcelled qualities that have the character of inseparability.[53]

He explains that the first line refers to the relative, and the second refers to the ultimate. Distorted phenomena, which are adventitious and separable from the nature of reality, are empty; they are the relative truth. The ultimate truth, however, is not empty of those qualities that are inseparable from the nature of reality.

In addition to the above stanza from the *Uttaratantra,* another source commonly cited to support the interpretation of the empty quality of Buddha-nature is found in Candrakīrti's autocommentary on the *Madhyamakāvatāra* (VI.95). In this citation, originally found in the *Laṅkāvatārasūtra,* Mahāmati asks the Buddha how Buddha-nature is different from the Self proclaimed by non-Buddhists, and the Buddha answers as follows:

> Mahāmati, my Buddha-nature teaching is not similar to the non-Buddhists' declaration of Self. Mahāmati, the Tathāgatas, Arhats, and completely perfect Buddhas teach Buddha-nature as the meaning of the words: emptiness, the authentic limit, nirvāṇa, non-arising, wishlessness, etc. For the sake of immature beings who are frightened by selflessness, they teach by means of Buddha-nature.[54]

Bötrül states that from the empty aspect, Buddha-nature is not like the Self of the non-Buddhists because it is inseparable from the great emptiness distinguished by the "three gates of liberation" (i.e., empty essence, signless cause, wishless effect). He says that from the aspect of appearance, Buddha-nature is not without qualities because it has a nature with the qualities of luminous clarity, distinguished by knowledge, love, and powers.

Thus, Buddha-nature is not like the Self of the non-Buddhists *due to its empty aspect.* The emphasis on the empty aspect of Buddha-nature reflects the ultimate in the two truths of appearance/emptiness, which Bötrül delineates as the manner that Candrakīrti posits the two truths, in accord with the middle wheel. The *unity* of the empty and appearing aspects of reality, known in authentic experience, reflects the ultimate in the two truths of authentic/inauthentic experience, which he delineates as the manner that the two truths are posited in the *Uttaratantra,* in accord with the last wheel. In this way, he integrates Candrakīrti's treatment of Buddha-nature in the *Madhyamakāvatāra* (which emphasizes the *empty* aspect) with the description from the *Uttaratantra* (which emphasizes the aspect of *appearance*).

Moreover, Bötrül regards both the *Madhyamakāvatāra* and *Uttaratantra* as expounding the view of Prāsaṅgika-Madhyamaka. He states that a unique quality of Prāsaṅgika-Madhyamaka is this noncontradiction, or unity, of (1) the empty essence and (2) the nature of clarity. This unity, described as "compassionate resonance" (*thugs rje*), reflects the characteristic triad of the Great Perfection: empty essence (*ngo bo stong pa*), natural clarity (*rang bzhin gsal ba*), and allpervasive compassionate resonance (*thugs rje kun khyab*). As with Mipam, Bötrül's interpretation of the exoteric scriptures of Sūtra is infused with the esoteric view of the Great Perfection. He also echoes the Great Perfection in his explanation of a verse from the Perfection of Wisdom Sūtras:

> The mind is devoid of mind;
> The nature of mind is luminous clarity.[55]

He states that the first line shows the empty essence and the second line shows the nature of clarity. Bötrül presents luminous clarity—the unity of appearance and emptiness—as the common subject matter of Sūtra and Mantra. In this way, his presentation of the unity of the two truths functions to synthesize Sūtra and Mantra.

Another way he shows the continuity between Sūtra and Mantra is by including both within a single integrated system. He states that the hierarchy of views in both cases of Sūtra and Mantra—in the philosophies (*grub mtha'*) and vehicles (*theg pa*)—is based on the manner of ascertaining the view, gradually or instantaneously. The higher views are distinguished from the lower views due to their being less gradual. Such an integration of Sūtra and Mantra, and attributing Mantra with a higher *view* than Sūtra, is a principal feature of Bötrül's Nyingma view.

Distinguishing the Middle Way View

Bötrül notably distinguishes his Nyingma view from (1) a view that considers the last wheel to be a provisional meaning and the Buddhanature to be a mere absence—like the mainstream Geluk presentation of Prāsaṅgika; and (2) a view of "other-emptiness" that considers Buddha-nature taught in the last wheel to be truly established, while rejecting Prāsaṅgika as inferior to the Great Middle Way—like the teachings of the Jonang school. By doing so, he makes an interpretative move similar to the one made by the fourteenth-century Sakya scholar

Gorampa in his text with a similar title, *Distinguishing the Views*.[56] In *Distinguishing the Views*, Gorampa places his own Sakya view, which he aligns with "the proponents of the freedom from extremes as the Middle Way," in contrast to the two extremes of "the proponents of eternalism as the Middle Way" of the Jonang and "the proponents of annihilationism as the Middle Way" of the Geluk.

An important way that Bötrül distinguishes the Nyingma tradition from these two traditions is through his characterization of emptiness. In Dölpopa's Jonang tradition, there is a distinction between "other-emptiness" and "self-emptiness" and a preference for "other-emptiness"—ultimate reality that is empty of relative phenomena. Ultimate reality is pure and unchanging in the Jonang tradition; it is "empty" only in the sense that it lacks all that is other—all the impure and impermanent phenomena that comprise relative reality. In contrast, the Geluk tradition following Tsongkhapa criticizes the Jonang. Proponents of the Geluk tradition consistently argue that the ultimate truth is necessarily a mere absence. According to a Geluk interpretation, emptiness is not an ultimate metaphysical presence that is above and beyond phenomenal reality; rather, emptiness means simply the *absence* of inherent existence in any particular phenomenon.

A third meaning of emptiness is articulated in the Nyingma tradition that Bötrül represents. According to Bötrül, emptiness is an inconceivable unity of appearance and emptiness. In this way, emptiness is represented in these three traditions as respectively (1) a real presence (Jonang), (2) an absence (Geluk), and (3) a nonconceptual unity (Nyingma).

Following Mipam, Bötrül expresses a unique quality of Nyingma exegesis by not taking an either/or position on either of the dichotomies of: (1) emptiness in the middle wheel versus Buddha-nature in the last wheel, and (2) Prāsaṅgika versus the "Great Middle Way" of other-emptiness. Rather, he integrates the two sides of these dichotomies into a tradition that he calls the "Great Prāsaṅgika" (*thal 'gyur chen po*). His depiction of the "Great Prāsaṅgika" and his treatment of the Prāsaṅgika-Svātantrika distinction are important topics in this section on the ground.

Distinguishing Prāsaṅgika and Svātantrika

In his characterization of Prāsaṅgika, Bötrül notably rejects Tsongkhapa's eight unique features of Prāsaṅgika[57] and distances himself from the more radical Svātantrika-Prāsaṅgika distinction that Tsongkhapa made. Bötrül depicts how Svātantrikas represent the empty nature of reality through qualifying the negation of phenomena, such that a negation of phenomenon is held to refer to its ultimate status, not its conventional existence. Indeed, he says that to negate appearances when the two truths are divided would be to overextend the object of negation (*dgag bya*), which is an extreme view of annihilationism. Nevertheless, he says that the unique Prāsaṅgika arguments negate appearances directly, without qualification. Thus, in establishing the nature of reality, Prāsaṅgikas cut straight to the empty nature of everything. In contrast, he depicts the process of coming to know reality for Svātantrikas as gradual.

Bötrül presents the main object of negation for Svātantrikas as true existence, not appearances. In this way, the Svātantrikas divide the two truths and their discourse distinguishes between the ultimately nonexistent and the conventionally existent. Also, they establish their claims of conventional existence and ultimate nonexistence through autonomous arguments (*rang rgyud kyi sbyor ba, svatantraprayoga*). Whereas the object of negation for a Svātantrika is merely true existence, the object of negation for a Prāsaṅgika is *any conceptual reference*. Consequently, the Prāsaṅgika's object of negation (i.e., all extremes) is more comprehensive than the Svātantrika's primary object of negation (i.e., extreme of existence).

While Svātantrikas separate the two truths, the two truths are not separated in the discourse that defines the Prāsaṅgikas. The unique discourse of Prāsaṅgikas—which emphasizes the way things are in meditative equipoise—has no claims and uses consequences to negate wrong views. The difference between Svātantrika and Prāsaṅgika, however, is not simply in logical form (i.e., autonomous arguments vs. consequences) but involves an emphasis on a distinctive view.

Moreover, what is established (*bsgrub bya*) for the Svātantrikas is the categorized ultimate, an absence of true existence, whereas what is established for the Prāsaṅgikas is the uncategorized ultimate. Bötrül's statements that Prāsaṅgikas have something to establish contrast with other prominent figures in his tradition, who distinguish Prāsaṅgika by stating that the Prāsaṅgikas only negate, but do not *establish* a freedom from constructs.[58] In any case, Bötrül states that there is no *referent object* established for the Prāsaṅgikas.

Bötrül not only distinguishes Prāsaṅgika in terms of ultimate emptiness, but also in terms of relative appearance. He makes a distinction between the way the relative truth is asserted in the traditions of (1) Mind-Only, (2) Yogācāra-Madhyamaka (Śāntarakṣita), and (3) Prāsaṅgika-Madhyamaka. He says that appearances are held to be mind in the Mind-Only tradition, and that the mind is conceived as truly established. In Yogācāra-Madhyamaka, the conventional mode of reality (*tha snyad gnas tshul*) is mind, but that mind is not held to be ultimately real. In Prāsaṅgika, the appearances of relative truth are "merely self-appearance" (*rang snang tsam*).

There is no reality *behind* conventional appearances to ground reality in the Prāsaṅgika tradition. In contrast to the way that conventional reality is presented in the Mind-Only and Yogācāra-Madhyamaka traditions, "merely self-appearance" seems to be the concise and comprehensive delineation of conventional truth in the context of what is a *uniquely* Prāsaṅgika account of conventional reality. We are not given an elaborate discussion of conventional truth beyond this—perhaps necessarily so—because when we engage in discourses that theorize about reality, we are no longer in the domain of Prāsaṅgika as it is defined: namely, within the domain of discourse that accords with the uncategorized ultimate, the "content" of nonconceptual meditative equipoise. Nevertheless, he explains that Prāsaṅgikas do make a distinction between what is correct and mistaken from merely a conventional perspective, and that self-appearance is constituted by mind. Yet significantly for Bötrül's Nyingma tradition, the unique arguments of Prāsaṅgika function to undermine the substantialist and discursive presumptions that system-building discourses such as Yogācāra involve.

Bötrül further argues against substantialist explanations of causality in the Prāsaṅgika tradition such as the "entity of disintegration" (*zhig pa dngos po*) set forth by Tsongkhapa among his eight distinguishing features of Prāsaṅgika. In contrast, Bötrül argues that the causality of dependently-arisen appearances *just is*; it cannot be conceived. The law of karma cannot be fully known, except by a Buddha.

Valid Cognition

As we saw above, valid cognition and the Middle Way are brought together within the two tiers of the two truths: the two ultimate and two conventional valid cognitions. The categories of valid cognition also come into play within Bötrül's threefold presentation of appearance and emptiness. He respectively delineates three types of appearance and emptiness and shows how each is validly known. Drawing from valid cognition's dichotomy of nonconceptual perception and conceptual inference—and supplementing what is unknowable (by ordinary means) as a third—he delineates three types of appearances:

- appearances that are manifest, which are known through valid cognitions of sense-faculty direct perceptions,

- appearances that are hidden objects, which are known by inference, and
- appearances that are extremely hidden, such as the causal processes of karma, which are known through valid testimony (e.g., scripture).

He makes a parallel division regarding emptiness, making a threefold distinction in terms of emptiness and delineating how each is respectively known:

- emptiness that is manifest, which is known in meditative equipoise through a Sublime One's yogic direct perception,
- emptiness that is hidden, which is known by the valid cognition that examines the categorized ultimate, and
- emptiness that is extremely hidden, which is known by the valid cognition that examines the uncategorized ultimate.

These three emptinesses can be seen to respectively correspond to other-emptiness (the Jonang), emptiness of true existence (the Geluk), and self-emptiness (the Great Prāsaṅgika of Nyingma).

Moreover, these three interpretations of emptiness are reflected in Bötrül's delineation of three types of Middle Way traditions based on how the object of negation is identified: (1) other-emptiness (Jonang/Yogācāra), (2) emptiness of true existence (Geluk/Svātantrika), and (3) self-emptiness (Nyingma/Prāsaṅgika). He states that the primary object of negation in "other-emptiness" is inauthentic experience, the primary object of negation for the Svātantrika is true existence, and the primary object of negation in "self-emptiness" (Prāsaṅgika) is any conceptual reference. Accordingly, he says that the two truths can be said to be (1) "different in the sense of negating that they are one," in the context of other-emptiness[59]; (2) "the same with different contradistinctions," in the contexts of Svātantrika discourse; and (3) "neither one nor many," in Prāsaṅgika discourse. In this way, he outlines three different approaches to emptiness in the Middle Way.

Reflections on the Ground

Despite the differences on the surface between these three traditions' discourses on emptiness, it would be a mistake to accept their often polemical rhetoric at face value. In fact, we find a lot in common within their interpretations. Aside from a varied degree of emphasis upon certain aspects of a Buddhist worldview, we do not necessarily find a substantial difference between the Jonang, Geluk, and Nyingma interpretations of emptiness. We can see this when we look beyond the language of self-emptiness and other-emptiness to see that all three traditions accept a fundamental appearance/reality distinction—the Buddhist doctrine of two truths—whereby it is held that (1) phenomena do not exist in the way they appear to an ordinary being, (in which case appearances do not accord with reality,) and (2) appearance and reality accord without conflict in the undistorted perception of a Buddha.

Also, all three traditions accept that: (1) the undistorted perception of ultimate truth is not the distorted appearance of relative truth (other-emptiness), (2) relative phenomena are not found when their ultimate nature is analyzed (emptiness of true existence), and (3) emptiness in essence is inexpressible (the uncategorized ultimate of Prāsaṅgika). Furthermore, in none of these traditions is emptiness the utter negation of everything—it is not utter nihilism because some type of *presence* remains. The nature and content of what remains may be where the more significant distinctions are found among these traditions, but such a discussion here would be a digression. The important point here is that while there are clearly distinctions among the views of these traditions to be acknowledged (and thus a distinctive Nyingma view to be sustained), at the same time, Bötrül configures the views of these different traditions in an ecumenical way, such that each has a legitimate place as an authentic representation of Buddhist truth. This is the key to the "non-sectarian" identity of this sectarian text.

Before moving on to the second main section of the text, the path, I should mention one more issue that Bötrül presents in the middle of this section on the two truths. In between his discussion of the ultimate and the relative truths, he presents an appended discussion of the legitimacy of the Nyingma tradition. He first addresses the Nyingma tradition as a legitimate path of liberation. Then he defends the legitimacy of the Nyingma tradition's vows of individual liberation. The fact that he places this appended defense of the Nyingma in between his discussion of the two truths is telling: it suggests that the Nyingma is the "middle way" between (1) those in the early generation (and the Jonang), who prioritize the ultimate truth and (2) those in the later generation (the Geluk), who prioritize the relative truth.[60] With this defense, we are reminded that one of Bötrül's central concerns is to show the authenticity of the Nyingma tradition.

Path: The Unity of the Two Accumulations

Presentations of the path play an important role in sustaining the narrative structure of a Buddhist worldview. The principal feature of Bötrül's structure of the path is a narrative of discovery—a path that is the discovery of the unity of the ground and the fruition of Buddhahood. While the preceding section on the ground depicts the integration of the two truths, the section on the path deals with an integration of the two accumulations, merit and wisdom. Also, while the section on the ground primarily relies on the *Madhyamakāvatāra* and the *Uttaratantra* as the primary textual sources, this section additionally draws from the *Abhisamayālaṃkāra*. Following Mipam, Bötrül seeks to integrate the disparate presentations of the path as laid out in various ways in different Buddhist *śāstras*.

His section on the path is comprised within two main headings: "abandonment" and "realization." In the first section, he discusses what is abandoned, which corresponds to the truth of cessation. He also explains at what stage on the path the various obscurations are abandoned. In the next section, he discusses the antidote, the truth of the path that brings forth realization.

What is abandoned is twofold: the afflictive obscurations (*nyon sgrib*) and cognitive obscurations (*shes sgrib*). He delineates these two obscurations in terms of cause, essence, and function:

- The cause of the afflictive obscurations is the apprehension of a self of persons; the cause of the cognitive obscurations is the apprehension of a self of phenomena.
- The essence of afflictive obscurations is the afflictive emotions—such as miserliness, anger, and desire; the essence of cognitive obscurations is the "concepts of the three spheres" (agent, object, action).
- The function of afflictive obscurations is to obstruct liberation; the function of cognitive obscurations is to obstruct omniscience.

In his discussion of cognitive obscurations, Bötrül delineates three types of conceptuality: (1) concepts of true existence, (2) concepts of reified signs, or objectification, and (3) concepts that are mere dualistic appearances. Each one is progressively more subtle: he states that the first is manifest for ordinary beings, the second is manifest in the postmeditations of bodhisattvas on the "impure grounds" (grounds

1–7), and the third is sometimes manifest for bodhisattvas on the "pure grounds" (grounds 8–10). He also mentions five types of "nonconceptuality" from the *Dharmadharmatāvibhāga*, which are distinguished from the genuine nonconceptuality of nonconceptual wisdom:

> [Nonconceptual wisdom] has the character of being free from the five types: (1) mental non-engagement, (2) complete transcendence, (3) quietism, (4) essential meaning, and (5) premeditated signs.[61]

In contrast to these five, nonconceptual wisdom realizes the uncategorized ultimate. It is significant that Bötrül argues that the uncategorized ultimate is a uniquely Mahāyāna realization. He says that the realization that the Mahāyāna shares with the Hīnayāna is merely that of the categorized ultimate. In this way, he shows a distinction between (1) the Hīnayāna realization of the Auditors and Self-Realized Ones and (2) the Mahāyāna realization of the bodhisattvas. By doing so, he directly opposes another one of Tsongkhapa's eight distinguishing features of Prāsaṅgika—namely, that Auditors and Self-Realized Ones realize the selflessness of phenomena (to the extent that bodhisattvas do).

We saw above how Bötrül associates Prāsaṅgika discourse with the uncategorized ultimate, the content of meditative equipoise. In this section of the path, he not only describes meditative equipoise in terms of the object (the uncategorized ultimate), but also in terms of the subject (wisdom). For his Nyingma tradition, this distinction between the subjectivity of conceptual consciousness and nonconceptual wisdom is paramount.

In contrast to an apprehension by consciousness, he states that there is no representational mode of apprehension (*rnam pa'i 'dzin sdangs*) at the time of wisdom's meditative equipoise—during which there is no conceptual apprehension, not even the apprehension of an object's lack of intrinsic existence. Thus, actual meditative equipoise is completely nonconceptual. Also, he explains that meditative equipoise is always without appearance; consequently, if there is an appearance, it is necessarily postmeditation. In this way, meditiative equipoise is the accumulation of wisdom without appearance; whereas merit, which is with appearance, is to be accumulated in postmeditation. Thereby, the path is the unity of the two accumulations of merit and wisdom.

Near the end of his lengthy explanation of various details of the path, he makes a distinction between two types of purity: (1) naturally abiding purity (*rang bzhin rnam dag*) and (2) purity that is freed from the adventitious defilements (*glo bur bral dag*). Naturally abiding purity is the innate nature of a Buddha within the minds of all sentient beings. This is the principal element in his presentation of the path as a narrative of discovery. From the aspect of this naturally abiding purity, there is no difference between sentient beings and Buddhas. However, there is a difference in the second purity. The purity that is freed from the adventitious defilements is the purity that is exclusive to Buddhas. Such purity is actualized only when all of the cognitive and afflictive obscurations have been completely abandoned.

Fruition: The Unity of the Two Exalted Bodies

In the section on fruition, Bötrül presents the unity of the two exalted bodies—the Truth Body and the Form Bodies. A key point to this section is the distinction between two types of fruition: (1) a freed effect (*bral 'bras*) and (2) a ripened effect (*rnam smin 'bras*). A freed effect is the result of removing something that was obscuring what was already there, like the sun freed from clouds. Such an effect is due to the naturally abiding purity. A ripened effect is a transformation, like a seed transforming into a sprout.

He states that transformation of a sentient being into a Buddha is merely apparent, according to the mode of appearance. In the reality of the way things are, there is no distinction between a Buddha and a sentient being. Consequently, in the way that things appear, a being is newly transformed into a Buddha; yet in the way that things really are, beings discover the Buddha that has *always already* been their nature from the beginning. In concluding this section on the fruition, Bötrül describes the "three mysteries" of a Buddha—the exalted body, speech, and mind—in a final delineation of the way Buddhas appear to sentient beings and the way they are in a Buddha's own perception.

Note on the Translation

The verses of Bötrül's original composition are offered in the first section as a stand-alone translation, followed by the verses interspersed with his autocommentary that he later wrote. The verses are terse and difficult to penetrate without his commentary, but since this text was originally a stand-alone composition, there is a beauty and integrity to it that tends to get lost when it is only read along with the commentary. Yet the commentary is indispensible to fully probe the layers of meaning and structure of the "root text," so I advise the reader to begin by reading the verses with the commentary (where you will also find my annotations), and later return to the following section and read the verses alone. In any case, feel free to flip back and forth between these forms of text, as I have done many times. I have consulted five editions of the Tibetan texts: a manuscript published by Mewa Khenpo Tupten (*rme ba mkhan po thub bstan*, 1928–2000), who was one of Bötrül's students; another edition published in Sichuan, China;[62] the edition published in his Collected Works;[63] and two editions published by Tarthang Tulku.[64]

My interpretation of this text is due in no small measure to Khenpo Kātyāyana, who taught me the entire text at the Ngagyur Nyingma Institute in the summer of 2004. The audio recording of Khenpo Chökhyap's oral commentary has also been an invaluable reference. In addition to identifying the targets of Bötrül's critiques, it has helped me more fully appreciate the lively flavor of this text. One of Khenpo Chökhyap's students, Khenpo Champa Lodrö, also helped me to appreciate several key points of this text. I also wish to thank him for giving me a photograph of his teacher and Bötrül's student, Khenpo Chökhyap, to print in this book. Another of Khenpo Chökhyap's students, Khenpo Tsülnam at the Sherapling monastic college in Bir, India, was most helpful in answering many of the questions I had after I had completed the initial draft of the translation in the summer of 2005. I wish to thank Khenpo Könchok Mönlam, too, for giving me a picture of Bötrül to print in this book, a photograph that he got from his teacher and Bötrül's student, Mewa Khenpo Tupten. I also owe a special thanks to Khenpo Tsültrim Lodrö, who answered several of my questions at Larung Gar in Serta. Several other Tibetan scholars have assisted me in interpreting this text, too many to mention by name. Others who gave me valuable feedback were Ryan Conlon, Cortland Dahl, Eric Lochner, Derek Maher, Michele Martin, Arthur McKeown, Krim Natirbov, Charlie Orzech, Gillian Parrish, Nathaniel Rich, Jann Ronis, Raul Schiappa-Pietra, and Gail Stenstad. This translation is dedicated to all my teachers, and to anyone who is navigating a middle way between a narrow-minded absolutism and spineless relativism. It is my sincere wish that this translation serve to sharpen our swords of insight in a blaze that brings both clarity and warmth, not fan the destructive flames of sectarian animosity.

Bötrül's student, Khenpo Chökhyap

Verses of *Distinguishing the Views and Philosophies*

A Lamp of Essential Points

namo mañjuśrīye! Homage to Mañjuśrī!

The doctrine of the ground, path, and fruition that unites Sūtra and Mantra
Is the greatly miraculous view and conduct of indivisible appearance and emptiness.
All the Buddha's Word and commentaries on the viewpoint, common and extraordinary,
Are taught through three valid measures (tshad ma)—may the assembly of Sublime Ones be victorious!

The explanation and practice of the Victorious One's teaching are the great maṇḍala of the sun and moon;
[Through] the generation of the miraculous intent, when the time was ripe
The chariot was drawn further and further north.
It became the splendor of beings of the Cool Land.

The earlier and later masterly scholars of the Land of Snow
Explained the distinctive traditions separately without mixing them.
Due to this, the four views and philosophies of Sakya, Geluk, Kagyü, and Nyingma
Are widely renowned as "the four transmissions of the teaching."

The source of the river of all the Victorious One's teachings in the Land of Snow
Is the school of early translations, endowed with the six qualities of greatness.

The profound essential points of its view, meditation, and conduct
Are much superior to the various philosophies of others.

One who knows well, without mixing, the delineations of philosophies of
The respective schools of Sakya, Geluk, Kagyü, and Nyingma, and
Is skilled at properly upholding one's own unique tradition,
Is certainly a being who upholds the teachings of the Victorious One.

Therefore, if you want to uphold the illustrious tradition of the early translations,
You should maintain all the profound key points of its view, meditation, and conduct—
Completely upholding the meaning of the profound essential points—
Without mixing in the slightest word of the various ordinary philosophies.

Alas! Due to various attitudes of these days,
Other than duḥkha (suffering) that is the strife of mutual attachment and aggression,
Repetition of various hearsays, and discourse on pleasant-sounding words,
It is rare that there is one who properly speaks the profound essential points of the views and philosophies.

Discernment is knowing how to distinguish the essential points concerning what is and is not doctrine,
Knowing the divisions between one's own and others' philosophies, and
Knowing elegant discourses from inferior discourses.
It is what scholars have, not hordes of fools!

Due to this, having completely given up the attitudes of attachment and aggression,
I will briefly expound upon a distinguishing lamp that completely illuminates
The mere mode of reality of the distinctive views and philosophies of the old and new schools—
Their unmixed appearing forms in accordance with their respective traditions.

The distinctive ways of assertion by the earlier and later masterly scholars
From the Land of Snow go beyond what can be expressed;
Concerning solely the distinction between Buddhists and non-Buddhists,
There are discordant ways of dividing them.

According to the way of assertion by the matchless Atīśa
Most of the masterly scholars of the new schools of translation
Make the distinction between Buddhists and non-Buddhists in terms of refuge—
By merely that, it is solely a division based upon the support.

According to the intended meaning of the scriptures of sūtra and tantra,
The school of early translations asserts immense distinctions—
Distinctions in terms of the support, view,
Meditation, conduct, and fruition.

Others make the distinction between the Mahāyāna and Hīnayāna
By only the generation of the mind [of awakening];
This is just a division of intention.
There is a vast difference in view, meditation, conduct, and fruition.

Some people claim that the views and philosophies of the two
Higher and lower vehicles are contradictory.
Also, others variously claim that while there is no distinction in view,
There are distinctions in the conduct and the fruition.

Our tradition, that of the scholars of the school of early translations,
Asserts immense distinctions between the higher and lower, and
Asserts the views and philosophies of the progression of vehicles
In the manner of the gradual and instantaneous.

Therefore, the four philosophies
Are in accord in accepting the seals that symbolize the Word;
However, in terms of the manner of (1) clarity, (2) extensiveness, and (3) completeness,
There is a great difference between the higher and lower.

Other people say: "Other than a distinction in method for Sūtra and Mantra,
There is no distinction in view."
Other than a view of a mere void selflessness,
There is no appearing aspect, no luminous clarity; therefore, it is faulty.

In our tradition, as for the manner of the vehicles of Sūtra and Mantra,
Although there is no distinction from the aspect of emptiness, the expanse of phenomena,

From the aspect of appearance, the spontaneous presence of luminous clarity,
The distinction in views is like the earth and space.

There is a vast distinction of clarity, extensiveness, and completion in the two:
(1) The luminous clarity of the Causal Vehicle,
The nature of mind which is Buddha-nature, and
(2) The spontaneously present luminous clarity of Mantra.

In short, the four philosophies of the Causal Vehicle
Have the profound distinction of the manner of completing the absence of self;
The four tantra sets of Secret Mantra
Have the profound distinction of the view of spontaneous presence.

The main point of this, the consummate meaning,
Is the way of perfecting, gradually or instantaneously,
The supreme view of the noncontradiction of appearance and emptiness—
The meaning of the great unity free from extremes.

Whoever holds appearance and emptiness with an influx of contradictions, and
Asserts emptiness as an emptiness of true existence—a mere nonentity—
Has difficulty explaining the divisions between the views
Of sūtra and tantra.

Other presentations of the provisional and definitive
In the three wheels that express
Claim that the first [wheel] is the provisional meaning, the middle [wheel] is the definitive meaning, and
The last [wheel] is exclusively the provisional meaning.

They accept the extreme that a provisional meaning topic
Is necessarily nonexistent conventionally.
Through this, the profound meanings of sūtra and tantra,
Such as the Buddha-nature, are said to not exist at all.

Some people say:"The first wheel
And the middle wheel are only provisional meanings.
The definitive meaning is exclusively the last [wheel];
Its topic is what is truly established."

Through two valid cognitions,
Based on two ways of dividing the two truths, which is the expressed,
In the three wheels of sūtras, which is the evaluated,
Our tradition asserts two manners of the provisional/definitive in this way.

The supreme object found by the valid cognition of ultimate analysis
From the two truths of appearance/emptiness,
Ultimate emptiness—which is the explicit teaching of the middle wheel—
Is asserted as the definitive meaning; and,

The supreme object found by the valid cognition of purity
From the two truths of authentic/inauthentic experience,
Ultimate luminous clarity—which is the explicit teaching of the last wheel—
Is asserted as the definitive meaning.

From the distinction of what is expressed being appearance or emptiness,
There are the manners of dividing the provisional and the definitive;
Due to distinct manners of division,
The definitive meaning middle and last wheels are asserted as noncontradictory.

In this way, the tradition of scholars in the school of early translations
Has distinctive ways of dividing the provisional and the definitive;
For the profound meaning intended by the sūtras and śāstras,
See my Key to the Provisional and Definitive.

Other presentations of śāstras
Claim that the explicit teaching of the Uttaratantra *is a provisional meaning.*
They accord with the assertion that the heritage is a mere emptiness
Relinquished of luminous clarity, the aspect of appearance.

Our tradition accepts the Uttaratantra
As the unexcelled definitive meaning—
A commentary on the viewpoint of the profound meaning of the [Buddha-]Nature Sūtras that
Emphasizes the supreme luminous clarity, the aspect of appearance, which is the intended meaning of the Great Prāsaṅgika.

Others explain the Abhisamayālaṃkāra *scripture*
As definitively a Svātantrika scripture.

The main reason is the fear that the eight [unique] assertions [of Prāsaṅgika]
Would [otherwise] collapse.

As for our tradition, the school of early translations, lord Mipam
Widely established [the Abhisamayālaṃkāra*] as just a source scripture of the Prāsaṅgika and Svātantrika*
With reasoned implications by the power of fact
In "the Rejoinders," etc.

These days, although people claim to be Nyingma,
They just repeat after others, without reason.
Our tradition, the tradition of the scholars of the early generation,
Is written in the Ornament of Maitreya's Viewpoint.

Others say that the scriptures of the Svātantrika-Madhyamaka
Conflict with the Great Prāsaṅgika.
Our tradition, [that of] the lord of doctrine, Mipam,
Accepts [Svātantrika] as a step toward the Great Prāsaṅgika.

Others explain the presentations of going for refuge in the three jewels differently—
Such as the classifications of the defining character, illustration,
Causal and resultant refuge, and
Temporary and consummate [refuge].

The translators and scholars of our tradition, the school of early translations,
Accept the classifications of the essence of refuge, which is the three jewels, and
Their illustrations and so on,
In accord with the scriptures of the Word and commentaries on their viewpoint.

The defining character of the Mahāyāna generation of the mind [of awakening] is also
Variously presented by others.
Our tradition explains in accord with the scriptural meaning
That is the viewpoint of the great chariots.

[Others] explain its illustrations as separate [and]
The viewpoints of the chariots as contradictory.

Our tradition, that of the great omniscient one [Longchenpa],
Accepts [their] noncontradiction as a single essential point.

Some claim that the generation of the mind
For mediocre and sharp faculties is bogus—mere words.
Our tradition accepts the Mahāyāna generation of the mind
For all three [faculties] to be genuine.

The assertions of our tradition, the scholars of the school of early translations,
Such as the classifications of the generation of mind in this way,
Are elucidated as such in the meaning-commentary of the Perfection of Wisdom—
See the Ornament of Maitreya's Viewpoint.

The two evaluating valid cognitions
Ascertain the evaluated objects, the two truths.
Due to this, there are the divisions of philosophies,
Views, meditations, actions, and fruitions.

There are different traditions, earlier and later,
Concerning the presentations of the evaluating valid cognitions.
Due to this, there are the distinctive discordant assertions
Of views and philosophies.

The later generation of scholars
Widely proclaims with one voice
Two valid cognitions, the ultimate and the conventional,
Which are the valid cognitions that analyze the two truths.

However, other than only the categorized ultimate
And the conventional of confined perception,
The valid cognition that analyzes the uncategorized [ultimate]
And [the conventional valid cognition of] pure vision are not explained.

They speak of the reasoned manner of valid cognition that analyzes the ultimate
In accord with the valid cognition of confined perception; [however,]
Other than its ultimate that is a nonentity,
It cannot establish what is profound, peaceful, and free from constructs.

The valid cognition that analyzes the conventional, too
Is none other than just a confined perception; therefore,
Other than the mere impure relative,
It cannot establish the pure relative.

The masterly scholars of the early generation
Accept two ultimate valid cognitions and
Two conventional valid cognitions
As reasonings that analyze the two truths.

The two ultimate valid cognitions are:
Those that analyze the categorized and the uncategorized.
The two conventional valid cognitions are:
The valid cognitions of confined perception and purity.

The lord Mipam elucidated these delineations
In accord with the quintessential instructions of the school of early translations
And the intended meaning of sūtras, tantras, and śāstras,
In the elegant discourse, Sword of Insight.

The categorized valid cognition analyzing the ultimate
Establishes the temporary categorized ultimate;
The valid cognition that analyzes the uncategorized
Establishes the consummate uncategorized.

The conventional valid cognition of confined perception
Establishes the mode of appearance—the impure relative;
The conventional valid cognition of purity
Establishes the mode of reality—the pure relative.

The valid cognition of ultimate analysis
Establishes all phenomena as lacking true existence, the great emptiness;
The conventional valid cognition
Separately discerns pure and impure appearances.

In this way, this thoroughly complete valid cognition—
At once evaluating the profound and vast intended meanings
Of the sūtras, tantras, and śāstras—
Is a distinctive quality of the early generation of scholars.

This is a stanza at the interlude between sections.

For the moment, I will forgo a presentation
Of the four views and philosophies of Buddhists
From the manners of perfecting the two truths, the evaluated objects,
In the traditions of earlier and later masterly scholars of the Land of Snow.

Here, I will briefly explain
The essential points of the views and philosophies of the ground, path, and fruition of
The supreme vehicle, the Great Middle Way,
In the distinctive traditions of the earlier and later masterly scholars of the Land of Snow.

Others explain the Middle Way as something in between
That is free from the two extremes.
For each of the ground, path, and fruition,
They make assertions that are not the Middle Way.

Their assertions fall apart through question and debate:
Such a Middle Way is which of the two truths?
In which sublime path is it cultivated—in meditative equipoise or in postmeditation?
At the consummate fruition, which of the two exalted bodies is it?

Our tradition accepts the abiding reality free from all extremes
As the Middle Way of the ground.
Through this, the path and fruition also
Are designated as the Middle Way.

In the scriptural tradition of the supreme vehicle, the Middle Way,
There are discordant ways of explaining
The two truths of appearance and emptiness, the evaluated objects,
From among the three: ground, path, and fruition.

Concerning the way of dividing the two truths in general,
Scholars accept two delineations of the two truths:
(1) The two truths of appearance/emptiness and
(2) The two truths of authentic/inauthentic experience.

These days, other than the two truths of appearance/emptiness
It is rare that the two truths of authentic/inauthentic experience is known.

Due to this, the profound intended meanings
Of the definitive meaning sūtras and tantras are cast far away.

By means of ultimate valid cognition analyzing the mode of reality,
Through the evaluated object being authentic or not
There is the twofold division of
Emptiness as the ultimate truth and appearance as the relative truth.

This manner is the unexcelled way
Of dividing the two truths in the scriptural tradition of
The definitive meaning sūtras of the middle wheel, tantras,
And Candrakīrti's meaning-commentary.

By means of the valid cognition of purity [evaluating] the mode of appearance
Through the evaluated object being authentic or not
There is the division of the ultimate as authentic experience
And the relative as inauthentic experience.

This manner is the unexcelled way
Of dividing the two truths in the scriptures of
The definitive meaning sūtras of the last wheel, tantras,
And the Mahāyāna-Uttaratantra.

Regarding this, the Svātantrika-Madhyamaka
Accepts the two truths of appearance/emptiness;
In the Prāsaṅgika texts, both delineations
Of the two truths are accepted without contradiction.

Therefore, both Candrakīrti's scriptures and
The Uttaratantra *scripture of the supreme regent [Maitreya]*
Are within one essential point, without contradiction,
Prāsaṅgika Mahāyāna scriptures.

Herein, the heritage of the basic element, Buddha-nature, etc.,
Is the supreme ultimate truth of authentic experience; however,
It has both the truths of appearance and emptiness
Through the way of dividing as appearance/emptiness.

Some people apply the two delineations of the two truths
To the Prāsaṅgika-Madhyamaka and Svātantrika-Madhyamaka separately.

They have difficulty realizing the noncontradictory intended meaning
Of either the middle or the last wheel.

Therefore, know the noncontradiction of both
Delineations of the two truths—
The meaning taught in the definitive meaning sūtras and śāstras
Of the Great Middle Way.

Thus, from among the two delineations of
Ways of dividing the two truths,
Here is what some people say is
The defining character of the two truths of appearance/emptiness:

"An object found by a valid cognition that analyzes
The conventional false seeings, and
An object found by a valid cognition that analyzes
The consummate authentic seeing."

Still, what is said to be Candrakīrti's tradition
Is a claim of a faulty defining character;
An appropriate analogy is a crow that ate filth, and
Wiped its beak on a clean place.

Others state as the defining character of the two truths:
"The apprehended object
Of authentic seeing's mode of apprehension, and
The apprehended object of false seeing's mode of apprehension."

They still claim that this is the intended meaning
Of Candrakīrti's scriptural tradition.
Here too there are the general faults of
No pervasion, over-pervasion, and impossibility.

Our tradition asserts the respective defining characters of the two truths as follows:
"The defining characters of the ultimate and relative are (1) the object of wisdom beyond mind in meditative equipoise—what is; and
(2) The object of conventional mind's seeing—whatever there is."

This way is the intended meaning of the definitive meaning sūtras
And the two magnificent masters;

The meanings shown through both inclusion and exclusion
Are the faultless defining characters.

Concerning the delineation of the illustrations, [some people claim,]
"Although from the perspective of an elderly person,
There is the correct and mistaken relative,
From [a Prāsaṅgika's] own perspective, other than the mistaken relative,
There is no correct relative."

Without differentiating the two truths,
They claim all sorts of conceptual fabrications.
In the glorious Candrakīrti from the Noble Land,
What delusion is posited, inside or out?

Yet [they] hold on, saying, "There is a common locus of
Deluded cognition and valid cognition."
A valid cognition like this—which is deluded omniscience—
Is quite amazing!

Our tradition accepts that from the perspective of the valid cognition of ultimate analysis,
There are no divisions of correct and mistaken phenomena; and
In the perspective of the conventional, relative truth,
The correct and mistaken are divided separately.

From the perspective of ultimate analysis,
All phenomena are certainly illusory, deluded perceptions.
However, by merely this, from the perspective of conventional truth
They are not delusions of the mistaken relative.

Although all phenomena are seen as an illusion
By the glorious Candrakīrti of the Noble Land,
From the perspective of his perception,
Conventionally, the color of the conch and moon

Perceived as white is the vision of the correct relative.
Turning away [this],
It is impossible [for him] to have a mistaken cognition, [such as]
Perceiving the conch and moon as yellow.

From the perspective of the mere illusion of the relative,
The world in postmeditation, Candrakīrti divides

The relative into two, correct and mistaken,
Through self-appearance being deluded or non-deluded.

There is no appearance left over
That is not negated by the valid cognition of ultimate analysis.
Due to that, there is no consequent fault
That the conventional is established by its own character.

Without understanding the critical points such as these, which are difficult to realize,
There are claims such as: "The conventional is stated following after the elderly people of the world," and
"Self-appearance is only the mistaken relative," and
"There is a common locus of deluded cognition and valid cognition."

This is a stanza at the interlude between sections.

[Some people say,] "There are four ultimates,
Subjective and objective,
Through the division of implicative and non-implicative negations, which are
The nominal and actual ultimates."

There is fault because this way lacks the freedom from constructs that is
Superior to the emptiness that is a non-implicative negation;
Other than being the categorized, such a non-implicative negation
Is not even a fraction of the uncategorized.

Our tradition asserts that the categorized [ultimate] is
An emptiness that is a negation of constructed extremes only partially, and that
The uncategorized ultimate is
Free from all subtle and gross constructed extremes.

Some people say, "The two truths are contradictory."
Still they say, "They are essentially the same identity
With different contradistinctions."
Stating a common locus of contradiction and relationship is very amazing!

Other than the understood meaning of merely the two truths
Of the categorized valid cognition,

This manner is not the intended meaning of the Prāsaṅgika view—
The uncategorized free from extremes.

Others say, "The two truths are neither
One-sidedly one nor many;
[Asserting that they are] essentially the same with different contradistinctions
Is the tradition of logicians."

Regarding this, the tradition of the Prāsaṅgika view
Is like that, free from being one or many;
However, why don't they explain the tradition of the Svātantrika view
In accord with the Bodhicittavivaraṇa *scripture?*

Our tradition asserts that the division of the two truths
As essentially the same with different contradistinctions
Is the object of valid cognition analyzing the categorized
In the tradition of the Svātantrika view.

In the tradition of the consummate Prāsaṅgika view,
The object of valid cognition analyzing the uncategorized
Is free from all concepts of
The two truths being essentially one or many.

Nevertheless, for the objects of the valid cognition of pure vision
In the two truths of authentic/inauthentic experience,
The phenomena that are pure and impure, authentic and inauthentic,
Are asserted as the negation of being one.

Regarding the sequence, [some people say], "After ascertaining the ultimate,
The relative appearances are ascertained."
Others say, "From the relative, which is the method,
The ultimate, which arises from the method, is ascertained. . ."

Our tradition asserts the progressive and instantaneous manners of ascertainment
From the four stages of the view of the Middle Way.
The Svātantrikas ascertain the two truths progressively;
Instantaneous ascertainment is the tradition of Prāsaṅgika.

Regarding this, the two: (1) the method and that which arises from method, and

(2) The sequence of ascertaining the two truths
Are alike but not to be mistaken—
Confusing them as the same is confusion at the core.

Although there is accord in the way of stating the words,
"Emptiness is the ultimate truth,"
There are different qualities in the evidence,
What is established, the objects, and what is negated.

Others say, "The arguments of the Great Prāsaṅgika-Madhyamaka
Are consequences."
However, [by this,] the unique [quality of] Prāsaṅgika—
Being free from all assertions—is reduced to words.

Our tradition asserts that the uncategorized ultimate
Is free from all assertions.
Therefore, the unique arguments of the Great Middle Way
Are the great consequences (thal 'gyur, prasaṅga).

Others claim, "The view is a non-implicative negation."
Look at the phenomenon established—a lack of true existence—that is implied
By the negation of true establishment, which is the object of negation;
Their arguments are merely implicative negations.

Our tradition asserts that by negating all constructed extremes,
No extremes of reference or constructed phenomena are implied whatsoever.
Due to this, the arguments are exclusively non-implicative negations, and
The view is the great freedom from extremes.

Others variously say that the essence of emptiness is
An entity or a nonentity;
Other than being relative truths,
These are not the emptiness that is the ultimate.

Some people say: "The ultimate emptiness is a nonentity—
A lack of true existence that is a non-implicative negation."
As such, other than the categorized ultimate,
It is not the uncategorized ultimate.

[Concerning] this, since valid cognitions of confined perception
Find objects that are entities and nonentities,

They say, "There is no third alternative in between a direct contradiction;
Therefore, emptiness is a nonentity."

Regarding this, (1) emptiness that is posited as a nonentity
And (2) appearance that is posited as an entity
Is merely the understood meaning of the reasoning in introductory logic primers;
Both are relative truths.

Others say, "There is a permanent truth
That withstands ultimate analysis."
Look to the following: "In a faulty view of emptiness
Those with little intelligence will be destroyed."

Our tradition asserts ultimate emptiness
As the great uncategorized ultimate,
The expanse beyond the constructed phenomena
Of the relative objects found by a valid cognition of confined perception.

Emptiness is not an entity;
While appearance is not reified,
That appearance abides as the great emptiness—
This is a critical point that destroys the clinging to entities.

Emptiness is not a nonentity;
While emptiness is not reified,
The self-lucidity of emptiness is appearing phenomena—
This is a critical point of the dawning of dependent arising.

Since it is not an entity, it is free from being a permanent entity;
Since it is not a nonentity, it is free from being the extreme of annihilation.
The expanse of luminous clarity—profound, peaceful, and free from constructs—
Is asserted as the great ultimate, the abiding reality.

This way is neither the domain of an analysis of the categorized ultimate nor
The domain of analysis of a conventional valid cognition of confined perception.
The great valid cognition that analyzes the uncategorized ultimate
Is the unique meaning established by Prāsaṅgika reasoning.

This is a stanza at the interlude between sections.

Others say: "All the relative appearances of entities are not empty;
They are not reasoning's object of negation.
However, they are the object of negation
Of the sublime path without dualistic appearance."

This view and philosophy with the ground and path in contradiction
Is a view that has separated the view and the meditation.
This manner is destroyed by
Candrakīrti's three great reasonings of the power of fact.

Regarding this, [some] say, "True establishment is the object of negation
For the valid cognition of ultimate analysis.
A phenomenon that is not merely an imputation of the conceptual mind
Is what is truly established."

Without negating conventional appearances,
This negation of something separate that is truly established
Is merely the understood meaning of the two truths divided
By a categorized valid cognition analyzing the ultimate.

In this, having divided the two truths,
After ascertaining relative appearances,
What is there that is truly established to be negated again
By a valid cognition of ultimate analysis?

Therefore, appearances themselves are analyzed and established as empty
From a perspective that is uncertain whether
These dualistic appearances of entities are either
(1) Actually established as they appear or (2) the relative.

In which of the two truths is [true establishment] the ground of analysis?
What is the use of leaving appearances as they are
And futilely analyzing whether or not there is
Something separate that is truly established?

The ground of analysis is all these various appearances of entities—
The ultimate of the realists and
The conventional world of the Middle Way [proponents]—
They are asserted as empty from the perspective of ultimate truth.

The way of emptiness in Candrakīrti's tradition is
To analyze appearances themselves through ultimate analysis and

Assert all appearances of entities to be empty,
Without asserting an ultimate pillar or pot.

Similarly, if an ultimate pillar or pot
Is not asserted,
The negation [of the ultimate status of these appearances] by the valid cognition of ultimate analysis' reasoning
Is good, followers of the path of reasoning!

[Others say,] "Due to being empty of another—true establishment—
There is no ultimate pillar or pot."
This bears a resemblance to the elimination of fear in a place where there are snakes,
By [the absence of] an elephant—amazing!

If you wish to negate something separate that is truly established at the time of the ground, and
Destroy dualistic appearances at the time of the path,
Then it is reasonable to hold the position that
When selflessness is seen, [merely] the permanent self is relinquished!

It is difficult for phenomena and suchness, and
Emptiness and dependent arising, to be feasible [when]
The two are: (1) selflessness that is solely an exclusion, a nonentity, and
(2) Non-empty relative entities.

Look at the proponents of other-emptiness (gzhan stong), whose emptiness
Leaves this shimmering appearance of solid duality as it is,
Without making it reasoning's object of negation.
[Their] object of negation, like horns, is something separate that is truly established.

This is a stanza at the interlude between sections.

Our tradition, the asserted viewpoint of the translators and scholars of the school of early translations—
[That of] Mipam, the lord of doctrine—
Asserts emptiness [and]
The reasoning of ultimate analysis' object of negation in this way:

Having divided the two truths,
If appearance has been ascertained as the illusory relative,

The nature of appearance is not negated again
By valid cognition's reasoned analysis.

As for the mere relative,
If the nature of appearance is also negated
By a reasoned analysis analyzing the conventional,
Then that is the great [extreme] view of nonexistence.

That which is asserted to be truly established is:
Appearances themselves that are [held as] ultimately established or
Phenomena that seem to withstand ultimate analysis
When the relative has not been ascertained as illusion.

Regarding this, the categorized valid cognition's object of negation is
The phenomena that are truly established ultimately.
The object of negation of the valid cognition that analyzes the uncategorized is
The gross and subtle constructed extremes, etc.

Without the slightest thing withstanding the analysis by
The reasoning consciousness of valid cognition's ultimate analysis,
All relative appearances of constructed phenomena
Are negated within the ultimate expanse free from extremes.

The fear that it becomes a view of annihilation
Because the object of negation is too encompassing (khyab ches)
Is a concern that realists have, the ones who do not know about dependent arising,
Not a fear of Middle Way proponents.

If relative appearances are negated by conventional valid cognition,
Then that is a view of annihilation.
The ultimate status of all phenomena is negated
By the valid cognition of ultimate analysis—even so, how is this annihilation?

This reasoning establishes that production, etc.
Does not withstand analysis even conventionally.
Due to being free from all assertions,
The constructs of appearance are directly severed.

If you realize all appearances as appearances of the nonexistent—forms of emptiness—and
Realize what is imputed by the conceptual mind as the nature of illusion,
Then [they do] not fetter and are not negated;
The nature of appearance is not negated.

Through this is the unexcelled definitive secret of ascertaining
Emptiness dawning as dependent arising;
The foundation of all the profound distinctions of philosophy
Is not known by ordinary, confined perception.

What is the use of negating something separate that is truly established?
Appearances that withstand analysis are negated in both of the two truths.
The nature of dependently-arisen appearances is not negated.
When this meaning is realized, the knot sealing the difficult points is unraveled.

This is a stanza of summation.

One may say: "Having divided the two truths,
It is a view of annihilation if relative appearances are negated,
Yet if appearances are not negated,
It is difficult for emptiness to be established."

In general, both Prāsaṅgikas and Svātantrikas
Divide the two truths from the perspective of conventional valid cognition.
However, their delineations of the essences of the two truths, and so forth,
Are dissimilar.

Here I will briefly explain the way of dividing
The categorized and uncategorized ultimates
Through the two truths separated or not
By the valid cognition of ultimate analysis.

Regarding this, it is widely renowned in India and Tibet
That there are two delineations of the valid cognition of ultimate analysis:
"The arguments common to Svātantrika and Prāsaṅgika," and
"The unique Prāsaṅgika arguments."

By this, from the two truths being divided or not
In Svātantrika and Prāsaṅgika,

There are the manners of ascertaining the view
In a Sublime One's meditative equipoise and postmeditation, from which

There emerge: the categorized and uncategorized ultimates,
The conventional established by its own character or not,
The distinction between reasons that are autonomous arguments and those that are consequences, and
Assertions of a view being present or not.

Regarding this, having separated the two truths, which is the evaluated object,
With the valid cognition of common arguments,
The Svātantrika-Madhyamakas
Establish the view of the categorized ultimate.

Therefore, in the stages of the view, constructs are progressively eliminated
By autonomous arguments—the common arguments
That analyze the categorized—
Through a manner of alternating between appearance and emptiness.

When analyzing the categorized ultimate,
The two truths are separated and
Appearances are not negated;
The object of negation, qualified as what is truly established, is negated.

Therefore, from the perspective of the authentic ultimate,
What is established in the Svātantrika view is
The establishment of merely the categorized—the emptiness of true existence.
In accord with this, some from the schools of later translations say,

"It is a view of annihilation if appearances are negated."
They know merely what is confined perception.
Negating an object of negation—something separate that is truly established—
They say, "We have ascertained the appearing mode of the object of negation!"

Regarding this, without dividing the two truths, which is the evaluated object,
The valid cognition of the unique arguments

Of the Great Prāsaṅgika-Madhyamaka
Establish the view of equality free from extremes.

Therefore, in the stage of the [Prāsaṅgika] view constructs are instantaneously negated
By consequences—the unique arguments
That analyze the uncategorized ultimate—
Without alternating between appearance and emptiness.

When analyzing the uncategorized,
All relative constructs are negated without dividing two truths;
Therefore, all constructed extremes are negated
Without qualifying the object of negation.

Therefore, in both of the two truths,
What is established in the Prāsaṅgika view is
The establishment of the uncategorized—free from extremes.
The school of early translations follows after this.

There are no faults of the inferior logicians
Relying on a valid cognition of confined perception—
Such as the object of negation being too encompassing or
The side of appearance being denigrated.

In short, in accord with the intended meaning of the Four Applications of Emptiness [Sūtra],
Svātantrika and Prāsaṅgika are the progressive and instantaneous ways
Of perfecting the four stages of the view
Free from the four constructed extremes.

Since form itself is empty, it is free from the extreme of existence—
Appearance abides as the great emptiness.
Since while empty, it appears, it is free from the extreme of nonexistence—
Emptiness dawns as the great dependent arising.

Since they are not different, it is free from [the extreme of] both—
Emptiness and dependent arising are the great unity.
Since appearance and emptiness are equal, it is free from [the extreme of] neither—
The equality free from extremes, Emaho!

One may be very learned and accomplished, yet not fully understand;
The fortunate ones who clearly realize this meaning are joyful!
I think of the kindness of the lineage of awareness-holders in the school of early translations—
My kind, glorious teacher is so compassionate!

This is a stanza at the interlude between sections.

Others explain different presentations,
Including what is and is not viable to exist
From the conventional and ultimate perspectives, and
The objects of negation by reasoning and the path.

Our tradition asserts the way of the early generation of scholars.
See the elegant discourses of Mipam, the lord of the doctrine,
Which accord with the quintessential instructions of the lineage of the omniscient one [Longchenpa]—
The great one endowed with a thousandfold scriptures, reasonings, and quintessential instructions.

Without mixing them, uphold the categories
Of the unique, elegant discourses such as these.
It is good to abandon pointless aggression and jealousy
Toward doctrines and individuals.

Alas! These days some people hold onto the gibberish that
"In the Nyingma's scriptural tradition of the great secret,
There is no liberation."
Others repeat after them.

The Great Sage taught the division
Of whether or not there is a supreme path of liberation
Through whether or not the profound view
Of the four seals that signify the Word is realized.

Therefore, show through reasoning
The way of contradicting the four seals that signify the Word!
We can debate over who contradicts the intended meaning of the four seals that signify the Word,
The early or later [schools of translations].

We can investigate whether or not there is liberation in that [tradition]
Which does not accept that all phenomena are empty,
But asserts the nonexistence of a pointless separate thing that is truly established
To be viable as emptiness!

In general, in the supreme vehicle of the Great Middle Way,
The root of the path of liberation is accepted as the lack of true existence,
So it is good to investigate whether or not that with the name "empty of true existence"
Is the emptiness of true existence.

The tradition of the school of early translations' lineage of the great secret
Is a lineage that progressed from the mouths to the ears of the sublime assemblies
Of Victorious Ones and their [bodhisattva] offspring;
Ordinary conceptual fabrications do not rival it.

Look at the countless scholars and accomplished ones
Who traverse the high grounds
Through this tradition of sūtra, tantra, and quintessential instructions—
The complete and unerring supreme path!

[Some people say,] "The continuity of vows in the lineage of the school of early translations
Is impure; its head is Nāgārjuna."
Widely renowned as a glorious, fully-ordained monk,
[Nāgārjuna] is praised in the scriptures of the Great Sage.

Look at the virtue of those with the audacity to say that
Lord Nāgārjuna, the great chariot who is
The sole ornament beautifying the world,
Is without vows, a fully-ordained monk [merely] by name!

Without understanding a mere fraction of the scriptural tradition
And with no reasoning to establish,
It is good for someone with the form of a religious practitioner
To relinquish the intolerable bad karma of rejecting the doctrine.

Although the manners of expression accord in mere name—
"Appearance is the relative truth,"

The early and later [schools of translations] have different ways of assertion—
Such as the presentations of appearance and reality, and the essence [of the relative].

Aside from the mode of appearance of the impure relative, which is the domain of the valid cognition of confined perception,
Others do not explain the pure mode of reality—
The domain of the valid cognition of purity.

Without both modes of appearance and reality,
There is no accordance or lack of accordance between appearance and reality;
The distorted cognitions of ordinary beings become valid cognition and
The visions of Sublime Ones become mistaken cognition.

Our tradition accepts two relative appearances—
The pure and the impure—
Due to the mode of appearance of impure delusion and
The mode of reality of the pure ground.

Those of the later generation posit the relative partially, too,
Through solely confined perception.
The scholars' tradition distinguishes the relative's appearance and reality
Through two valid cognitions.

Concerning the mode of appearance, which is relative appearance,
Some say it is conceptually imputed yet established by valid cognition,
Others say it is the indivisibility of appearance and mind.
The scholars' tradition asserts it as self-appearance.

For those who assert that the conventional is conceptually imputed yet established by valid cognition, or
Who assert that appearance and mind are the same,
It is difficult to have a reasonable presentation of the conventional—
What is valid and what is invalid, etc.

Due to one's self-appearance being distorted or not,
There are the delineations of conventional objects being true or false,
Valid or invalid, and so forth;
Conventional presentations are most refined.

Concerning the manners of asserting the phenomena of self-appearance,
The tradition of Mind-Only (1) posits the mode of appearance as
Cognition and matter that are the category of the imagined nature (kun btags), and
(2) Accepts the mode of reality, which is the essence of the consummate dependent nature (gzhan dbang), as mind.

Śāntarakṣita's tradition (1) posits the mere mode of appearance, such as cognition and matter,
As relative phenomena that are [established by their] own characters, and
(2) Accepts as the conventional mode of reality (tha snyad gnas tshul)
That all appearances are mind.

Candrakīrti's tradition is that the mode of appearance, all phenomena of self-appearance,
Appear to the mind and are produced by the mind;
Therefore, self-appearances, the great forms of emptiness,
Are alike as illusions.

The unmatched elegant discourse,
Separating this into appearance (snang ba) and appearing objects (snang yul),
Is the assertion of the omniscient lord of doctrine [Longchenpa]
Elucidated in his great commentary, the White Lotus.

When appearances are asserted as mind,
The universal ground and reflexive awareness (rang rig) are indispensable;
In the assertion [of appearances] as merely self-appearance,
No deliberate refutation or affirmation is made.

Regarding this, from the conventional perspective of the mode of appearance,
One's own limitless perceptions of various environments and inhabitants—
Which are dependently arisen from the pure and impure mind itself—
Arise from karma.

Regarding this, other traditions throw out the support of the causality of karma,
Which are the entities of dependent arising,
Saying that, "A nonentity is established as the entity of disintegration;
That itself is the support of the causality of karma."

With the disintegration of the entity of disintegration (zhig pa dngos po),
The first moment of a phenomenon that is a cause and
The second moment of a phenomenon that is the effect
Are contradictory in progressive and simultaneous modes of production.

[Some say:] "An effect is not suitable to arise
From the cause itself disintegrating or not disintegrating."
When we debate the issue of whether or not a cause and effect meet,
What is the use of disintegration?

When food does not satisfy the stomach,
How can the food's entity of disintegration satisfy?
When the eyes do not see forms,
Do the eyes' entity of disintegration see?

When the aggregate of old age and death is relinquished,
Investigate whether or not the entity of disintegration is old age and death.
If it is, from that is only ignorance;
If it is not, the entity of disintegration is the Buddha!

At the time of nirvāṇa when the aggregates have disintegrated
[They] prostrate to the common locus of a permanent phenomenon and an entity!
The great chariot, Nāgārjuna,
Asserted that nirvāṇa is unconditioned.

For realists, an entity as the support
For the causality of karma is indispensable.
Svātantrikas and others follow after them;
Proponents of the Great Middle Way assert dependent arising.

The cause of a sprout is a seed;
The ripening cause is karma itself—
Because karma is unceasing,
Until an effect arises from it.

By the infallible truth of dependent arising
The causality of karma does not perish in a hundred aeons;
When [the causes] are gathered and the time comes,
It is certain that the effect will ripen.

Since causality is extremely hidden (shin tu lkog gyur)
It is said to be an inconceivable phenomenon.
In this, even contemplation is shunned
Regarding causal processes such as support, meeting, and so forth.

In this way, the issue of whether or not there is an assertion of a view
On conventional causality and so forth,
Others explain one-sidedly;
Our tradition explains having divided the two truths.

Some people say: "The way of asserting the conventional
Follows after the elderly people of the world—
Those who have not turned their minds to emptiness,
Nor have been influenced by philosophies."

Our tradition asserts "in the perspective of the world"
As the perspective of the conventional truth of the world—
From yogis and masterly scholars in the world
Down to ordinary idiots.

We accept the conventional as
Facts that are renowned and established in the world—
That which is seen, heard, and known
Without examination by ultimate analysis.

Superimposed phenomena such as the Principle (gtso, prakṛti) and the self,
Which are imputed by Buddhist and non-Buddhist philosophies,
Are neither the relative truth of the world
Nor in accord with conventional fact.

See the Ornament of Candrakīrti's Viewpoint,
The meaning-commentary on the Madhyamakāvatāra,
Which elucidates the intended meaning of lord Mipam—
The illustrious tradition unmixed with the eight main [unique features of Prāsaṅgika or] any of those [other assertions just mentioned].

The mode of reality of pure appearance,
Which is the great meaning revealed by the scriptures of sūtra and tantra, is
The heritage of the basic element, the nature of luminous clarity, etc.—
Whatever pure appearances there are.

Regarding this, other than a constructed extreme of existence or nonexistence, permanence or annihilation,
Masterly scholars of the later generation do not know
The nature of the essential nature, the heritage of the basic element,
Which is profound, peaceful, and stainless.

Some people take the position that the Mahāyāna heritage
Is an entity that is the ultimate truth.
They say: "The sūtras, tantras, and śāstras *that explicitly teach emptiness free from extremes*
Are the provisional meaning."

This heritage that is a common locus of a permanent phenomenon and an entity
Conflicts with the path of reasoning.
Such a heritage that is an entity of true permanence
Is not the illustrious tradition of the Lion of the Śākyas.

Some people say, "The Mahāyāna heritage is
Merely an ultimate nonentity.
The sūtras, tantras, and śāstras *that explicitly teach the appearing aspect of luminous clarity*
Are the provisional meaning."

Is a heritage of the basic element that is a permanent nonentity,
Eloquent to those who know reasoning, or what?
Such a heritage that is annihilation, nothing at all,
Is not the illustrious tradition of the Buddha.

Some people assert the heritage as
A common locus of what is unconditioned and conditioned—
A unity of both (1) the nonentity that is emptiness and
(2) The entity that is the clarity of mind.

There are no sūtras, tantras, or śāstras *that state*
A naturally abiding heritage (rang bzhin gnas rigs) that is conditioned.
Are they asserting this conditioned heritage of clarity
To be the developing heritage (rgyas 'gyur rigs)?

Some people fear that if they assert the heritage as either existent or nonexistent,
Then it will contradict reasoning.

They speak of [heritage] in the manner of a cause that potentially emerges,
Like butter from milk.

Such a manner of a cause that potentially emerges
Is said to be conditioned by proponents of reasoning.
This heritage of the basic element—which was not present before, but potentially emerges—
Is not the tradition of the omniscient one, father and son.

Other than merely the valid cognitions analyzing the categorized ultimate and
Conventional confined perception,
They do no have the valid cognition of purity;
Therefore, there is fault.

Ordinary philosophies do not know of
This luminous clarity, which is the abiding reality of the mind.
It is the great meaning revealed by the scriptures of sūtra and tantra, and
Is present in the tradition of the scholars of the early generation.

It is the great, profound meaning, purposefully expressed
By the Guide, the Lion of Men,
"Profound, peaceful, free from constructs, and luminously clear—
The identity of the unconditioned."

It is the supreme, revealed meaning widely taught
In the definitive meaning sūtras of the middle and last wheel:
"The mind is devoid of mind;
The nature of mind is luminous clarity."

The suchness of mind free from extremes
Is the great indivisibility of the expanse and wisdom.
It is luminously clear, profound, peaceful, free from constructs,
Self-existing, unconditioned, and spontaneously present.

Its nature cannot be known or expressed by a confined intellect,
Like that which is an entity or a nonentity.
Therefore, since it transcends the extremes of purity, bliss, permanence, and the self,
It is the transcendent perfection.

The property of the essential nature, the abiding reality pure from the beginning,

Has the identity of three distinctive qualities:
It is essentially empty, naturally clear, and
Its nature is all-pervasive compassionate resonance (thugs rje).

The supreme definitive meaning of the middle wheel
Is the expanse of phenomena endowed with the three gates of liberation.
"The mind is devoid of mind. . ."
The essence of mind itself abides as empty.

From the two truths as appearance/emptiness,
The ultimate emptiness is the supreme freedom from constructs.
Since it is the object found by the valid cognition of ultimate analysis,
It is free from the extreme of the truth of permanent entities.

The supreme definitive meaning of the last wheel
Is the heritage of the Buddha endowed with knowledge, love, and powers.
". . . The nature of mind is luminous clarity"
Is the nature that abides as the great luminous clarity.

From the two truths of authentic/inauthentic experience,
It is the supreme ultimate of the concordant modes of appearance and reality.
Since it is the object found by the conventional valid cognition of purity,
It is free from the extreme of annihilation as nothing at all.

The supreme noncontradiction of the middle and last wheels
Is the unity of appearance and emptiness—the basic element of the essential nature.
From the purity and impurity of mind itself,
It abides as the great interdependent arising of compassionate resonance.

It is the supreme meaning of the noncontradiction of the two truths
Of appearance/emptiness and authentic/inauthentic experience.
Since it is not the domain of confined valid cognition,
It is free from all adventitiously constructed phenomena.

This is unlike ordinary other-emptiness
Because [it] cannot withstand the analysis of ultimate valid cognition;
Due to being the object found by the valid cognition of pure [vision],
It is not rivaled by the ordinary emptiness of true existence.

Regarding this, through three distinct objects of negation
Of reasoning by a valid cognition of ultimate analysis,

Three conventions of the Middle Way are made:
(1) Emptiness of true existence, (2) other-emptiness, and (3) self-emptiness.

Regarding this, [the proponents of] emptiness of true existence and other-emptiness
Explain the middle and last wheels as contradictory.
The great school of early translations' Middle Way, free from extremes,
Accepts the middle and last wheels as the definitive meaning;

They are accepted without contradiction as a single essential point,
Having elegantly distinguished between the ways of dividing the two truths—
The two truths of appearance/emptiness and
Authentic/inauthentic experience.

This is the intended meaning of the Victorious Ones and their [bodhisattva] offspring;
It is the unexcelled, distinctive assertion
Of the powerful victor, Longchenpa, and
The omniscient Lochen Dharmaśrī.

If this meaning, as it is, is understood well,
The definitive meaning [sūtras] of the middle and last wheels,
Candrakīrti's texts and the Uttaratantra, *etc.,*
Dawn without contradiction as a single essential point.

Through this, know the immeasurable profound meanings
Of the tantras of Secret Mantra, such as
The natural maṇḍala of spontaneous presence and
The abiding reality, which is the innate mind.

An extremely clear presentation of this is
Elucidated in the Lion's Roar: Exposition [of Buddha-Nature].
If you want to know its difficult points,
See the Notes [on the Essential Points of the Exposition] *that I wrote.*

This does not withstand ultimate analysis,
Nor is it an object found by a conventional valid cognition of confined perception;
It is the meaning established by the uncategorized ultimate analysis, and
Is the object found by the conventional valid cognition of purity.

This is a stanza at the interlude between sections.

Such an evaluated object is an extremely hidden phenomenon;
It is inconceivable to a valid cognition of confined perception.
It is seen by the omniscient valid cognition of purity
Who said it in the scriptures, so trust it.

There are three for each
Of the evaluated objects that are the two truths of appearance/emptiness.
The three are: (1) what is evident, (2) what is hidden, and
(3) What is extremely hidden.

The objects of evident appearance, such as forms,
Are ascertained by the direct perceptions of sense-faculty valid cognitions of confined perception.
Objects of hidden appearance, such as impermanence,
Are ascertained by the mental inferences of confined perception.

The phenomena of extremely hidden appearance—
Such as the causality of karma, the heritage of the basic element, and the innate mind—
Are ascertained through the valid cognition that relies upon the testimony
Of those who possess pure vision.

At the time of meditative equipoise on emptiness that is evident,
There is ascertainment by the valid cognition of yogic direct perception in a Sublime One's continuum.
Emptiness that is hidden and the mere absence of self
Are ascertained by the valid cognition analyzing the categorized.

Emptiness that is extremely hidden
Is the uncategorized ultimate itself.
It is ascertained by the valid cognition that analyzes the uncategorized—
The great, unique arguments of Prāsaṅgika.

Within the path of cultivation, there is both abandonment and realization:
Abandonment is the truth of cessation;
Realization is the truth of the path.
Cessation and path are the two, abandonment and realization.

Regarding this, there is the nature of the abandonments and
The way of actually perfecting them. From these,
Within abandonment—which is the nature of the truth of cessation—
There are the objects of abandonment and the way of abandonment.

The objects of abandonment have the nature of afflictive emotions and cognitive [obscurations].
Asserting a presentation of this,
Masterly scholars of the later generation
Explain the essence of the two obscurations as follows.

"The classes that mainly obstruct
Liberation and omniscience."
[By this] one can understand merely the defining character of their functions,
However, it is not a complete [presentation].

Regarding this, the obscurations are said to have a fixed number of two:
(1) Afflictive obscurations and (2) cognitive obscurations.
Due to this, it is said, "The obscurations to absorption also are
Either afflictive or cognitive [obscurations]."

However, since it is not an obscuration
To liberation or omniscience,
A third, called "the obscurations to absorption,"
Was asserted by the undefeated protector [Maitreya].

Some people assert, "The illustrations of a cognitive obscuration
Are only non-concurrent formations" (ldan min gyi 'du byed).
A concept that is a non-concurrent formation
Is not in the tradition of scholars in India or Tibet.

All Mahāyāna sūtras and śāstras,
In a single viewpoint with one voice,
Assert that cognitive obscurations are
Concepts of the three spheres.

Some people say: "Afflictive obscurations alone entirely encompass
Apprehensions of the three spheres as truly existent;
Only the latency for this
Is a cognitive obscuration."

The mere latency for that afflictive emotion
Can be understood as a cognitive obscuration itself;
However, [by this alone] the presentation of the nature of the two obscurations
Still is not completely understood.

Some people explain the stage as follows: "Up to the seventh impure ground,
Only afflictive obscurations are abandoned.
On the pure grounds,
Only cognitive obscurations are abandoned."

The presentations of what is to be abandoned and
The antidotes have been greatly confused.
They have strayed far from the presentation of the grounds and paths
In the Mahāyāna sūtras and śāstras.

In order to avoid the fault that the great Sublime Ones who previously traversed a lesser path
Would have nothing to abandon
On the seven impure grounds,
Some people say: "They abandon the obscurations of thorough stupidity, etc."

As such, which of the two obscurations is it?
Through question and debate,
The positions such as [these] assertions of defining character,
Fixed number, stage, etc., are left far behind.

Some people say: "A bodhisattva on the first ground
Has completely abandoned what Auditors and Self-Realized Ones have abandoned.
Still they have latencies
Which are called 'afflictive obscurations.' "

As such, which is it? An afflictive or cognitive [obscuration]?
Through question and debate, the position is destroyed.
The scholars of India and Tibet do not accept
Innate afflictive obscurations to be discards of the Path of Seeing.

In accord with the elegant discourse of the lineage of the omniscient one [Longchenpa],
The expert at singing the song of the noncontradiction of
All the illustrious traditions of the great chariots,
Mipam, the lord of the doctrine, explains as follows.

Regarding this, the defining character of what is abandoned
Is posited for both of the two obscurations, the afflictive and cognitive,

From the general to the specific,
By means of cause, essence, and function.

The causes are the two apprehensions of true existence—
The apprehensions of a self of phenomena and persons.
Apprehending phenomena as truly existent is a cognitive obscuration;
Apprehending persons as truly existent is an afflictive obscuration.

The essences are as follows: attachment, and so forth, are afflictive obscurations;
Concepts of the three spheres are cognitive obscurations.
Their functions are as follows: having the characters of obstructing
Liberation and omniscience.

Therefore, genuine obscurations
Are asserted within a fixed number of two;
The third, obscuration to absorption,
Is just nominally enumerated as an obscuration.

The illustrations for both afflictive and cognitive [obscurations]
Are concepts—mental phenomena.

Thus, there are four types of apprehended-apprehender concepts:
(1) Thorough affliction, (2) complete purification, (3) substantial, and (4) imputed.

The three types of concepts of the three spheres
Are definitely cognitive obscurations:
(1) Concepts of true existence, (2) concepts of reified signs, and
(3) Concepts that are merely dualistic appearances.

The first is manifest for ordinary beings;
The second is manifest at the time of the seven impure [grounds];
The third at times is even manifest
In the postmeditation of those on the pure grounds.

When these are manifest,
It is called a Sublime One's "lax postmeditation";
The six transcendent perfections, etc., that are polluted by these
Are just "worldly transcendent perfections."

Concerning the way of abandonment, for both of the obscurations
There is a twofold division: the imputed and the innate [aspects].

Also for the innate [aspects], there is (1) what is potential
And (2) its extremely subtle latency.

Therefore, the imputed [aspects] of both obscurations
Are held to be only discards of the Path of Seeing.
The sublime spiritual community of bodhisattvas who have abandoned these
Are endowed with the eight qualities of awareness and freedom.

If someone says: "This assertion that cognitive obscurations are discards of the Path of Seeing
Is not the tradition of Candrakīrti.
It is the Svātantrika tradition, such as [said in] the Abhisamayālaṃkāra*;*
It is not the consummate hidden meaning."

A hidden meaning [like theirs] does not account for:
The distinctive features of the Mahāyāna Path of Joining,
The discards of the Path of Seeing, the accomplishment of the accumulations of antidotes,
The summit of the uninterrupted Path of Seeing, and so on.

The distinctive feature of a Prāsaṅgika like theirs
Is a consummate hidden meaning of the Mother [Perfection of Wisdom]
That has not been renowned previously in Tuṣita Heaven,
Nor to scholars of India or Tibet!

Regarding the way of abandoning the innate potentials,
The discards, such as the great of the great discards,
Are abandoned by the nine antidotes,
Such as the lesser of the lesser Path of Meditation.

Their extremely subtle latencies
Are difficult to demolish by an ordinary path of training;
They are abandoned by the uninterrupted path's summit—
The supreme uninterrupted [path] of only a Buddha.

In this, we assert the potentials for afflictive emotions
As what are discarded by the path on the seven impure grounds, and
The cognitive obscurations that are their latencies
As discards of the pure grounds.

Therefore, there are two types of cognitive obscurations—
Those that are latencies for afflictive emotions and those that are not.

Without knowing the division of these,
It is difficult to explain the great scriptural tradition.

Some scriptural traditions of the great chariot assert,
"Some obscurations with the name 'afflictive emotions'
Are discards of the pure grounds."
Nevertheless, they are not potentials for the obscurations that are afflictive emotions.

Rather, the latencies for afflictive emotions
Are merely designated with the name "afflictive emotions."
It widely appears as such
In the great Mahāyāna sūtras and śāstras.

If this meaning is understood,
Then the hardships of abandoning jointly
The nine types of cognitive obscurations on the impure grounds
Will be easily removed.

Therefore, in presentations of the abandonment of the two obscurations,
The lord of the doctrine, Mipam,
Holds the position that all the scriptural traditions of the great chariots
"Have a viewpoint that only accords."

The intended meaning of the great chariots such as this
Was explained by the lord of the doctrine, Mipam.
Therefore, know the immense scriptural traditions
From his elegant discourses.

The apprehensions of thorough affliction and complete purification, which are the apprehended-concepts, and
The apprehensions of a substantial or imputed person, which are the apprehending-concepts,
Are, in short, themselves the root
Of all afflictive and cognitive obscurations to be abandoned.

The root of the antidote is the clear realization of the selflessness of persons
And the complete selflessness of phenomena.
In short, the antidote to the darkness
Of the afflictive emotions and cognitive obscurations is selfless emptiness.

These are clarifying stanzas at the interlude.

In this way, as for the antidote—the truth of the path,
Which is the perfection of the types of realization of selflessness—
I will briefly explain the divisions
Of the ways of the antidote and clear realizations.

Some people say: "The intelligence that realizes
The mere nonentity that is the lack of true existence—
A type of realization shared with the Auditors and Self-Realized Ones—
Cannot accomplish the destruction of cognitive obscurations.

Therefore, the clear realization, [like a] firefly,
That realizes the mere nonentity that is the lack of true existence
Still needs an accompaniment to accomplish
The destruction of the great darkness of cognitive obscurations."

The type of realization that knows a nonentity
Has no power by itself to destroy cognitive obscurations.
It is impossible for it to be accompanied by the assistance of another power—
Even if it were, what would it do?

Even the realization of the common, mere categorized emptiness
Is not the direct antidote for cognitive obscurations.
The unique direct antidote for cognitive obscurations
Is the clear realization of the uncategorized.

When there dawns a clear realization [like] the Sun King,
Born from churning the ocean of the unified accumulations,
That itself destroys the darkness of ignorance,
Without needing to depend on another accompaniment.

In this way, in the stages of clear realization
Of the truth of the path, which is the antidote,
There is a twofold division:
The sublime path of meditative equipoise and postmeditation.

There are also two types of meditative equipoise:
Meditative stabilization with appearance and without appearance.
Likewise, there are two types of postmeditation:
Worldly postmeditation and transcendent postmeditation.

Others say regarding the nature of meditative equipoise:
"The object is a nonentity that is an emptiness of true existence.

The subject, which is the entity of mind,
Meditates with a mode of apprehension ('dzin stangs).

Such is the understood meaning
Of a valid cognition of confined perception; however,
It is not even a fraction of the profound nonconceptual wisdom
Of the meditative equipoise of a great Sublime One.

Our tradition asserts that from the perspective of the wisdom of meditative equipoise,
There is no appearance and no cognition;
The appearance of wisdom is inconceivable.
The essence of luminous clarity—profound, peaceful, and free from constructs—

Is the supreme, ultimate wisdom,
Which is the unity of the great expanse and wisdom.
In this, the difference between subject and object
Is just mental imputation.

Regarding the distinctive object, others say,
"The object of meditative equipoise is a mere emptiness of true existence."
Other than a categorized lack of true existence, which is [an object of] consciousness,
This is not the object of profound wisdom.

The domain of the wisdom of reflexive awareness
Is the unique ultimate, the nature of great purity.
It is the supreme mother of the Victorious Ones—
Unspeakable, inconceivable, and inexpressible.

Others say: "The subject,
Which is a dualistic mind, is wisdom itself."
They know merely basic logic primers [that say]
"Mind (blo), awareness (rig), and cognition (shes) are equivalents."

Our tradition asserts the wisdom of the Sublime Ones
As the wisdom of reflexive awareness;
The mind is devoid of mind, but
Its nature is the great luminous clarity.

The mind (sems) is the dualistic mind of perceived-perceiver;
As such, it is only a valid cognition of confined perception.

Wisdom (ye shes) is nondual, the great luminous clarity;
It is the valid cognition of pure vision.

"The ultimate is not the domain of mind;
It is the domain of the wisdom of reflexive awareness."
In accord with the meaning of the words of sūtra,
The scholars' tradition distinguishes mind (sems) and awareness (rig).

Others explain the essence [of nonconceptual wisdom] as follows: "It is only free from concepts
That apprehend words and objects as mixed."
Such nonconceptuality is a property of all [direct perception] cognitions;
It is not unique.

The nonconceptual wisdom of meditative equipoise
Is explained in sūtras to have the character
Of a unique nonconceptuality
That is not mixed with the five kinds of common nonconceptuality.

Concerning the meaning of whether or not there is a representational mode of apprehension,
Others say: "[Meditative equipoise] definitely has a mode of apprehension.
All perceived-perceiver duality dissolves
While there is a mode of apprehension of nonexistence."

Our tradition asserts that the mind that meditates on the mere categorized ultimate
Has a mode of apprehension; [however,]
In the great clear realization of the uncategorized
It is free from all modes of apprehension.

Regarding the way of being free from the dualistic appearances of perceived-perceiver,
Others explain: "Subjects and objects exist, but
Are merely not apprehended by the mind;
This is the meaning of the absence of dualistic appearances."

Still they say: "The subject and object are indivisible,
[Like] water poured into water."
Such a meditative equipoise that is mistaken cognition—
With appearance and reality in discord—is a disgrace!

Therefore, from the perspective of the wisdom of meditative equipoise,
The entirety of perceived-perceiver duality dissolves into the expanse.
The expanse that transcends the constructed phenomena of the relative
Abides as the ultimate—the great luminous clarity.

As postmeditation's dualistic appearances
And cognitions dissolve into the expanse,
Luminous clarity—the self-lucidity of the mind devoid of mind—
Manifests.

Although it is beyond appearances and cognitions,
It is not like the time of being unconscious;
The wisdom appearances of luminous clarity—profound, peaceful, and stainless—
Are inconceivable.

Regarding this, we assert that the sublime path of meditative equipoise is twofold:
Meditative stabilization with and without appearance.
Yogic direct perception that is a meditative equipoise with appearance
Is asserted as postmeditation's meditative stabilization with appearance.

Regarding this, some people say without reason:
"The Svātantrika-Madhyamakas accept the sublime path
Of meditative equipoise with appearance;
The Prāsaṅgikas accept without appearance."

In the scriptural tradition of the scholars of the early generation,
It is said that both the Svātantrika-Madhyamakas and the Prāsaṅgika-Madhyamakas
Accept both meditative stabilizations—
With and without appearance.

Some people say: "The meaning of with appearance and without appearance
Is the presence or absence of dualistic appearances."
Is this tenable for a tradition that asserts
That the wisdom that knows whatever there is has appearances?

A meditative stabilization that manifests whatever there is in the relative
Is with appearance;
A meditative stabilization that actualizes the ultimate as it is
Is without appearance.

Therefore, in a simultaneous way of the two truths,
No Sublime One on a ground of training
Can know the appearance of whatever there is
While in meditative equipoise on the meaning of what is.

In a manner of alternating between meditative equipoise and postmeditation—
From churning the ocean of the unified accumulations—
The great darkness of the two obscurations is utterly dispelled and
The maṇḍala of the unified two exalted bodies is perfected.

Meditative stabilization that is meditative equipoise without appearance
Engages the meaning of the ultimate as it is;
Meditative stabilization that is postmeditation with appearance
Engages the meaning of whatever there is in the relative.

The profound vajra-*like meditative stabilizations, such as [the meditations on]*
Selflessness, the sixteen emptinesses,
And the sequence of the nature of nonentities,
Are meditative equipoises without appearance.

All illusory meditative stabilizations, such as [the meditations on]
Retention and courageous eloquence, the thorough trainings, the qualities of the grounds,
And the sequence of the six transcendent perfections,
Are postmeditations with appearance.

The mother of the Victorious Ones—the nondual,
Nonconceptual meditative equipoise—
Is the ultimate mind of awakening.
It is expressed as "the accumulation of wisdom without appearance."

Meditative stabilizations of postmeditation that are
Without concepts of the three spheres, such as magical acts of generosity,
Are transcendent perfections that transcend the world.
They are expressed as "the accumulation of merit with appearance."

In postmeditation, acts of generosity, etc., with reference—
Constricted by reified signs of the three spheres and
Manifest concepts that apprehend duality—
Are "worldly transcendent perfections."

Concerning the distinctive types of realization, most of the later generation say,
"The three Sublime Ones have the same type of realization."
The type of realization that is a non-implicative negation is the same, [but]
What does the trouble of proving that do?

The Mahāyāna's unique type of realization—
Giving rise to the nonconceptual wisdom of phenomena—[comes from]
Completely pleasing virtuous spiritual friends and
Completely gathering the accumulations of merit and wisdom.

It would be very amazing if
All of a sudden, an Auditor abruptly perfects
The Mahāyāna's unique type of realization,
Without the causes and conditions preceding it!

Others say: "Even the irreducibles, which are difficult to realize,
Are realized [by Auditors and Self-Realized Ones];
However, their types of realization are distinguished by some [phenomena] that are easy to realize."
They have a tradition proclaiming that there is no liberation in the Abhidharma scriptures!

In general, selfless emptiness is the nondual door of pacification;
It is the mother of the four Sublime Ones.
Therefore, in order to liberate beings,
Its twofold division is stated.

The partial selflessness, which is merely categorized,
Is the type of realization of the Sublime Auditors and Self-Realized Ones;
Merely that is a type of realization shared with
The Sublime Ones of the Mahāyāna.

The type of realization unique to the Mahāyāna
Is the great uncategorized ultimate.
The distinctive type of realization of selflessness is unexcelled—
Clearly, extensively, and completely.

If someone says: "This distinction among types of realization
Is that of the Svātantrika tradition, such as the Abhisamayālaṃkāra.
This is not a unique feature
Of the Prāsaṅgika Mahāyāna."

Go ahead and explain a hidden meaning that does not account for
The distinctive features of the Mahāyāna Path of Joining,
The greatness of the unique knowledge of the path, and
The distinctive knowledge of the ground, such as the distinctive signs!

Go ahead and profess a Prāsaṅgika tradition
That was not previously explained by the supreme regent [Maitreya]
Nor even was Candrakīrti's viewpoint of
The hidden meaning of sūtras!

Concerning the ways of perfecting the types of realization,
Others say: "The Mahāyāna type of realization
Has the distinctive feature of being perfected in the continuum
Of those who have not entered the Mahāyāna path."

Some people claim: "A bodhisattva on the first ground
Has perfected the type of realization of the Auditors and Self-Realized Ones."
Such elegant discourses as these, which do not accord with either
The Middle Way or Mind-Only, are a disgrace!

The illustrious tradition of the Lion of the Śākyas,
From the scriptural tradition of scholars of the school of early translations,
Explains the delineation of the grounds and paths, and
The ways of perfecting abandonment and realization, as follows.

Regarding this, abandonment and realization is twofold:
The truth of the path and the truth of cessation.

Nāgārjuna asserted that the truth of cessation, emptiness, and the ultimate
Have the same meaning;
Therefore, selflessness, emptiness, and the authentic limit
Are just the same meaning.

Regarding this, there are two:
(1) Natural purity and (2) purity that is free from the adventitious [obscurations].

Within the natural purity of selflessness,
There is the twofold selflessness: of phenomena and persons.
From the ways of clearly realizing these,
There are two truths of the path: Mahāyāna and Hīnayāna.

Within abandonment, the purity that is free from the adventitious,
There are two cessations: the abandonment of the afflictive and cognitive [obscurations].
From the ways of manifestly attaining these,
There are two nirvāṇas: Mahāyāna and Hīnayāna.

This meaning is twofold: (1) the way of realization temporarily and
(2) The way of perfecting abandonment and realization consummately.

Regarding this, natural purity is seen
On the Path of Seeing, from the [first] ground of Sublime Joy.

At [the seventh ground,] Gone Afar,
Abandonment and realization is shared with the Auditors and Self-Realized Ones:
The cessation is the abandonment of afflictive obscurations and
The perfection of the truth of the path is the selflessness of persons.

However, since the consummate cessation and path—
The selflessness of phenomena and abandonment freed from cognitive obscurations—
Have not been perfected,
The Victorious Ones rouse them from cessation.

When perfecting, ripening, and training have been completed,
There is the consummate great freedom from the adventitious;
Abandonment free from cognitive obscurations and
The antidote, the selflessness of phenomena, are perfected.

The truth of cessation that is the perfection of abandonment
Is the nature of the Essential Body;
The great truth of the path of perfect realization
Is the discovery of the consummate Wisdom Truth Body.

This is a quintessential instruction
From the matchless spiritual friend—
A lineage from the mouth to the ears not propagated to others.
We are fortunate!

Concerning the way of attaining the fruition,
Those of the later generation explain a presentation of the path and fruition; however,

They do not account for the profound meaning of [the modes of] reality and appearance—
Abiding purity and transformation.

Our tradition, the tradition of the scholars of the early generation,
Asserts by means of the modes of (1) reality and (2) appearance:
(1) Abiding purity, which is a freed effect, and
(2) Transformation, which is a ripened effect.

In the explanation of the unique mode of reality
By the conventional valid cognition of purity,
The consummate fruition is the naturally abiding purity—
The abiding purity that is the effect freed from the adventitious [defilements].

In the common explanation of the mode of appearance
By the conventional valid cognition of confined perception,
The causal phenomena are completely transformed in time (gnas skabs)—
The effect is asserted as a transformation into a ripened effect.

Due to [the modes of] reality and appearance—
Freed and ripened from the natures of the two causal accumulations—
We assert the Truth Body's qualities as a freed effect and
The accomplishment of the Form Bodies as a ripened effect.

Concerning the nature of the fruition, others say,
"The identity of the three exalted bodies of the Buddha
Is an object of a mind of confined perception—
Limited to matter, cognition, and non-concurrent [formations]."

Such a common locus of sentient beings and Buddhas,
Which is not beyond the phenomena of aggregates and constituents, and
Has not relinquished the activity of mental feeling (sems tshor),
Is a disgrace!

The nature of the three exalted bodies
Stated in the profound, definitive meaning sūtras
Is free from the aggregates and
Transcends the constituents and sense-fields.

Therefore, it is said that anyone who regards [the nature of the Buddha]
As a form or as a sound

Has entered into the mistaken path of conceptuality;
That one does not know this nature.

Therefore, the nature of the three mysteries
Is the display of great wisdom;
The omniscience of a perfect Buddha
Is solely the nature of the Truth Body.

The displays of the Guides' Form Bodies
Are appearances that are like forms, [but]
Are not material phenomena composed of particles.
View them as the self-lucidity of the expanse of phenomena.

In this way, profound suchness
Is not what is known by logicians.
A mind of confined perception
Is not able to fully know these.

Others' perceptions are
A limitless array of a variety of exalted bodies
Simultaneously appearing in each part of every particle;
[A Buddha's] own perception is the changeless wisdom body.

Others' perceptions are
A manifold array of as many languages as there are in the six classes of beings,
Simultaneously resounding.
[A Buddha's] own perception is the unobstructed wisdom speech.

Others' perceptions are
An array of a mind that knows everything instantly—
Simultaneously seeing objects of knowledge.
[A Buddha's] own perception is the unwavering wisdom mind.

When a valid cognition of confined perception
Investigates the nature of the omniscient subject,
Due to knowing entities,
Omniscience is asserted as conditioned in the mere mode of appearance.

However, wisdom's self-appearance is the great luminous clarity,
Profound, peaceful, and free from constructs.
It is self-existing, unconditioned, and spontaneously present—
The great freedom from the extremes of purity, bliss, self, and permanence.

Regarding omniscience's domain, the assertions:
"Omniscience itself does not perceive impure phenomena of delusion," and
"Omniscience does perceive—a Buddha's own perception also has deluded perceptions,"
Are confusion at the core.

[Deluded perceptions are seen] in the way that someone with superknowledge
Sees the phenomena of deluded perceptions in another's dream.
However, they are not his own perceptions;
His own perceptions are his waking perceptions.

Likewise, omniscience itself sees and knows
All the impure fields of others' perceptions.
However, they are not [a Buddha's] own perception;
A Buddha's own perception is the pure field.

When perfecting, ripening, and training have been completed,
And when the three realms are a manifest, perfect Buddha,
The three exalted bodies are perfected in the field of the Victorious Ones, and
The viewpoints of Sūtra and Mantra are integrated indivisibly.

The mode of appearance is the impurity of others' perceptions and
All the phenomena of appearance, resonance, and cognition;
The mode of reality is the pure field of [the Buddha's] own perception and
The perfect array of exalted body, speech, and mind.

Objects, faculties, and awareness abide as pure and
The qualities of transformation know no end.
Although it may not taste good in the perceptions of others,
It appears in [the Buddha's] own perception as the supreme taste of purity.

The way of knowing that sees appearance and emptiness as equality
Knows the pure and impure simultaneously.
The one taste of knower and known
Is inconceivable and inexpressible by a mind of confined perception.

There are two objects of knowledge: (1) what is and (2) whatever there is.
Within the appearing phenomena of whatever there is, there are two:
(1) [A Buddha's] own perception, which is the pure mode of reality, and
(2) The perceptions of others, which are the modes of appearance of the six classes of beings.

Although there are five wisdoms that know,
There are two: (1) the wisdom of what is and (2) the wisdom of whatever there is.
Through this, know the infinite definitive mystery of
The way in which wisdom knows the objects of knowledge.

In this way, without pollution of the poisons of attachment and aggression,
This was a concise lamp that elucidates the mode of reality—
The distinctive essential meanings, without mixing them—
Distinguishing the early and later traditions of masterly scholars in the Land of Snow.

In the dominion of the kingdom of the school of early translations' doctrine of the great secret—
Which is the supreme, illustrious tradition of the Victorious One, the Lion of the Śākyas—
With the pretense of staying a long time, I held a begging bowl of the three faiths
At the threshold of the vast and profound feast of doctrine.

Due to this, the fortune that this inquisitive youth attained well is
This fortune of food from the feast of doctrine.
In order to repay the kindness of my glorious teachers,
And in order to benefit some honest people with discerning minds,

Sākya[muni]'s monk from the eastern region of Dakpo,
The one called "Dongak Tenpé Nyima,"
Wrote clearly from the path of authentic reasoning,
In accordance with the scriptures of sūtra and tantra, and the quintessential instructions of my teacher.

By this virtue, may all beings that exist, equal to [the extent of] space,
Enjoy the splendor of the seven qualities of high birth.
Having completely entered the path of the three beings,
May they all attain unexcelled awakening!

May I also, from now until the extent of existence,
Enter the realms of beings in a variety of forms
And play in the sacred light, without parting from the sole refuge,
The infallible youth with the top-knot [Mañjughoṣa]!

May the light of the wheels of explanation and practice of the Victorious Ones' teaching
Pervade all the kingdoms of the vast territories and regions!
May we abide in discipline and perfect study, contemplation, and meditation,
Beautifying the Capable One's teaching with exposition, debate, and composition!

Ornament of Mañjughoṣa's Viewpoint

An Explanation of the Words and Meanings of *Distinguishing the Views and Philosophies*

A Lamp of Essential Points

namo mañjuśrīye! Homage to Mañjuśrī!

In the vast spatial expanse of the Truth Body, the profound peace free from constructs,
The luminous clarity of the self-radiance of wisdom and love is the perfect rapture (longs spyod rdzogs)
Endowed with the radiant brilliance of splendorous enlightened activity that trains beings in whatever ways are needed—
May the omniscient illuminator of beings be victorious on the crown of my head!

The assembly upholding the teachings impartially—
The bodhisattvas such as Mañjughoṣa and Maitreya, the eight close sons[1] *and the sixteen elders,*
The six ornaments,[2] *the two supreme ones,*[3] *the three Mañjughoṣas,*[4] *etc.—*
Are my objects of veneration.

The essential points of the views and philosophies of the earlier and later masterly scholars of the Land of Snow
Are one taste in the oceanic expanse of the consummate viewpoint;

Yet for the time being, the distinctive four rivers of transmission of the Buddha's Word
Will be delineated by elaborating the words and meanings of scripture.

Herein lies all the oceans of viewpoints within the doctrines of Sūtra and Mantra, which are the precious teachings of the guide who is a lion among men. This is an elucidation of the distinctive views and philosophies in accord with the way the masterly scholars of Tibet such as the three Mañjughoṣas explained through the four rivers of transmission of the Buddha's Word.

To explicate this lamp of essential points of delineation, in *Distinguishing the Views and Philosophies*—which is a meaning-commentary on [Mipam's] *Beacon of Certainty*—there are three parts: (1) the sections of composition, (2) the composed scripture, and (3) the concluding meaning of the completed composition.

1. The Sections of Composition

The first section has two parts: (1) the expression of worship and (2) the resolve to compose.

1. Expression of Worship

namo mañjuśrīye! Homage to Mañjuśrī!

This is an expression of worship to the supreme exalted deity, Mañjughoṣa. Then, there is a statement of the greatness of the early translations, the topic of the body of the treatise, in an expression of worship to the assembly of Sublime Ones who thoroughly taught those [doctrines]:

The doctrine of the ground, path, and fruition that unites Sūtra and Mantra
Is the greatly miraculous view and conduct of indivisible appearance and emptiness.
All the Buddha's Word and commentaries on the viewpoint, common and extraordinary,
Are taught through three valid measures (tshad ma)—may the assembly of Sublime Ones be victorious!

The distinctive meaning in general is the unity of all the excellent paths of Sūtra and Mantra in the precious teachings of the Victorious One. Specifically, the distinctive view of the ground is the unity of the two truths; the distinctive training on the path is the unity of the two accumulations; and the distinctive fruition to be attained is the unity of the two exalted bodies. In either context of Sūtra or Mantra, there is the greatness of ascertaining the grand unity of the indivisible appearance and emptiness within all presentations of the topics of the ground, path, and fruition, without an influx of contradictions regarding the two truths, such as the partiality of separating appearance and emptiness.

In particular, the miraculous view is associated with the view of the glorious sublime master of Nāgas [Nāgārjuna], whose unequalled chariot of the Great Middle Way is the profound school among the four great Buddhist philosophies.[5] The miraculous conduct is associated with the way of conduct of the great preceptor, Śāntarakṣita, whose Sarvāstivāda tradition of upholding the Vinaya is distinctively wonderful among the four schools of the great Vinaya traditions in the Noble Land of India.[6] In short, the greatness of the meaning of what is expressed has the distinction of being the paramount view, meditation, conduct, and fruition.

The scriptures that express this topic are also distinctive: In general, there are three precious scriptural sections of the common scriptures of the Buddha's Word.[7] Specifically, there are the ocean-like scriptural sections of Mantra of the awareness-holders, and in particular, the extraordinary precious yogas of the three inner-tantras.[8] The entirety of the oceanic sūtras and tantras of the Word of the Victorious One, together with the commentaries on their viewpoint, has the distinction of complete perfection, of comprehensiveness without error.

The way of instruction in all these wonderfully unique, good words and meanings—the character of what is expressed and the means of expression—is also distinctive by means of (1) the valid measure of the scripture of the Victorious One, which is the Word of sūtra and tantra; (2) the valid measure of reasoning, which is its power of fact itself; and (3) the valid measure of the quintessential instructions, which is the oral testimony of a sacred teacher. In this way, the instruction is characterized by the three valid measures.

"May the sublime assembly of Victorious Ones and their offspring be completely victorious!" is an expression of worship in general to the supreme teacher, who is the master sage, together with the assembly of the eight close sons, the sixteen elders, and so forth. Specifically, it is to the great scholars and accomplished ones of India such as the six ornaments and the two supreme ones. In particular, it is to their emanations, the Preceptor [Śāntarakṣita], the Master [Padmasambhava], and the Dharma [King Trisong Detsen], together with the emanated assembly of great translators and scholars. These distinctions should be known through the previous histories of doctrine in general, and specifically, through the writings of the glorious Rongzom—and in particular, in [Mipam's] *Aspiration for the Expansion of the Teachings*[9] and so forth.

Also, expressing worship in this way accords with how the great chariots of the past composed treatises, and follows the quintessential instructions of sacred beings. The topic of the body of the treatise expresses the greatness of the doctrine of the early translations; it praises and venerates the assembly of Sublime Ones who gave these teachings.

2. *Resolve to Compose*

The second section has two parts: (1) the manner of composition and (2) the actual resolve.

1. Manner of Composition

The explanation and practice of the Victorious One's teaching
are the great maṇḍala of the sun and moon;
[Through] the generation of the miraculous intent, when the
time was ripe
The chariot was drawn further and further north.
It became the splendor of beings of the Cool Land.

The earlier and later masterly scholars of the Land of Snow
Explained the distinctive traditions separately without mixing
them.
Due to this, the four views and philosophies of Sakya, Geluk,
Kagyü, and Nyingma
Are widely renowned as "the four transmissions of the
teaching."

The source of the river of all the Victorious One's teachings in
the Land of Snow

Is the school of early translations, endowed with the six qualities of greatness.
The profound essential points of its view, meditation, and conduct
Are much superior to the various philosophies of others.

One who knows well, without mixing, the delineations of philosophies of
The respective schools of Sakya, Geluk, Kagyü, and Nyingma, and
Is skilled at properly upholding one's own unique tradition,
Is certainly a being who upholds the teachings of the Victorious One.

Therefore, if you want to uphold the illustrious tradition of the early translations,
You should maintain all the profound key points of its view, meditation, and conduct—
Completely upholding the meaning of the profound essential points—
Without mixing in the slightest word of the various ordinary philosophies.

Alas! Due to various attitudes of these days,
Other than duḥkha *(suffering) that is the strife of mutual attachment and aggression,*
Repetition of various hearsays, and discourse on pleasant-sounding words,
It is rare that there is one who properly speaks the profound essential points of the views and philosophies.

Discernment is knowing how to distinguish the essential points concerning what is and is not doctrine,
Knowing the divisions between one's own and others' philosophies, and
Knowing elegant discourses from inferior discourses.
It is what scholars have, not hordes of fools!

The precious teachings of the Victorious One, the Lion of the Śākyas, are a great maṇḍala that integrates the sun and moon of explanation and practice. The source of the doctrine, which is the universal splendor of beings, is the Noble Land of India. The supreme teacher, the master sage himself, generated the intent for the doctrine to come to be the splendor of the disciples in the dark region—the Land of Snow.

Following the prophesy that the precious teachings of the Victorious One would spread further and further north, there was a woman who tended chickens, Saṃvarī, the daughter of Selé, who had sons who were emanated bodhisattvas. Thinking of the future, they made a resolve when they built the great Jarung Khashor Stūpa.[10] In accord with their generated intent and aspirations—the strength of which was like a chariot made of wind—the sun and moon of the precious teaching went north when the time was ripe. Accordingly, the doctrine was brought further and further north from the Noble Land of India.

As the universal splendor of beings, the doctrine came to our cool land of snow mountains due to the power of the sheer kindness of the former Dharma King, the emanated scholars, and emanated translators. In this Land of Snow, Tibet, all of the masterly scholars who came earlier and later merged into the river of the single viewpoint—the consummate expanse of equality free from constructs. However, out of necessity—at times to destroy the quality of thorough affliction or to develop the quality of complete purification—there are manners of distinctive commentaries that emphasize the quality of appearance or the quality of emptiness, without mixing the asserted meanings. This is stated in [Mipam's] overview of the *Madhyamakālaṃkāra*.[11]

Due to this, the four types of views and philosophies of the Sakya, Geluk, Kagyü, and Nyingma are widely renowned as "the four transmissions of the teaching." Moreover:

- the Sakya, endowed with glory, is the transmission of the explanation of the vast and profound
- the Geluk, endowed with virtue, is the transmission of the reasoning of the scriptural collections
- the Kagyü, protector of beings, is the transmission of the accomplishment of practice, and
- the Nyingma, Secret Mantra, is the transmission of sūtra, tantra, and the quintessential instructions

Furthermore, there are various ways of presenting the qualities of the four transmissions, such as:

- Geluk, "the transmission of Sūtra"
- Nyingma, "the transmission of Mantra"
- Sakya, "the transmission of explanation," and
- Kagyü, "the transmission of practice"

In this way, the source of the river of teachings for every specific teaching of the Victorious One that exists in Tibet, the Land of Snow, is superior due to six greatnesses: (1) the greatness of the place where they were translated, (2) the greatness of the sponsors having great wealth, (3) the greatness of the flower [of wealth] that was a support for the request, (4) the greatness of the scholars who facilitated the translations, (5) the greatness of the translators who wrote them down, and (6) the greatness of the doctrines that were translated. An extensive presentation of this can be known from the elegant discourses of the glorious Rongzom, etc.

Due to this, the unique and profound essential points of the view, meditation, and conduct of the school of early translations are much superior to other various philosophies. The manner of superiority by means of view and meditation will be explained below.

Also, one should know the many ways that the conduct has essential points of profound distinction such as: the practice of the three foundations of the Vinaya[12] in general; and specifically, the direction of the patchings, etc., of the religious robes, the way of wrapping the lower skirt, as well as many distinctions down to the color of the hats—and in the ritual tradition of Secret Mantra in particular, even the body posture and the manner of chanting.

In general, anyone with a fine intellect having individually known, without aggression, all the delineations of the distinctive philosophies of the respective Sakya, Geluk, Kagyü, and Nyingma traditions without mixing them—and who upholds one's own tradition properly without mixing it with the others—is a scholar. That person is certainly able to be a great being upholding the teaching—one who upholds, sustains, and develops the Victorious One's precious teachings through explanation, debate, and composition. On the other hand, one with attachment and aggression—who is argumentative, sectarian, and jealous—and competes for power and influence, is just as is said:

"While not knowing the teachings, it is a disgrace to boast to be an upholder of the teachings."

For this reason, if you want to properly uphold the tradition of the early translations of Nyingma itself, you should maintain all the profound key points such as the distinctive view, meditation, and conduct of the school of early translations, completely upholding the meaning of the distinctive essential points without mixing in even a single word of all the other various ordinary philosophies. Otherwise, alas! In this current era, the five degenerations[13] of the age of strife (*rtsod ldan, kaliyuga*) are booming greater and greater. Due to this, and the influence of various conceptual attitudes such as attachment and aggression, most monastic traditions create an abundance of *duḥkha* from argumentation and strife. They are mutually attached to their own factions and have intolerable aggression toward other factions. Although there are a few that appear to be engaged in study and explanation, other than merely following the hearsay of others, they do not at all stand on their own; they are not self-reliant.

Even if they are not like that, they do not even turn their minds in the slightest to the meaning of the great scriptures. Without analysis, they mainly prattle upon a few pleasant-sounding, fancy words of a mere memorized phrase of scripture or a few parts of a commentary on the words. Other than that, it appears to be rare, nearly impossible, for someone to have realized the profound essential points of the views and philosophies for oneself as they are, and with an understanding of the meaning of the scriptures, speak properly with an altruistic mind.

However, without any reason at all, people think that their own factions are the pure doctrine. They think to themselves, and proclaim to others, "All the other factions have impure doctrines. They don't even have the path of liberation." Likewise, they hold as divine "this which is the profound philosophy of my own tradition!" And they view the other factions as demonic. They praise their own mere monastic textbooks as elegant discourses and heedlessly curse the authentic Word [of the Buddha] and *śāstras* of the other factions. Although there are many who accomplish the causes of the inexhaustible bad karma of rejecting the doctrine, when analyzed well, the mind-treasuries of those great, masterly scholars—those with an eye for doctrine and perfect instinct and training—have the discernment of knowing how to differentiate the essential points of what is pure and impure doctrine, the divisions between the philosophies of their own and others' traditions, and the respective distinctions between elegant and inferior discourses. Otherwise, this is not the domain of knowledge of a hoard of fools! Since they are without the opportunity [to know], it would be good if they refrained from that talk.

2. Actual Resolve

Due to this, having completely given up the attitudes of attachment and aggression,
I will briefly expound upon a distinguishing lamp that completely illuminates
The mere mode of reality of the distinctive views and philosophies of the old and new schools—
Their unmixed appearing forms in accordance with their respective traditions.

Due to this in general, any doctrine or person that falls within the Sakya, Geluk, Kagyü, and Nyingma—all the precious teachings of the guiding sage—have the same taste, like honey and molasses; they are the sacred refuge for now and the future. So I will expound a discourse having completely given up negative conceptual attitudes—the causes of what will ripen in the future without perishing—such as attachment and aggression by means of partiality and bias, clinging with attachment to my own faction and being hostile toward another faction, wishing to refute it, etc. This is a concise summary, a distinguishing lamp that completely illuminates the mere mode of reality of the distinctive views and philosophies of the old and new schools free from superimposition and denigration—and the features of the radiantly appearing, unmixed forms in accord with the scriptural traditions of the respective masterly scholars. This is my resolve to compose.

2. The Composed Scripture

This section has two parts: (1) the distinctions between the views and philosophies of the vehicles and (2) distinguishing the distinctive views and philosophies.

1. Distinctions Between the Views and Philosophies of the Vehicles

This section has two parts: (1) the distinction between the Buddhist and non-Buddhist philosophies and (2) distinguishing between higher and lower vehicles in particular.

1. Distinction Between the Buddhist and Non-Buddhist Philosophies

The distinctive ways of assertion by the earlier and later masterly scholars
From the Land of Snow go beyond what can be expressed;
Concerning solely the distinction between Buddhists and non-Buddhists,
There are discordant ways of dividing them.

According to the way of assertion by the matchless Atīśa
Most of the masterly scholars of the new schools of translation
Make the distinction between Buddhists and non-Buddhists in terms of refuge—*
By merely that, it is solely a division based upon the support.

According to the intended meaning of the scriptures of sūtra and tantra,
The school of early translations asserts immense distinctions—
Distinctions in terms of the support, view,
Meditation, conduct, and fruition.

In general, the respective distinctions among the ways of assertion by the earlier and later masterly scholars from the Land of Snow are beyond what can be expressed. However, concerning just this context here, there are many distinctions among discordant assertions regarding the way of dividing solely the difference between Buddhists and non-Buddhists. Some masterly scholars of the schools of later translations say, as stated in *Philosophical Systems: Lion's Song Abandoning Delusion*:† "The distinctive teaching, teacher, and view are two: Buddhist and non-Buddhist. . . ." They make the distinction between Buddhists and non-Buddhists by means of:

- the distinctive teaching—whether or not the four seals[14] are transgressed, and whether or not it is endowed with the three trainings of the path[15] or not

*According to Bötrül's student, Khenpo Chökhyap, this view is said to primarily concern the Geluk (*dge ldan pa*).

†This is a text written by the Geluk scholar, Jamyang Zhepa (*'jam dbyangs bshad pa*, 1648–1722), *grub mtha' rnam par bzhag pa 'khrul spong gdong lnga'i sgra dbyangs kun mkhyen lam bzang gsal ba'i rin chen sgron me*. See English translation in Jeffrey Hopkins, *Maps of the Profound* (Ithaca: Snow Lion Publications, 2003), 25–55.

- the distinctive teacher—whether or not the Great Sage [Buddha] is held to be the teacher, and
- the distinctive view—whether or not a creator such as Īśvara is accepted or not

Moreover, some people, in accord with what is stated in the *Bodhisattvapiṭaka,* also make the distinction between Buddhists and non-Buddhists by means of the view—whether or not the four seals that signify the Word are accepted, etc. Since these traditions are in fact in accord with our tradition, I do not convey a distinction.

Also, some people express the words of the matchless Atīśa's *Lamp of the Path of Awakening*:[16] "Buddhists and non-Buddhists have a difference in refuge." In general, in accord with this way of asserting that the distinction between Buddhists and non-Buddhists also must be made by means of refuge, most masterly scholars of the schools of later translations make the distinction between Buddhists and non-Buddhists only by refuge. In the monastic textbooks of philosophical systems such as *The Great View and Philosophy*, the difference between Buddhists and non-Buddhists is made in terms of refuge: "The defining character of a Buddhist is one who authentically accepts the source of refuge, the three jewels, and does not search for another refuge apart from this. The opposite of this is the defining character of a non-Buddhist."* This way merely makes a distinction by means of refuge—the specific foundational support, which is a distinction in the manner of excluding [properties] that are not endowed (*mi ldan rnam gcod*).[17]

However, some people refute this, saying, "It is not legitimate to make a distinction between Buddhists and non-Buddhists by means of the view of the four seals that signify the Word. The distinction between the two needs to be made *solely* by refuge." Most followers of the old and new schools make these statements in an attuned voice.

However, these ones with eyes of partiality have not even seen a fraction of all the profound and subtle teachings on the distinction between Buddhists and non-Buddhists within the great sūtras and *śāstras*. They just know how to mouth the mere words of the great scriptures that make the division in terms of the support of refuge.

---

*The text that Bötrül cites in paraphrase here is apparently the voluminous text by the Geluk scholar, Changkya Rolpé Dorjé (*lcang skya rol pa'i rdo rje*, 1717–1786), *Presentation of Philosophical Systems* (*grub pa'i mtha' rnam par bzhag pa gsal bar bshad pa thub bstan lhun po'i mdzes rgyan*). See parallel discussion of refuge in Changkya Rolpé Dorjé, *Presentation of Philosophical Systems*, 11.

Due to this, precisely in accord with the intended meaning of the oceanic scriptures of sūtra and tantra, the proponents of the Nyingma school of early translations assert immense distinctions between the philosophies of Buddhists and non-Buddhists. A fivefold distinction is spoken in scriptures such as [Longchenpa's] *Precious Wish-Fulfilling Treasury:*

- the distinction of the support of refuge
- the distinction of the view of the abiding reality
- the distinction of the cultivation of meditation
- the distinction of the conduct that is performed and
- the distinction of the fruition that is attained

In general, in the great sūtras and *śāstras* such as the *Bodhisattvapiṭaka,* and in particular, in the *White Lotus,* the omniscient lord of doctrine's [Longchenpa's] great commentary [on the *Wish-Fulfilling Treasury*], these manners can now be known extensively.[18]

Regarding this, some people claim: "The distinction between Buddhists and non-Buddhists must be made in terms of the refuge; it is not reasonable to make a distinction between the two in terms of the view of the four seals that signify the Word because that would contradict both scripture and reasoning. Firstly, it would contradict scripture because of contradicting such texts as the *Lamp of the Path* [*of Awakening*] by Atīśa."

They do not understand the essential point. The intention of that scripture in this context is an authentic means of establishing the distinction of the *support* of refuge—the first among the five distinctive features. However, it does not state, "other than refuge alone, there are no other distinctions," by excluding the endowment of other [properties] (*gzhan ldan rnam gcod*).[19] How do these [other four properties] conflict with the scriptures? Following in accord with this, some people cite the *Great Array of Ati* (*a ti bkod pa chen po*)[20] scripture as a source to establish the distinction between the two [Buddhists and non-Buddhists] needing to be made in terms of refuge*; this is merely a claim that establishes what has already been established.

*This statement is attributed to Khenpo Gangshar (*gang shar dbang po*, 1925–1958/9), by Bötrül's student, Khenpo Chökhyap.

One may say: "Secondly, it would contradict reasoning, too, because if it were necessary to make a distinction between Buddhists and non-Buddhists by means of whether or not the view of the [four] seals that signify the Word are accepted, then that would not encompass a basis of the property (*mtshan gzhi*)—a sponsor of Buddhism. This follows because although a sponsor of Buddhism is necessarily a Buddhist, he does not [necessarily] know how to accept the four seals."

[In response:] Well, it would [absurdly] follow that it would also not be reasonable to make a distinction between Buddhists and non-Buddhists by means of whether or not one authentically accepts the source of refuge, the three jewels, because that does not encompass a basis of the property—a sponsor of Buddhism. This follows because a basis of the property [a sponsor of Buddhism] also does not [necessarily] know the way of authentically accepting the source of refuge—the three jewels. The *Great Exposition of the Stages of the Path* by the lord [Tsongkhapa] states:

> The way of accepting refuge is necessarily endowed with four properties: knowing the qualities of the three jewels, knowing [their] distinction, accepting [them], and not propounding otherwise.[21]

Hence, it is also difficult for a sponsor of Buddhism, who does not know even the manner of accepting the four seals, to authentically accept the source of refuge—the three jewels—by means of knowing the qualities of the three jewels and so forth. Moreover, from a sūtra:

> Most people who are scared through fear,
> Go for refuge in a mountain,
> A forest, or a big tree;
> That refuge is not foremost. . . .[22]

This shows the necessity of going for refuge by means of accepting the nature of the profound reality of the four truths—knowing that all contaminated phenomena are suffering, etc.—without transgressing the intended meaning of the four seals. Otherwise, how could going for refuge as such be a property that distinguishes Buddhists and non-Buddhists?

Moreover, some people contend: "If you say a Buddhist is someone who accepts the four seals, and otherwise, one is not a Buddhist, then it would [absurdly] follow that the five Mahāsaṃmata schools[23] would not be Buddhist because they do not accept the four seals. This follows because they assert the personal self (*gang zag gi bdag*) to be substantially established."

[In response:] Well, it would [absurdly] follow that the subject, Buddhist realists (*dngos po smra ba*),[24] would necessarily have a philosophy that does not accept the four seals because they do not assert all phenomena to be empty. This follows because they accept what is substantially established, such as the two irreducibles (*cha med gnyis*),[25] which are the subtle self of phenomena. Therefore, at the time of the third council, following the *Sūtra Revealing the Prophesy of the Dream of King Kṛkī*[26] and others, all the eighteen schools of the Auditors had been established to be philosophies of a pure path to liberation by means of similarly accepting the Buddhist view of the four seals that signify the Word.

Accordingly, the five Mahāsaṃmata schools also ascertain the selflessness of persons as it is. Although they accept the four seals, they do not know to posit the referent of the view of self as nominally existent; they use the mere word *substantially existent*. Even so, how could this be like the non-Buddhist's self that is a permanent entity? Likewise, the proponents of Mind-Only in the Mahāyāna also assert the complete selflessness of phenomena from the most subtle,[27] and accept a truly existent basis of appearance—the dependent nature (*gzhan dbang, paratantra*). Even so, one should also know the various distinctions between them and the Vaibhāṣikas, and so forth. Although there is a lot that needs to be said here, for the moment, I will leave it at that.

Thus, [Mipam's] *Gateway to Scholarship* also makes a minimal distinction between Buddhists and non-Buddhists by means of refuge.[28] However, the distinction between the philosophies of Buddhists and non-Buddhists, as was just explained, accords with what is spoken in such texts as the *Summary of the Philosophies*[29] by the lord of doctrine, Mipam.

2. Distinguishing Between Higher and Lower Vehicles in Particular

This section has two parts: (1) the general and (2) the specific views and philosophies.

1. The General

Others make the distinction between the Mahāyāna and Hīnayāna
By only the generation of the mind [*of awakening*];

This is just a division of intention.
There is a vast difference in view, meditation, conduct, and fruition.

Other masterly scholars claim that the distinction between the Mahāyāna and Hīnayāna needs to be made *solely* by means of the generation of the mind [of awakening] because it is said: "Mahāyāna and Hīnayāna are distinguished by the generation of the mind [of awakening]." Although this is the case, it is not reasonable to assume that there is no other distinction besides just this.

The meaning of the scriptural statement, "Mahāyāna and Hīnayāna are distinguished by the generation of the mind [of awakening]," is just that a distinction is made also by means of the intention—the generation of the mind [of awakening]. However, there are other distinctions between the two as well in such statements as the presence of the distinctions by means of the seven greatnesses in the *Precious Wish-Fulfilling Treasury*, in accord with the viewpoint of the *Sūtrālaṃkāra*.[30] They are boundless, but to summarize the essential points, extremely vast distinctions are accepted by means of:

- view—whether or not it has perfected the twofold selflessness
- meditation—whether or not its method and insight are distinctive
- conduct—whether or not it is endowed with the six transcendent perfections, and
- fruition—whether or not it accomplishes the great awakening

It was stated thus by the lord of the doctrine [Longchenpa]:

The view is like space—the eighteen emptinesses.[31]

The meditation is luminous clarity—the thirty-seven factors.[32]

The conduct is faultless—the six transcendent perfections.[33] And,

The fruition is unexcelled—the accomplishment of awakening.[34]

2. The Specific Views and Philosophies

This section has two parts: (1) distinguishing the views and philosophies of the higher and lower vehicles and (2) distinguishing the views of Sūtra and Mantra in particular.

1. Distinguishing the Views and Philosophies of the Higher and Lower Vehicles

Some people claim that the views and philosophies of the two
*Higher and lower vehicles are contradictory.**
Also, others variously claim that while there is no distinction in view,
There are distinctions in the conduct and the fruition.

Our tradition, that of the scholars of the school of early translations,
Asserts immense distinctions between the higher and lower, and
Asserts the views and philosophies of the progression of vehicles
In the manner of the gradual and instantaneous.

Therefore, the four philosophies
Are in accord in accepting the seals that symbolize the Word;
However, in terms of the manner of (1) clarity, (2) extensiveness, and (3) completeness,
There is a great difference between the higher and lower.

Some philosophers claim that, due to the extreme contradictions between the views and philosophies of the two scriptural traditions of the higher and lower vehicles, there is no liberation in the scriptural traditions of the lower vehicle. Also, others accept that the three Sublime Ones[35] have a single type of realization. They accept that the type of realization, the view, is without distinction for (1) a person of the lower vehicle who is a person that has attained realization on the path, such as Śāriputra, and (2) a bodhisattva of the Mahāyāna abiding on the tenth ground. However, they variously claim that

*This is attributed to the Geluk by Bötrül's student, Khenpo Chökhyap. He states how the Geluk view of Mind-Only is incompatible with their view of the Middle Way, and how they view Prāsaṅgika and Svātantrika as incompatible.

there is a distinction in the conduct—whether or not it is endowed with the six transcendent perfections, and the fruition, whether or not the nirvāṇa of the Mahāyāna or Hīnayāna is attained. Extensive presentations of these manners appear in the Wisdom Chapter [of the *Bodhicaryāvatāra*] in the contexts such as the Gone Afar[36] section, and also in the corresponding "Rejoinders."[37]

Regarding this, our tradition, that of the masterly scholars of the early translations, asserts as follows: The views and philosophies of the higher and lower philosophies and the progression of vehicles are not contradictory from the aspect of the ascertainment of selflessness and meditation on that meaning. However, by means of their path being gradual, the Hīnayāna—with a view that ascertains only a selflessness of persons, and meditation on the meaning of that [selflessness of persons]—is the means to accomplish the fruition of a mere nirvāṇa. Compared to that, through the manner of an instantaneous path, the Mahāyāna—with a view that ascertains both selflessnesses and meditation on the meaning of that [twofold selflessness]—is the means to accomplish the consummate fruition of great awakening. Thus, immense distinctions are also accepted between the higher and lower vehicles.

For this reason, not only are the higher and lower vehicles [not contradictory], but since the four philosophies also are in accord in accepting the four seals that signify the Word—and since the lower ones are steps toward the higher ones—the four philosophies certainly are not contradictory. However, from the distinction of whether or not they are able to ascertain (1) clearly, (2) extensively, and (3) completely in the context of ascertaining the view, we accept extremely vast distinctions between the four higher and lower views and philosophies.

2. Distinguishing the Views of Sūtra and Mantra in Particular

Other people say: "Other than a distinction in method for
Sūtra and Mantra,
*There is no distinction in view."**

*This view is attributed to the Geluk and Sakya stemming from Sakya Paṇḍita (*sa skya paṇḍita*, 1182–1251), by Bötrül's student, Khenpo Chökhyap. For Tsongkhapa's statements on Sūtra and Mantra not having a different view, see Tsongkhapa, *Great Stages of Mantra* (*sngags rim chen mo*), 18; English translation in Jeffrey Hopkins, trans. and ed., *Tantra in Tibet*, 110. For Sakya Paṇḍita's statement, see note 42 below.

Other than a view of a mere void selflessness,
There is no appearing aspect, no luminous clarity; therefore, it is faulty.

In our tradition, as for the manner of the vehicles of Sūtra and Mantra,
Although there is no distinction from the aspect of emptiness, the expanse of phenomena,
From the aspect of appearance, the spontaneous presence of luminous clarity,
The distinction in views is like the earth and space.

There is a vast distinction of clarity, extensiveness, and completion in the two:
(1) The luminous clarity of the Causal Vehicle,
The nature of mind which is Buddha-nature, and
(2) The spontaneously present luminous clarity of Mantra.

In short, the four philosophies of the Causal Vehicle
Have the profound distinction of the manner of completing the absence of self;
The four tantra sets of Secret Mantra[38]
Have the profound distinction of the view of spontaneous presence.

The main point of this, the consummate meaning,
Is the way of perfecting, gradually or instantaneously,
The supreme view of the noncontradiction of appearance and emptiness—
The meaning of the great unity free from extremes.

Whoever holds appearance and emptiness with an influx of contradictions, and
Asserts emptiness as an emptiness of true existence—a mere nonentity—
Has difficulty explaining the divisions between the views
Of sūtra and tantra.

It appears that other masterly scholars say: "Other than a distinction between the two, Sūtra and Mantra, in the aspect of method (solely whether or not it is embraced by the co-emergent wisdom of great bliss), there is no distinction whatsoever in the view." Other than stating a mere void selflessness that is a view indicated by the

Middle Way in both contexts of Sūtra and Mantra, this way does not explain the appearing aspect of the ground (such as the maṇḍalas of luminous clarity's exalted bodies and wisdoms) in the context of Mantra. Therefore, it is faulty.

Our own tradition, the Nyingma school of early translations, accepts a distinction of view in the manner of the vehicles of Sūtra and Mantra. Yet when evaluated from the side of solely the empty aspect, the expanse of phenomena (*chos kyi dbyings, dharmadhātu*), there is no distinction. All of these are merely synonyms with the same meaning:

- the great emptiness—the ultimate expressed in the contexts of the Great Middle Way
- the great equality—the ultimate of the Mahāyoga tradition
- Samantabhadrī, the primordial maṇḍala as it is—the ultimate of Anuyoga, and
- the great primordial purity—the ultimate of Atiyoga

This is stated in the canon of early translations and commentaries on its viewpoint in general, and in [Mipam's] *Beacon of Certainty* in particular:

> The glorious Candrakīrti in the Noble Land [of India]
> And Rongzom Chözang in Tibet
> Established with one viewpoint and one voice
> The great emptiness of primordial purity.[39]

And:

> The two: this [the Great Middle Way free from constructs] and the Great Perfection
> Are just synonyms with the same meaning.[40]

This is established in limitless scriptures, such as [Mipam's] *Overview of the Guhyagarbha*,[41] and it is also established by reasoning. Intending this, Sapaṇ stated:

> If there were a view superior to the freedom from constructs of the Perfection [Vehicle], then [that view would possess constructs].[42]

However, when evaluated from the aspect of appearance, even these names are not mentioned in the Vehicle of Characteristics:

- The view of the great purity of the relative, the nature of luminous clarity, which is the appearing aspect in the glorious Mahāyoga tradition,
- The Samantabhadra maṇḍala of the deities of the three seats,[43] which is the view of Anuyoga from the aspect of appearance, and
- The spontaneously present maṇḍala of the ground-appearance, the profound view of Atiyoga.

Therefore, in Nyingma scriptures in general, the difference between the views of Sūtra and Mantra is like the earth and space. Specifically, as it appears extensively in the works of the lord of doctrine, Mipam, the difference in view can also be established by reasoning.[44]

Moreover, in the tradition of Kriyāyoga in the lower tantras, the appearing aspect of the relative transforms into a divine maṇḍala; a view that ascertains this potential transformation is not present in the path of Sūtra. In this, those who claim that the view does not concern the side of the relative have already been eliminated.[45]

Regarding this, some people claim: "It follows that it is not reasonable to say that the subject, objects of knowledge, are superior to Sūtra in the view of Mantra by means of luminous clarity, the aspect of appearance, because in sūtras it is also explained as such; luminous clarity is the definitive meaning Buddha-nature."

By only this there is no entailment because there is a distinction of (1) clarity, (2) extensiveness, and (3) completeness in the two luminous clarities of Sūtra and Mantra: (1) the aspect of appearance, or aspect of luminous clarity, in the context of the Causal Vehicle—such as the ten [Buddha-]Nature Sūtras and the *Uttaratantra*—is the intrinsic nature of mind, the Buddha-nature; and (2) in the general tradition of tantras of Mantra, the aspect of appearance is luminous clarity, and in Atiyoga, the aspect of appearance is the spontaneously present maṇḍala. If [one says the reason is] not established, [then in response]:

1. There is a distinction in *clarity* because in the Mantrayāna, appearances are clearly revealed to be divine maṇḍalas by means of the reasonings of the five subsequent analogies and the reasonings of the five previous actualities.[46]

2. There is a distinction in *extensiveness* because in the Mantrayāna, each and every pattern of thought (*rtog tshogs*)—such as the aggregates, constituents, and sense-fields—are extensively explained as divine maṇḍalas.

3. And there is a distinction in *completeness* because the Mantrayāna states that appearances, resonances, and cognitions, etc., are complete as the maṇḍalas of the three seats.

Such distinctions are not present in the Causal Vehicle because [luminous clarity] is not taught other than: (1) as a mere illustration by means of a metaphor, (2) as a mere brief summary of the possession of Buddha-nature, and (3) as a mere luminous clarity that is the suchness of mind.

Regarding this, some people claim: "It is not reasonable to state that there is no difference in view between Sūtra and Mantra from the aspect of emptiness, the side of the expanse of phenomena, because some of our tradition's monastic textbooks say that there is also a difference from the side of emptiness."[47]

However, their intent is as follows: From the side of emptiness, too, when [emptiness] is distinguished by the aspect of appearance—luminous clarity—it is expressed as if there were a distinction [in the empty aspect] because it is the emptiness endowed with all supreme aspects (*rnam kun mchog ldan gyi stong nyid*). Due to this, it is also expressed as if there were a difference in view also by means of the great unity of appearance and emptiness, etc. However, all the essential points come down to only the aspect of appearance, distinguished by luminous clarity as shown in this context; one should not think otherwise.

To summarize all the essential points of the features of the higher and lower vehicles: The views and philosophies of the proponents of the four Causal Vehicle philosophies have the profound distinction of the manner of completing selflessness—from the selflessness of persons in the Vaibhāṣika tradition to the full completion of the selflessness of phenomena in the view of the Great Middle Way. Likewise, there is an extremely great distinction between the views of the higher and lower tantras among the views of the four tantras of Secret Mantra—the quality of luminous clarity which is the aspect of appearance—from the Kriyātantra view of the relative, which is potentially established to be the great divine maṇḍala, to the full completion of the spontaneously present ground-appearance in Atiyoga.

Some people say: "It is not appropriate to apply the doctrinal language of 'spontaneous presence' (*lhun grub*) also to the lower tantras such as Mahāyoga."*

Without seeing the target of the defendant, where is the challenger shooting the arrow? I distinguish these distinctively. As for the necessity of the syllables *luminous clarity* in the lower tantras and *spontaneous presence* in Atiyoga, "From the aspect of appearance, the spontaneous presence of luminous clarity . . ." and ". . . (2) The spontaneously present luminous clarity of Mantra." While clearly present, it is not known by you; the insight that discerns this is not spontaneously present!

In general, that the doctrinal language of "spontaneous presence" does not appear at all in the lower tantras is a grounds for investigation; not only in the lower tantras, but "unconditioned and spontaneously present"[48] is also stated in the *Uttaratantra*—even so, you have not seen it! Anyway, since there is no point in such types of disputes, I do not intend a lengthy response.

As for the distinction between the views of Sūtra and Mantra, the main essential point of this, the consummate meaning, is a feature of the supreme noncontradiction of appearance and emptiness, the profound view. The distinction comes from the way of perfecting the meaning of this great unity free from extremes—whether it is ascertained gradually or instantaneously, without progression. Otherwise, those upholding any philosophy that brings forth contradictions between appearance and emptiness, and anyone who asserts the essence of emptiness as a mere nonentity that is an emptiness of true existence, obviously have difficulty explaining the extremely profound division between the views of sūtra and tantra.

2. *Distinguishing the Distinctive Views and Philosophies*

This section has two parts: (1) the scriptures that express and (2) the scriptural meaning expressed.

1. The Scriptures that Express

This section has two parts: (1) distinguishing the provisional and definitive Word and (2) distinguishing the *śāstras*—the commentaries on the viewpoint.

This view is attributed to Jamyang Khyentsé Chökyi Lodrö ('jam dbyangs mkhyen brtse chos kyi blo gros*, 1893–1959) by Bötrül's student, Khenpo Chökhyap.

1. Distinguishing the Provisional and Definitive Word

Other presentations of the provisional and definitive
In the three wheels that express
Claim that the first [wheel] is the provisional meaning, the middle [wheel] is the definitive meaning, and
*The last [wheel] is exclusively the provisional meaning.**

They accept the extreme that a provisional meaning topic
Is necessarily nonexistent conventionally.
Through this, the profound meanings of sūtra and tantra,
Such as the Buddha-nature, are said to not exist at all.

Some people say: "The first wheel
And the middle wheel are only provisional meanings.
The definitive meaning is exclusively the last [wheel];
Its topic is what is truly established."†

Through two valid cognitions,
Based on two ways of dividing the two truths, which is the expressed,
In the three wheels of sūtras, which is the evaluated,
Our tradition asserts two manners of the provisional/definitive in this way.

The supreme object found by the valid cognition of ultimate analysis
From the two truths of appearance/emptiness,
Ultimate emptiness—which is the explicit teaching of the middle wheel—
Is asserted as the definitive meaning; and,

The supreme object found by the valid cognition of purity
From the two truths of authentic/inauthentic experience,
Ultimate luminous clarity—which is the explicit teaching of the last wheel—
Is asserted as the definitive meaning.

---

*The view that the last wheel is provisional and the middle wheel is definitive is a Geluk view. See, for instance, Changkya Rolpé Dorjé, *Presentation of Philosophical Systems*, 341–42; see also Jeffrey Hopkins, *Meditation on Emptiness*, 426–27.

†This view is attributed to the Kagyü and Jonang by Bötrül's student, Khenpo Chökhyap.

From the distinction of what is expressed being appearance or emptiness,
There are the manners of dividing the provisional and the definitive;
Due to distinct manners of division,
The definitive meaning middle and last wheels are asserted as noncontradictory.

In this way, the tradition of scholars in the school of early translations
Has distinctive ways of dividing the provisional and the definitive;
For the profound meaning intended by the sūtras and śāstras,
See my Key to the Provisional and Definitive.[49]

Regarding presentations of the provisional and definitive in the three wheels of the Word that express, other scholars say: "The first wheel, the wheel of the four truths, is the provisional meaning; the middle wheel, the wheel of the absence of attributes, is the definitive meaning; and the last wheel, the wheel that thoroughly differentiates the ultimate, is exclusively the provisional meaning."

They think it is acceptable to formulate the extreme such that if it is a topic of the provisional meaning, then it is necessarily something that does not exist even conventionally. Due to this, they say that the meanings indicated in the profound sūtras and tantras, such as the aspect of appearance of Buddha-nature, the aspect of luminous clarity, and the universal ground (*kun gzhi, ālaya*) are "not even conventionally existent because they are provisional meaning topics"; they claim these to be utterly nonexistent.

Also, other people make the claim, "Not only is the first wheel of the Word, but also the middle wheel is exclusively the provisional meaning." They say that only the last wheel of the Word is the definitive meaning. Moreover, they claim: "Its topic, Buddha-nature, is truly established; it is not empty of its own essence." Regarding this, some people say: "It should be asserted as such because this is how the master Asaṅga taught the delineation of the provisional and the definitive in scripture; one should follow after that."

Without understanding the meaning of the essential point, what is it that they say? In accord with the master Asaṅga's scriptural teaching of various delineations of the provisional and definitive, the last Word is distinctly separated into sūtras of (1) Mind-Only and (2) Middle Way:

1. Following the four Mind-Only Sūtras,[50] such as the *Saṃdhinirmocana*, Asaṅga forged the tradition of vast activity—in which the definitive meaning is accepted as the sūtras that teach three consummate vehicles, and those which mainly teach that tradition's three natures as the topic; the opposite of these are accepted as the provisional meaning.

2. And, following the ten [Buddha-]Nature Sūtras,[51] such as the *Dhāraṇīśvararājaparipṛcchāsūtra*, he wrote a commentary on the root scripture of the *Uttaratantra*, which is a commentary on their viewpoint—in which the definitive meaning is accepted as the sūtras that teach a single consummate vehicle, and those which mainly teach the heritage (*rigs*) of the essential nature, the basic element, as the topic; the opposite is accepted as the provisional meaning.

However, by this fact, the outlines of the provisional and definitive asserted by master Nāgārjuna, father and son [Candrakīrti], are not erased. Nor is there a single mixture of the provisional/definitive of each respective tradition of the Mind-Only and Middle Way—by which the definitive meaning Buddha-nature is taught to be truly established. [They may wonder,] "Then what?" It is obvious that they need to perfect their analysis.

Our Nyingma tradition, the school of early translations, accepts the defining character of the provisional meaning in general as that which has all three complete: (1) a basis in [another] intention, (2) a purpose, and (3) explicit invalidation; the opposite of this is accepted as the definitive meaning. Demonstrating a summary of the essential points in the viewpoint of the school of the early translations' scriptural tradition, the gentle protector, [Mipam] Rinpoché, stated in his [*Sword of Insight:*] *Ascertaining the Meaning:*

> Since it is stated with a basis in [another] intention upon which it is intended,
> Like the eight: [four] covert intentions (*ldem dgongs*) and [four] intentions (*dgongs pa*),[52]
> Because the literal meaning is invalidated by valid cognition, and
> Because of having a purpose,
> Therefore, there are the four philosophies. . . .[53]

Sūtras of covert intention and sūtras of intention are illustrations [of the provisional meaning].

There are three ways of dividing the provisional and definitive; these can also be condensed by means of:

1. the ground—whether or not it is the consummate abiding reality
2. the path—whether or not it is the consummate object of cultivation, and
3. the fruition—whether or not it is the consummate result

The way of positing the provisional and definitive in this context, however, is distinguished by means of the ground—whether or not it is the consummate abiding reality.

In general, for a proponent of any of the four philosophies, the sūtras that mainly teach their respective ultimate as the topic are posited as the definitive meaning, and the sūtras that mainly teach the relative as the topic are posited as the provisional meaning. Since the context here is the philosophy of the Middle Way, for the way of dividing the provisional and definitive in this tradition, I will give a concise demonstration, an extensive explanation, and a summary.

1. Concise Demonstration

The distinctive topics of the respective three wheels of the Word, the evaluated, are evaluated by means of the two valid cognitions that analyze the ultimate and the conventional. Within the ways of dividing the two truths by means of appearance/emptiness and authentic/inauthentic experience, there are two manners of positing the provisional and the definitive; ". . . our tradition asserts in this way," is the concise demonstration.

2. Extensive Explanation

To elaborate extensively, the manner of positing the topic as the definitive meaning by means of appearance/emptiness in the middle Word is as follows: By means of emptiness, the object found by valid cognition of ultimate analysis being supremely authentic or not, there is the way of dividing the two truths in which relative phenomena are [posited] from the aspect of appearance, and ultimate phenomena are [posited] from the empty aspect. From this, sūtras with emptiness, the ultimate truth, as the main topic of explicit teaching—the Perfection of Wisdom Sūtras of the middle wheel—are the definitive meaning. Oppositely, sūtras that teach the aspect of appearance, the relative truth, as their main topic are accepted as provisional meanings—like the first Word, the wheel of doctrine of the four truths—because of:

1. having a basis in [another] intention—intended to [refer to] existence only conventionally
2. having a purpose—for the sake of taking care of those with the Auditor heritage, and
3. having a literal teaching that is invalidated by ultimate valid cognition—such as teaching the topic of the inherent existence of the aggregates, constituents, and sense-fields.

Otherwise, without distinguishing the valid cognitions, people are unsure what to do, wondering why it is not suitable to explain literally the explicit teachings of the first Word—topics like the sequence of accepting and rejecting [within] the four truths, and the trainings of discipline, such as maintaining the vowed disciplines of a fully-ordained monk as a cause for higher states and definitive goodness. It becomes a joke!

Furthermore, the manner of positing the topic as the definitive meaning by means of whether or not appearances accord with reality [i.e., authentic/inauthentic experience] in the last Word is as follows: By means of the object found by the conventional valid cognition of pure [vision] being supremely authentic or not, there is the way of dividing the two truths in which relative phenomena are [posited] from the aspect of being appearances that do not accord with reality [i.e., inauthentic experience], and ultimate phenomena are [posited] from the aspect of being appearances that accord with reality [i.e., authentic experience]. From this, sūtras with luminous clarity, the ultimate truth, as the main topic of explicit teaching—the sūtras teaching Buddha-nature of the last wheel—are accepted as the definitive meaning. Oppositely, [sūtras] that teach the relative that is inauthentic experience as the main topic are posited as provisional meanings—like the first Word, the wheel of doctrine of the four truths—because of:

1. having a basis in [another] intention—intending merely the manner of impure appearances
2. having a purpose—for the sake of the aversion toward *saṃsāra* for Auditors, etc.

3. having a literal teaching that is a topic invalidated by thoroughly conventional valid cognition based on pure vision—such as the teaching that impure phenomena (the aggregates, constituents, and the like) are inherently existent

Due to this, in the tradition of the Great Middle Way, in accord with the meaning of the viewpoint of sūtras such as the *Akṣayamatisūtra*[54] and great *śāstras* such as the *Madhyamakāvatāra*, the middle Word is accepted as the definitive meaning; and in accord with the meaning of the viewpoint of sūtras such as the *Dhāraṇīśvararāja*[55] and great *śāstras* such as the *Uttaratantra*, sūtras of the last wheel that teach Buddha-nature are accepted as the definitive meaning. The meaning of the viewpoint within a single essential point, without contradiction, is the general [way of] Nyingma scriptures (*snying gzhung spyi*).

Specifically, in the commentary on the [three] vows by the Minling (*smin gling*) lord of doctrine [Lochen Dharmaśrī], a variable language is used: "The middle Word is accepted as half-definitive and half-provisional, or definitive for the time being."[56] Two manners of accepting the definitive meaning are shown perforce: (1) in the Mind-Only tradition, the middle Word is asserted as half-definitive and half-provisional and (2) in the tradition of the Middle Way, [the middle Word is asserted as] the definitive meaning. In short, in the tradition of the Great Middle Way, both the middle Word and the last Word are accepted as the definitive meaning.

In particular, in just the way that the masterly scholars of the school of early translations, like the great omniscient one [Longchenpa], expressed the scriptural meaning, both the middle and last Word are in general said to be definitive meaning sūtras in [Mipam's] *Lion's Roar: Exposition* [*of Buddha-Nature*].[57] Moreover, it is not everything in the last Word, but it is the sūtras that teach the [Buddha-]nature that are said to be the definitive meaning; in this context, the viewpoint of these statements is expressed as the complete [viewpoint]. However, those who have not perfected analysis of the essential points and have an inverted understanding of "the four reliances"[58] may spout various chatter, appearing to refute the scriptures of the omniscient one, father and son, and in particular, the presentations of the definitive and provisional meanings explained by Mipam, the lord of doctrine. Beware at this time!

3. Summary

The meaning of the essential points of the definitive and provisional meanings taught in this way is summarized as follows: In short, as for the topic of the middle and last Word, based on the distinctive ways of stating the main topic of the explicit teaching—Buddha-nature from the aspect of appearance or the expanse of phenomena from the empty aspect—the middle wheel is posited as the definitive meaning, and the last wheel is posited as the definitive meaning. The nature of this is based on the level of emphasis upon the topic: Other than just the distinctive ways in which they are respectively distinguished temporarily, as for the consummate meaning, the two are also accepted within a single essential point, without contradiction, as definitive meaning sūtras. There are a great many scriptural citations for this; yet being weary with words, I have not elaborated them at this moment.

In this way, in accord with the meaning of the profound viewpoint of the Mahāyāna Sūtras of the Word and the *śāstras* which are the commentaries on their viewpoint, the exceptional manner of dividing the definitive and provisional meanings in the tradition of the scholars of the school of early translations is clear in my *Key to the Provisional and Definitive.* "See that!" is a reference.

2. Distinguishing the Manners of Asserting Śāstras—*The Commentaries on the Viewpoint*

Other presentations of śāstras
Claim that the explicit teaching of the Uttaratantra *is a provisional meaning.*
They accord with the assertion that the heritage is a mere emptiness
Relinquished of luminous clarity, the aspect of appearance.

Our tradition accepts the Uttaratantra
As the unexcelled definitive meaning—
A commentary on the viewpoint of the profound meaning of the [Buddha-]Nature Sūtras that
Emphasizes the supreme luminous clarity, the aspect of appearance, which is the intended meaning of the Great Prāsaṅgika.

Others explain the Abhisamayālaṃkāra *scripture*
*As definitively a Svātantrika scripture.**

*This view is attributed to the Geluk by Bötrül's student, Khenpo Chökhyap. Tsongkhapa wrote his commentary on the *Abhisamayālaṃkāra*, the *Golden Rosary of Elegant Discourse* (*legs bshad gser phreng*), before he developed his unique Prāsaṅgika position in his later years.

The main reason is the fear that the eight [*unique*] *assertions*
  [*of Prāsaṅgika*]
Would [*otherwise*] *collapse.*

As for our tradition, the school of early translations, lord Mipam
Widely established [*the* Abhisamayālaṃkāra] *as just a source*
  scripture of the Prāsaṅgika and Svātantrika
With reasoned implications by the power of fact
In "the Rejoinders," etc.

These days, although people claim to be Nyingma,
They just repeat after others, without reason.
Our tradition, the tradition of the scholars of the early
  generation,
Is written in the Ornament of Maitreya's Viewpoint.

Others say that the scriptures of the Svātantrika-Madhyamaka
Conflict with the Great Prāsaṅgika.
Our tradition, [*that of*] *the lord of doctrine, Mipam,*
Accepts [*Svātantrika*] *as a step toward the Great Prāsaṅgika.*

Also, concerning the manner of asserting the presentation of *śāstras*, the commentaries on the viewpoint, some other masterly scholars assert that the *Mahāyāna-Uttaratantraśāstra* is in general a Prāsaṅgika Mahāyāna scripture. However, they explain that the topic of its explicit teaching is a provisional meaning because "its basis of intention is emptiness. . . ."* The [above] word "claim" (*lo*) is used as just an embellishing word to express that this is the assertion

*Sakya Paṇḍita states that Buddha-nature taught in the *Uttaratantra* has emptiness as its basis of intention. See Sakya Paṇḍita, *Clear Differentiation of the Three Vows*, I.138–9. Published in Jared Douglas Rhoton, trans., *A Clear Differentiation of the Three Codes*, 285. Tsongkhapa says that emptiness is the basis of intention of the Buddha-nature that was taught in the *Laṅkāvatārasūtra* and in the *Madhyamakāvatāra* (under VI.95). See Tsongkhapa, *Essence of Eloquence* (*drang nges legs bshad snying po*), in *Collected Works*, vol. 14, 92a–95b; see also Tsongkhapa, *Thoroughly Illuminating the Viewpoint*, 325–26. In his commentary on the *Uttaratantra*, the Geluk scholar, Gyeltsapjé (*rgyal tshab rje dar ma rin chen*, 1364–1432), says that emptiness is the basis of intention of the Buddha-nature taught as a universal ground separate from the six collections of consciousness. See Gyeltsapjé, *theg pa chen po rgyud bla ma'i ṭīka*, *Collected Works*, vol. 3, 75a–78b. For further discussion of Geluk interpretations of Buddha-nature, see David S. Ruegg, *Three Studies in the History of Indian and Tibetan Madhyamaka Philosophy*, 75–6n171.

of another. As for the reason for needing to explain in that way, it appears to be just done in accord with a philosophy that relinquishes luminous clarity in the traditions of Mahāyāna, without accepting it, while asserting a mere non-implicative negation (*med dgag*)—a lack of true existence—as heritage and accepting that.

Our tradition, the Nyingma school of early translations, accepts the *Uttaratantra*, one of the "Five Treatises of Maitreya,"[59] as the unexcelled definitive meaning that is a commentary on the intent of the ten [Buddha-]Nature Sūtras specific to the last Word; it emphasizes the quality of the supreme luminous clarity—the appearing aspect of the Buddha-nature, the heritage of the basic element—which is the intended meaning of the Great Prāsaṅgika Mahāyāna.

If one says, "But is it not said: 'Its basis of intention is emptiness'?"

The meaning of this statement is as follows: From the aspect of appearance, unlike the Nirgrantha,[60] [Buddha-nature] is distinguished by the qualities of the luminous and clear nature—knowledge, love, and powers; and from the empty aspect, unlike the Self of the non-Buddhists, [Buddha-nature] is distinguished by the essence of great emptiness—the three gates of liberation[61]—from which it is indivisible. This is the meaning intended by the statement. The words do not show that the explicit teaching is a provisional meaning because, while the distinctions of a basis of intention and a purpose are stated, it is not a statement of explicit invalidation by valid cognition, which is the cause for positing a provisional meaning. In this way, it makes the same essential point as what is intended in the statements from the root text and [auto]commentary of the *Madhyamakāvatāra,* too—that the nature of Buddha-nature is not like the Self of the non-Buddhists; it is distinguished by the three gates of liberation.[62]

If one says: "In that context, there is a distinctive teaching that the definitive meaning Buddha-nature is nonexistent even conventionally."

Are you able to maintain a complete entailment such that whatever is a provisional meaning topic is necessarily nonexistent conventionally? In this instance, there is a lot that needs to be said, but that is all for now.

Likewise, regarding the *Abhisamayālaṃkāra,* the Perfection of Wisdom scripture, most other masterly scholars explain it as one-sidely a Svātantrika-Madhyamaka scripture. The reason for doing this is that the meaning of the eight main features of the tradition of Prāsaṅgika-Madhyamaka, which are explained in their scriptures, are feared to collapse due to invalidation if they were to accept the *Abhisamayālaṃkāra* as a Prāsaṅgika scripture. There is no greater invalidation than the *Abhisamayālaṃkāra* itself for the positions asserting that (1) the distinctive realization is that the three Sublime Ones have one type of realization and (2) the distinctive abandonment is that cognitive obscurations are not relinquished until the eighth ground.

Our tradition, the school of early translations, asserts as follows: Lord Mipam, with reasoned implications that engage the power of fact, widely established [the *Abhisamayālaṃkāra*] as just a source scripture common to both the Prāsaṅgika and Svātantrika in his texts such as *Rapsel Rejoinder*[63] and *Eliminating Doubts*.[64] In the sections analyzing the three Sublime Ones' types of realization and the stages upon which the cognitive obscurations are relinquished, others say that even though such presentations as the existence of distinctive types of realization for the three Sublime Ones are explained in the *Abhisamayālaṃkāra*, this is because it is the tradition of Svātantrika. In response, [Mipam states that] it is not established that the *Abhisamayālaṃkāra* is exclusively a Svātantrika scripture, etc. One can also know this from the way the "Five Treatises of Maitreya" are presented in [Mipam's] commentary on the *Dharmadharmatāvibhāga*.[65]

If one says: "Well, these texts establish [the *Abhisamayālaṃkāra*] as merely a scripture common to the Prāsaṅgika and Svātantrika. However, it is not established as a source scripture because a "source" (*phyi mo*) needs to be that which is the root, or basis of division; whereas the two, Prāsaṅgika and Svātantrika, did not split from there."

The *Mūlamadhyamakakārikā*, a commentary on the viewpoint of the explicit teaching of emptiness, is posited as a source scripture of the Middle Way because there became a split into two [Prāsaṅgika and Svātantrika] due to the discordant ways that the respective Prāsaṅgika and Svātantrika masters explained its viewpoint. In the same way, the *Abhisamayālaṃkāra*, a commentary on the viewpoint of the hidden meaning of clear realization, is established as a source scripture of the Middle Way because there similarly was a split into two due to the discordant ways that the respective Prāsaṅgika and Svātantrika masters in both India and Tibet explained its viewpoint.

These days, for no reason at all, people who claim to be Nyingma say that the *Abhisamayālaṃkāra* is definitively a Svātantrika scripture.[66] There appears to be many who repeat after others without reason.

Regarding this, one may say: "It is reasonable to explain the subject, the *Abhisamayālaṃkāra*, as only a Svātantrika scripture because it was explained as such by both Vimuktasena and Haribhadra." [In response:] Well, it [absurdly] follows that it is reasonable to explain the subject, the *Mūlamadhyamakakārikā*, as only a Svātantrika scripture because it was explained as such by the Svātantrika masters. Regarding this, I have composed the distinctive tradition of the scholars of the early generation in the meaning-commentary on the Perfection of Wisdom, the *Ornament of Maitreya's Viewpoint*—know it from there.

Furthermore, other scholars say: "The distinctive scriptural tradition of the Svātantrika-Madhyamaka is in conflict with the Great Prāsaṅgika Mahāyāna because there is debate between them."

As for our tradition, the Nyingma position: The gentle protector Mipam, the lord of the doctrine, asserted that the scriptural tradition of the Svātantrika, such as the *Madhyamakālaṃkāra*, temporarily emphasizes the categorized ultimate, based on which it becomes a step toward the consummate Great Prāsaṅgika. He widely established this in the context of his overview to the *Madhyamakālaṃkāra*, etc.[67]

2. The Scriptural Meaning Expressed

This section has two parts: (1) the gateway to the path of what is expressed and (2) the actual scriptural meaning—the nature of what is expressed.

1. The Gateway to the Path of What is Expressed

This section has two parts: (1) the foundation of the path—going for refuge and (2) the gateway to the Mahāyāna path—generating the mind [of awakening].

1. The Foundation of the Path—Going for Refuge

Others explain the presentations of going for refuge in the three jewels differently—
Such as the classifications of the defining character, illustration,
Causal and resultant refuge, and
Temporary and consummate [*refuge*].

The translators and scholars of our tradition, the school of early translations,
Accept the classifications of the essence of refuge, which is the three jewels, and
Their illustrations and so on,
In accord with the scriptures of the Word and commentaries on their viewpoint.

Concerning the foundation of the path, going for refuge, there appear to be various distinctive assertions. The following is an explanation of the defining character of the three jewels, which is the object of refuge.

Some people say: "The defining character of the Buddha-jewel is: (1) the consummate expanse endowed with the twofold purity and (2) the body with the threefold endowment—knowledge, love, and powers. . . ." And, "The defining character of the dharma-jewel is (1) the truth of uncontaminated, complete purification comprised by either the path or cessation that is endowed with the eight qualities of inconceivability and so on."[68] Or, some people say: "[The defining character of the dharma-jewel] is the truth of uncontaminated, complete purification comprised by either the path or cessation." As the defining character of the saṅgha-jewel, they say, for instance: "The truth of uncontaminated, complete purification within the continuum of a sublime bodhisattva that is comprised by either the path or cessation. . . ." Or, "A sublime [bodhisattva] child of the Victorious Ones endowed with the eight qualities of awareness and freedom."[69]

Also, for the essence of the illustrations of the three jewels, they posit the nature of a mere entity or nonentity set forth by confined perception. They do not explain the division between the causal and resultant refuge. In the context of positing the three temporary refuges, they identify solely the three jewels of the Mahāyāna in general. However, when positing the sole consummate refuge, they say that the Hīnayāna dharma and saṅgha are not the consummate refuge and do not say anything about whether or not these two Mahāyāna [dharma and saṅgha] are the consummate refuge or not. They just arbitrarily say, "The refuge is solely the Buddha. . ."[70] Others explain presentations differently in various other ways.

As for our tradition, the translators and scholars of the early generation posit the essence of the defining character of the three jewels, the object of refuge, in just the same way as the scriptural meaning of the *Mahāyāna-Uttaratantra*. In general:

- The defining character of the Buddha-jewel is that which is endowed with the twofold benefit [of self and other] and eight qualities.[71]
- The defining character of the dharma-jewel is the path and cessation endowed with the eight qualities.
- And the defining character of the saṅgha-jewel is that which is endowed with the eight qualities of awareness and freedom.

If one says: "Well, it follows that the subject, the Sublime Buddha, is the defined term (*mtshon bya*) of both the dharma and the saṅgha because of [having] their defining characters." I accept—remember the words of the [*Uttaratantra*] scripture: "Because of being the consummated assembly, too. . . ."[72]

Regarding this, in the context of dividing the three temporary refuges, one posits as part of the defining character: That which is (1) a temporary object of refuge and (2) endowed with the eight qualities of the path and cessation is the defining character of the dharma-jewel; and, that which is (1) a temporary object of refuge and (2) endowed with the eight qualities of awareness and freedom is the defining character of the saṅgha-jewel.

People say concerning this, "This is not reasonable as the defining character of the dharma-jewel because a convergence of the path and cessation is impossible. Therefore, as part of the defining character, one needs to use 'either the path or cessation.' "

However, this is merely the meaning understood in the path of reasoning of introductory logic primers, viewing appearance and emptiness as contradictory. It is apparent that they have not understood the profound meaning of the noncontradiction of appearance and emptiness.

Likewise, the distinctive illustrations are posited as follows:

- The distinctive Buddha-jewel—the inseparability of abandonment, which is the Essential Body (*ngo bo nyid sku, svabhāvikakāya*), and realization, which is the Wisdom Truth Body—is the identity of what is profound, peaceful, free from constructs, and unconditioned.

- The distinctive dharma-jewel is (1) the essence of the truth of cessation, which is emptiness free from extremes, and (2) its self-lucidity (*rang mdangs*), which is the essence of luminous clarity actualized in time (*re zhig*), accepted as a quality of the path.

- The distinctive saṅgha-jewel is the identity of the Sublime [bodhisattva] children of the Victorious Ones endowed with the defining character of the eight qualities of awareness and freedom from the first ground on.

We also assert a twofold distinction of going for (1) causal refuge and (2) resultant refuge. Causal refuge is going for refuge in the cause of refuge—what has already become the continuum of another being, as is taught. Resultant refuge is going for refuge in the result of refuge—the three jewels of one's own continuum, as is taught.

Moreover, the distinction between the temporary and consummate refuge is as follows: Just like the intended meaning of the *Uttaratantra,* there is a division of the three temporary [refuges] based upon the three Mahāyāna jewels. However, "The refuge is solely the Buddha,"[73] asserts that the Buddha-jewel is the sole refuge and that the other two are temporary refuges, etc. There are limitless distinctions explained in accord with the Mahāyāna Word and commentaries on their viewpoint.

2. The Gateway to the Mahāyāna Path—Generating the Mind [of Awakening]

The defining character of the Mahāyāna generation of the
mind [of awakening] is also
Variously presented by others.
Our tradition explains in accord with the scriptural meaning
That is the viewpoint of the great chariots.

[Others] explain its illustrations as separate [and]
*The viewpoints of the chariots as contradictory.**
Our tradition, that of the great omniscient one [Longchenpa],
Accepts [their] noncontradiction as a single essential point.

Some claim that the generation of the mind
For mediocre and sharp faculties is bogus—mere words.
Our tradition accepts the Mahāyāna generation of the mind
For all three [faculties] to be genuine.

The assertions of our tradition, the scholars of the school of
early translations,
Such as the classifications of the generation of mind in this
way,
Are elucidated as such in the meaning-commentary of the
Perfection of Wisdom—
See the Ornament of Maitreya's Viewpoint.

Concerning the way of positing the defining character of the generation of the mind [of awakening], the gateway to enter the

*This refers to the Geluk, as stated by Bötrül's student, Khenpo Chökhyap.

Mahāyāna path, some people say: "[The defining character of the mind of awakening is] that which (1) appears as the essence of complete benefit for others and perfect awakening and (2) is the main awareness concurrent with the wish that observes perfect awakening for the sake of others." Other people say: "The main awareness concurrent with the wish that observes, in the manner of activated experience, perfect awakening for the sake of others." Also, some people say: "That which (1) is a main awareness and (2) occurs concurrently with the wish that observes perfect awakening for the sake of others." And people say: "The main awareness that occurs concurrently with the aspiration that is a wish, for the sake of others, that either oneself or another attains perfect awakening."* Statements of various presentations appear in the commentaries on the scriptures.

As for the assertion of our tradition, in just the way the intended meaning of the great chariot, Maitreyanātha, is in such texts as the *Abhisamayālaṃkāra*, the concise essential meaning of the great omniscient one's [Longchenpa's] *Precious Wish-Fulfilling Treasury* and the Minling lord of doctrine's [Lochen Dharmaśrī's] *Three Vows* [*Commentary*]: *Cluster of Supreme Intentions* is explained as follows: The defining character of the generation of the mind [of awakening] is the exceptional method and insight endowed with the twofold benefit.

Likewise, regarding the essence of the illustration of that generation of the mind [of awakening], others explain the viewpoints of the chariots, fathers and sons, as contradictory. They say, "Due to the main mind (*gtso sems*) and mental state (*sems byung*) being separate, the two assertions of: (1) Asaṅga and his [half-]brother [Vasubandhu] accepting the mind of awakening as a mental state and (2) both Vimuktasena and Haribhadra accepting it as a main mind, are in internal contradiction."

However, our tradition, that of the great omniscient one, accepts that the main mind and the mental state are both illustrations of the generation of the mind [of awakening]. Other than being mere explanations that are explicit or implicit, these scriptures of the chariots, fathers and sons, are in fact without contradiction as one essential point.

Concerning the distinctive delineations of the genuine and nominal [mind of awakening], some masterly scholars appear to state: "In general, the sūtras say that there are three generations of the mind

*These views are attributed to the Geluk by Bötrül's student, Khenpo Chökhyap. For an example of a Geluk scholar, Paṇchen Sonam Drakpa (*paṇ chen bsod nams grags pa*, 1478–1554), supporting the view that the mind of awakening is a main mind and not a mental state, see Paṇchen Sonam Drakpa, *Clear Lamp (rnam bshad snying po rgyan gyi don rigs lam bzhin du gsal bar 'chad pa'i yum don yang gsal sgron me)*, 121.7–122.4.

[of awakening]: (1) the shepherd-like generation of mind for those of sharp faculties, (2) the ferryman-like generation of mind for those of mediocre faculties, and (3) the king-like generation of mind for those of dull faculties.[74] However, the generations of mind for both the sharp and mediocre faculties are merely nominally existent; they are not the genuine generation of the mind because, respectively, (1) it is impossible for there to be a time when oneself becomes a Buddha after having previously established all sentient beings in the state of Buddhahood, because the time when all sentient beings have become Buddha is impossible; likewise, (2) the assertion that both oneself and others become Buddhas together is also not established; such a time is impossible because a time when *saṃsāra* is emptied is impossible. Therefore, these two generations of mind are bogus; in fact, other than mere words, such assertions are not established."*

Well, it would [absurdly] follow that the subject, the sacred generation of the mind of those with dull faculties that is the king-like great wish, also would be an assertion as such [not established] due to that [same] reason; it is impossible for there to be a time to establish all sentient beings in the state of Buddhahood after oneself has become a Buddha because the time when *saṃsāra* is emptied is impossible—they assert this entailment. Moreover, it would [absurdly] follow that the subject, immeasurable compassion, would merely be nominal because such is impossible. This follows because (1) it is an aspiration that all sentient beings be freed from suffering and (2) such is impossible—similar implications follow.

Our tradition accepts the three generations of the mind [of awakening] found in sūtras to be genuine without qualification. The assertions of our tradition, the scholars of the school of early translations—such as the classifications of the generation of mind in this way—are elucidated in this way in the meaning-commentary on the the *Abhisamayālaṃkāra*, the Perfection of Wisdom scripture. See the *Ornament of Maitreya's Viewpoint*.

2. The Actual Scriptural Meaning—The Nature of What is Expressed

This section has two parts: (1) the delineation of the evaluating valid cognitions and (2) distinguishing the evaluated objects—the ground, path, and fruition.

---

*This view is attributed to the Geluk by Bötrül's student, Khenpo Chökhyap.

1. The Delineation of the Evaluating Valid Cognitions

The two evaluating valid cognitions
Ascertain the evaluated objects, the two truths.
Due to this, there are the divisions of philosophies,
Views, meditations, actions, and fruitions.

There are different traditions, earlier and later,
Concerning the presentations of the evaluating valid cognitions.
Due to this, there are the distinctive discordant assertions
Of views and philosophies.

The later generation of scholars
Widely proclaims with one voice
Two valid cognitions, the ultimate and the conventional,
Which are the valid cognitions that analyze the two truths.

However, other than only the categorized ultimate
And the conventional of confined perception,
The valid cognition that analyzes the uncategorized [ultimate]
And [the conventional valid cognition of] pure vision are not explained.

They speak of the reasoned manner of valid cognition that analyzes the ultimate
In accord with the valid cognition of confined perception; [however,]
Other than its ultimate that is a nonentity,
It cannot establish what is profound, peaceful, and free from constructs.

The valid cognition that analyzes the conventional, too
Is none other than just a confined perception; therefore,
Other than the mere impure relative,
It cannot establish the pure relative.

The masterly scholars of the early generation
Accept two ultimate valid cognitions and
Two conventional valid cognitions
As reasonings that analyze the two truths.

The two ultimate valid cognitions are:
Those that analyze the categorized and the uncategorized.
The two conventional valid cognitions are:
The valid cognitions of confined perception and purity.

The lord Mipam elucidated these delineations
In accord with the quintessential instructions of the school of early translations
And the intended meaning of sūtras, tantras, and śāstras,
In the elegant discourse, Sword of Insight.

The categorized valid cognition analyzing the ultimate
Establishes the temporary categorized ultimate;
The valid cognition that analyzes the uncategorized
Establishes the consummate uncategorized.

The conventional valid cognition of confined perception
Establishes the mode of appearance—the impure relative;
The conventional valid cognition of purity
Establishes the mode of reality—the pure relative.

The valid cognition of ultimate analysis
Establishes all phenomena as lacking true existence, the great emptiness;
The conventional valid cognition
Separately discerns pure and impure appearances.

In this way, this thoroughly complete valid cognition—
At once evaluating the profound and vast intended meanings
Of the sūtras, tantras, and śāstras—
Is a distinctive quality of the early generation of scholars.

This is a stanza at the interlude between sections.

Regarding this, there are three sections: (1) a concise demonstration, (2) an extensive explanation, and (3) a summary.

1. Concise Demonstration

In general, any philosopher with an eye for the doctrine ascertains the evaluated objects, the two truths, by means of one's own two evaluating valid cognitions. Due to this fact, divisions are made from the Auditors to the Vajrayāna among distinctive philosophies, views, meditations, actions, and fruitions. Therefore:

> To engage the mind that ascertains without error
> The nature of the two truths,
> You should supremely establish the good eye
> Of the two stainless valid cognitions.[75]

As is said, to definitively discern the nature of the evaluated objects, the two truths, you need to be learned in the delineations of the evaluating valid cognitions, the cause without which [definitive discernment] will not arise—this is an essential point.

[2. Extensive Explanation]

For the presentations of the evaluating valid cognitions in general, there are different traditions of the respective early and later masterly scholars. Due to this fact, assertions of views and philosophies are also distinct and discordant. The later generation of masterly scholars, as if in one voice, widely proclaims two valid cognitions that analyze the two truths: "the valid cognition that analyzes the ultimate" and "the valid cognition that analyzes the conventional." However, in the system of some traditions, other than only (1) the ultimate valid cognition that analyzes the categorized ultimate that accords with the manner of the Svātantrika and (2) the conventional valid cognition of confined perception taught in the logicians' (*rtog ge*) scriptures, there is no literal explanation of the valid cognition that analyzes the uncategorized ultimate, the unique argument of the Prāsaṅgika tradition. In particular, none of them explain the thoroughly conventional valid cognition that relies upon pure vision.

Due to this, the reasoned way of ultimate valid cognition becomes a valid cognition of confined perception—it is similar to the manner of not negating the subject, sound, but needing to negate sound's permanence on the occasion of stating, "It follows that the subject, sound, is not permanent because it is a functioning entity." This follows because even in the context of ultimate analysis, they say: "A pot is not empty of pot; a pot is empty of true existence. The subject, pot, is not negated; one must negate its true establishment." However, other than the evaluated object, the ultimate that is merely a categorized nonentity, which is the ultimate explained in the context of Svātantrika, this way cannot establish the uncategorized ultimate as it is—as it is said, "Profound, peaceful, free from constructs, and unconditioned"[76]—which is the great equality of emptiness and appearance. One should know these manners extensively from texts like [Mipam's] *Commentary on the Difficult Points of the Word in General.*[77]

Likewise, concerning the valid cognition that analyzes the conventional: Other than just a valid cognition of confined perception, the way of teaching in the general Hīnayāna scriptures and the *Pramāṇavārttika*, etc., the conventional valid cognition of pure vision is not explained. Therefore, the evaluated object, the relative, also is none other than the mere impure relative of the aggregates, constituents, and sense-fields, which is the ground as taught in the corpus of Abhidharma. Thus, it cannot be established as the pure relative, the maṇḍala of the deities of the three seats, which is the ground as taught in the awareness-holders' corpus of Mantra. Therefore, in both contexts of Sūtra and Mantra, they say such things as: "The ultimate is only a non-implicative negation," "There is no view superior to merely impure appearance, which is the relative ground," and, "The innate mind is a conditioned phenomenon."

The masterly scholars of the early generation make a primary division within the reasoning that analyzes the two truths in general, with a fixed number of two: (1) the valid cognition that analyzes ultimate emptiness and (2) the valid cognition that analyzes conventional appearance. Nevertheless, when divided, there is also a twofold division made within the valid cognition that analyzes the ultimate: (1) the valid cognition that analyzes the categorized and (2) the valid cognition that analyzes the uncategorized—and a twofold division made within the valid cognition that analyzes the conventional: (1) the conventional valid cognition of confined perception and (2) the conventional valid cognition of purity. The essence and divisions of each of these distinctive evaluating valid cognitions, the delineations of dispelling objections, etc., are known from the lord Mipam's great elegant discourses—such as the *Sword of Insight: Ascertaining the Meaning*—which accord with the intention of both sūtras and tantras of the Word, the great *śāstras*, and the quintessential instructions of the school of early translations.

Furthermore, due to dividing the valid cognition of ultimate analysis into two, all the views and philosophies of the lower vehicles are not disregarded due to provisionally accepting an ultimate analysis that is a valid cognition analyzing the categorized. From the selflessness of persons of the Vaibhāṣika tradition, etc., up to the concordant ultimate of the Svātantrika tradition, there is precise ascertainment of the emptiness qualified as the categorized ultimate and as selflessness.

And the lower vehicles also are explained, directly and indirectly, to be authentic paths to liberation and omniscience.

By means of accepting the valid cognition that analyzes the uncategorized ultimate, the great empty essence—which is the ultimate distinguished as the uncategorized—is completely ascertained without superimposition or denigration. And the unexcelled, distinctive path to liberation and omniscience is established—from the great empty ultimate of the Prāsaṅgika tradition, through the ultimate great equality of the glorious Mahāyoga tradition, up to the primordial purity of the ground-expanse of Atiyoga, the Great Perfection.

Similarly, due to dividing conventional valid cognition into two: by means of accepting the valid cognition of confined perception, the modes of appearance of the impure relative are ascertained without superimposition or denigration—such as the aggregates, elements, and sense-fields comprised within the causality of [the truths of] suffering and origin in the tradition of the Vehicle of Characteristics. By means of accepting the valid cognition of conventional purity, the relative, distinguished by the luminous and clear nature of great purity, is completely established without superimposition or denigration—from the appearing aspect of Buddha-nature, the relative of luminous clarity, etc., which is the definitive meaning in the tradition of the Vehicle of Characteristics, through the relative great purity of the glorious Mahāyoga tradition, to the spontaneous presence of the ground-appearance of Atiyoga, the Great Perfection.

Otherwise, as soon as there is no conventional valid cognition of pure vision, there is no valid cognition found as a means to establish the existence of the great purity of the relative, as shown in the *Māyājāla Guhyagarbha* and so forth, other than a mere assertion because (1) ultimate valid cognition is not only simply unable to establish that; even if it were said to just exist as not empty in that perspective [of ultimate valid cognition], it would be truly established, and (2) confined conventional valid cognition establishes only the impurity of the aggregates, fire to be hot and burning, and earth to be hard and obstructive, etc. How could confined conventional valid cognition establish the five aggregates to be the five Buddha families and the five elements to be the maṇḍalas of the five goddesses?[78]

Therefore, there are reasons of the five previous actualities and the reasons of the five subsequent analogies, etc., as is said: "The sole cause and the manner of the syllable. . . ."[79] By means of the manners of direct perception and inference, the valid cognition analyzing the uncategorized ultimate establishes the empty essence—the distinctive great equality of the ultimate—from the aspect of emptiness. However, from the aspect of appearance, there is nothing else observed to establish the aspect of natural luminous clarity—the distinctive great purity of the relative—other than the conventional valid cognition of pure vision.

Thus, in short, the valid cognition of ultimate analysis establishes all phenomena comprising the ground, path, and fruition—from form up to omniscience—as lacking true existence and as the great emptiness in the [respective] temporary and consummate manners. The thoroughly conventional valid cognition distinguishes the respective impure and pure appearances by means of the modes of appearance and reality.

One may think regarding this: "The conventions of valid cognition analyzing the ultimate and the conventional are the traditions of the lower philosophies such as Svātantrika. However, it is not appropriate to use the conventions of valid cognition in the Prāsaṅgika tradition."

It is not established that the Prāsaṅgika tradition does not have the conventions of valid cognition because there are four valid cognitions in Candrakīrti's *Prasannapadā*: the four valid cognitions are those of direct perception, inference, scripture, and analogy.[80] Since the enumeration of four valid cognitions is asserted as his own tradition, a presentation of valid cognition is also present in general. And specifically, he also accepts a distinction between the valid cognition of confined perception and the valid cognition of pure vision because:

> Just as the observation by one with an eye-disorder
> Does not invalidate the cognition by someone without an
> eye-disorder,
> Likewise, a mind that has relinquished stainless wisdom
> Cannot invalidate a stainless mind.[81]

And in his autocommentary on this:

> The cognition of an ordinary being devoid of uncontaminated wisdom also cannot invalidate the uncontaminated vision. . . .[82]

Similarly, he also accepts that, compared to the valid cognition of pure vision, confined perception is not a mind of valid cognition:

> The eye, ear, and nose are not valid cognitions. . . .[83]

And:

> If the world sees thusness, then what need is there for other Sublime Ones?
> What would be the use of the sublime path?[84]

And from his autocommentary:

> In the analysis of thusness itself, only the Sublime Ones are valid cognition. . . .[85]

He also clearly shows the presentation of what is and is not valid cognition conventionally; ultimately, he ascertains without observing any of the constructed categories of what is and is not valid cognition.

3. SUMMARY

The following is a summary of this section. In this way, concerning the intended meaning of the Word—the sūtras comprised by the three wheels and precious tantras—together with the *śāstras*, which are the commentaries on the viewpoint: (1) That which is taught in the manner of the twofold selflessness of persons and phenomena is the profound aspect of the categorized and uncategorized ultimate, and (2) that which is taught by means of the twofold modes of appearance and reality is the vast aspect of the impure and pure relative. Without needing to reject either by means of denigration, they all can be evaluated simultaneously:

- the ultimate valid cognitions that are all the valid cognitions that analyze the categorized in the perceptions of impure confined perception taught in scriptures from the Svātantrika on down
- the ultimate valid cognitions that are all the uncategorized valid cognitions taught in the scriptures of sūtra and tantra, such as in the context of Prāsaṅgika
- the valid cognition of impure confined perception taught in the scriptures such as the seven treatises on valid cognition,[86] and
- the valid cognition of pure vision taught in the contexts of the *Uttaratantra* and the *Guhyagarbha*, etc.

The thoroughly complete entirety of all these evaluating valid cognitions is a unique quality of the early generation of scholars.

This is a stanza at the interlude between sections.

2. Distinguishing the Evaluated Objects—The Ground, Path, and Fruition

This section has two parts: (1) a concise demonstration and (2) an extensive explanation.

1. *Concise Demonstration*

For the moment, I will forgo a presentation
Of the four views and philosophies of Buddhists
From the manners of perfecting the two truths, the evaluated objects,
In the traditions of earlier and later masterly scholars of the Land of Snow.

Here, I will briefly explain
The essential points of the views and philosophies of the ground, path, and fruition of
The supreme vehicle, the Great Middle Way,
In the distinctive traditions of the earlier and later masterly scholars of the Land of Snow.

Regarding this in general, a sūtra says:

> The knower of the world [taught] the two truths.
> Don't listen to the division from another; know it oneself.

And from the *Madhyamakaśāstra*:

> The doctrine taught by the Buddha
> Is completely based upon the two truths.[87]

As is said, from the distinctive manners of perfecting, in a progressive or instantaneous way, the nature of the two truths—the evaluated objects of the three wheels of the Word—there are distinctive traditions of the four views and philosophies of the Buddhists [explained] by earlier and later masterly scholars of the Land of Snow.

For example, there are distinctions regarding whether or not the teachings of the four truths and their sixteen [aspects] of impermanence, etc.,[88] are asserted as the subtle selflessness of phenomena in the Vaibhāṣika system. There are distinctions regarding the presentations of universals and particulars, objects and cognitions, etc., [in the Sautrāntika system]. And there are distinctions as to the ways of identifying the essences of the three natures, etc., in the Mind-Only system. Although there are many distinctive traditions, I will forgo a presentation of differentiating them for the moment; I will not elaborate.

In this context, I will explain a brief presentation of the essential points of the view and philosophy of the ground, path, and fruition in the Prāsaṅgika tradition—the Great Middle Way that is the supreme vehicle—in the tradition of the earlier and later masterly scholars who came to the Land of Snow.

2. *Extensive Explanation*

This section has two parts: (1) the nature of the supreme vehicle, the Middle Way, and (2) distinguishing its ground, path, and fruition.

1. THE NATURE OF THE SUPREME VEHICLE, THE MIDDLE WAY

Others explain the Middle Way as something in between
*That is free from the two extremes.**
For each of the ground, path, and fruition,
They make assertions that are not the Middle Way.

Their assertions fall apart through question and debate:
Such a Middle Way is which of the two truths?
In which sublime path is it cultivated—in meditative equipoise or in postmeditation?
At the consummate fruition, which of the two exalted bodies is it?

Our tradition accepts the abiding reality free from all extremes
As the Middle Way of the ground.

---

*This view is attributed to the Geluk scholar, Pari Rapsel (*dpa' ris blo bzang rab gsal*, 1840–1910), by Bötrül's student, Khenpo Chökhyap. For an example of such a view represented in Pari Rapsel's works, see Pari Rapsel, *Ornament of Mañjughoṣa's Viewpoint*, 387–89. See also Karma Phuntsho, *Mipham's Dialectics and the Debates on Emptiness*, 156.

Through this, the path and fruition also
Are designated as the Middle Way.

Concerning the manner of identifying the Middle Way, or middle, some people take a position saying, "Relative appearance imputed by the conceptual mind is the very subtle extreme of permanence. Ultimate emptiness that is a non-implicative negation is the very subtle extreme of annihilation. However, neither of these individually is the Middle Way. The Middle Way is necessarily something in between these two, in the middle. However, neither the ground, the path, nor the fruition individually is the Middle Way because (1) the ground is not the Middle Way and (2) neither the path nor the fruition is the Middle Way. . . ."

Following after this, some supreme scholars also make a refutation, saying: "The identification of the Middle Way shown in the context of Mipam Rinpoché's commentary on the *Madhyamakālaṃkāra* is not reasonable."* In response, from [Mipam's] *Eliminating Doubts*: "Those who say that neither one of the three—ground, path, or fruition—is the Middle Way are lost. . . ."[89] And similarly in the *Rapsel Rejoinder* as well, extensive statements are made refuting other traditions and identifying the tradition of the Middle Way, in response to the supreme scholar Lozang Rapsel's[90] statement: "You are not a follower of the Middle Way because you do not even abide in the middle. Therefore, you need to abide in the middle, or in something in between."[91]

Consequently, it appears that the assertion of a Middle Way that abides in between the two truths falls apart through question and debate such as: "At the time of the ground, which of the two truths is it?" And, "At the time of the path, in which sublime path is it cultivated, in meditative equipoise or in postmeditation?" And, "At the consummate fruition, which exalted body is it posited as?"

Our tradition is as follows: "The abiding reality free from all extremes is the Middle Way of the ground. . . ."[92] It is spoken many times in the *Rapsel Rejoinder*. Also in *Eliminating Doubts*, [Mipam] states that the Middle Way of the ground is established as the genuine Middle Way, and through this, he asserts the way that the path and fruition are also established to be designated as the Middle Way.[93] Accordingly, we assert the Middle Way of the ground as the abiding reality free from all constructed extremes. Through this, we show that both the path and the fruition are also designated as the Middle Way.

---

*This refers to the Nyingma scholar, Dodrup Damchö (*rdo grub dam chos*).

2. DISTINGUISHING ITS GROUND, PATH, AND FRUITION

This section has three parts: (1) the nature of the ground—the two truths, (2) the essence of the path—the distinctive abandonments and realizations, and (3) the consummate fruition—distinguishing the two exalted bodies.

1. Nature of the Ground—The Two Truths

This section has three parts: (1) a concise demonstration, (2) an extensive explanation, and (3) a summary.

1. Concise Demonstration

In the scriptural tradition of the supreme vehicle, the Middle Way,
There are discordant ways of explaining
The two truths of appearance and emptiness, the evaluated objects,
From among the three: ground, path, and fruition.

In general, in the scriptural tradition of the supreme vehicle, the Great Middle Way, from among the three—(1) the ground, which is the two truths, (2) the path, which is abandonment and antidote, and (3) the fruition, which is the two exalted bodies—there is discord from the onset concerning the ways of explaining the essence, and so forth, of the two truths of appearance and emptiness, which are the evaluated objects. This was the concise demonstration.

2. Extensive Explanation

This section has three parts: (1) a general demonstration of the way of dividing the two truths, (2) the specific division of the two truths of appearance/emptiness, and (3) an extensive presentation of the two truths.

1. General Demonstration of the Way of Dividing the Two Truths

This section has three parts: (1) a concise demonstration, (2) an extensive explanation, and (3) a summary.

1. Concise Demonstration

Concerning the way of dividing the two truths in general,
Scholars accept two delineations of the two truths:
(1) The two truths of appearance/emptiness and
(2) The two truths of authentic/inauthentic experience.

In the great scriptures in general, concerning the way of dividing the two truths, which is the ground, (1) the two truths of appearance/emptiness are posited by means of the modes of appearance and emptiness and (2) the two truths of authentic/inauthentic experience are posited by means of whether the modes of appearance and reality are in accord or not. The scholars of India and Tibet accept these two delineations as the ways of positing the two truths.

2. Extensive Explanation

This section has two parts: (1) refuting other traditions and (2) presenting our tradition.

1. Refuting Other Traditions

These days, other than the two truths of appearance/emptiness
*It is rare that the two truths of authentic/inauthentic experience is known.**
Due to this, the profound intended meanings
Of the definitive meaning sūtras and tantras are cast far away.

These days, it seems that only the two truths of appearance and emptiness is widely known, but it is extremely rare for one to know the profound two truths of whether or not appearance accords with reality [i.e., authentic/inauthentic experience]. Due to this, the profound intended meanings of the definitive meaning sūtras and tantras—the positions that accept the indivisibility of appearance and emptiness—are cast far away, such as:

- the presentation of Buddha-nature, which is the unity of appearance and emptiness, as ultimate, and

*This refers to the traditions of the Sakya and Geluk, according to Bötrül's student, Khenpo Chökhyap.

- the presentation of the indivisibility of purity and equality as the ultimate truth in the Mahāyoga tradition

2. Presenting Our Tradition

This section has two parts: (1) the way of dividing the two truths as appearance/emptiness and (2) the way of dividing the two truths as authentic/inauthentic experience.

1. Way of Dividing the Two Truths as Appearance/Emptiness

By means of ultimate valid cognition analyzing the mode of reality,
Through the evaluated object being authentic or not
There is the twofold division of
Emptiness as the ultimate truth and appearance as the relative truth.

This manner is the unexcelled way
Of dividing the two truths in the scriptural tradition of
The definitive meaning sūtras of the middle wheel, tantras,
And Candrakīrti's meaning-commentary.

Furthermore, in the great scriptures such as the *Madhyamakāvatāra* in general, as stated in [Mipam's] overview of the *Madhyamakālaṃkāra*,[94] the two truths are divided by means of appearance and emptiness through the evaluated object of ultimate valid cognition analyzing the mode of reality being authentic or not: emptiness, which is the authentic evaluated object, is "ultimate truth," and appearances, which are not authentic, are "relative." In this way, the manner of positing the two truths by means of appearance/emptiness is the viewpoint of the profound, definitive meaning sūtras of the middle Word of signlessness, such as the extensive, middling, and condensed Mother [Perfection of Wisdom Sūtras], because of mainly teaching the topic—the positing of all appearances from form to omniscience as relative phenomena, and emptiness, which is the nonestablished essence of those, as the ultimate truth. This follows because of being widely renowned in India and Tibet as "the sūtras that teach the explicit teaching of emptiness."

Not only in those [sūtras], but this is also the viewpoint of tantra sets such as the glorious Mahāyoga:

- In the context of Mahāyoga, the two truths are posited by means of appearance/emptiness—from the aspect of appearance is "the great purity of the relative," and from the aspect of emptiness, "the great equality of the ultimate."
- Likewise, the two truths are divided in the context of Anuyoga—from the aspect of appearance, the relative is "the maṇḍala of the deities of the three seats," and from the aspect of emptiness, the ultimate is "the primordial maṇḍala as it is."
- Also, in the context of Atiyoga—from the aspect of appearance, the relative is posited as the ground-appearance that is spontaneously present by nature, and from the aspect of emptiness, the ultimate is posited as the nature of the primordially pure essence of the ground-expanse.

There is no way of positing all these manners of explanation other than as the two truths of appearance/emptiness.

The viewpoint of the root text and [auto]commentary of Candrakīrti, which is the meaning-commentary[95] on the great *śāstra*, the *Prajñāmūlamadhyamaka*[-*kārikā*], is also the two truths as appearance and emptiness; it is not seen otherwise. From the *Madhyamakāvatāra:*

> [Buddha] said that all entities found by authentic and false seeing are apprehended as two essences:
> That which is the object of authentic seeing is ultimate; false seeings are relative truths.[96]

Authentic seeing, which is only the emptiness that is an object of the wisdom of meditative equipoise, is posited as the ultimate; false seeings, all illusory and dreamlike aspects of appearance, are posited as the relative. Such an emptiness, which is the ultimate truth, is ascertained through the ultimate valid cognition that analyzes the mode of reality [through] the negation of production by means of the four extremes, etc. However, there is not a single word in the "Collection of Reasonings" of the Middle Way,[97] or the root text and [auto]commentary of the *Madhyamakāvatāra*, that is a presentation that posits the two truths in which the ultimate is nirvāṇa and the relative is *saṃsāra* by means of the pure conventional valid cognition analyzing the mode of appearance. Therefore, it is established that this way of dividing the two truths as appearance/emptiness is the unsurpassed viewpoint of these scriptures.

2. Way of Dividing the Two Truths as Authentic/Inauthentic Experience

> *By means of the valid cognition of purity* [*evaluating*] *the mode of appearance*
> *Through the evaluated object being authentic or not*
> *There is the division of the ultimate as authentic experience*
> *And the relative as inauthentic experience.*
>
> *This manner is the unexcelled way*
> *Of dividing the two truths in the scriptures of*
> *The definitive meaning sūtras of the last wheel, tantras,*
> *And the* Mahāyāna-Uttaratantra.

Moreover, in scriptures such as the *Uttaratantra*, as is also stated in [Mipam's] overview of the *Madhyamakālaṃkāra*,[98] the two truths are divided by means of the evaluated object being authentic or not at the time of evaluation by the conventional valid cognition of pure vision analyzing the mode of appearance: (1) as the authentic mode of the abiding reality, both appearance and emptiness are ultimate, such as the emptiness-object and the wisdom-subject for which appearance is in accord with reality, and (2) as inauthentic modes of appearance, the aspects of distortion are relative, such as the subjects and objects for which appearance is not in accord with reality.

In this way, the manner of positing the two truths by means of whether or not appearance accords with reality is [the viewpoint] of the definitive meaning sūtras of the last Word, such as the ten [Buddha-]Nature Sūtras, for which:

- the quality of the definitive meaning Buddha-nature is asserted as the ultimate which is appearance in accord with reality—from the empty aspect, it is the nature endowed with the three gates of liberation, the essentially empty, objective expanse of phenomena (*yul chos kyi dbyings*); and from the aspect of appearance, it is inseparable from the qualities of knowledge, love, and powers, the natural luminous clarity of the subjective wisdom (*yul can ye shes*), and

- the aspect of adventitious defilements, the distorted appearances which are the nature of *saṃsāra*—the subjects and objects that are the separable aspects that do not abide in the foundational nature of reality—are asserted as the relative which are appearances that do not accord with reality

This follows because of being renowned like the wind in India and Tibet as "the sūtras that explicitly teach the definitive meaning Buddha-nature."

Not only in those [sūtras], but this is also the viewpoint of precious tantra sets such as the glorious Mahāyoga:

- In the context of Mahāyoga, both appearance and emptiness are posited as the ultimate of authentic experience—the indivisibility of purity and equality called "the great seven ultimate treasures."[99] The opposite of this, all the aspects of inauthentic experience, are posited as the relative called "the relative of imputed delusion."
- Likewise, in the context of Anuyoga, the indivisibility of appearance and emptiness—the ultimate of authentic experience—is the great ultimate of the unity of the two truths called "the maṇḍala of the awakened mind." The opposite of this, the aspect of inauthentic experience, is called "the relative of impure delusion."
- Also, in the context of Atiyoga, the unity of primordial purity and spontaneous presence—the ultimate of authentic experience—is called "the ultimate truth of self-existing wisdom abiding within the ground." The aspect of inauthentic experience, the deluded phenomena of dualistic perception, is called "the relative of impure ground-appearance."

For these distinctive assertions, no way to explain them is seen other than as the two truths of authentic/inauthentic experience.

Moreover, in the context of the *Mahāyāna-Uttaratantra* also, ". . . But not empty of the unexcelled qualities that have the character of inseparability,"[100] shows as ultimate: the luminous clarity that is the self-lucidity of the empty essence, the Buddha-nature—the heritage (*rigs*) which is the basic element—inseparable from the qualities of the Truth Body that is a freed effect; and, "The basic element is empty of those adventitious [phenomena] that have the character of separability,"[101] shows as relative: the defilements which do not abide in the foundational nature—the distorted phenomena of perceived-perceiver [duality]—which are separable through the power of training in the path of the antidote.

This is the viewpoint of the ascertainment of Buddha-nature—the essence of primordially pure nirvāṇa—by means of the valid cognition of conventional purity, such as the reasons of efficacy, dependency, and the nature of things as taught in "Because the body of the perfect Buddha is radiant. . . ."[102] It is not seen to be other than this. Therefore, this way of dividing the two truths by means of authentic/inauthentic experience is established as the unexcelled viewpoint of these scriptures.

3. *Summary*

This section has three parts: (1) a demonstration of the delineations of different ways of assertion in general, (2) refuting the mistaken conceptions of others whose claims are one-sided, and (3) a summary of the essential points of the noncontradiction of scriptural meaning.

1. Demonstration of the Delineations of Different Ways of Assertion in General

Regarding this, the Svātantrika-Madhyamaka
Accepts the two truths of appearance/emptiness;
In the Prāsaṅgika texts, both delineations
Of the two truths are accepted without contradiction.

Therefore, both Candrakīrti's scriptures and
The Uttaratantra *scripture of the supreme regent* [*Maitreya*]
Are within one essential point, without contradiction,
Prāsaṅgika Mahāyāna scriptures.

Herein, the heritage of the basic element, Buddha-nature, etc.,
Is the supreme ultimate truth of authentic experience; however,
It has both the truths of appearance and emptiness
Through the way of dividing as appearance/emptiness.

Regarding this, from among the two ways of dividing the two truths in general, the Svātantrika tradition only accepts the two truths of appearance/emptiness, through positing the relative as the appearing aspect of all phenomena and the ultimate as the empty aspect. This is the way it is stated according to [Mipam's] overview of the *Madhyamakālaṃkāra*.[103]

In the scriptures of the Prāsaṅgika tradition, as was just explained, both ways of positing the two truths are accepted as one essential point without contradiction because:

1. the commentaries on the middle Word—such as the "Collection of Reasonings" and the root text and [auto]commentary of the *Madhyamakāvatāra*—posit the two truths by means of appearance and emptiness, and
2. the commentaries on the last Word—such as the root text and commentary of the *Uttaratantra*—posit the two truths by means of whether appearance is in accord with reality or not

Only accepting one of these and rejecting the other is not done. For this reason, both: (1) scriptures of Candrakīrti, such as the root text and [auto]commentary of the *Madhyamakāvatāra*, and (2) the *Uttaratantra* scripture of the supreme, great regent, Maitreyanātha, also are within one essential point, without contradiction, scriptures of the Prāsaṅgika Mahāyāna.

In general, Buddha-nature, etc., is said to be the ultimate in the great scriptures. Also, sometimes the empty essence is stated as the ultimate, and natural clarity is stated as the relative. Their viewpoint is as follows: Both the appearing and empty aspects of heritage, the basic element, [Buddha-]nature, etc. are posited as ultimate from the aspect of appearance in accord with reality [authentic experience]; however, through the manner of delineating the relative from the aspect of appearance and the ultimate from the empty aspect, it has [aspects of] both the truths of appearance and emptiness.

2. Refuting the Mistaken Conceptions of Others Whose Claims are One-Sided

Some people apply the two delineations of the two truths
To the Prāsaṅgika-Madhyamaka and Svātantrika-Madhyamaka separately.
They have difficulty realizing the noncontradictory intended meaning
Of either the middle or the last wheel.

Concerning this, some people apply them separately, saying, "As for the two delineations of the two truths divided by means of (1) authentic/inauthentic experience and (2) appearance/emptiness, the first is the two truths in the Prāsaṅgika tradition, and the second is the two truths in the Svātantrika tradition. Therefore, in the Svātantrika tradition, other than the two truths of appearance/emptiness, the two truths of authentic/inauthentic experience are not accepted. Likewise, in the Prāsaṅgika tradition, other than only the two truths of authentic/inauthentic experience, there are no two truths of appearance/emptiness."

However, it appears that if there were nothing other than a restricted, one-sided manner of positing the two truths in the Prāsaṅgika tradition, then it would be difficult to realize or explain the profound intended meaning of either the middle wheel or the last wheel of the Word as the noncontradictory two truths of appearance/emptiness and authentic/inauthentic experience.

3. Summary of the Essential Points of the Noncontradiction of Scriptural Meaning

Therefore, know the noncontradiction of both
Delineations of the two truths—
The meaning taught in the definitive meaning sūtras and
śāstras
Of the Great Middle Way.

For this reason, the meaning taught in the profound, definitive meaning sūtras of the middle and last wheels of the Word, and the commentaries on their viewpoint, such as the root text and [auto]commentary on the *Madhyamakāvatāra* and the *Uttaratantra*, is stated in two delineations of the two truths—appearance/emptiness and authentic/inauthentic experience. Know this manner that the Prāsaṅgika tradition accepts both without contradiction, as a single essential point.

2. Specific Division of the Two Truths of Appearance/Emptiness

This section has four parts: (1) the defining character of the two truths of appearance/emptiness, (2) the delineation of the illustrations of the two truths of appearance/emptiness, (3) the essence of the two truths of appearance/emptiness, and (4) the sequence of ascertaining the two truths of appearance/emptiness.

1. *Defining Character of the Two Truths of Appearance/Emptiness*

This section has two parts: (1) refuting other traditions and (2) presenting our tradition.

1. Refuting Other Traditions

Thus, from among the two delineations of
Ways of dividing the two truths,
Here is what some people say is
The defining character of the two truths of appearance/ emptiness:

"An object found by a valid cognition that analyzes
The conventional false seeings, and
An object found by a valid cognition that analyzes
*The consummate authentic seeing."**

Still, what is said to be Candrakīrti's tradition
Is a claim of a faulty defining character;
An appropriate analogy is a crow that ate filth, and
Wiped its beak on a clean place.

Others state as the defining character of the two truths:
"The apprehended object
Of authentic seeing's mode of apprehension, and
The apprehended object of false seeing's mode of apprehension."

They still claim that this is the intended meaning
Of Candrakīrti's scriptural tradition.
Here too there are the general faults of
No pervasion, over-pervasion, and impossibility.

As was just explained, from among the two delineations of ways of dividing the two truths, this context concerns the manner of explaining the defining character of the two truths of appearance/emptiness. In the tradition of some monastic textbooks, the defining characters of the relative and ultimate truths are respectively explained as follows: "The defining character of the relative truth is an object found by a

*This view is attributed to the Geluk by Bötrül's student, Khenpo Chökhyap.

valid cognition analyzing the conventional—that is, false seeings; the defining character of the ultimate truth is an object found by a valid cognition analyzing the consummate—that is, authentic seeing."

Still, although such defining characters are the intended meaning of Candrakīrti's scriptural tradition, they are just so *ordinarily* (*spyir btang tsam*). This follows because although they encompass the manners of evaluating objects for Sublime Ones in training, for whom meditative equipoise and postmeditation are distinct, they are faulty defining characters that do not encompass the way of the simultaneous evaluation of the two truths by a Sublime Buddha, in each respective [wisdom that knows] what is and [wisdom that knows] whatever there is. It is explained according to the words of the great being, Sapaṇ, in an appropriate analogy:

> A crow that ate filth
> Wipes its beak on a clean place. . . .[104]

By means of the way of seeing the objects of knowledge of the two truths, wisdom with a single essence is divided into two: [the wisdom that knows] what is and [the wisdom that knows] whatever there is. Yet they do not present in Candrakīrti's texts [the wisdom that knows] what is, for instance, to be both wisdoms—[the wisdom that knows] what is and [the wisdom that knows] whatever there is. Therefore, they are unable to establish the defining characters in Candrakīrti's tradition as faultless.

Other defining characters of the two truths are respectively stated as follows: "[The defining character of the relative truth is] an object found by a conventional valid cognition that is valid in relation to that conventional valid cognition; and [the defining character of the ultimate truth is] an object found by a reasoning consciousness's valid cognition that is valid in relation to that valid cognition of reasoning consciousness."* Also, some people say for these two defining characters, respectively: "Phenomena (*chos can*) that are infallible from the perspective of a reasoning relative mind; and suchness (*chos nyid*) that is infallible from the perspective of a reasoning ultimate mind." And some people say: "The defining character of the relative is an

*This reflects the defining character of the two truths given by the Geluk scholar, Sera Jetsün Chökyi Gyeltsen (*se ra rje btsun chos kyi rgyal mtshan*, 1469–1546), in his *Necklace for Fortunate Ones: Exposition of the Middle Way* (*dbu ma'i rnam bshad legs bshad skal bzang mgul rgyan*). Sera Jetsün Chökyi Gyeltsen's defining character is cited and translated in Karma Phuntsho, *Mipham's Dialectics and the Debates on Emptiness*, 117.

object found together with suitably appearing constructs by means of a valid cognition of its explicit realization; and the defining character of the ultimate is an object found without the perception of suitably appearing constructs by means of a valid cognition of its explicit realization."

Although there are many ways to describe them, in this [Prāsaṅgika] tradition, if it is a defining character of the two truths, it should be demonstrated in the scriptures of the Great Prāsaṅgika masters, Candrakīrti and Śāntideva. Since it is easy to realize that all others are not the Prāsaṅgika tradition, I will not elaborate upon distinguishing their qualities.

Moreover, some other omniscient masterly scholars say: "The defining characters of the ultimate and relative truths, respectively, are (1) the apprehended object of authentic seeing's mode of apprehension and (2) the apprehended object of false seeing's mode of apprehension." Although it is said that this itself is the intended meaning of the great texts of the glorious Candrakīrti, the tradition of the *Madhyamakāvatāra*, when this defining character is examined slightly, it appears to have general faults:

- If this defining character of the ultimate is the defining character of the general ultimate, then it does not encompass the uncategorized ultimate.
- If this defining character is only the ultimate in this context [of the uncategorized ultimate], then there is over-pervasion of the categorized ultimate, which is not the meaning of the defined term.
- And, it is not possible for the defined term to be the uncategorized ultimate.[105]

2. Presenting Our Tradition

Our tradition asserts the respective defining characters of the two truths as follows:
"The defining characters of the ultimate and relative are (1) the object of wisdom beyond mind in meditative equipoise—what is; and
(2) The object of conventional mind's seeing—whatever there is."

This way is the intended meaning of the definitive meaning sūtras
And the two magnificent masters;
The meanings shown through both inclusion and exclusion
Are the faultless defining characters.

The way of asserting the respective defining characters of the two truths in our tradition is as follows: The defining character of the ultimate truth is that which is the abiding reality of what is, and is an object of the wisdom of meditative equipoise beyond mind; and the defining character of the relative truth is that which is a mode of appearance of whatever there is, and is an object perceived by a conventional mind.

The manner of such defining characters is the unexcelled viewpoint of the definitive meaning sūtras in general, and the commentaries on the viewpoint by the great scholars, the pundits and accomplished ones, namely, the two magnificent masters—glorious Candrakīrti of the magnificent view and Śāntideva of the magnificent conduct. In the root text and [auto]commentary of the *Madhyamakāvatāra*, the defining character of the ultimate is posited by means of inclusion (*yongs gcod*);[106] in the context of the Wisdom Chapter of the *Bodhicaryāvatāra*, the defining character of the ultimate is indicated by means of exclusion (*rnam gcod*).[107] Both scriptures indicate the defining character of the relative by means of inclusion.[108] In this way, the faultless defining characters of the two truths are shown by means of both inclusion and exclusion.

In general, in order to realize the actual ultimate, which is the direct object of exclusively the wisdom of meditative equipoise, the ultimate is said to be the domain of wisdom beyond mind, having distinguished as separate (1) the dualistic mind of perceived-perceiver and (2) the nondual wisdom without perceived-perceiver. In order to know that the relative truth is what is realized by either the mind (*blo*) or wisdom (*ye shes*), with or without the duality of perceived-perceiver, its defining character is posited by means of it being the domain of mind *in general*, without being distinguished [as the exclusive domain of a dualistic mind]. Know this essential meaning.

2. Delineation of the Illustrations of the Two Truths of Appearance/Emptiness

This section has two parts: (1) the delineation of the relative and (2) the delineation of the ultimate.

1. Delineation of the Relative

This section has two parts: (1) refuting other traditions and (2) presenting our tradition.

1. Refuting Other Traditions

Concerning the delineation of the illustrations, [*some people claim,*] *"Although from the perspective of an elderly person,*
There is the correct and mistaken relative,
From [*a Prāsaṅgika's*] *own perspective, other than the mistaken relative,*
*There is no correct relative."**

Without differentiating the two truths,
They claim all sorts of conceptual fabrications.
In the glorious Candrakīrti from the Noble Land,
What delusion is posited, inside or out?

Yet [*they*] *hold on, saying, "There is a common locus of*
Deluded cognition and valid cognition."†
A valid cognition like this—which is deluded omniscience—
Is quite amazing!

Concerning the manner of asserting the delineations of the illustrations for the two truths, some masterly scholars say: "The correct and mistaken relatives are posited in the Svātantrika tradition; however, a unique assertion of this [Prāsaṅgika] tradition is as follows: The division of the relative into correct and mistaken is accepted for the world, namely, in the perspective of an elderly person's consciousness. However, in Candrakīrti's own perspective, other than only the

*This view is attributed to the Geluk by Bötrül's student, Khenpo Chökhyap. This position is represented in a statement by the Geluk scholar, Changkya Rolpé Dorjé, in his *Presentation of Philosophical Systems*, 321. See translation in note on page 141.

†This position is attributed to the Geluk by Bötrül's student, Khenpo Chökhyap. In his commentary on the *Bodhicaryāvatāra*, the Geluk scholar, Gyeltsapjé, states that what is established by valid cognition—forms and so on—are negated by a Sublime One's valid cognition. Gyeltsapjé, *Gateway to the Bodhisattvas (rgyal sras 'jug sngogs)*, 355. Such is the case with the conventional valid cognition of confined perception in Bötrül's own tradition, too; in the end, it is a deluded cognition. Apparently, the difference lies with the presence of a second conventional valid cognition—pure vision. Since there is no such valid cognition of pure vision in the opponent's tradition, he argues that they are left with this contradiction.

mistaken relative, there is no correct relative. If there were a correct relative, then there would be the consequent fault that the relative would be established by its own character."*

However, although there is neither a correct nor a mistaken relative in the perspective of ultimate truth in the Great Prāsaṅgika tradition, they speak all sorts of conceptual fabrications without clearly differentiating the two truths—such as saying that the manner of positing the correct and mistaken relative is only in the perspective of conventional truth for the world. Due to this, [they say that] the own perspective of the glorious Candrakīrti from the Noble Land is the delusion of the sole perception of the mistaken relative, without any perception of the correct relative.

What delusion, inside or outside, is there posited in the root text and [auto]commentary of the *Madhyamakāvatāra*? They should examine this. Still, they claim a common locus of deluded cognition and valid cognition in this [Prāsaṅgika] tradition. In Candrakīrti's own perspective, a valid cognition like this—omniscience that is delusion subsumed within the mistaken relative—appears to be quite amazing!

2. *Presenting Our Tradition*

This section has three parts: (1) a concise demonstration, (2) an extensive explanation, and (3) dispelling objections.

1. CONCISE DEMONSTRATION

Our tradition accepts that from the perspective of the valid
cognition of ultimate analysis,
There are no divisions of correct and mistaken phenomena; and
In the perspective of the conventional, relative truth,
The correct and mistaken are divided separately.

---

*This statement is attributed to the Geluk by Bötrül's student, Khenpo Chökhyap. The Geluk scholar, Changkya Rolpé Dorjé, made a statement that reflects Bötrül's target: "The assertion that evaluated objects [that is, forms and so forth] are false even conventionally is due to not accepting that they are established by way of their own characters even conventionally. Other proponents of the Middle Way accept a correct and incorrect relative, but this is due to their accepting that phenomena are established by way of their own characters conventionally. . . . The correct and incorrect is posited in dependence upon the perspective of the cognitions of people in the world; our own tradition of Prāsaṅgika does not distinguish between the incorrect and correct." Changkya Rolpé Dorjé, *Presentation of Philosophical Systems*, 321. See also Newland, *The Two Truths*, 117–23.

Regarding this, our tradition accepts as follows: In the Svātantrika tradition in general, the two truths are divided from the perspective of the valid cognition of ultimate analysis. From the perspective of that [ultimate] valid cognition, while the correct and mistaken relatives are not negated, those [relative phenomena] being truly established, and so on, are negated. However, in this unique [Prāsaṅgika] tradition, from the perspective of ultimate analysis there are no divisions at all between relative phenomena that are correct and mistaken, in accord with the statement, "Through this reasoning [production] is not reasonable even conventionally. . . ."[109] However, "I speak from the perspective of the world,"[110] and:

> That which is apprehended by the six unimpaired
> faculties
> Is understood by the world;
> What is beyond the truth of the world,
> The world presents as mistaken.[111]

In accord with the intended meaning of the root text and [auto]commentary of the *Madhyamakāvatāra*, we accept a separate division of the correct and mistaken [relative truths]. From the perspective of the conventional, relative truth: the correct relative is that which appears that is unpolluted by adventitious delusion such as the sight of a white conch and the view of the causality of karma; and the mistaken relative is what appears polluted by adventitious delusion, such as the sight of a yellow conch and the view that there is no causality of karma.

2. EXTENSIVE EXPLANATION

> *From the perspective of ultimate analysis,*
> *All phenomena are certainly illusory, deluded perceptions.*
> *However, by merely this, from the perspective of conventional*
> *truth*
> *They are not delusions of the mistaken relative.*
>
> *Although all phenomena are seen as an illusion*
> *By the glorious Candrakīrti of the Noble Land,*
> *From the perspective of his perception,*
> *Conventionally, the color of the conch and moon*
>
> *Perceived as white is the vision of the correct relative.*
> *Turning away* [*this*],

It is impossible [for him] to have a mistaken cognition, [such as]
Perceiving the conch and moon as yellow.

From the perspective of the mere illusion of the relative,
The world in postmeditation, Candrakīrti divides
The relative into two, correct and mistaken,
Through self-appearance being deluded or non-deluded.

Regarding this, from the perspective of ultimate analysis, all appearances of phenomena are certainly illusory, deluded perceptions that do not withstand analysis. However, [by] merely this, all relative appearances are not posited as solely the mistaken relative—delusion—from the perspective of the truth of the conventional world. This follows because as a handprint [result] of the glorious Candrakīrti from the Noble Land seeing ultimate emptiness, he saw all phenomena as illusory, deluded perceptions. However, by merely this, from Candrakīrti's perspective, it is not possible to have a deluded cognition—having turned away from all perceptions of the correct relative conventionally, such as the perceptions of a white conch and a white moon—and perceiving only the mistaken relative as all that is perceived, such as the perceptions of a yellow conch and a yellow moon. Therefore, from the perspective of the mere illusion of the relative, the conventional world in postmeditation, the glorious Candrakīrti makes a twofold division of the relative—the correct and the mistaken—due to the power of deluded or non-deluded self-appearance.

3. DISPELLING OBJECTIONS

There is no appearance left over
That is not negated by the valid cognition of ultimate analysis.
Due to that, there is no consequent fault
That the conventional is established by its own character.

Without understanding the critical points such as these, which are difficult to realize,
There are claims such as: "The conventional is stated following after the elderly people of the world," and
"Self-appearance is only the mistaken relative," and
"There is a common locus of deluded cognition and valid cognition."

This is a stanza at the interlude between sections.

If someone says: "If this [Prāsaṅgika] tradition's correct and mistaken relative is not posited as only in the perspective of the world, but as Candrakīrti's own perspective, then it would follow that the conventional would be established by its own character—just like it is for the Svātantrikas."

This [Prāsaṅgika] tradition's "correct relative" is not like the appearances left over that are not negated even by the valid cognition of ultimate analysis, as in the Svātantrika. Therefore, there is no consequent fault at all to be sought after that the conventional would be established by its own character. Without understanding these profound difficult points, claims such as these appear: "All of the conventional should be spoken following after the elderly people of the world," and, "There is nothing other than the mistaken relative in Candrakīrti's self-appearance," and, "In this [Prāsaṅgika] tradition, although there is a common locus of deluded cognition and valid cognition, there is no contradiction."

This is a stanza at the interlude between sections.

2. Delineation of the Ultimate

This section has two parts: (1) refuting other traditions and (2) presenting our tradition.

1. *Refuting Other Traditions*

> [*Some people say,*] *"There are four ultimates,*
> *Subjective and objective,*
> *Through the division of implicative and non-implicative negations, which are*
> *The nominal and actual ultimates."**
>
> *There is fault because this way lacks the freedom from constructs that is*
> *Superior to the emptiness that is a non-implicative negation;*

*This view is attributed to the Geluk by Bötrül's student, Khenpo Chökhyap. The Geluk scholar, Changkya Rolpé Dorjé, mentions four such ultimates: two subjective ultimates and two objective ulimates. See Changkya Rolpé Dorjé, *Presentation of Philosophical Systems*, 244. For the fourfold ultimates presented in the Geluk tradition, see Elizabeth Napper, *Dependent Arising and Emptiness*, 429–40; see also Newland, *The Two Truths*, 161–62.

Other than being the categorized, such a non-implicative negation
Is not even a fraction of the uncategorized.

Concerning the distinctive identification of the illustrations of the categorized (*rnam grangs*) and the uncategorized (*rnam grangs ma yin pa*) ultimates, there are some people who distinctively posit an objective emptiness as the actual (*rnam grangs ma yin pa*) ultimate, and the subject that realizes that as the nominal (*rnam grangs*) ultimate.[112] The way that this is also appropriate in our tradition is stated in the *Rapsel Rejoiner*,[113] so I will not express differences.

However, regarding this, it appears that some masterly scholars explain that the way the categorized and uncategorized ultimates occur in the Svātantrika texts, such as the *Satyadvaya*,[114] is here [in the Prāsaṅgika], too. They say, "Different means of expression are divided for each of the two respective nominal and actual ultimates. There are four ultimates when the ultimate is divided by different means of expression because there are two objective ultimates when divided in terms of the object and two in terms of the subject. Divided in terms of the object:

1. An implicative negation (*ma yin dgag*), such as the assembled meaning of a sprout and its lack of true existence, is the objective concordant ultimate; that [implicative negation] and the objective nominal ultimate have the same meaning.
2. A non-implicative negation (*med dgag*) that is the lack of true existence of a sprout is the actual objective ultimate. That [non-implicative negation] and the objective actual ultimate have the same meaning.

And divided in terms of the subject:

3. An inference that realizes emptiness through the manner of an object-universal (*don spyi*) is the subjective concordant ultimate; that [inference] and the subjective nominal ultimate have the same meaning;
4. The valid cognition that directly perceives emptiness is the actual subjective ultimate; that [direct perception] and the subjective actual ultimate have the same meaning."

However, with this way in which the actual (uncategorized) ultimate must be identified as a non-implicative negation, the profound freedom from constructs in the tradition of the Great Middle Way that is superior to a non-implicative negation is not explained. Consequently, there is fault. When examined, such an emptiness that is a non-implicative negation merely partially negates constructed extremes. As is stated in [Mipam's] *Madhyamakālaṃkāra* commentary, other than being merely the categorized ultimate of the Svātantrika tradition, it is not even a fraction of the uncategorized ultimate of the Prāsaṅgika tradition.

2. Presenting Our Tradition

Our tradition asserts that the categorized [ultimate] is
An emptiness that is a negation of constructed extremes only partially, and that
The uncategorized ultimate is
Free from all subtle and gross constructed extremes.

Our tradition, the school of early translations, asserts as follows: In general, we posit the categorized ultimate as the Svātantrika tradition's emptiness that is a negation of constructed extremes only partially, and the uncategorized ultimate as the Prāsaṅgika tradition's emptiness that is free from all subtle and gross constructed extremes. When distinguished in detail, the categorized ultimate is provisionally emphasized in the Svātantrika tradition. In the end, since they conclusively settle upon the uncategorized, both are accepted. The provisional ultimate is not accepted in the Prāsaṅgika tradition, as is taught extensively in such [texts] as [Mipam's] commentary on the Wisdom [Chapter of the *Bodhicaryāvatāra*]:

> One should know that there is no twofold distinction of the categorized and uncategorized ultimates in this [Prāsaṅgika] tradition.[115]

3. *Essence of the Two Truths of Appearance/Emptiness*

This section has two parts: (1) refuting other traditions and (2) presenting our tradition.

1. Refuting Other Traditions

Some people say, "The two truths are contradictory."

Still they say, "They are essentially the same identity
*With different contradistinctions."**
Stating a common locus of contradiction and relationship is very amazing!

Other than the understood meaning of merely the two truths
Of the categorized valid cognition,
This manner is not the intended meaning of the Prāsaṅgika view—
The uncategorized free from extremes.

Others say, "The two truths are neither
One-sidedly one nor many;
[Asserting that they are] essentially the same with different contradistinctions
Is the tradition of logicians."†

Regarding this, the tradition of the Prāsaṅgika view
Is like that, free from being one or many;
However, why don't they explain the tradition of the Svātantrika view
In accord with the Bodhicittavivaraṇa *scripture?*

Concerning the distinction of the two truths as essentially the same with different contradistinctions, in the tradition of some masterly scholars, it is asserted as follows: "The self-contradistinctions (*rang ldog*) of the two truths are in general contradictory. The self-contradistinctions of the two—(1) a relative entity such as a pot and (2) its emptiness of true existence, which is a nonentity—are contradictory. However, if phenomena were essentially different from their suchness, namely, their emptiness of true existence, then they would be truly established. Therefore, we assert that the two—(1) that which lacks true existence

---

*This view is attributed to the Geluk by Bötrül's student, Khenpo Chökhyap. For Tsongkhapa's depiction of the relationship between the two truths as "essentially the same with different contradistinctions," see Tsongkhapa, *Thoroughly Illuminating the Viewpoint*, 176.

†This view is attributed to the Sakya scholar, Gorampa, by Bötrül's student, Khenpo Chökhyap. For Gorampa's argument against the two truths being essentially the same, see Gorampa, *Completely Elucidating the Definitive Meaning*, 114.3–116.5.

and (2) that which relatively exists—are essentially the same with different contradistinctions. From the *Bodhicittavivaraṇa:*

> Apart from the relative
> The ultimate is not observed;
> The relative is said to be emptiness.
> Emptiness itself is the relative because
> Without one there is certainly not the other—
> Like a product and an impermanent phenomenon.[116]

"Therefore, that which is relatively existent is itself essentially the same as what is empty of true existence. Also, that which is empty of true existence is itself essentially the same as what is relatively existent. There is no emptiness of true existence other than what is relatively existent; and there is no relative existence other than what is empty of true existence. This itself is explained as the viewpoint of the *Four Applications of Emptiness Sūtra* [*Heart Sūtra*].

"In the *Saṃdhinirmocana* it is said that the assertion of [the ultimate and relative as] either the same or different each has four faults.[117] And all the statements such as, 'the character free from being the same or different,'[118] express the same viewpoint as this. However, the *Mūlamadhyamakakārikā* states, 'neither different nor the same'[119] due to intending what is free from being *truly established* as one or many; it is not the same as this [literal meaning]."

In short, they assert for the two truths a common locus of relationship and contradiction. Other than the Svātantrika tradition's understood meaning of the mere two truths that are the objects found by the valid cognition analyzing the categorized, such a way of explanation is not said to be the intended meaning of the Prāsaṅgika view, which is the great uncategorized ultimate that is free from extremes.

Other great all-seeing ones say, "Based on the perspective of wisdom's vision, the two truths are definitely neither the same nor different. Saying otherwise—that they are 'essentially the same with different contradistinctions'—is merely the way of presenting products and impermanent phenomena in the logicians' tradition of valid cognition." And there is also the way of saying that the two truths are "merely conventionally, different in the sense of negating that they are one."

In general, the two truths are accepted to be neither the same nor different in this way in the tradition of the Prāsaṅgika view. Nevertheless, in the tradition of the Svātantrika view, why don't they explain according to the tradition of the *Bodhicittavivaraṇa* [namely, that the two truths are essentially the same with different contradistinctions]? I think that it is reasonable to [also] explain in that way.

2. Presenting Our Tradition

Our tradition asserts that the division of the two truths
As essentially the same with different contradistinctions
Is the object of valid cognition analyzing the categorized
In the tradition of the Svātantrika view.

In the tradition of the consummate Prāsaṅgika view,
The object of valid cognition analyzing the uncategorized
Is free from all concepts of
The two truths being essentially one or many.

Nevertheless, for the objects of the valid cognition of pure vision
In the two truths of authentic/inauthentic experience,
The phenomena that are pure and impure, authentic and inauthentic,
Are asserted as the negation of being one.

Although other traditions of explanation are spoken in that way, the Nyingma's own tradition, that of the school of early translations, asserts as follows: As is stated in the scriptural commentaries in general, based upon the Svātantrika tradition's ultimate that depends upon two truths—which is the object of valid cognition analyzing the categorized [ultimate]—it is not appropriate for the two truths to be divided other than as essentially the same with different contradistinctions (*ngo bo gcig la ldog pa tha dad*). However, the two truths are asserted as neither one nor many in relation to the consummate Prāsaṅgika tradition's view of the ultimate, which is the object of valid cognition analyzing the uncategorized.

Nevertheless, in certain contexts concerning the two truths of phenomena that appear in accordance with reality—which are the objects of the conventional valid cognition of pure vision—by means of whether or not they are established in the mode of reality, the two: (1) the phenomena of nirvāṇa, which is the natural purity of appearances in accord with reality, and (2) the phenomena of *saṃsāra*, which is the natural impurity of appearances that do not accord with reality, are asserted, like an entity and a nonentity, as the negation of being one (*gcig pa bkag pa*). However, it appears that in [Mipam's] *Exposition* [*of Buddha-Nature*] and so forth, the two—*saṃsāra* and nirvāṇa—are also asserted to be neither one nor many in the manner of phenomena (*chos can*) and suchness (*chos nyid*).[120]

4. Sequence of Ascertaining the Two Truths of Appearance/Emptiness

This section has two parts: (1) refuting other traditions and (2) presenting our tradition.

1. Refuting Other Traditions

> *Regarding the sequence,* [*some people say*], *"After ascertaining the ultimate,*
> *The relative appearances are ascertained."**
> *Others say, "From the relative, which is the method,*
> *The ultimate, which arises from the method, is ascertained. . . ."†*

Concerning the sequence of ascertaining the two truths, other supreme scholars assert the manner of ascertaining the two truths as follows: "First one negates the true establishment of appearances by means of [the reasoning of] being neither one nor many, etc. As a handprint [result] of ascertaining the ultimate, which is the emptiness of true existence, then one must ascertain the relative—all appearances of phenomena—as merely conceptual imputations." Also, others appear to say, "In dependence upon the method, which is the relative, one must ascertain the ultimate, which arises from the method."

2. Presenting Our Tradition

> *Our tradition asserts the progressive and instantaneous manners of ascertainment*
> *From the four stages of the view of the Middle Way.*[121]
> *The Svātantrikas ascertain the two truths progressively;*
> *Instantaneous ascertainment is the tradition of Prāsaṅgika.*

---

*This refers to Svātantrikas (and equated with the Geluk) by Bötrül's student, Khenpo Chökhyap.

†This view is attributed to the Sakya scholar, Gorampa, by Bötrül's student, Khenpo Chökhyap. For Gorampa's statements on the relative and ultimate truths as the method and that which arises from the method, see Gorampa, *Completely Elucidating the Definitive Meaning*, 54.5–55.2.

Regarding this, the two: (1) the method and that which arises from method, and
(2) The sequence of ascertaining the two truths
Are alike but not to be mistaken—
Confusing them as the same is confusion at the core.

Our tradition asserts (1) the manner of conclusive ascertainment by the four stages of the Middle Way view progressively and (2) the manner of instantaneous-like ascertainment. From among these, the Svātantrikas ascertain appearance as empty; and after determining the mere categorized ultimate, they must then ascertain the emptiness dawning as dependently-arisen relative [phenomena] that are established by their own characters. There is nothing else suitable in a progressive ascertainment of the two truths.

By means of [the reasoning of] being neither one nor many, etc., the [followers of the] Great Middle Way directly ascertain appearance as the great uncategorized ultimate free from extremes—the equality that is the unity of emptiness and appearance. This instantaneous ascertainment—without relying on alternation between appearance and emptiness—is established as the Prāsaṅgika tradition.

If it is said, "This is not reasonable because these two are the method and that which arises from method."

Regarding this, there is a statement, "The relative truth, which is the method, and the ultimate truth, which is that which arises from method." The two appear as similar: (1) that which is taught as the method and that which arises from method concerning *what is needed to ascertain* the ultimate (that which arises from method), from the method for ascertaining the ultimate (such as the Middle Way reasonings); and (2) *the sequence for ascertaining* the two truths shown in this context [that is, progressive and instantaneous]. Based on this, to confuse them as the same is a great confusion at the core.

3. Extensive Presentation of the Two Truths

This section has two parts: (1) distinguishing ultimate emptiness—the mode of reality and (2) distinguishing relative phenomena—the mode of appearance.

1. Distinguishing Ultimate Emptiness—The Mode of Reality

This section has two parts: (1) a concise demonstration and (2) an extensive presentation.

1. Concise Demonstration

Although there is accord in the way of stating the words,
"Emptiness is the ultimate truth,"
There are different qualities in the evidence,
What is established, the objects, and what is negated.

Here in the context of explaining the view of the ground—the two truths of appearance/emptiness—there is accord in merely the way of stating the words, "Emptiness is the ultimate truth." However, there are different qualities in that assertion, such as: the way of formulating the establishing evidence, the nature of the emptiness that is established, and the explanation of the distinctive object of negation by means of whether or not there are commonly appearing objects.

2. Extensive Explanation

This section has four parts: (1) the arguments, (2) what is established, (3) the object of negation, and (4) the delineations of Prāsaṅgika and Svātantrika.

1. Arguments

This section has two parts: (1) the distinction between consequences and autonomous arguments and (2) the distinctive arguments and views.

1. Distinction Between Consequences and Autonomous Arguments

Others say, "The arguments of the Great Prāsaṅgika-
Madhyamaka
*Are consequences."**
However, [by this,] the unique [quality of] Prāsaṅgika—
Being free from all assertions—is reduced to words.

Our tradition asserts that the uncategorized ultimate
Is free from all assertions.

*This claim is attributed to the Geluk by Bötrül's student, Khenpo Chökhyap. This claim is an implication of one of Tsongkhapa's eight unique assertions of Prāsaṅgika, namely, that autonomous arguments (*rang rgyud kyi sbyor ba, svatantraprayoga*) are not accepted to be able generate the view of thusness in the continuum of an opponent.

Therefore, the unique arguments of the Great Middle Way
Are the great consequences (thal 'gyur, prasaṅga).

From the mouths of others, the scholars who are the crown-ornaments of the Land of Snow, it is said, "In the context of the Great Prāsaṅgika-Madhyamaka, arguments must be formulated as only consequences. Formulating arguments that are consequences is the unique quality of this tradition."

However, as is said in such texts as [Mipam's] *Difficult Points of Scriptures in General,*[122] when considering the way of asserting evidence in their tradition, phenomena—objects such as pots—are not negated. Therefore, it is difficult for unique Prāsaṅgika arguments to be free from assertions by means of there being no commonly appearing objects with the realists. Thus, [Prāsaṅgika] is reduced to mere words.

Our tradition asserts as follows: From the perspective of the uncategorized ultimate, which is the profound domain of the wisdom of meditative equipoise, entities that are commonly appearing objects, such as pillars and pots, are not observed. And all gross and subtle constructed phenomena, which are the objects of negation, are negated without reference, while there is not even the slightest referent object of existence or nonexistence that is established as an implication of the negation; there are no assertions at all. Because of this, the arguments in this Great Middle Way are uniquely Prāsaṅgika arguments: such as the evidence, entailment, and assertions of the opponent being inferences renowned to another, etc. They have the greatness of being formulated as unique arguments that are consequences precisely because an opponent's wrong understandings are overturned by means of exclusively these unique Prāsaṅgika arguments.

2. Distinctive Arguments and Views

*Others claim, "The view is a non-implicative negation."**
Look at the phenomenon established—a lack of true existence—
that is implied

---

*This claim is attributed to the Geluk by Bötrül's student, Khenpo Chökhyap. Tsongkhapa emphasized that the ultimate truth is a non-implicative negation. See, for instance, Tsongkhapa, *The Lesser Exposition of the Stages of the Path,* 396.6. A non-implicative negation is characterized as an explicit negation that does not imply anything else; for instance, "Brahmins should not drink alcohol." In contrast, an implicative negation is characterized as an explicit negation that implicates something else; for instance, "the fat Devadatta does not eat during the day." This negation implies something else, namely, that Devadatta eats at night. In contrast to implicative negations, the connotative force of a non-implicative negation is denial rather than an implied affirmation.

By the negation of true establishment, which is the object of negation;
Their arguments are merely implicative negations.

Our tradition asserts that by negating all constructed extremes,
No extremes of reference or constructed phenomena are implied whatsoever.
Due to this, the arguments are exclusively non-implicative negations, and
The view is the great freedom from extremes.

Other masterly scholars claim: "The Prāsaṅgika view needs to be a non-implicative negation. If it is stated to be free from constructs, it becomes the tradition of Hvashang.[123] The arguments also need to be formulated as consequences."

When examined, however, other than merely implicative negations, it is difficult for their arguments to be pure consequences. Look at their way of formulating evidence: without negating the object, such as a pot, the lack of true existence—the phenomenon established—is implied by the negation of true establishment, which is the object of negation. Their arguments have the complete defining character of implicative negations.

Our tradition asserts as follows: In the context of ascertaining the ultimate of this [Prāsaṅgika] tradition, due to not accepting commonly appearing objects such as pots, there is no extreme of reference at all that is a constructed phenomena, such as existence or nonexistence, implied by the negation of all the subtle and gross constructed extremes posited by individual opponents. Therefore, the argument is exclusively a non-implicative negation because its defining character is complete. In the context of formulating an argument that negates the four extremes of production in the *Prasannapadā*, the realist [Bhāvaviveka] says: "You proponents of the Middle Way undoubtedly assert production from another as an implication of the refutation of self-production." Then Candrakīrti states, "This is in terms of a non-implicative negation,"[124] stating that the argument in this context is a non-implicative negation.

Since the argument is a non-implicative negation, the view is free from all extremes because there is not even the slightest constructed phenomenon, existent or nonexistent, implied by the negation.

2. What is Established

This section has two parts: (1) refuting other traditions and (2) presenting our tradition.

1. Refuting Other Traditions

This section has two parts: (1) a concise demonstration and (2) an extensive explanation.

1. Concise Demonstration

> *Others variously say that the essence of emptiness is*
> *An entity or a nonentity;**
> *Other than being relative truths,*
> *These are not the emptiness that is the ultimate.*

Concerning the manner of asserting the essence of the ultimate emptiness, others speak variously: some say it is an entity and others say it is a nonentity. However, as is stated extensively in the great scriptures, other than being mere relative truths, these entities and nonentities are not the emptiness that is the uncategorized ultimate.

2. Extensive Explanation

This section has two parts: (1) refuting the constructed extreme of emptiness as a nonentity and (2) refuting the constructed extreme of emptiness as an entity.

1. Refuting the Constructed Extreme of Emptiness as a Nonentity

> *Some people say: "The ultimate emptiness is a nonentity—*
> *A lack of true existence that is a non-implicative negation."*†

---

*The view that emptiness is an entity is that of the Kagyü tradition, and the Jonang scholar, Dölpopa. The view that emptiness is a nonentity is that of the Geluk (Svātantrika) and also the Sakya, according to Khenpo Chökhyap's oral commentary.

†This view is attributed to the Geluk by Bötrül's student, Khenpo Chökhyap. Tsongkhapa consistently emphasized that the ultimate truth is solely a (non-implicative) negation. See, for instance, Tsongkhapa, *The Lesser Exposition of the Stages of the Path (lam rim chung ba)*, 396.6.

As such, other than the categorized ultimate,
It is not the uncategorized ultimate.

[Concerning] this, since valid cognitions of confined perception
Find objects that are entities and nonentities,
They say, "There is no third alternative in between a direct contradiction;
Therefore, emptiness is a nonentity."

Regarding this, (1) emptiness that is posited as a nonentity
And (2) appearance that is posited as an entity
Is merely the understood meaning of the reasoning in introductory logic primers;
Both are relative truths.

Some monastic textbooks say: "The ultimate emptiness in the Great Middle Way tradition is only a nonentity—a lack of true existence that is a non-implicative negation."

However, other than the categorized ultimate of the Svātantrika tradition, such an emptiness is not the uncategorized ultimate because: "Since arising, etc., is negated . . ."[125] and, "Actually, it is free from all assemblages of constructs"[126]; if even Svātantrika texts state that the great ultimate needs to be free from all extremes, then it is needless to mention about the Prāsaṅgika tradition.

Consequently, this manner of asserting emptiness as a nonentity is as follows: The evaluated object found by a valid cognition of confined perception is necessarily either an entity or a nonentity—one or the other of a dichotomy. Therefore, they say: "They are a direct contradiction, so necessarily there is no third alternative in between which is neither of the two. Hence, if emptiness is not an entity, then it must be a nonentity."

However, in general, positing emptiness as a nonentity and appearance as an entity is merely the understood meaning of the basic reasoning in introductory logic primers. It is taught in order to extend the wide hand of compassion to trainees with such intellects. However, the way that this is not the consummate emptiness was stated by the second Victorious One, the great lord Tsongkhapa, in a scroll sent to Rendawa:[127]

> Great emptiness is in accord with the consummate meaning,
> "entities and nonentities are conditioned. . . ."[128]

As is stated, both of these [entities and nonentities] are merely relative truths.

2. Refuting the Constructed Extreme of Emptiness as an Entity

Others say, "There is a permanent truth
That withstands ultimate analysis."
Look to the following: "In a faulty view of emptiness
Those with little intelligence will be destroyed."

Also, other scholars say, "Emptiness, the essence of the [Buddha-]nature, is a permanent truth that is not empty; it withstands even ultimate analysis."* However, [to them I say] look to the following:

> In a faulty view of emptiness,
> Those with little intelligence will be destroyed.[129]

2. *Presenting Our Tradition*

This section has three parts: (1) a concise demonstration, (2) an extensive explanation, and (3) a summary of the meaning established in the Great Middle Way free from extremes.

1. Concise Demonstration

Our tradition asserts ultimate emptiness
As the great uncategorized ultimate,
The expanse beyond the constructed phenomena
Of the relative objects found by a valid cognition of confined perception.

Regarding this, our tradition asserts the essence of the ultimate truth as the great uncategorized ultimate, the expanse of phenomena

---

*This refers to the Jonang scholar, Dölpopa, and "proponents of other-emptiness" (*gzhan stong*), as stated by Bötrül's student, Khenpo Chökhyap. For Jonang Tāranātha's statements on the truly established ultimate that withstands analysis and is not empty of its own essence, see Tāranātha, *Essence of Other-Emptiness (gzhan stong snying po)*, in *Collected Works*, vol. 18, 180.2–180.4; 190.2–190.3.

beyond all constructed phenomena of the relative, such as entities and nonentities, which are objects found by a valid cognition of confined perception.

2. Extensive Explanation

Emptiness is not an entity;
While appearance is not reified,
That appearance abides as the great emptiness—
This is a critical point that destroys the clinging to entities.

Emptiness is not a nonentity;
While emptiness is not reified,
The self-lucidity of emptiness is appearing phenomena—
This is a critical point of the dawning of dependent arising.

The essence of ultimate emptiness is not existent and not an entity; while the appearances of all the appearing relative phenomena are not reified, the essence of appearance abides as the great emptiness. In this there is a critical point that pacifies all constructs of clinging to relative entities. The essence of this emptiness is not nonexistent and not a nonentity either; while the emptiness of the empty essence of ultimate suchness is not reified, the self-lucidity of emptiness is phenomena appearing unceasingly. This is a distinctive critical point of the dawning of dependent arising.

3. Summary of the Meaning Established in the Great Middle Way Free from Extremes

Since it is not an entity, it is free from being a permanent entity;
Since it is not a nonentity, it is free from being the extreme of annihilation.
The expanse of luminous clarity—profound, peaceful, and free from constructs—
Is asserted as the great ultimate, the abiding reality.

This way is neither the domain of an analysis of the categorized ultimate nor
The domain of analysis of a conventional valid cognition of confined perception.

The great valid cognition that analyzes the uncategorized ultimate
Is the unique meaning established by Prāsaṅgika reasoning.

This is a stanza at the interlude between sections.

Therefore, since the essence of ultimate emptiness is not an entity, it is free from all the extremes of permanent entities. Since its essence is not a nonentity, it is also free from all the extremes of nonexistent annihilation. Hence, in accord with the intended meaning of the *Lalitavistarasūtra*, its essence is the expanse of luminous clarity—profound, peaceful, and free from constructs—asserted as the great ultimate, the abiding reality that is free from all extremes.

The following is a summary of this section: The profound way of such an abiding reality free from extremes is neither the domain of valid cognition analyzing the categorized ultimate nor the domain of analysis of a conventional valid cognition of confined perception; these cannot evaluate it. However, it is not that there is no establishing valid cognition; it is the meaning established that arises as a handprint [result] of negation by exclusion through the unique Prāsaṅgika reasoning—the ultimate valid cognition that analyzes the uncategorized ultimate.

This is a stanza at the interlude between sections.

3. Object of Negation

This section has three parts: (1) refuting other traditions, (2) presenting our tradition, and (3) dispelling objections.

1. Refuting Other Traditions

Others say: "All the relative appearances of entities are not empty;
They are not reasoning's object of negation.
However, they are the object of negation
*Of the sublime path without dualistic appearance."**

---

*This view is attributed to the Geluk by Bötrül's student, Khenpo Chökhyap. This is an implication of the Geluk position that phenomena are not the objects of negation for reasoning; only true establishment is the object of negation. In other words, a pot is not reason's target; rather, it is the pot conceived as truly established.

This view and philosophy with the ground and path in contradiction
Is a view that has separated the view and the meditation.
This manner is destroyed by
Candrakīrti's three great reasonings of the power of fact.

Regarding this, [some] say, "True establishment is the object of negation
For the valid cognition of ultimate analysis.
A phenomenon that is not merely an imputation of the conceptual mind
Is what is truly established."

Without negating conventional appearances,
This negation of something separate that is truly established
Is merely the understood meaning of the two truths divided
By a categorized valid cognition analyzing the ultimate.

In this, having divided the two truths,
After ascertaining relative appearances,
What is there that is truly established to be negated again
By a valid cognition of ultimate analysis?

Therefore, appearances themselves are analyzed and established as empty
From a perspective that is uncertain whether
These dualistic appearances of entities are either
(1) Actually established as they appear or (2) the relative.

In which of the two truths is [true establishment] the ground of analysis?
What is the use of leaving appearances as they are
And futilely analyzing whether or not there is
Something separate that is truly established?

The ground of analysis is all these various appearances of entities—
The ultimate of the realists and
The conventional world of the Middle Way [proponents]—
They are asserted as empty from the perspective of ultimate truth.

The way of emptiness in Candrakīrti's tradition is
To analyze appearances themselves through ultimate analysis and
Assert all appearances of entities to be empty,
Without asserting an ultimate pillar or pot.

Similarly, if an ultimate pillar or pot
Is not asserted,
The negation [of the ultimate status of these appearances] by the valid cognition of ultimate analysis' reasoning
Is good, followers of the path of reasoning!

[Others say,] "Due to being empty of another—true establishment—
There is no ultimate pillar or pot."
This bears a resemblance to the elimination of fear in a place where there are snakes,
By [the absence of] an elephant—amazing!

If you wish to negate something separate that is truly established at the time of the ground, and
Destroy dualistic appearances at the time of the path,
Then it is reasonable to hold the position that
When selflessness is seen, [merely] the permanent self is relinquished!

It is difficult for phenomena and suchness, and
Emptiness and dependent arising, to be feasible [when]
The two are: (1) selflessness that is solely an exclusion, a nonentity, and
(2) Non-empty relative entities.

Look at the proponents of other-emptiness (gzhan stong), whose emptiness
Leaves this shimmering appearance of solid duality as it is,
Without making it reasoning's object of negation.
[Their] object of negation, like horns, is something separate that is truly established.

This is a stanza at the interlude between sections.

Regarding the distinctive identification of the valid cognition of ultimate analysis' object of negation, in the tradition of some other masterly scholars, it is said: "At the time of ascertaining the view of the ground, appearances—all conventionally appearing phenomena, which are the appearances of relatively existent entities—are not empty of their own essences and are not the object of negation of the valid cognition of ultimate analysis. This follows because if they were negated, it would be a view of annihilation. Therefore, appearances are not reasoning's object of negation. However, they are the path's object of negation because they should be asserted as the object of negation of the path—such as that of the wisdom of a Sublime One's meditative equipoise."

In this way, (1) the time of ascertaining the view of the ground and (2) the time of practicing meditation on the path are a view and philosophy in contradiction. As they have expressed the faults of other traditions' assertions in some texts, [their own tradition has] a view that has separated the view and the meditation. For the reasoning that destroys this manner, as spoken by other masterly scholars, the way of invalidation is shown in the scripture of the glorious Candrakīrti by the three great reasonings of the power of fact.[130]

Regarding this, in their tradition they say, "The object of negation for the reasoning of ultimate analysis should only be what is truly established." The criterion that they explain for true establishment is a unique quality of this tradition: "That which is not merely imputed by the conceptual mind is posited as what is truly established."

This way of not negating conventional appearances, while negating something separate that is truly established, is merely the understood meaning in the context of ascertaining emptiness in the Svātantrika-Madhyamaka tradition: the categorized valid cognition of ultimate analysis divides the two truths, and without negating the conventional appearances such as pots, negates the ultimate status of the pillars and pots.

When examining this manner in general, having divided the two truths, when all appearing phenomena such as pillars and pots have been ascertained as the illusory relative, whoever has ascertained them as such does not accept their existence as truly established, whether they are an ordinary being or a Sublime One. Therefore, what is there that is truly established to be negated again by a valid cognition of ultimate analysis? It becomes the fault of establishing what has already been established.

For this reason, the ground of analysis is the status of these appearances themselves, from the perspective of an opponent who is not certain whether or not all these various appearances—the appearances of dualistic entities such as pillars and pots—are either (1) ultimately established as they appear or (2) existent as the essence of merely relative illusion. Through investigation by the valid cognition of ultimate analysis, these appearances need to be established as emptiness—as not ultimately established. Otherwise, in which perspective of the two truths does [something truly established] exist—in that of the realists or that of the Middle Way [proponents]? Without establishing the appearances themselves—such as the two irreducibles that are the grounds of analysis—as ultimately nonexistent, what is the use of an analysis of whether or not there is a pointless truly established thing that is separate from these [appearances], which are left as they are?

Therefore, the ground of analysis is the various appearances of entities, such as the two irreducibles, which the realists assert as ultimately existent and, hence, truly established. The Middle Way proponents assert that these relative appearances are established only from the perspective of the conventional world, and are empty from the ultimate perspective. Is this not the case?

Concerning the way of being ultimately empty, it is not like it is in the Svātantrika tradition. The valid cognition of ultimate analysis examines whether or not these relative appearances are ultimately existent or not. An ultimate pillar or pot is not accepted, and likewise, all such relative phenomena, the appearances of entities, are negated as ultimately nonexistent. Accepting appearances themselves as empty is the tradition of Candrakīrti, isn't it?

Therefore, in precise accordance with Candrakīrti, if you do not accept appearances such as pillars and pots as ultimately existent, then the manner in which there are ultimately no appearances of pillars and pots is through ultimate valid cognition's reasoning that these appearances themselves are ultimately nonexistent. If the ultimate status of these appearances is negated by reasoning, it is good, followers of the path of reasoning! However, as with speaking without knowing the reason, without ascertaining by reasoning the way that pillars and pots, etc., ultimately do not exist, stating their nonexistence is just making an arbitrary claim, isn't it?

If a realist were to ask a proponent of the Middle Way, "In your Middle Way tradition, are these appearances of pillars and pots ultimately existent or not?" When you do not respond, "These appearances of pillars and pots do not ultimately exist; they are empty," but say, "Pillars and pots do not ultimately exist due to their being empty of another, true establishment." This bears a resemblance to an amazing fact of the five Mahāsaṃmata schools' tradition. Candrakīrti states:

While seeing one's own house as a lair of snakes
To eliminate fear, saying: "There are no elephants here."
And by this to also eradicate the dread of snakes,
Is alas, a laugh for others.[131]

In consideration of this, when the ground is ascertained, merely something separate that is truly established is negated; and when the path is practiced, all dualistic appearances are claimed to be destroyed. When the Mahāsaṃmatas ascertain the ground, which is the observation of a view of self, they say that the self is the aggregates; and when they see selflessness on the path, they make the claim that they have given up simply the permanent self. This position is suitable for you to hold!

In short, the two: (1) a mere nonentity that is solely an exclusion—a lack of true existence that is the negation of something separate that is truly established—and (2) the entities of relative appearance, which are not known to be empty even from the perspective of ultimate valid cognition, are like (1) rabbit horns, nonentity exclusions that do not exist, and (2) cattle horns, existent entities. An extensive presentation of the way that these two are not suitable as phenomena and suchness, and are also difficult to be feasible in the way that emptiness dawns as dependent arising, etc., should be known from [Mipam's] *Difficult Points of Scriptures in General*,[132] etc.

The following is a summary of the section: Look at this way of professing an emptiness of another, true establishment, in phenomena such as pots. While they view the side of the proponents of other-emptiness as the enemy, they are in accord with them! As it is said in [Changkya] Rolpé Dorjé's *Song of the View* (*lta mgur*),[133] they accept, as the object of negation of that [ultimate] valid cognition, an emptiness that is empty of something separate that is truly established—like horns. Without making this shimmering appearance of solid duality the object of negation of ultimate analysis' reasoning, it remains unchanged—left as it is.

This is a stanza at the interlude between sections.

2. Presenting Our Tradition

Our tradition, the asserted viewpoint of the translators and scholars of the school of early translations—
[That of] Mipam, the lord of doctrine—
Asserts emptiness [and]
The reasoning of ultimate analysis' object of negation in this way:

Having divided the two truths,
If appearance has been ascertained as the illusory relative,
The nature of appearance is not negated again
By valid cognition's reasoned analysis.

As for the mere relative,
If the nature of appearance is also negated
By a reasoned analysis analyzing the conventional,
Then that is the great [extreme] view of nonexistence.

That which is asserted to be truly established is:
Appearances themselves that are [held as] ultimately established or
Phenomena that seem to withstand ultimate analysis
When the relative has not been ascertained as illusion.

Regarding this, the categorized valid cognition's object of negation is
The phenomena that are truly established ultimately.
The object of negation of the valid cognition that analyzes the uncategorized is
The gross and subtle constructed extremes, etc.

Without the slightest thing withstanding the analysis by
The reasoning consciousness of valid cognition's ultimate analysis,
All relative appearances of constructed phenomena
Are negated within the ultimate expanse free from extremes.

In accord with the asserted viewpoint of the great translators and scholars of the school of early translations, our tradition asserts the means of ascertaining emptiness and the object of negation of ultimate analysis in this way: In the context of the Great Middle Way, one should speak having distinguished the contexts of (1) directly negating appearances and (2) the manner of not negating them. One should not speak arbitrarily.

Therefore, as a handprint [result] of a previous ultimate analysis, the two truths are divided. By means of ascertaining all relative phenomena as not established from the perspective of the ultimate great emptiness, whatever phenomena appear are all ascertained as illusory. Having already determined this, there is no other thing that is truly established to negate again, nor is the nature of appearance that has been ascertained as empty and dependently-arisen to be negated. As for the mere relative conventionally, if the nature of appearances such as the causality of karma is also negated by a reasoning consciousness analyzing the conventional, then it becomes the great [extreme] view of nonexistence.

If you think, "Well, didn't you explain that appearances should be negated directly?"

This is from the perspective of a mind that was not preceded by a reasoning valid cognition of ultimate analysis, for which:

- appearing phenomena themselves are held to be ultimately established in the way they appear, or
- the relative has not been ascertained as illusory phenomena, and phenomena seem to withstand analysis even from the perspective of ultimate analysis

We accept this to be the criteria for what is truly established because it is explained like this in [Mipam's] *Difficult Points of the Scriptures in General*, etc.

In general, as for the object of negation in the Svātantrika tradition's valid cognition analyzing the categorized, what is negated is what is ultimately established, or what is actually, truly established—having divided the two truths and not negating relative appearances. As for the object of negation in the Prāsaṅgika tradition's valid cognition analyzing the uncategorized, from the perspective of great emptiness, there is no qualification at all that gross constructed extremes, such as what is truly established, are to be negated, whereas subtle constructed extremes of mere appearances are not to be negated. This way of negation is stated in the *Prasannapadā*, and the root text and [auto]commentary of the *Madhyamakāvatāra*, etc.

Therefore, from the perspective of one who has not ascertained the great emptiness—that there is nothing ultimately established—all appearances of relative constructed phenomena, such as the gross and subtle constructed extremes, are negated within the expanse of the great ultimate free from extremes, without the slightest thing withstanding the analysis of the reasoning of valid cognition's ultimate analysis.

3. Dispelling Objections

The fear that it becomes a view of annihilation
Because the object of negation is too encompassing (khyab ches)

Is a concern that realists have, the ones who do not know about dependent arising,
Not a fear of Middle Way proponents.

If relative appearances are negated by conventional valid cognition,
Then that is a view of annihilation.
The ultimate status of all phenomena is negated
By the valid cognition of ultimate analysis—even so, how is this annihilation?

This reasoning establishes that production, etc.
Does not withstand analysis even conventionally.
Due to being free from all assertions,
The constructs of appearance are directly severed.

If you realize all appearances as appearances of the nonexistent—forms of emptiness—and
Realize what is imputed by the conceptual mind as the nature of illusion,
Then [they do] not fetter and are not negated;
The nature of appearance is not negated.

Through this is the unexcelled definitive secret of ascertaining
Emptiness dawning as dependent arising;
The foundation of all the profound distinctions of philosophy
Is not known by ordinary, confined perception.

What is the use of negating something separate that is truly established?
Appearances that withstand analysis are negated in both of the two truths.
The nature of dependently-arisen appearances is not negated.
When this meaning is realized, the knot sealing the difficult points is unraveled.

This is a stanza of summation.

If someone says: "If appearances are directly negated in this way, then it will become a denigrating view of annihilation because reasoning's object of negation is too encompassing."

Such is the fear of realists who do not know the manner of emptiness dawning as dependent arising even to the slightest degree. Yet such a vulgar fear does not occur to those who have realized for themselves, and explain to others, the profound viewpoint of the supreme vehicle, the Great Middle Way.

The "view of annihilation" refers to an assertion by means of a conventional valid cognition that the relative causality of karma, and all appearances such as pillars and pots, do not exist from the perspective of conventional truth until they are imputed by a conceptual mind. This is the view of annihilation. However, from the standpoint of an opponent who has not ascertained that these constructed phenomena of relative appearance do not exist from the perspective of ultimate emptiness:

- By which valid cognition are they negated? By valid cognition of ultimate analysis.
- From the perspective of which of the two truths? From the perspective of the ultimate.
- What is the object of negation? All appearing phenomena of the relative.
- In what way are they negated? Without applying a qualifier, such as "ultimately," to the object of negation.

Even though all gross and subtle constructed extremes are negated, how does this become annihilation? As is said:

> By this reasoning, if [production] is not reasonable even conventionally, then what is your production?[134]

The reasoning consciousness of ultimate analysis establishes all appearances of constructs—such as production even just conventionally—as not able to withstand analysis. Since there are no assertions in the perspective of great emptiness, such as "this is empty; this is not empty," all constructs of appearance are directly severed.

In this way, as the handprint [result] of ascertaining the great ultimate emptiness, emptiness dawns as dependent arising. As is said:

> For one whom emptiness is suitable,
> Everything is suitable.[135]

By means of this, if you realize that all the phenomena of relative appearance are appearances of the nonexistent—forms of emptiness—and that all conceptual imputations are the nature of illusion, then they do not fetter, nor are they refuted; there is no need to negate the mere nature of relative appearances. Through this is the unexcelled secret of ascertaining emptiness dawning as dependent arising. The profound definitive secret of ascertaining the foundation of all the profound distinctions superior to the lower philosophies is not known by ordinary minds of logicians with valid cognitions of confined perception.

The following is a summary of this section: In short, in this tradition of the Great Middle Way, what is the use for ordinary beings or Sublime Ones to qualify the object of negation and merely negate something separate that is truly established, like the Svātantrikas? Therefore, since whatever appears itself should be ascertained as empty, negation is done without accepting an appearance that withstands analysis within either of the two truths. However, there is no negation of the nature of the dependently-arisen appearances that arises as the handprint [result] of appearances that have been ascertained as empty.

Therefore, before emptiness has been ascertained as dependently arisen by the valid cognition of ultimate analysis, Svātantrikas, etc., do not negate appearances, but negate what is truly established, etc., upon those [appearances]. After ascertaining those appearances themselves to be empty, conventionally, Prāsaṅgikas do not negate the mere appearances that have been ascertained as empty and dependently arisen, etc. If you realize this tradition's profound meaning as it is, the sealed knot of the difficult points of the respective scriptural meanings will unravel itself.

This is a stanza that summarizes the section.

4. Delineations of Prāsaṅgika and Svātantrika

This section has two parts: (1) the actual delineations and (2) supplementary topics.

1. The Actual Delineations

This section has three parts: (1) a concise demonstration of the views and philosophies of Prāsaṅgika and Svātantrika, (2) an extensive explanation of these respective delineations, and (3) a summary of the essential meaning of the division in this way.

1. Concise Demonstration of the Views and Philosophies of Prāsaṅgika and Svātantrika

One may say: "Having divided the two truths,
It is a view of annihilation if relative appearances are negated,
Yet if appearances are not negated,
It is difficult for emptiness to be established."

In general, both Prāsaṅgikas and Svātantrikas
Divide the two truths from the perspective of conventional valid cognition.
However, their delineations of the essences of the two truths, and so forth,
Are dissimilar.

Here I will briefly explain the way of dividing
The categorized and uncategorized ultimates
Through the two truths separated or not
By the valid cognition of ultimate analysis.

Regarding this, it is widely renowned in India and Tibet
That there are two delineations of the valid cognition of ultimate analysis:
"The arguments common to Svātantrika and Prāsaṅgika," and
"The unique Prāsaṅgika arguments."

By this, from the two truths being divided or not
In Svātantrika and Prāsaṅgika,
There are the manners of ascertaining the view
In a Sublime One's meditative equipoise and postmeditation, from which

There emerge: the categorized and uncategorized ultimates,
The conventional established by its own character or not,
The distinction between reasons that are autonomous arguments and those that are consequences, and
Assertions of a view being present or not.

Regarding this, one may say: "When ascertaining emptiness in the Middle Way tradition in general, it is a view of annihilation to divide the two truths and negate not only an ultimate pillar, but also negate its relative appearance. Yet if these relative appearances are not negated by a valid cognition of ultimate analysis, then it is extremely difficult for these appearances to be established as the profound emptiness—as not ultimately established."

In general, both the Prāsaṅgikas and the Svātantrikas make a division by distinguishing the two truths as separate from the perspective of conventional valid cognition. However, the delineations of the respective essences, and so forth, of the two truths in the Prāsaṅgika and Svātantrika are dissimilar. Moreover, in this context, I will briefly explain the way of dividing the ultimate into two by means of: (1) ascertaining the categorized ultimate, having divided the two truths by means of an ultimate valid cognition analyzing the abiding reality, and (2) ascertaining the uncategorized ultimate without separating the two truths, also from the perspective of that [ultimate] valid cognition.

In general, it is renowned like the wind in India and Tibet that there are two delineations of the valid cognition of ultimate analysis: (1) "the arguments common to the Prāsaṅgika and the Svātantrika,"[136] and (2) "the unique Prāsaṅgika arguments."[137] Due to this, the following are the ways that the Prāsaṅgikas and Svātantrikas ascertain emptiness.

When Svātantrikas ascertain emptiness, due to the fear of a view of annihilation if appearances were negated without dividing the two truths, they separate the two truths and do not negate conventional appearances. Also, they qualify [the object of negation] as "truly established" and establish the mere categorized ultimate.

When Prāsaṅgikas ascertain emptiness, they do not separate the two truths. Since relative appearances become [held as] truly established if they are not directly negated without separating the two truths, all conventional appearances are established as the great uncategorized ultimate, without applying any qualifier such as "truly established." Due to this feature, there are distinctions between Prāsaṅgika-Madhyamaka and Svātantrika-Madhyamaka as a result of the [respective] manners of ascertainment (1) in accord with the view in the meditative equipoise of the Sublime Ones and (2) in accord with the view of their postmeditation. Through this, there are the distinctions of:

- the categorized or uncategorized ultimate
- the conventional established by its own character or not
- formulating arguments as autonomous arguments or consequences, and
- assertions of a view being present or not

2. Extensive Explanation of These Respective Delineations

This section has two parts: (1) the view and philosophy of Svātantrika-Madhyamaka and (2) distinguishing the view of the consummate Prāsaṅgika.

1. *View and Philosophy of Svātantrika-Madhyamaka*

This section has three parts: (1) a concise demonstration, (2) an extensive explanation, and (3) refuting its concordant positions.

1. CONCISE DEMONSTRATION

Regarding this, having separated the two truths, which is the evaluated object,
With the valid cognition of common arguments,
The Svātantrika-Madhyamakas
Establish the view of the categorized ultimate.

In general, in the Svātantrika tradition:

- by means of the distinctive common arguments—the valid cognition of autonomous [arguments]
- [analyzing] the distinctive evaluated object—the two truths separated
- the distinctive view is established—the mere categorized ultimate

2. EXTENSIVE PRESENTATION

This section has three parts: (1) the progressive stages of the Svātantrika view, (2) presenting the object of negation of the valid cognition that separates the two truths, and (3) what is established—the categorized ultimate.

1. PROGRESSIVE STAGES OF THE SVĀTANTRIKA VIEW

Therefore, in the stages of the view, constructs are progressively eliminated
By autonomous arguments—the common arguments
That analyze the categorized—

Through a manner of alternating between appearance and
emptiness.

The way of eliminating constructs in this Svātantrika tradition is as follows: The four constructs are progressively eliminated in the stages of the view by the valid cognition of autonomous [arguments], the common arguments that analyze the categorized ultimate. In a manner of alternating between appearance and emptiness, first appearance is ascertained as empty—merely the categorized emptiness—then the dependently-arisen appearances are posited as established by their own characters, etc.

2. PRESENTING THE OBJECT OF NEGATION OF THE VALID COGNITION THAT SEPARATES THE TWO TRUTHS

When analyzing the categorized ultimate,
The two truths are separated and
Appearances are not negated;
The object of negation, qualified as what is truly established, is
negated.

Concerning the distinctive object of negation in this [Svātantrika] tradition, at the time of [analysis] by a valid cognition analyzing the categorized ultimate, the two truths are separated and the relative constructed appearances are not directly negated. The object of negation is qualified as "ultimate," etc., and merely what is truly established is negated.

3. WHAT IS ESTABLISHED—THE CATEGORIZED ULTIMATE

Therefore, from the perspective of the authentic ultimate,
What is established in the Svātantrika view is
The establishment of merely the categorized—the emptiness of
true existence.

The distinctive object established in the Svātantrika tradition is as follows: Due to this reason [stated above], from the authentic perspective, or the ultimate perspective, what is emphasized is merely the categorized ultimate. The emptiness of true existence is the object established; this establishment is the view of the Svātantrika tradition.

3. REFUTING ITS CONCORDANT POSITIONS

In accord with this, some from the schools of later translations say,
*"It is a view of annihilation if appearances are negated."**
They know merely what is confined perception.
Negating an object of negation—something separate that is truly established—
They say, "We have ascertained the appearing mode of the object of negation!"

Similarly, some on the side of the schools of later translations are also in accord with this; they say: "It is a view of annihilation if the valid cognition of ultimate analysis negates appearances."

However, they know merely the way of the valid cognition of confined perception. That approach qualifies the object of negation and negates something separate that is truly established. Still, they appear to say: "We have also ascertained the appearing mode of the object of negation!"

2. *Distinguishing the View of the Consummate Prāsaṅgika*

This section has three parts: (1) a concise demonstration, (2) an extensive explanation, and (3) presenting our concordant tradition.

1. CONCISE DEMONSTRATION

Regarding this, without dividing the two truths, which is the evaluated object,
The valid cognition of the unique arguments
Of the Great Prāsaṅgika-Madhyamaka
Establish the view of equality free from extremes.

---

*This view is attributed to the Geluk by Bötrül's student, Khenpo Chökhyap. Khenpo Chökhyap stated that true establishment, like a truly established pot, is the object of negation for Svātantrikas, but the pot itself is negated by Prāsaṅgikas. Tsongkhapa devotes a section of his *Great Exposition of the Stages of the Path* to a view that takes appearances as the object of negation. He says that such a position is an overextension of the object of negation. See Tsongkhapa, *Great Exposition of the Stages of the Path*, 580–643. For a discussion of Tsongkhapa's position on this point, see Napper, *Dependent Arising and Emptiness*, 101–22.

In the Great Prāsaṅgika-Madhyamaka tradition:

- by the distinctive arguments—the valid cognition of the unique, great consequences
- [analyzing] the distinctive evaluated object—the two truths that are not distinguished separately
- the distinctive view is established—the uncategorized ultimate, the great equality free from extremes

2. EXTENSIVE EXPLANATION

This section has three parts: (1) the instantaneous stage of the Prāsaṅgika view, (2) presenting reasoning's object of negation without dividing two truths, and (3) through this, showing what is established—the uncategorized.

1. INSTANTANEOUS STAGE OF THE PRĀSAṄGIKA VIEW

Therefore, in the stage of the [Prāsaṅgika] view constructs are instantaneously negated
By consequences—the unique arguments
That analyze the uncategorized ultimate—
Without alternating between appearance and emptiness.

The way of eliminating constructs in the stage of the view of this Great Middle Way tradition is asserted as follows: Due to this reason [stated above], the stage of the view is the instantaneous elimination of constructs by means of consequences—the unique arguments that analyze the uncategorized ultimate—without alternating between appearance and emptiness. Whatever phenomena appear are within the manner of the unity of emptiness and dependent arising—the great equality.

2. PRESENTING REASONING'S OBJECT OF NEGATION WITHOUT DIVIDING TWO TRUTHS

When analyzing the uncategorized,
All relative constructs are negated without dividing two truths;
Therefore, all constructed extremes are negated
Without qualifying the object of negation.

Concerning the distinctive object of negation in this [Prāsaṅgika] tradition, at the time of [analysis by] the valid cognition analyzing the uncategorized ultimate, all the relative, constructed appearances are directly negated without dividing two truths as separate. Therefore, all gross and subtle constructed extremes are negated without qualifying the object of negation as "truly established," etc., like the Svātantrikas.

3. *WHAT IS ESTABLISHED—THE UNCATEGORIZED*

Therefore, in both of the two truths,
What is established in the Prāsaṅgika view is
The establishment of the uncategorized—free from extremes.

The distinction of what is established in this Great Prāsaṅgika tradition is as follows: Due to this reason, what is established in both of the two truths is the unity of appearance and emptiness. The view of the Great Prāsaṅgika is the establishment of the great uncategorized ultimate free from extremes.

3. PRESENTING OUR CONCORDANT TRADITION

The school of early translations follows after this.
There are no faults of the inferior logicians
Relying on a valid cognition of confined perception—
Such as the object of negation being too encompassing or
The side of appearance being denigrated.

Regarding this, the school of early translations follows after this great philosophy itself. The statements of fault by inferior logicians, who rely upon only the valid cognition of confined perception—such that it becomes the view of annihilation because the object of negation is too encompassing, or that it denigrates the side of appearance—have no opportunity to access this.

3. SUMMARY OF THE ESSENTIAL MEANING OF THE DIVISION IN THIS WAY

In short, in accord with the intended meaning of the Four Applications of Emptiness Sūtra,
Svātantrika and Prāsaṅgika are the progressive and instantaneous ways

Of perfecting the four stages of the view
Free from the four constructed extremes.

Since form itself is empty, it is free from the extreme of existence—
Appearance abides as the great emptiness.
Since while empty, it appears, it is free from the extreme of nonexistence—
Emptiness dawns as the great dependent arising.

Since they are not different, it is free from [the extreme of] both—
Emptiness and dependent arising are the great unity.
Since appearance and emptiness are equal, it is free from [the extreme of] neither—
The equality free from extremes, Emaho![138]

One may be very learned and accomplished, yet not fully understand;
The fortunate ones who clearly realize this meaning are joyful!
I think of the kindness of the lineage of awareness-holders in the school of early translations—
My kind, glorious teacher is so compassionate!

This is a stanza at the interlude between sections.

In short, both the Prāsaṅgika and Svātantrika accord with the intended meaning of the *Four Applications of Emptiness Sūtra* [*Heart Sūtra*]. There is a distinction between their [respective] ways of perfecting the four stages of the Middle Way view progressively or instantaneously by means of ascertaining emptiness free from the four constructed extremes of existence and nonexistence.

In general, appearance itself abides as emptiness, as is said in the first line of the *Four Applications of Emptiness Sūtra:* "Form is empty." Therefore, free from the extreme of entities and existence, the first of the four extremes, there is the first of the four stages of the view—appearance ascertained as empty. Even while empty, forms, etc., appear without ceasing—as is said in the second line of the *Four Applications of Emptiness Sūtra:* "Emptiness is form." Therefore, free from the extreme of nonentities and nonexistence, the second of the four extremes, there is the second of the four stages of the view—emptiness dawning as dependent arising.

The two truths of appearance and emptiness are not different, as is said in the third line of the *Four Applications of Emptiness Sūtra:* "There is no emptiness other than form." Therefore, free from the third of the four extremes, the extreme of both existence and nonexistence, there is the third of the four stages of the view—the unity of emptiness and dependent arising. The two truths of appearance and emptiness are equal without contradicting, as is said in the fourth line of the *Four Applications of Emptiness Sūtra:* "There is no form other than emptiness." Therefore, free from the fourth extreme, the extreme of neither [existence nor nonexistence], there is freedom from all extremes—the great unified equality. Since the profound Middle Way view is amazing and miraculous, the words of wonderment, "Emaho!" are expressed. And then:

> One may be very learned and accomplished, yet not fully understand;
> The fortunate ones who clearly realize this meaning are joyful!
> I think of the kindness of the lineage of awareness-holders in the school of early translations—
> My kind, glorious teacher is so compassionate!

This is spoken as a stanza at the interlude between sections.

2. *Supplementary Topics*

This section has two parts: (1) the actual supplementary topics and (2) an appended [explanation].

1. Actual Supplementary Topics

> *Others explain different presentations,*
> *Including what is and is not viable to exist*
> *From the conventional and ultimate perspectives, and*
> *The objects of negation by reasoning and the path.*
>
> *Our tradition asserts the way of the early generation of scholars.*
> *See the elegant discourses of Mipam, the lord of the doctrine,*
> *Which accord with the quintessential instructions of the lineage of the omniscient one* [Longchenpa]—

The great one endowed with a thousandfold scriptures,
reasonings, and quintessential instructions.

Without mixing them, uphold the categories
Of the unique, elegant discourses such as these.
It is good to abandon pointless aggression and jealousy
Toward doctrines and individuals.

Moreover, concerning individual scholars' distinct ways of assertion, it is said that for most of the early generation, what is conventionally existent is not viable to exist, whereas not existing ultimately is viable as not existing.* For most of the later generation, it is said that what is relatively existent is viable as existent, whereas not existing ultimately is not viable as not existing. Our tradition has the distinctive assertions that what is conventionally existent is viable as conventionally existent, but not viable as ultimately existent; and not existing ultimately is viable as not existing ultimately, but not as nonexistent conventionally.

Furthermore, others explain in different ways, such as stating, "Although appearance is not analysis' object of negation, it is the path's object of negation." However, our tradition, the tradition of the early generation of scholars, is elucidated in accord with the quintessential instructions of the lineage of the omniscient one [Longchenpa]—the one endowed with a thousandfold scriptures, reasonings, and quintessential instructions—by the lord of doctrine, Mipam, in his elegant discourses such as the *Rapsel Rejoinder*. "Look there!"

In short, if you uphold the tradition of the school of early translations, uphold the unmixed categories of the unique elegant discourses, such as these that have been shown above in mere illustration, by means of the authentic path of reasoning that affirms and negates. Otherwise, it is clearly good to abandon pointless attachment and aversion, by means of which there is intolerable, aggressive jealousy toward the elegantly spoken doctrines of those on the sacred path of our Buddhist scriptures, such as those on the side of the Geluk, and toward valid individuals such as the gentle protector Tsongkhapa—who is like the second omniscient Victorious One—father and sons.[139]

---

*These positions of the early generation of Madhyamaka refer to Maja Changchup Dzöndrü (*rma bya byang chub brtson 'grus*, ca. twelfth century) and Tsang Nakpa (*gtsang nag pa*, ca. twelfth century), who were disciples of Patsap (*pa tshab nyi ma grags*, ca. eleventh century), as stated by Khenpo Chökhyap. For more on these figures, see David Ruegg, *Three Studies in the History of Indian and Tibetan Madhyamaka Philosophy*, 39–55.

2. Appended [Explanation]

This section has two parts: (1) establishing the supreme path of liberation and (2) refuting misconceptions about the continuity of the vows of individual liberation.

1. *Establishing the Supreme Path of Liberation*

Alas! These days some people hold onto the gibberish that
"In the Nyingma's scriptural tradition of the great secret,
*There is no liberation."**
Others repeat after them.

The Great Sage taught the division
Of whether or not there is a supreme path of liberation
Through whether or not the profound view
Of the four seals that signify the Word is realized.

Therefore, show through reasoning
The way of contradicting the four seals that signify the Word!
We can debate over who contradicts the intended meaning of the four seals that signify the Word,
The early or later [schools of translations].

We can investigate whether or not there is liberation in that [tradition]
Which does not accept that all phenomena are empty,
But asserts the nonexistence of a pointless separate thing that is truly established
To be viable as emptiness!

In general, in the supreme vehicle of the Great Middle Way,
The root of the path of liberation is accepted as the lack of true existence,
So it is good to investigate whether or not that with the name "empty of true existence"
Is the emptiness of true existence.

---

*This view is attributed to the Geluk scholar, Pari Rapsel, by Bötrül's student, Khenpo Chökhyap. In Pari Rapsel's critique of Mipam's presentation of an ultimate truth that is not a referent of the mind, he says that Mipam's presentation of the ultimate—which does away with valid cognition and its observed object—does nothing other than lead those who seek liberation down the wrong path. See Pari Rapsel, *Ornament of Mañjughoṣa's Viewpoint*, 394–95.

The tradition of the school of early translations' lineage of the great secret
Is a lineage that progressed from the mouths to the ears of the sublime assemblies
Of Victorious Ones and their [bodhisattva] offspring;
Ordinary conceptual fabrications do not rival it.

Look at the countless scholars and accomplished ones
Who traverse the high grounds
Through this tradition of sūtra, tantra, and quintessential instructions—
The complete and unerring supreme path!

Alas! These days some people speak gibberish without thinking, saying, "There is not even the slightest path of liberation in the Nyingma's scriptural tradition of the great secret." Most others repeat after them. However, in the illustrious tradition of Buddhism in general, the division of whether or not there is a supreme path of liberation is the distinction of whether or not the profound meaning of the view of the four seals that signify the Word has been realized. The Great Sage said this in the sūtras. Therefore, in saying such things as, "The Nyingma tradition has no path of liberation because it contradicts the intended meaning of the four seals that signify the Word"—show by reasoning the manner of this contradiction!

When examined well, it appears that we can debate over which tradition, the early or later [schools of translations], contradicts the intended meaning of the four seals that signify the Word. This follows because it is reasonable to analyze whether or not there is liberation in a tradition that: (1) says such things as "form is not empty of form" yet does not accept a single phenomenon of the ground, path, or fruition to be ultimately empty, but (2) accepts the non-implicative negation of a pointless, separate, truly established thing in those [phenomena] to be viable as emptiness.

In general, in the tradition of the supreme vehicle of the Great Middle Way, the root of the path of liberation is accepted as the realization of the lack of true existence. So it is good to investigate whether or not that with the name "empty of true existence," which is an emptiness of a separate object of negation, is the emptiness of true existence that is the nature of emptiness and selflessness—one of the four seals that signify the Word.

In contrast, the illustrious tradition of the school of early translations' lineage of the great secret is a lineage that progressed from the mouths to the ears of the sublime assembly of Victorious Ones and their [bodhisattva] offspring. Ordinary conceptual fabrications do not rival it because it is established by the valid cognitions of scripture, reasoning, and quintessential instructions. Look at the authentic manner of the signs of fruition, such as "the visible tradition of the lineage"—the countless scholars and accomplished ones of the past who traverse the high grounds based upon the complete and unerring supreme path, the scriptures of sūtra and tantra, and the quintessential instructions of lamas! This is spoken as merely a brief illustration.

2. Refuting Misconceptions About the Continuity of the Vows of Individual Liberation

[Some people say,] "The continuity of vows in the lineage of the school of early translations
Is impure; its head is Nāgārjuna."
Widely renowned as a glorious, fully-ordained monk,
[Nāgārjuna] is praised in the scriptures of the Great Sage.

Look at the virtue of those with the audacity to say that
Lord Nāgārjuna, the great chariot who is
The sole ornament beautifying the world,
Is without vows, a fully-ordained monk [merely] by name!

Without understanding a mere fraction of the scriptural tradition
And with no reasoning to establish,
It is good for someone with the form of a religious practitioner
To relinquish the intolerable bad karma of rejecting the doctrine.

Similarly, there are many who say that the continuity of vows of the school of early translations' lineage is impure. Initially, the great, noble brahmin of the past[140] said:

As of yesterday, I was not a fully-ordained monk;
From today onwards, I am a fully-ordained monk.
The supreme, fully-ordained monk, the glory of the Heruka. . . .[141]

An accusation was made that the way that master Nāgārjuna was ordained was faulty—that the vow's head, Nāgārjuna, was impure.

In the middle, the threesome, Ma, Yo, and Tsang,[142] were supplemented by two fully-ordained Chinese monks. An accusation was made that the way that Lachen Gongpa Rapsel[143] was ordained was faulty; they said that Lachen Gongpa Rapsel's vows were impure. In the end, some Nyingma mantra-holders act as preceptors for the liturgy of the vows of individual liberation. Inferring from this, it is apparent that it is said, "The continuity of all Nyingma vows is certainly impure."

However, first of all, master Nāgārjuna is praised in the scriptures of the Great Sage, such as:

> Widely renowned as a glorious, fully-ordained monk, his name will be called 'Nāga'. . . ."[144]

Look at the virtue of those with the audacity to say that lord Nāgārjuna, the great chariot and sole ornament beautifying the world, is without vows, a fully-ordained monk [merely] by name! Other such statements are also in accord with this manner.

In short, without having understood even a mere fraction of the profound intended meaning of a scriptural tradition like the Nyingma school of early translations, and also without reasoning to establish the way that a path is impure, it is clearly good for someone with the form of a religious practitioner to relinquish accomplishing the cause of such intolerable bad karma as rejecting the doctrine.

2. Distinguishing Relative Phenomena— The Mode of Appearance

This section has two parts: (1) a concise demonstration and (2) an extensive explanation.

1. Concise Demonstration

> *Although the manners of expression accord in mere name—*
> *"Appearance is the relative truth,"*
> *The early and later [schools of translations] have different ways of assertion—*
> *Such as the presentations of appearance and reality, and the essence [of the relative].*

Concerning the distinctive ways of asserting the relative truth of appearance, in general the manners of expression accord in mere name—"appearance is the relative truth." However, there are various traditions of the early and later [schools of translations] in Tibet concerning the presentations of the division of the conventional relative itself into two, appearance and reality, and the ways of asserting the essence of the relative, and so forth.

2. Extensive Explanation

This section has two parts: (1) a general demonstration of the way of dividing appearance and reality and (2) an extensive explanation of the nature of these respective delineations.

1. General Demonstration of the Way of Dividing Appearance and Reality

Aside from the mode of appearance of the impure relative,
which is the domain of the valid cognition of confined perception,
Others do not explain the pure mode of reality—
*The domain of the valid cognition of purity.**

Without both modes of appearance and reality,
There is no accordance or lack of accordance between appearance and reality;
The distorted cognitions of ordinary beings become valid cognition and
The visions of Sublime Ones become mistaken cognition.

Our tradition accepts two relative appearances—
The pure and the impure—
Due to the mode of appearance of impure delusion and
The mode of reality of the pure ground.

Those of the later generation posit the relative partially, too,
Through solely confined perception.

*This is attributed to the Geluk and Sakya by Bötrül's student, Khenpo Chökhyap. The reason for this attribution is apparently because the mainstream proponents of these traditions do not accept the qualities of the Buddha, such as the powers and so forth, to exist when one is a sentient being.

The scholars' tradition distinguishes the relative's appearance and reality
Through two valid cognitions.

In general, in the traditions of other masterly scholars, there is no conventional valid cognition other than the conventional valid cognition of confined perception. Therefore, the relative truth, which is its evaluated domain, is also merely the mode of appearance of the impure relative—the aspect of the impure appearances of the aggregates, constituents, and sense-fields. Other than that, there is no pure mode of reality of the ground, which is the evaluated domain of the conventional valid cognition of purity. They cannot explain the profound intended meaning such as, "The limbs of the *vajra*-aggregates are renowned as the five perfect Buddhas. . . ."[145]

In this way, at the time of ascertaining the ground, if there are not two: (1) a pure relative which is the mode of reality and (2) an impure relative which is the mode of appearance, then there will also not be (1) what is valid by means of the concordant modes of appearance and reality and (2) what is invalid by means of the discordant modes of appearance and reality. In this way, there is nothing else suitable other than (1) the impure perceptions of ordinary beings' distorted cognitions becoming valid cognition and (2) the pure perceptions of Sublime Ones' visions becoming mistaken cognition. As it is taught in sūtra: "The eye, ear, and nose are not valid cognitions. . . ."[146]

Concerning the appearances of the relative truth in general, our tradition asserts two types for just the conventional—the authentic and the impure—due to: (1) the impure, deluded mode of appearance, such as the deluded perceptions of the six classes of beings, and (2) the pure mode of reality of the ground, such as a Buddha's own perception.

In short, the later generation posits merely the relative of the impure mode of appearance, setting forth the relative partially by means of solely a valid cognition of confined perception. The scholars' tradition distinguishes the relative's appearance and reality by means of both valid cognitions of (1) conventional confined perception and (2) conventional purity.

2. Extensive Explanation of the Nature of These Respective Delineations

This section has two parts: (1) explaining the mode of appearance of the impure relative and (2) explaining the mode of reality of pure appearance.

1. Explaining the Mode of Appearance of the Impure Relative

This section has four parts: (1) the nature of whatever appears, (2) appearance as such relies upon dependent arising and the causality of karma, (3) due to this, whether or not there is an assertion of a view, and (4) the way of accepting the conventional, dependently-arisen appearances.

1. The Nature of Whatever Appears

This section has three parts: (1) a demonstration differentiating the distinctive assertions, (2) respectively refuting other unreasonable positions on this, and (3) a demonstration elaborating upon the differentiation of the reasonable position's philosophies.

1. A Demonstration Differentiating the Distinctive Assertions

Concerning the mode of appearance, which is relative appearance,
*Some say it is conceptually imputed yet established by valid cognition,**
Others say it is the indivisibility of appearance and mind.†
The scholars' tradition asserts it as self-appearance.

Concerning the mode of appearance, which is mere relative appearance, some people assert that in the own tradition of the Prāsaṅgika, all appearances of the relative are merely conceptual imputations that are established by valid cognition—they appear as the opponents in [Mipam's] *Light of the Sun Rejoinder*,[147] etc. There is also the position of some people who assert that relative phenomena are the indivisibility of appearance and mind, as was put forward as the opponents in [Longchenpa's *Precious*] *Wish-Fulfilling Treasury*, etc.[148] It is evident that the scholars' tradition asserts that relative phenomena are merely self-appearance.

*This view is attributed to the Geluk by Bötrül's student, Khenpo Chökhyap. We can see this, for instance, in the works of the Geluk scholar, Changkya Rolpé Dorjé, when he states that the self and the person are established by valid cognition (*tshad mas grub*) yet exist merely as imputation (*btags pa tsam du yod*). See Changkya Rolpé Dorjé, *Presentation of Philosophical Systems*, 304.

†This view is attributed to the Sakya by Bötrül's student, Khenpo Chökhyap.

2. Respectively Refuting Other Unreasonable Positions on This

For those who assert that the conventional is conceptually imputed yet established by valid cognition, or
Who assert that appearance and mind are the same,
It is difficult to have a reasonable presentation of the conventional—
What is valid and what is invalid, etc.

Regarding this, for the traditions that assert that the conventional is conceptually imputed yet established by valid cognition, or assert that appearance and mind are the same, it is difficult to have a reasonable conventional presentation—such as delineations of what is valid and what is invalid. This manner is extensively stated, for instance, in the first chapter of the *Precious Wish-Fulfilling Treasury* and in the *Light of the Sun Rejoinder*.

3. A Demonstration Elaborating Upon the Differentiation of the Reasonable Position's Philosophies

This section has three parts: (1) a concise demonstration, (2) an extensive explanation, and (3) supplementary topics.

1. CONCISE DEMONSTRATION

Due to one's self-appearance being distorted or not,
There are the delineations of conventional objects being true or false,
Valid or invalid, and so forth;
Conventional presentations are most refined.

It is said that the position that accepts [whatever appears] as merely self-appearance is able to posit in a most refined way all conventional presentations without fail. Due to the perspective of merely self-appearance being distorted or not, there are the delineations regarding: (1) conventional objects, such as the distinction between the truth of an appearance of a white conch and the falsity of the appearance of a yellow one; and (2) the subjects (*yul can*) also, such as positing the apprehension of it as white as valid cognition and as yellow as invalid.

2. EXTENSIVE EXPLANATION

Concerning the manners of asserting the phenomena of self-appearance,
The tradition of Mind-Only (1) posits the mode of appearance as
Cognition and matter that are the category of the imagined nature (kun btags), and
(2) Accepts the mode of reality, which is the essence of the consummate dependent nature (gzhan dbang), as mind.

Śāntarakṣita's tradition (1) posits the mere mode of appearance, such as cognition and matter,
As relative phenomena that are [established by their] own characters, and
(2) Accepts as the conventional mode of reality (tha snyad gnas tshul)
That all appearances are mind.

Candrakīrti's tradition is that the mode of appearance, all phenomena of self-appearance,
Appear to the mind and are produced by the mind;
Therefore, self-appearances, the great forms of emptiness,
Are alike as illusions.

The unmatched elegant discourse,
Separating this into appearance (snang ba) and appearing objects (snang yul),
Is the assertion of the omniscient lord of doctrine [Longchenpa]
Elucidated in his great commentary, the White Lotus.

In this way, although all proponents of the Middle Way and Mind Only are not different in so far as asserting [whatever appears as] merely self-appearance, when distinguished specifically, the manners of asserting the phenomena of self-appearance are as follows:

- As is said in the Mind-Only scriptures in general and [Mipam's] *Eliminating Doubts of Damchö* in particular, the Mind-Only Mahāyāna tradition (1) posits an unmixed presentation of the mode of appearance, which is the essence of merely the imagined nature—the categories of matter and cognition, etc., which are the aggregates, constituents, and sense-fields; and (2) by means of such evidence as the necessity of simultaneous observation [of a perceived object and a perceiving mind], accepts the mode of reality as mind, which is the consummate essence of the dependent nature.

- Also, Śāntarakṣita's tradition of Yogācāra-Madhyamaka: (1) posits relative phenomena as established by their own characters—such as matter and cognition, fire and heat—merely in the mode of appearance and (2) from the perspective of simply the conventional mode of reality, accepts all appearances as mind like the proponents of Mind-Only.
- Also, the glorious Candrakīrti's own unexcelled tradition accepts the mode of appearance from the perspective of merely self-appearance, in which all phenomena of relative appearances appear to the mind, and arise from the karma accumulated by the mind. As is said in the *Madhyamakāvatāra*, all the worlds of environments and inhabitants appear from the mind:

> The mind itself establishes the limitless varieties
> Of these worlds of sentient beings and these worlds of
> environments.[149]

Therefore, the forms of emptiness, which are self-appearances, are accepted to be equal to the manner of the eight examples of illusion.[150]

Due to this, the omniscient lord of doctrine [Longchenpa] also states:

> The mind makes formations and the mind accumulates
> all karma.
> These appear to the mind and are imputed by the mind;
> Therefore, strive to tame the deluded mind.[151]

And:

> When one is intoxicated by *dhatura,*
> Even though different appearances variously arise,

They all are deluded forms and not real.
Likewise, know that by means of connection with a deluded mind,
Whatever deluded perceptions of the six classes of beings there are,
All of them without exception are appearances of the nonexistent—forms of emptiness.[152]

In this way, appearance and appearing objects are distinguished as separate. All the aspects of appearance that appear to the mind are the mind. However, the mind's appearing objects, which are the appearances of the nonexistent, phenomena that are forms of emptiness—such as mountain ranges, houses, homes—are not the substance of mind, etc. The unrivaled elegant discourse that demonstrates the respective distinctions between what is and is not mind is the assertion of the omniscient lord of doctrine [Longchenpa]; it is elucidated in the *White Lotus,* the great commentary on the *Wish-Fulfilling Treasury.*[153]

3. SUPPLEMENTARY TOPICS

When appearances are asserted as mind,
The universal ground and reflexive awareness (rang rig) are indispensable;
In the assertion [of appearances] as merely self-appearance,
No deliberate refutation or affirmation is made.

The following concerns the distinction between whether or not the universal ground and reflexive awareness are accepted in the Great Middle Way tradition in general: As it is stated in [Mipam's] commentary on the *Madhyamakālaṃkāra,* in the tradition of the great scholar Śāntarakṣita, the universal ground and reflexive awareness are indispensable when appearances are asserted as mind.[154] As is stated in [Mipam's] commentary on the Wisdom [Chapter of the *Bodhicaryāvatāra*], in the Great Prāsaṅgika tradition's assertion of merely self-appearance, no deliberate refutation or affirmation is made of the universal ground or reflexive awareness.[155]

2. Appearance As Such Relies Upon Dependent Arising and the Causality of Karma

This section has two parts: (1) a concise demonstration and (2) an extensive explanation.

1. Concise Demonstration

Regarding this, from the conventional perspective of the mode of appearance,
One's own limitless perceptions of various environments and inhabitants—
Which are dependently arisen from the pure and impure mind itself—
Arise from karma.

Regarding this, from merely the conventional perspective of the mode of appearance, one's own vastly limitless perceptions of a variety of environments and inhabitants—such as happiness and sadness, the good and the bad, pure and impure, and so on—arise from karma. These dependently arise from the virtuous karma of a pure mind and the unvirtuous karma of an impure mind, as is said in the sūtras and in the great *śāstras*, such as the *Madhyamakāvatāra.*

2. Extensive Explanation

This section has three parts: (1) refuting other traditions, (2) presenting our tradition, and (3) dispelling objections.

1. REFUTING OTHER TRADITIONS

Regarding this, other traditions throw out the support of the causality of karma,
Which are the entities of dependent arising,
Saying that, "A nonentity is established as the entity of disintegration;
*That itself is the support of the causality of karma."**

With the disintegration of the entity of disintegration (zhig pa dngos po),
The first moment of a phenomenon that is a cause and
The second moment of a phenomenon that is the effect

*The entity of disintegration (*zhig pa dngos po*) is a Geluk assertion, and one of the eight unique assertions of Prāsaṅgika according to Tsongkhapa. For references to discussions of the entity of disintegration in Geluk texts, see José Cabezón and Geshe Lobsang Dargyay, *Freedom from Extremes,* 290n79.

Are contradictory in progressive and simultaneous modes of
production.

[Some say:] "An effect is not suitable to arise
From the cause itself disintegrating or not disintegrating."
When we debate the issue of whether or not a cause and effect
meet,
What is the use of disintegration?

When food does not satisfy the stomach,
How can the food's entity of disintegration satisfy?
When the eyes do not see forms,
Do the eyes' entity of disintegration see?

When the aggregate of old age and death is relinquished,
Investigate whether or not the entity of disintegration is old
age and death.
If it is, from that is only ignorance;
If it is not, the entity of disintegration is the Buddha!

At the time of nirvāṇa when the aggregates have disintegrated
[They] prostrate to the common locus of a permanent
phenomenon and an entity!
The great chariot, Nāgārjuna,
Asserted that nirvāṇa is unconditioned.

Regarding this, some masterly scholars in the Land of Snow ignore the support of the causality of karma in the Great Prāsaṅgika-Madhyamaka tradition—throwing it out. For them, the mere entities of dependently-arisen causality are not sufficient. They say: "The support of causality is the entity of disintegration itself, which is the nonentity after a cause has disintegrated. This is established by scriptures that state that old age and death is a condition of birth, etc., and by reasoning, such as the fact that a child will die due to not eating."

However, upon examination, there is contradiction. To illustrate, in a second moment [of a phenomenon] for instance, the cause disintegrates in the first moment. When the effect is produced in the second moment, the two—(1) the entity of disintegration that is the disintegration following the first instant of the causal phenomenon and (2) the resultant phenomenon that follows in the second instant after the cause—are contradictory in a progressive or simultaneous mode of production.

If produced progressively, then the cause disintegrates in the first instant, producing the entity of disintegration in the second instant. After that, if the sprout is produced, then the effect of the sprout is in the third instant, not in the second instant. There is also the fault that the cause and the effect do not meet. It is also not suitable to assert that the sprout is produced in the second instant because if the entity of disintegration of the second instant did not disintegrate, then it would be permanent. And if it did disintegrate, then there would be disintegration of disintegration [ad infinitum] until the end of existence; there would be no opportunity found for the production of a sprout.

If there were a simultaneous production of the two—(1) the effect of the sprout that follows after the disintegration of its cause in the first moment and (2) the entity of disintegration, which is another—then it follows that the entity of disintegration is not needed because the cause, the seed itself, can produce its effect, the sprout.

Furthermore, realists say to Middle Way proponents: "In your tradition propounding the Middle Way, too, an effect is not suitable to arise from either the cause itself disintegrating or not disintegrating."

Similarly, when debating the issue of it being unreasonable for an effect to arise in either case of the cause and effect meeting or not—in response to this, they posit the entity of disintegration as a support for the causality of karma, in order that such a fault does not apply. However, what is the use of the entity of disintegration here?

In order to avoid fault [they say:] "Although a cause and effect seem to meet, as when the body feels a tangible object, the fault does not apply—namely, that the cause and effect are the same due to the cause and effect meeting—because the disintegration intercedes between those two."

It would [absurdly] follow that the stomach would not be satisfied by food, but the stomach would need to be satisfied by food that was the entity of disintegration of food. Likewise, a child would also not die due to not eating food!

Again, in order to avoid fault [they say:] "Although the cause and effect seem to not meet, as when the eye apprehends a form, there is no fault of the consequence that the two do not meet because the entity of disintegration conjoins them."

It would [absurdly] follow that the eye entity would not see forms, but the entity of disintegration, which is the already disintegrated eye entity, would see forms. Likewise, even a blind person whose eyes have disintegrated would see forms! Furthermore, at the time of nirvāṇa, when the aggregate of old age and death has been relinquished through the power of cultivating the path, investigate the issue of whether or not old age and death is the disintegrated old age and death's entity of disintegration. If such an entity of disintegration were old age and death, then the sublime Buddha would also have the continuity of old age and death. Also, it would be reasonable for ignorance to arise from that [entity of disintegration].

If they say: "The entity of disintegration that relinquishes old age and death is nirvāṇa, not old age and death."

Such an entity of disintegration would also be the Buddha! Therefore, it would be reasonable [for them] to prostrate to that common locus of a permanent phenomenon and an entity—the great nirvāṇa that is the disintegration of the aggregates! As for the manner of being a permanent phenomenon and an entity in general, (1) disintegration is established as an entity by [their] assertion and (2) the disintegration that is nirvāṇa is established as unconditioned by scriptures—the great chariot, Nāgārjuna, stated in the *Mūlamadhyamakakārikā*: "nirvāṇa is unconditioned."[156]

2. PRESENTING OUR TRADITION

This section has two parts: (1) a concise demonstration and (2) an extensive explanation.

1. CONCISE DEMONSTRATION

For realists, an entity as the support
For the causality of karma is indispensable.
Svātantrikas and others follow after them;
Proponents of the Great Middle Way assert dependent arising.

In general, previously in India ordinary non-Buddhists asserted the entity of disintegration as the support for the causality of karma. For realists, an indestructible entity is indispensable as a support for the causality of karma. For instance, Vaibhāṣikas assert acquisition (*thob pa*); some of their specific subsects assert the imperishable substance (*chud mi za ba'i rdzas*); Sautrāntikas assert the mental continuum; and proponents of Mind-Only assert the universal ground. Most Middle Way proponents, such as the higher and lower Svātantrikas, follow after them; however, proponents of the Great Middle Way, the Prāsaṅgikas, assert mere dependent arising.

2. *EXTENSIVE EXPLANATION*

The cause of a sprout is a seed;
The ripening cause is karma itself—
Because karma is unceasing,
Until an effect arises from it.

By the infallible truth of dependent arising,
The causality of karma does not perish in a hundred aeons;
When [the causes] are gathered and the time comes,
It is certain that the effect will ripen.

As for the way of illusory, dependent arising, the cause that has a sprout as its effect is just a seed, and the ripening cause of an effect is just karma—virtuous or evil. It is sufficient that there is no entity that supports the causality of karma other than this, as is said in the *Madhyamakāvatāra*:

> Since karma is without inherently existent cessation
> Therefore, even without the universal ground this can be established.[157]

Although an action (karma) such as taking life seems to cease, due to the fact that there is no inherently existent cessation of karma, the ripened effect is suitable to emerge until the time when the ripening has been experienced. Although there is nothing like the universal ground to support the causality of karma, due to the infallible truth of dependent arising, it will not perish for even a hundred aeons, until the karma's effect. When the causes and conditions are gathered, and the time comes to experience the ripening, it is certain that the effect will infallibly ripen. As is said in the *Karmaśataka*:[158]

> The karma of embodied beings
> Will not perish for even a hundred aeons.
> When [the causes] gather and the time comes,
> The effect will ripen.

3. DISPELLING OBJECTIONS

Since causality is extremely hidden (shin tu lkog gyur)
It is said to be an inconceivable phenomenon.
In this, even contemplation is shunned

Regarding causal processes such as support, meeting, and so forth.

If someone says: "Without a support for the causality of karma, such as the universal ground or disintegration, it is not reasonable for ripened effects to be experienced."

It is not necessary to investigate in this way because this presentation of the causality of karma is an extremely hidden object of evaluation. Therefore, karma and the ripening of karma is said to be inconceivable among the four types of inconceivable phenomena.[159] Hence, investigation by mere confined perception—examining whether or not there is a support for the causality of karma, and whether or not causes and effects meet, and so on—becomes a cause for denigrating the causality of karma; such thinking is even shunned in sūtras. Due to this, the *Madhyamakāvatāra* also says: "Regarding the causality of karma, even contemplation is shunned. . . ."[160]

However, it is not at all that there is no evaluating valid cognition. By the power of knowing karma and the ripening of karma, the wisdom that knows whatever there is sees the subtle manner of the causality of karma. The first Word, the wheel of doctrine of the four truths, teaches: (1) the causality of the contaminated, which is thorough affliction, and (2) the causality of the uncontaminated, which is complete purification. It is said that one should gain certainty in the belief of karma by following after sūtras that teach the subtle details of the process of causality.

3. Whether or Not There is an Assertion of a View

In this way, the issue of whether or not there is an assertion of a view
On conventional causality and so forth,
Others explain one-sidedly;
Our tradition explains having divided the two truths.

In this way, concerning the issue of whether or not there is an assertion of a view on the existence or not of the causality of karma and so forth conventionally, others explain partially. They explain the Middle Way as one-sidedly having assertions or one-sidedly not having assertions. However, our tradition, that of the omniscient lord of the doctrine [Longchenpa], explains the way [of assertion] and so on, having divided the two truths: (1) there are no assertions at the time of ascertaining the ultimate and (2) there are assertions in the Great Middle Way at the time of ascertaining the conventional.[161]

4. Way of Accepting the Conventional, Dependently-Arisen Appearances

This section has three parts: (1) refuting other traditions, (2) presenting our tradition, and (3) advice to know from elsewhere also.

1. Refuting Other Traditions

Some people say: "The way of asserting the conventional
Follows after the elderly people of the world—
Those who have not turned their minds to emptiness,
Nor have been influenced by philosophies."

Concerning the way of asserting the conventional in the Great Middle Way tradition, some people claim to be Middle Way proponents following elderly people, saying: "One should follow after the elderly people of the world—those who have not turned their minds to emptiness, nor have been influenced by philosophies."

However, the way that this is unreasonable is stated extensively in [Mipam's] commentary on the *Madhyamakālaṃkāra*.[162]

2. Presenting Our Tradition

Our tradition asserts "in the perspective of the world"
As the perspective of the conventional truth of the world—
From yogis and masterly scholars in the world
Down to ordinary idiots.

We accept the conventional as
Facts that are renowned and established in the world—
That which is seen, heard, and known
Without examination by ultimate analysis.

Superimposed phenomena such as the Principle (gtso, prakṛti) and the self,
Which are imputed by Buddhist and non-Buddhist philosophies,
Are neither the relative truth of the world
Nor in accord with conventional fact.

Concerning the Middle Way tradition that is the school following after what is renowned in the world, our tradition asserts the intended meaning of accepting a conventional presentation from the mere perspective of the world, as in, "I speak from the perspective of the world . . ."[163] as follows: From the perspective of the world, conventional appearances are accepted without examination by ultimate analysis; they are the factual objects (*don mthun*) seen, heard, and known:

- from the presentations of the grounds and paths, etc., renowned to masterly scholars and yogis of the world
- to the world of relative entities renowned and established to ordinary idiots

Regarding this, the superimposed phenomena such as the Principle and the self imputed by Buddhist and non-Buddhist philosophies are neither the correct relative of (1) the relative truth of the world nor (2) conventional fact. However, they are posited as merely the mistaken relative.

3. Advice to Know from Elsewhere Also

> *See the* Ornament of Candrakīrti's Viewpoint,
> *The meaning-commentary on the* Madhyamakāvatāra,
> *Which elucidates the intended meaning of lord Mipam—*
> *The illustrious tradition unmixed with the eight main [unique features of Prāsaṅgika or] any of those [other assertions just mentioned].*

In general, there are distinctive discordant assertions like those just mentioned. Specifically, there are the distinctive assertions of other traditions that accept eight main unique features of the Great Middle Way tradition: The unique ways of (1) refuting a universal ground that is separate from the six collections [of consciousnesses] and (2) refuting reflexive awareness; (3) not accepting that autonomous arguments generate the view of thusness in an opponent's continuum, (4) like cognition, also not [*sic!*] asserting external objects;[164] (5) accepting that Auditors and Self-Realized Ones completely realize the selflessness of phenomena; (6) positing the apprehension of a self of phenomena as an afflictive obscuration; (7) accepting disintegration as an entity; and (8) the consequent unique manner of positing the three times.

See the *Ornament of Candrakīrti's Viewpoint*,[165] an explanation of the *Madhyamakāvatāra*, which is a discourse that elucidates the intended meaning of Mipam, the lord of doctrine, and others—the illustrious tradition that is not mixed with these eight main unique features.

2. *Explaining the Mode of Reality of Pure Appearance*

This section has three parts: (1) a concise demonstration, (2) an extensive presentation, and (3) advice to realize the profound meaning.

1. Concise Demonstration

> *The mode of reality of pure appearance,*
> *Which is the great meaning revealed by the scriptures of sūtra and tantra, is*
> *The heritage of the basic element, the nature of luminous clarity, etc.—*
> *Whatever pure appearances there are.*

Regarding this, "the mode of reality of pure appearance," which is the great meaning revealed by scriptures of sūtra and tantra, is the basic element of heritage, the Buddha-nature, the maṇḍala that is the nature of luminous clarity, etc.—whatever pure appearances there are of the abiding reality of the ground.

2. Extensive Explanation

This section has three parts: (1) refuting other traditions, (2) presenting our tradition, and (3) a summary of the essential meaning of that [mode of reality of pure appearance].

1. Refuting Other Traditions

This section has three parts: (1) a concise demonstration, (2) an extensive explanation, and (3) a summary.

1. CONCISE PRESENTATION

> *Regarding this, other than a constructed extreme of existence or nonexistence, permanence or annihilation,*
> *Masterly scholars of the later generation do not know*
> *The nature of the essential nature, the heritage of the basic element,*
> *Which is profound, peaceful, and stainless.**

*Those of the later generation refer to the Kagyü, Sakya, and Geluk, as stated by Bötrül's student, Khenpo Chökhyap.

Regarding this, other than either a constructed extreme of existence or nonexistence, permanence or annihilation, it appears that most masterly scholars of the later generation do not know the profound abiding reality as it is—the profound, peaceful, and stainless nature of the heritage of the basic element—which is Buddha-nature.

2. EXTENSIVE EXPLANATION

This section has four parts: (1) refuting the extreme of entities, (2) refuting the extreme of nonentities, (3) refuting the extreme of both, and (4) refuting the extreme of neither.

1. *REFUTING THE EXTREME OF ENTITIES*

Some people take the position that the Mahāyāna heritage
*Is an entity that is the ultimate truth.**
They say: "The sūtras, tantras, and śāstras *that explicitly teach emptiness free from extremes*
Are the provisional meaning."

This heritage that is a common locus of a permanent phenomenon and an entity
Conflicts with the path of reasoning.
Such a heritage that is an entity of true permanence
Is not the illustrious tradition of the Lion of the Śākyas.

Regarding this, as was set forth as an opponent in [Mipam's] *Lion's Roar: Exposition [of Buddha-Nature]*, some philosophers make the claim that the Mahāyāna heritage, which is the intended meaning of the last Word, is a truly established entity that is not ultimately empty. They explain all sūtras, tantras, and *śāstras* that explicitly teach the empty essence—the emptiness that is free from all extremes—as the provisional meaning.

As such, this heritage that is a common locus of a permanent phenomenon and an entity conflicts with the path of reasoning. Such a heritage that is an entity of true permanence conflicts with the scrip-

*This view is attributed to the Kagyü and "proponents of other-emptiness," such as the Jonang scholar Dölpopa, by Bötrül's student, Khenpo Chökhyap.

tures of the Victorious One, the Lion of the Śākyas. Therefore, one should know the extensive presentation of scripture and reasoning as to the manner that it cannot be established as the Buddha's illustrious tradition from the *Lion's Roar: Exposition* [*of Buddha-Nature*].[166]

2. REFUTING THE EXTREME OF NONENTITIES

Some people say, "The Mahāyāna heritage is
Merely an ultimate nonentity.
The sūtras, tantras, and śāstras *that explicitly teach the appearing aspect of luminous clarity*
*Are the provisional meaning."**

Is a heritage of the basic element that is a permanent nonentity,
Eloquent to those who know reasoning, or what?
Such a heritage that is annihilation, nothing at all,
Is not the illustrious tradition of the Buddha.

Also, some people say that the Mahāyāna heritage is a mere nonentity that is the emptiness of what is truly established ultimately. They explain all the sūtras, tantras, and *śāstras* that explicitly teach the manner of the nature of luminous clarity's appearing aspect as the provisional meaning.

However, since a heritage of the basic element that is devoid of qualities—and a nonentity, unconditioned, with a permanent nature—conflicts with reasoning by the power of fact, is it eloquent to those who know reasoning, or what? Moreover, such a heritage as this—an annihilation that is nothing at all—also conflicts with the scriptures of the Victorious One, the perfect Buddha. Therefore, it cannot be established as his illustrious tradition. Know the extensive manner of this also from the *Lion's Roar: Exposition* [*of Buddha-Nature*].[167]

---

*This view is attributed to the Geluk by Bötrül's student, Khenpo Chökhyap. For a Geluk view on Buddha-nature as an absence, the aspect of the mind's lack of true establishment, see Khedrupjé, *rgyud sde spyi'i rnam par bzhag pa rgyas par bshad pa* in Ferdinand Lessing and Alex Wayman, *Mkhas grub rje's Fundamentals of the Buddhist Tantras*, 52–53. See also David Ruegg, "On the dGe lugs pa Theory of the *tathāgatagarbha*," in *Pratidānam*, ed. J.C. Heesterman, 505. For more on Geluk interpretations of Buddha-nature, see David S. Ruegg, *Three Studies in the History of Indian and Tibetan Madhyamaka Philosophy*, 75–76n171.

3. REFUTING THE EXTREME OF BOTH

Some people assert the heritage as
A common locus of what is unconditioned and conditioned—
A unity of both (1) the nonentity that is emptiness and
*(2) The entity that is the clarity of mind.**

There are no sūtras, tantras, or śāstras *that state*
A naturally abiding heritage (rang bzhin gnas rigs) that is conditioned.
Are they asserting this conditioned heritage of clarity
To be the developing heritage (rgyas 'gyur rigs)?

Also, some people assert the Mahāyāna heritage as a unity of both the unconditioned and the conditioned—a common locus of the two: (1) the emptiness that is the absence of constructed entities and (2) the conditioned entity that is the clarity of mind.

However, a naturally abiding heritage that is conditioned is not at all stated in the scriptures of sūtra, tantra, or *śāstra* that assert the definitive meaning of the supreme vehicle, the Great Middle Way. Also, when examining this by reasoning, is this conditioned aspect of the heritage of clarity asserted as merely the developing heritage? This manner also appears extensively in the *Lion's Roar: Exposition* [*of Buddha-Nature*].[168]

4. REFUTING THE EXTREME OF NEITHER

Some people fear that if they assert the heritage as either existent or nonexistent,
Then it will contradict reasoning.

---

*This view is attributed to the Sakya, and Rongtön Sheja Künrik (*rong ston shes bya kun rig*, 1367–1449) in particular, by Bötrül's student, Khenpo Chökhyap. Ngawang Jorden explains Buddha-nature as the indivisibility of the emptiness and clarity of mind as the view of the Sakya scholar, Gorampa, in "Buddha-nature: Through the Eyes of Go rams pa bsod rnams seng ge in Fifteenth-Century Tibet," 125. Jorden cites the Sakya scholar, Mangtö Ludrup Gyatso (*mang thos klu sgrub rgya mtsho*, 1523–1596), from a manuscript of *rnam bshad nor bu'i phreng ba*, a commentary on Gorampa, in his thesis, p.124n252: "In short, the unity of clarity and emptiness is posited as Buddha-nature because *saṃsāra* and nirvāṇa are comprised within the mind (*sems*) and the mind also is free from constructs, empty of true existence; therefore, the abiding nature of objects primordially abides as the unity of clarity and emptiness" (translation mine).

They speak of [heritage] in the manner of a cause that potentially emerges,
Like butter from milk.†

Such a manner of a cause that potentially emerges
Is said to be conditioned by proponents of reasoning.
This heritage of the basic element—which was not present before, but potentially emerges—
Is not the tradition of the omniscient one, father and son.

Also, some people fear that if they say that the heritage is either existent or nonexistent, then it will conflict with reasoning. Due to this, they speak of the Mahāyāna heritage as well in merely the way of a cause that potentially emerges but lacks qualities beforehand—like butter potentially emerging from milk. When this is examined by reasoning, such a cause that potentially emerges—but has no qualities beforehand—is accepted as conditioned by proponents of reasoning. Therefore, there is the consequent fault that heritage would be conditioned. It also contradicts scripture: In general, such a heritage of the basic element—that potentially emerges but has no qualities beforehand—is not the assertion of the omniscient, perfect Buddha. Specifically, it is not the assertion of Longchenpa, father and son, nor is it that of the lord of doctrine, Minling, father and son.[169]

3. SUMMARY

Other than merely the valid cognitions analyzing the categorized ultimate and
Conventional confined perception,

---

†This apparently is addressed to a Sakya position. For instance, the Sakya scholar, Rongtön, in his commentary on the famous verse from the *Uttaratantra* I.155 that states, "The basic element is empty of those adventitious [phenomena] that have the character of separability, but not empty of the unexcelled qualities that have the character of inseparability," glossed the second line, which literally states that the basic element is not empty of qualities, by saying that it is "not empty due to not being empty of the twofold self." Rongtön, *Commentary on the Uttaratantra* (*rgyud bla ma'i 'grel pa*), 145. See also Shenpen Hookham, *The Buddha Within*, 40–41. He thus explained the heritage as an absence, without affirming positive qualities of a Buddha to innately exist when one is a sentient being. Rongtön also portrayed the heritage as a cause as follows: "The basic element is the potential (*sa bon*) for transcendent qualities; it is a cause because the three jewels arise in dependence upon the defilements becoming purified through properly directing the mind toward it." Rongtön, *Commentary on the Uttaratantra*, 108.

They do no have the valid cognition of purity;
Therefore, there is fault.

Other than only the mere valid cognition that analyzes the categorized ultimate for ultimate valid cognition, and the mere valid cognition of confined perception for conventional valid cognition, those who propound [the heritage of Buddha-nature] in these ways do not have an account of the conventional valid cognition of purity. Therefore, there is fault.

2. *Presenting Our Tradition*

This section has three parts: (1) a concise demonstration, (2) an extensive explanation, and (3) a summary.

1. CONCISE DEMONSTRATION

Ordinary philosophies do not know of
This luminous clarity, which is the abiding reality of the mind.
It is the great meaning revealed by the scriptures of sūtra and tantra, and
Is present in the tradition of the scholars of the early generation.

It is the great, profound meaning, purposefully expressed
By the Guide, the Lion of Men,
"Profound, peaceful, free from constructs, and luminously clear—
The identity of the unconditioned."

It is the supreme, revealed meaning widely taught
In the definitive meaning sūtras of the middle and last wheel:
"The mind is devoid of mind;
The nature of mind is luminous clarity."

The suchness of mind free from extremes
Is the great indivisibility of the expanse and wisdom.
It is luminously clear, profound, peaceful, free from constructs,
Self-existing, unconditioned, and spontaneously present.

Its nature cannot be known or expressed by a confined intellect,

Like that which is an entity or a nonentity.
Therefore, since it transcends the extremes of purity, bliss,
permanence, and the self,
It is the transcendent perfection.

Regarding this, this abiding reality of the mind free from superimposition and denigration—luminous clarity, the heritage of the basic element, which is Buddha-nature—is not known of by ordinary philosophies. This great meaning revealed by the scriptures of sūtra and tantra—the heritage of the basic element as it is—is lucidly present in the tradition of scholars of the early generation. Moreover, it is the great, profound meaning purposefully expressed by the Victorious One, the Guide and Lion of Men, in the *Lalitavistarasūtra:*

Profound, peaceful, free from constructs, luminously clear, and unconditioned,
I have found a nectar-like truth. . . .[170]

It is the supreme revealed meaning taught widely in definitive meaning sūtras of the middle and last wheels of the Word:

The mind is devoid of mind;
The nature of mind is luminous clarity.

Buddha-nature—the suchness of mind free from extremes—is the great indivisible unity of (1) the expanse of emptiness taught in the middle Word and (2) the wisdom of natural, luminous clarity taught in the last Word. It is distinguished as self-existing, unconditioned, and with spontaneously present qualities—as is explicitly taught in the *Mahāyāna-Uttaratantra:* "profound," "peaceful," "free from constructs," "luminously clear," "self-existing," "unconditioned," "spontaneously present," and so on. Its nature is not expressed or conceived by an intellect of confined perception, like that which is an entity or a nonentity. Therefore, it is the transcendent perfection, free from all extremes of purity, bliss, permanence, and the self that are posited by a valid cognition of confined perception.

2. EXTENSIVE EXPLANATION

This section has two parts: (1) the essence (*ngo bo*) of the essential nature free from extremes and (2) differentiating its nature (*rang bzhin*).

1. *ESSENCE OF THE ESSENTIAL NATURE FREE FROM EXTREMES*

The property of the essential nature, the abiding reality pure from the beginning,
Has the identity of three distinctive qualities:
It is essentially empty, naturally clear, and
Its nature is all-pervasive compassionate resonance (thugs rje).

The essence of such a heritage is asserted to be (1) the abiding reality that is the primordially pure property of the essential nature (2) bearing the identity that is the endowment of the three distinctive qualities—the nature of empty essence, natural clarity, and all-pervasive compassionate resonance. In short, the defining character of heritage is: the abiding reality which is the primordially pure property of the essential nature endowed with the three distinctive qualities. When divided by means of support, one should also know the way of the threefold division, and so on, as intended in the statement:

Like the sequence of pure, impure/pure, and completely pure,
There is the sequence of sentient beings, bodhisattvas, and Buddhas.[171]

2. *DIFFERENTIATING ITS NATURE*

This section has three parts: (1) empty essence—the intended meaning of the middle wheel, (2) nature of clarity—the intended meaning of the last wheel, and (3) showing the noncontradiction of the middle and last [wheels] as all-pervasive compassionate resonance.

1. Empty Essence—The Intended Meaning of the Middle Wheel

The supreme definitive meaning of the middle wheel
Is the expanse of phenomena endowed with the three gates of liberation.
"The mind is devoid of mind. . . ."
The essence of mind itself abides as empty.

From the two truths as appearance/emptiness,
The ultimate emptiness is the supreme freedom from constructs.
Since it is the object found by the valid cognition of ultimate analysis,
It is free from the extreme of the truth of permanent entities.

The distinctive empty essence is as follows: From the aspect of the empty essence of Buddha-nature, the nature of the expanse of phenomena is emptiness endowed with the three gates of liberation—as intended in the supreme, definitive meaning, and profound sūtras of the middle wheel of the Word. The essence of mind itself abides as emptiness, in accord with the intended meaning of the statement, "The mind is devoid of mind. . . ." From the manner of dividing the two truths as appearance/emptiness—which is the way of the middle wheel—this is the identity of emptiness that is the supreme ultimate truth free from extremes. Also, without the slightest thing withstanding the analysis of valid cognition analyzing the ultimate abiding reality, it is the consummate object found—dawning as the handprint [result] of negation by exclusion. Therefore, it is free from the extreme of the truth of permanent entities.

2. Nature of Clarity—The Intended Meaning of the Last Wheel

The supreme definitive meaning of the last wheel
Is the heritage of the Buddha endowed with knowledge, love,
and powers.
". . . The nature of mind is luminous clarity"
Is the nature that abides as the great luminous clarity.

From the two truths of authentic/inauthentic experience,
It is the supreme ultimate of the concordant modes of
appearance and reality.
Since it is the object found by the conventional valid cognition
of purity,
It is free from the extreme of annihilation as nothing at all.

The distinctive nature of luminous clarity is as follows: From the aspect of the nature of clarity, the heritage of the basic element is endowed with knowledge, love, and powers; it is the identity of the heritage of the Buddha—as intended in the supreme, definitive meaning sūtras of the last Word. The nature abides as the great luminous clarity, as is the intended meaning of the statement, ". . . The nature of mind is luminous clarity." From the manner of dividing the two truths as authentic/inauthentic experience—which is the way of the last wheel of the Word—this is the essence of authentic experience that is the supreme ultimate. Also, it is established as the consummate object found by the conventional valid cognition of purity. Therefore, it is naturally free from the extreme of annihilation as nothing at all.

3. Showing the Noncontradiction of the Middle and Last [Wheels] as All-Pervasive Compassionate Resonance

The supreme noncontradiction of the middle and last wheels
Is the unity of appearance and emptiness—the basic element of the essential nature.
From the purity and impurity of mind itself,
It abides as the great interdependent arising of compassionate resonance.

It is the supreme meaning of the noncontradiction of the two truths
Of appearance/emptiness and authentic/inauthentic experience.
Since it is not the domain of confined valid cognition,
It is free from all adventitiously constructed phenomena.

The viewpoint of the supreme noncontradiction of the middle and last wheels is as follows: Compassionate resonance, abiding as the great interdependent arising, shines everywhere due to the power of the purity and the impurity of the mind itself; it is the self-expression of the basic element of the essential nature—the Buddha-nature—which is the unity of appearance and emptiness. This manner—the noncontradictory two truths distinguished as appearance/emptiness and authentic/inauthentic experience—is the identity of the supreme ultimate truth. Since it is beyond the domain of the valid cognition of confined perception, it is naturally free from all adventitiously constructed phenomena such as existence and nonexistence, permanence and annihilation.

3. SUMMARY

This is unlike ordinary other-emptiness
Because [it] cannot withstand the analysis of ultimate valid cognition;
Due to being the object found by the valid cognition of pure [vision],
It is not rivaled by the ordinary emptiness of true existence.

From the aspect of the nature of luminous clarity, this heritage of the basic nature abides as the identity indivisible with all the qualities of the Truth Body, which is a freed effect. However, it is not the case that by appearing, it cannot be empty, for it abides as the empty essence that is unable to withstand analysis by the valid cognition of ultimate analysis. Therefore, it is not like some [claim of the proponents of an] ordinary other-emptiness, who are the opponents in the *Lion's Roar: Exposition [of Buddha-Nature]*.[172]

From the aspect of emptiness, it abides as empty of true existence, as the great freedom from constructs. However, it is not the case that by being empty, it cannot appear; it abides as the great nature of luminous clarity that is the object found by the conventional valid cognition of purity. Therefore, it is also not rivaled by the ordinary [claim of the proponents of] emptiness of true existence, who are the opponents in the *Lion's Roar: Exposition [of Buddha-Nature]*.[173]

Summary of the Essential Meaning of That [Mode of Reality of Pure Appearance]

This section has three parts: (1) distinguishing three conventions of the Middle Way, (2) describing their ways of explaining the Word's viewpoint, and (3) through this, advice to realize the immeasurable profound meaning.

1. Distinguishing Three Conventions of the Middle Way

Regarding this, through three distinct objects of negation
Of reasoning by a valid cognition of ultimate analysis,
Three conventions of the Middle Way are made:
(1) Emptiness of true existence, (2) other-emptiness, and (3) self-emptiness.

In general, there are nominal distinctions, such as emptiness of true existence, etc. However, in this context there are three operative distinctions widely renowned in Tibet, the Middle Ways of: (1) emptiness of true existence, (2) other-emptiness, and (3) self-emptiness. It is clear that these are made by means of three distinct ways of identifying the object of negation of reasoning by a valid cognition analyzing the ultimate.

2. Describing Their Ways of Explaining the Word's Viewpoint

Regarding this, [the proponents of] emptiness of true existence and other-emptiness

Explain the middle and last wheels as contradictory.
The great school of early translations' Middle Way, free from extremes,
Accepts the middle and last wheels as the definitive meaning;

They are accepted without contradiction as a single essential point,
Having elegantly distinguished between the ways of dividing the two truths—
The two truths of appearance/emptiness and
Authentic/inauthentic experience.

This is the intended meaning of the Victorious Ones and their [bodhisattva] offspring;
It is the unexcelled, distinctive assertion
Of the powerful victor, Longchenpa, and
The omniscient Lochen Dharmaśrī.

If this meaning, as it is, is understood well,
The definitive meaning [sūtras] of the middle and last wheels,
Candrakīrti's texts and the Uttaratantra, *etc.,*
Dawn without contradiction as a single essential point.

The proponents of the Middle Way of emptiness of true existence and the proponents of the Middle Way of other-emptiness explain the intended meaning of the middle and last wheels of the Word as contradictory. However, the school of early translations' Middle Way, free from extremes, distinguishes well the ways of dividing: (1) the ultimate accepted as the nature of the empty essence from the division of the two truths into appearance/emptiness, and (2) the ultimate that is the identity of the nature of luminous clarity from the division of the two truths into authentic/inauthentic experience. The viewpoint of both the definitive meaning [sūtras] of the middle and last wheels of the Word are accepted as a single essential point—the consummate great unity that is the noncontradiction of appearance and emptiness.

This is also shown by the Victorious One, the Lion of the Śākyas: The quality of the empty essence is extensively taught in the middle Word and the quality of the nature of luminous clarity is extensively elucidated in the last Word. The great [bodhisattva] offspring of the Victorious Ones, Mañjughoṣa and Maitreyanātha, as well emphasized the profound emptiness and the vast nature of luminous clarity. The powerful victor, Longchenpa, also asserted the intended meaning of (1) the middle Word as the empty essence and (2) the last Word as the identity of the luminous and clear nature.

In particular, the omniscient Lochen Dharmaśrī, in his great commentary on the [three] vows, asserted that the commentaries on the viewpoint of the middle Word, such as the Middle Way "Collection of Reasonings," literally state the empty essence; and that these are given the name "the Middle Way of self-emptiness." He asserted that commentaries on the viewpoint of the last Word, such as the *Uttaratantra*, literally elucidate the quality of the luminous and clear nature.[174] He also gave these the name "the Middle Way of other-emptiness," intended just *nominally*. However, this is not at all like the *operative* other-emptiness that is widely renowned these days because it is only intended nominally. This follows because he applied the name "other-emptiness of phenomena" (*chos can gzhan stong*) to proponents of Mind-Only as well.[175] Moreover, for the explicit teaching of the *Uttaratantra:*

> The basic element is empty of those adventitious [phenomena] that have the character of separability,
> But not empty of the unexcelled qualities that have the character of inseparability.[176]

He also applied the mere name "other-emptiness of suchness" (*chos nyid gzhan stong*), intending simply that in the literal intended meaning, the ultimate expanse—the Buddha-nature—is not empty of its own essence from the perspective of the valid cognition of pure vision; while it is empty of what is other, namely, the adventitious defilements that are abandoned.

However, this is not at all like ordinary other-emptiness because it is explicitly clear from his texts that he accepts, without dividing or excluding, the viewpoints of the definitive meaning sūtras of the middle and last Word, and the commentaries on their viewpoint, such as Nāgārjuna's "Collection of Reasonings" and Maitreyanātha's *Uttaratantra*. Moreover, he does not put forward even a single word in line with those who say that (1) the middle Word is a provisional meaning or that (2) the chariot tradition of Nāgārjuna, the father and sons who are the commentators on its viewpoint, is a view of annihilation. Due to this, he accepts the ultimate Buddha-nature as the indivisibility of appearance and emptiness.

Also, what is called "indivisible" in general is divided into three types of indivisibility:

1. "partial indivisibility," like a black and white thread intertwined
2. "nominal indivisibility," like a multicolored rope being empty of a snake, which is the emptiness of the imagined nature in the dependent nature within the Mind-Only system, and
3. "genuine indivisibility," like the indivisible essence of fire and heat

From among these three, "the indivisibility of purity and equality" is not merely partial or imputed indivisibility; the way that it must be asserted as genuine indivisibility is stated in [Lochen's] texts such as *Words [of the Lord of Secrets]*[177]—this is the same essential point. Therefore, other than merely the way they use words, I see both this manner and that of the omniscient lord of doctrine [Longchenpa] as the same essential point. Consequently, I say that it is "the unexcelled, distinctive assertion of the omniscient one and his lineage."

Accordingly, in the great summary of philosophies by Getsé Paṇchen, one should know the way that he too stated that the viewpoint of the middle and last Word should be realized as one—like the tastes of honey and molasses.[178] Otherwise, by considering just the way of word usage without even seeing where the profound viewpoint of scriptural meaning lies, one gets involved in various painstaking hardships of negating and affirming, which is a cause for wasting [a life with] leisure and advantages.

In short, having ascertained the viewpoint of the middle and last Word as noncontradictory—not in mere words, but realizing the great indivisibility of appearance and emptiness—whatever words are used become the essential point of the viewpoint of the omniscient one and his lineage; otherwise, it seems to be difficult. If the essential point of the meaning of this is understood well, as it is, then all the essential *meanings*—not mere *words*—of the definitive meaning sūtras of the middle and last wheel, and the likes of Candrakīrti's texts and the *Uttaratantra* as well, dawn without contradiction as a single essential point.

3. Advice to Realize the Immeasurable Profound Meaning

Through this, know the immeasurable profound meanings
Of the tantras of Secret Mantra, such as

The natural maṇḍala of spontaneous presence and
The abiding reality, which is the innate mind.

An extremely clear presentation of this is
Elucidated in the Lion's Roar: Exposition [of Buddha-Nature].
If you want to know its difficult points,
See the Notes [on the Essential Points of the Exposition] *that I wrote.*

This does not withstand ultimate analysis,
Nor is it an object found by a conventional valid cognition of confined perception;
It is the meaning established by the uncategorized ultimate analysis, and
Is the object found by the conventional valid cognition of purity.

This is a stanza at the interlude between sections.

As illustrated by what has been explained, know also the vastly immeasurable, profound meanings revealed by the great tantras of Secret Mantra—such as the ground that is the natural maṇḍala of spontaneous presence, and the abiding reality, which is the innate mind (*gnyug sems*).

In this way, there is a very clear presentation of this definitive meaning Buddha-nature elucidated in the *Lion's Roar: Exposition* [*of Buddha-Nature*]. If you want to know just a little bit about its difficult points, also see the *Notes* [*on the Essential Points of the Exposition*] that I wrote.

The stanza that summarizes the section is as follows: Revealed in this way, the essential nature, the heritage of the basic element, does not withstand the valid cognition of ultimate analysis. It is also not an object found by a conventional valid cognition of confined perception. However, it is the meaning established in the ascertainment of the great empty essence, through the valid cognition of the uncategorized ultimate having negated all extremes by exclusion. The quality of luminous clarity, its self-lucidity, is the object found by the conventional valid cognition of purity. This is a stanza at the interlude between sections.

1. *Advice to Realize the Profound Meaning*

Such an evaluated object is an extremely hidden phenomenon;
It is inconceivable to a valid cognition of confined perception.
It is seen by the omniscient valid cognition of purity
Who said it in the scriptures, so trust it.

Extremely hidden phenomena are profound evaluated objects difficult to realize, like the definitive meaning Buddha-nature and the profound causality of karma. They are inconceivable to a mere valid cognition of confined perception. The omniscient valid cognition of purity directly sees them by the power of knowing the various constituents, and by the power of knowing karma and the ripenings of karma, etc.[179] Consequently, they are spoken in the valid scriptures, pure by means of the three analyses,[180] by the valid being himself—the supreme teacher who possesses the valid cognition of such seeing—so trust it.

3. *Summary*

There are three for each
Of the evaluated objects that are the two truths of appearance/ emptiness.
The three are: (1) what is evident, (2) what is hidden, and
(3) What is extremely hidden.

The objects of evident appearance, such as forms,
Are ascertained by the direct perceptions of sense-faculty valid cognitions of confined perception.
Objects of hidden appearance, such as impermanence,
Are ascertained by the mental inferences of confined perception.

The phenomena of extremely hidden appearance—
Such as the causality of karma, the heritage of the basic element, and the innate mind—
Are ascertained through the valid cognition that relies upon the testimony
Of those who possess pure vision.

At the time of meditative equipoise on emptiness that is evident,

There is ascertainment by the valid cognition of yogic direct perception in a Sublime One's continuum.
Emptiness that is hidden and the mere absence of self
Are ascertained by the valid cognition analyzing the categorized.

Emptiness that is extremely hidden
Is the uncategorized ultimate itself.
It is ascertained by the valid cognition that analyzes the uncategorized—
The great, unique arguments of Prāsaṅgika.

In short, when coming to know the abiding reality of the ground, which is the object of evaluation, there should be ascertainment by means of three domains of evaluated objects. In general, one should ascertain three domains of the evaluated objects for each of the two truths of appearance and emptiness. The three are: (1) what is evident, (2) what is hidden, and (3) what is extremely hidden.

From among these three, for an ordinary person who does not have superknowledge, the appearances of the relative truth are:

1. evident appearances, such as forms, which can be ascertained by means of the valid cognition of the direct perceptions that apprehend them—such as an eye-consciousness that ascertains its own object

2. hidden appearances, such as the appearing aspects of impermanence and suffering, which can be ascertained by the confined perception of the valid cognition of mental inference by means of ascertaining evidence—such as being a product establishing it to be an impermanent phenomenon; and

3. phenomena of extremely hidden appearances—such as the profound causality of karma, the heritage of the basic element's aspect of luminous clarity, and the innate mind—which are difficult to realize. The valid cognition that ascertains these needs to rely on the testimony (*lung*) of those who possess pure vision, such as the valid cognition of omniscience. Otherwise, they cannot be ascertained. Therefore, when you move to this third domain of evaluated objects, the general approach of the proponents of reasoning is only to negate and affirm in

dependence upon scriptures that are pure by means of the three analyses.

Likewise, for the ultimate truth of emptiness also, objects of evaluation are:

1. the evident nature of emptiness, which can be ascertained by the valid cognition of yogic direct perception in a Sublime One's continuum at the time of meditative equipoise. However, its nature cannot be directly perceived by ordinary beings
2. the slightly hidden emptiness, which is the emptiness in the Auditor's tradition and the mere character of the absence of self. As for what ascertains it, this can be ascertained by the mere valid cognition that analyzes the categorized; and
3. the emptiness that is extremely hidden, which is the uncategorized ultimate itself. As for the valid cognition that ascertains it, the valid cognition that analyzes the uncategorized—the great, unique arguments of Prāsaṅgika—can ascertain it as a mere handprint [result] of the negation of all gross and subtle constructed extremes by means of exclusion. However, it is extremely difficult to realize through establishing it by means of inclusion.

These are stanzas that summarize the section.

2. Essence of the Path—
The Distinctive Abandonments and Realizations

This section has two parts: (1) a concise demonstration and (2) an extensive explanation.

1. Concise Demonstration

Within the path of cultivation, there is both abandonment and realization:
Abandonment is the truth of cessation;
Realization is the truth of the path.
Cessation and path are the two, abandonment and realization.

In general, there is both abandonment and realization in the path of cultivation. In this, "abandonment" is the nature of the truth of cessation, the freedom from obscurations. "Realization" is the essence of the truth of the path, which is the realization of the selfless abiding reality. Thus, both abandonment and realization are comprised within cessation and the path.

2. Extensive Explanation

This section has two parts: (1) distinguishing the nature of cessation—abandonment and (2) distinguishing the nature of the path—the antidote.

1. Distinguishing the Nature of Cessation—Abandonment

This section has two parts: (1) a concise demonstration and (2) an extensive explanation.

1. Concise Demonstration

Regarding this, there is the nature of the abandonments and
The way of actually perfecting them. From these,
Within abandonment—which is the nature of the truth of cessation—
There are the objects of abandonment and the way of abandonment.

In general, there is (1) the distinctive nature of the abandonments and (2) the distinctive way of actually perfecting them. From these, within abandonment also—which is the nature of the truth of cessation—it is necessary to ascertain (1) the distinctive objects of abandonment and (2) the way of abandonment.

2. Extensive Explanation

This section has two parts: (1) refuting other traditions and (2) presenting our tradition.

1. Refuting Other Traditions

This section has two parts: (1) the objects of abandonment and (2) the stages of abandonment.

1. Objects of Abandonment

This section has two parts: (1) a concise demonstration and (2) an extensive explanation.

1. Concise Demonstration

> *The objects of abandonment have the nature of afflictive emotions and cognitive [obscurations].*
> *Asserting a presentation of this,*
> *Masterly scholars of the later generation*
> *Explain the essence of the two obscurations as follows.*

In general, the obscurations that are the objects to be abandoned have the nature of both afflictive emotions and cognitive [obscurations]. Asserting a presentation of this, masterly scholars of the later generation explain the essence of the two obscurations, and so forth, as follows. This was a concise demonstration.

2. Extensive Explanation

> *"The classes that mainly obstruct*
> *Liberation and omniscience."**
> *[By this] one can understand merely the defining character of their functions,*
> *However, it is not a complete [presentation].*
>
> *Regarding this, the obscurations are said to have a fixed number of two:*
> *(1) Afflictive obscurations and (2) cognitive obscurations.*
> *Due to this, it is said, "The obscurations to absorption also are*
> *Either afflictive or cognitive [obscurations]."*
>
> *However, since it is not an obscuration*
> *To liberation or omniscience,*
> *A third, called "the obscurations to absorption,"*
> *Was asserted by the undefeated protector [Maitreya].*

---

*This position primarily refers to the Geluk, as stated by Bötrül's student, Khenpo Chökhyap. For more on the two obscurations in the Geluk tradition, see José Cabezón and Geshe Lobsang Dargyay, *Freedom from Extremes,* 290n82.

Some people assert, "The illustrations of a cognitive obscuration
Are only non-concurrent formations" (ldan min gyi 'du byed).
A concept that is a non-concurrent formation
Is not in the tradition of scholars in India or Tibet.

All Mahāyāna sūtras and śāstras,
In a single viewpoint with one voice,
Assert that cognitive obscurations are
Concepts of the three spheres.

Some people say: "Afflictive obscurations alone entirely encompass
Apprehensions of the three spheres as truly existent;
Only the latency for this
*Is a cognitive obscuration."**

The mere latency for that afflictive emotion
Can be understood as a cognitive obscuration itself;
However, [by this alone] the presentation of the nature of the two obscurations
Still is not completely understood.

Regarding this, some people say: "These are the defining characters of the two obscurations: (1) the defining character of an afflictive obscuration is that which abides as the class that mainly obstructs liberation and (2) the defining character of a cognitive obscuration is that which abides as the class that mainly obstructs omniscience."

Through these defining characters, one can understand merely the defining characters posited *by means of function* in the great scriptures. However, [by just this] one is not able to completely explain such presentations as the defining characters [posited] by means of cause and essence.

As for an illustration of obscurations that are definite in number, in general, an obscuration must be posited within a fixed enumeration of two obscurations. Due to this, some people say: "Obscurations to absorption also must be ascertained as either an afflictive or a cognitive [obscuration]; between these two, it is a cognitive obscuration."

---

*This view is attributed to the Geluk by Bötrül's student, Khenpo Chökhyap. Tsongkhapa states that the apprehension of true existence is an afflictive obscuration, and the latency (*bag chags*) for the potential (*sa bon*) to apprehend true existence is a cognitive obscuration. See Tsongkhapa, *Thoroughly Illuminating the Viewpoint*, 25b, 59a.

However, it is not fully qualified as that which obstructs liberation or omniscience. Therefore, it is merely a category of obscuration in general. Both afflictive and cognitive obscurations obscure special insight (*lhag mthong, vipaśyanā*); consequently, they are to be abandoned. The undefeated protector [Maitreya] asserted a third "obscuration to absorption" because it merely obscures calm abiding (*zhi gnas, śamatha*), the actual foundation of meditative concentration; consequently, it is to be abandoned.

Concerning the illustration of the essence of the obscurations, when identifying the illustration of a cognitive obscuration in the great commentary on the *Madhyamakāvatāra*, in reliance upon a mere statement that the latency for afflictive emotions is a cognitive obscuration,* some followers of Lord [Tsongkhapa] accept that cognitive obscurations are cognitions. However, since this also accords with our tradition, there is nothing to distinguish.

Most holders of the lineage [of Tsongkhapa] do not accept that cognitive obscurations are cognitions. Therefore, the manner that there are two traditions in this way is also stated in detail in Changkya's *Great Views and Philosophies*.[181] As is stated, the tradition that does not accept that cognitive obscurations are cognitions has the viewpoint that they are suitable to be nothing other than non-concurrent formations. Thus, some masterly scholars state that the illustrations of a cognitive obscuration are only non-concurrent formations. However, upon analysis, a non-concurrent formation that is the essence of a concept is not in the tradition of scholars in India or Tibet.

If it is said, "It is not established that cognitive obscurations are concepts."

All Mahāyāna sūtras and *śāstras*, in a single viewpoint with one voice, state: "Concepts of the three spheres are asserted as cognitive obscurations."[182] Therefore, cognitive obscurations are not suitable to be asserted as other than just concepts. However, it appears that some masterly scholars state: "This scripture designates latency with the name *concept*." In the great Middle Way tradition in particular, some masterly scholars say: "The apprehension of the three spheres as truly existent is necessarily an afflictive obscuration. The latency for that is a cognitive obscuration."

Cognitive obscurations that are the mere latencies for afflictive emotions can be understood partially by that. However, [by this] the presentation of the nature of the two obscurations still cannot be completely understood.

---

*See footnote on page 219.

2. *Stages of Abandonment*

This section has two parts: (1) refuting error regarding the stage of abandoning cognitive obscurations and (2) refuting error regarding the stage of abandoning afflictive obscurations.

1. Refuting Error Regarding the Stage of Abandoning Cognitive Obscurations

Some people explain the stage as follows: "Up to the seventh impure ground,
Only afflictive obscurations are abandoned.
On the pure grounds,
*Only cognitive obscurations are abandoned."**

The presentations of what is to be abandoned and
The antidotes have been greatly confused.
They have strayed far from the presentation of the grounds and paths
In the Mahāyāna sūtras and śāstras.

In order to avoid the fault that the great Sublime Ones who previously traversed a lesser path
Would have nothing to abandon
On the seven impure grounds,
Some people say: "They abandon the obscurations of thorough stupidity, etc."

As such, which of the two obscurations is it?
Through question and debate,
The positions such as [these] assertions of defining character,
Fixed number, stage, etc., are left far behind.

Concerning the stages of abandoning the two obscurations, the traditions of some masterly scholars accept that on the seven impure

*This view is attributed to the Geluk by Bötrül's student, Khenpo Chökhyap. Tsongkhapa states that cognitive obscurations have been relinquished only on the three pure grounds, after all the afflictive obscurations are relinquished. Tsongkhapa, *Thoroughly Illuminating the Viewpoint*, 59a.

grounds, other than exclusively afflictive obscurations, no cognitive obscurations are relinquished whatsoever. They explain that on the three pure grounds, only cognitive obscurations are abandoned, which are the latencies for those [afflictive emotions].

Regarding this, other masterly scholars have said: "This presentation of what is abandoned and the antidotes has been greatly confused. There is the fault of having strayed far from all the presentations of the grounds and paths in the great Mahāyāna sūtras and *śāstras*."

When this fault is stated in this way, some people claim to avoid the fault that there is nothing to abandon on the seven impure grounds for the Sublime Ones who were Arhats that previously traversed a lesser path and [later] engage in the Mahāyāna path. To avoid that fault, they explain that they abandon the twenty thorough stupidities (*shin rmongs*) and the eleven assumptions of negative states (*gnas ngan len*) as stated in the *Saṃdhinirmocanasūtra*.[183] Moreover, they say that they abandon the obscurations that obstruct the hundred and twelve qualities.

Also, some people respond to the consequence that there would be nothing abandoned on the seven [impure] grounds by stating: "I accept." Moreover, they also accept that there is no distinction between the uninterrupted path (*bar chad med lam*) and the path of release (*rnam grol lam*). Still, they appear to say that the qualities of the path develop from the lower to the higher grounds.

However, to those who say that bodhisattvas who previously traversed a lesser path abandon obscurations on the lower grounds (the seven impure grounds), I question and debate, "The obscuration of thorough stupidity must be one of the two obscurations. Which of the two is it?"

If they say: "It is an obscuration that obstructs liberation and omniscience; however, it is an illustration of neither an afflictive nor a cognitive [obscuration]," then it fails the presentation of the defining character. If such an obscuration is asserted to not obstruct liberation or omniscience, nor be an illustration of an afflictive or cognitive [obscuration], then the presentation of the fixed number [of two] fails. If it is asserted as either an afflictive or a cognitive [obscuration]—then (1) if it [is said to be] an afflictive obscuration, then since it has already been abandoned by a previous lesser path, then there is the fault that there would be nothing to abandon [on the seven impure grounds]; and (2) if it is said to be a cognitive obscuration, then the position of asserting the stage of abandonment [to be only on the three pure grounds], and so on, is left far behind.

2. Refuting Error Regarding the Stage of Abandoning Afflictive Obscurations

Some people say: "A bodhisattva on the first ground
Has completely abandoned what Auditors and Self-Realized Ones have abandoned.
Still they have latencies
*Which are called 'afflictive obscurations.' "**

As such, which is it? An afflictive or cognitive [obscuration]?
Through question and debate, the position is destroyed.
The scholars of India and Tibet do not accept
Innate afflictive obscurations to be discards of the Path of Seeing.

Also, some omniscient masterly scholars assert, "A bodhisattva on the first ground has completely abandoned whatever Auditors and Self-Realized Ones have abandoned. Still, obscurations—which are latencies for afflictive emotions designated with the name *afflictive emotions*—also exist on the higher grounds. Therefore, this is the intent of what is said in the root text and [auto]commentary on the *Madhyamakāvatāra*, etc., that afflictive obscurations exist on the higher [grounds]."

However, on the higher grounds, the presence of such a latency with the name *afflictive emotion* needs to be ascertained as one of the two obscurations—either an afflictive or cognitive [obscuration]. Therefore, through question: "Which of the two is it?" and debate: (1) if it is an afflictive obscuration, then by that, the position asserting that they are already abandoned on the first ground is destroyed; and (2) if it is a cognitive obscuration, then it needs to be accepted that as such it is abandoned without remainder on the eighth ground, because the *Madhyamakāvatāra* states: "On the eighth ground, these afflictive emotions, together with their root, are completely pacified. . . ."[184] If one says: "I accept," then the position of explaining that there are still

*This view is attributed to the Sakya scholar, Gorampa, by Bötrül's student, Khenpo Chökhyap. In his commentary on the *Abhisamayālaṃkāra,* Gorampa asserts that bodhisattvas on the first ground have completely abandoned and realized what Auditors and Self-Realized Ones have. See Gorampa, *Open Treasury of the Profound Hidden Meaning* (*shes rab kyi pha rol tu phyin pa'i man ngag gi bstan bcos mngon rtogs rgyan gyi gzhung snga phyi'i 'brel dang dka' ba'i gnas la dbyad pa spas don zab mo gter gyi kha 'byed*), *Collected Works,* vol. 7, 40.1–40.3.

latencies for afflictive emotions to be abandoned on the three pure grounds in the root text and [auto]commentary of the *Madhyamakāvatāra* is destroyed.

Moreover, scholars in India and Tibet do not assert that the entirety of innate afflictive obscurations are simply discards of the Path of Seeing (*mthong spang*).

2. Presenting Our Tradition

This section has three parts: (1) a concise demonstration, (2) an extensive explanation, and (3) advice to know elsewhere also.

1. *Concise Demonstration*

In accord with the elegant discourse of the lineage of the omniscient one [Longchenpa],
The expert at singing the song of the noncontradiction of
All the illustrious traditions of the great chariots,
Mipam, the lord of the doctrine, explains as follows.

Therefore, the elegant discourse of the lineage of the omniscient one, the expert at singing the song of elegant sayings, is the way in which the viewpoint of what is abandoned and the way of abandonment are a single point without contradiction in the illustrious traditions of all the fathers and sons of the great chariots (the chariot of the explicit teaching of emptiness and the chariot of the hidden meaning of clear realization). Accordingly, Mipam, the lord of doctrine, explains as follows.

2. *Extensive Explanation*

This section has three parts: (1) defining character, (2) illustration, and (3) the way of abandonment.

1. Defining Character

Regarding this, the defining character of what is abandoned
Is posited for both of the two obscurations, the afflictive and cognitive,
From the general to the specific,
By means of cause, essence, and function.

The causes are the two apprehensions of true existence—
The apprehensions of a self of phenomena and persons.
Apprehending phenomena as truly existent is a cognitive obscuration;
Apprehending persons as truly existent is an afflictive obscuration.

The essences are as follows: attachment, and so forth, are afflictive obscurations;
Concepts of the three spheres are cognitive obscurations.
Their functions are as follows: having the characters of obstructing
Liberation and omniscience.

Regarding this, the defining characters of the two obscurations to be abandoned in our tradition are as follows: [Mipam's] commentary on the [*Madhyamaka-*]*alaṃkāra* shows extensively how the essence of the two obscurations, shown by means of cause, essence, and function, is a single essential point in the great scriptures.[185] Accordingly, there are mere general obscurations to be abandoned by means of cause, essence, and function, which are divided into the two specific afflictive and cognitive obscurations. Regarding the way of dividing the obscurations by means of cause, the causes of all the afflictive and cognitive obscurations are the two apprehensions of true existence: (1) the apprehension of a self of phenomena and (2) the apprehension of a self of persons.

The essence of the apprehension of a self of phenomena is a cognitive obscuration; and all its results of subtle and gross stupidity are posited as cognitive obscurations. The essence of the apprehension of a self of persons is an afflictive obscuration; and all its results of the afflictive emotions are posited as afflictive obscurations. This is the viewpoint of the great *śāstras* and sūtras such as the *Laṅkāvatārasūtra*.

The way of division by means of essence is as follows: From the *Uttaratantra:*

Concepts such as miserliness
Are asserted as afflictive obscurations;
Concepts of the three spheres
Are asserted as cognitive obscurations.[186]

In accord with this viewpoint, by means of essence, concepts that are the essence of attachment and so forth are posited as afflictive obscurations; and concepts of phenomena that are the essence of the stupidity of the three spheres are posited as just cognitive obscurations.

The way of division by means of function is as follows: In accord with the viewpoint of the *Sūtrālaṃkāra*, etc., obscurations that obstruct liberation are afflictive obscurations, and obscurations with the character of obstructing omniscience are posited as cognitive obscurations.

2. Illustration

This section has two parts: (1) the enumeration of the illustration and (2) the essence of the illustration.

1. *Enumeration of the Illustration*

> *Therefore, genuine obscurations*
> *Are asserted within a fixed number of two;*
> *The third, obscuration to absorption,*
> *Is just nominally enumerated as an obscuration.*

Due to this reason [stated above], if the genuine obscurations are those that obstruct liberation and omniscience, then the fixed number of obscurations is asserted as two—as is the viewpoint of the *Madhyāntavibhāga*.[187] The third, the obscuration to absorption, is just nominally designated as an enumeration of an obscuration—in just a manner of speech; it merely obstructs the actual foundation of meditative concentration, calm abiding.

2. *Essence of the Illustration*

This section has two parts: (1) a general explanation and (2) a specific explanation of cognitive obscurations.

1. General Explanation

> *The illustrations for both afflictive and cognitive [obscurations]*
> *Are concepts—mental phenomena.*

All the sūtras and *śāstras* state, in a single viewpoint with one voice, that the essences of the illustrations for both afflictive and cognitive obscurations are concepts—mental phenomena.

2. SPECIFIC EXPLANATION OF COGNITIVE OBSCURATIONS

This section has three parts: (1) the categories, (2) the stages, and (3) supplementary topics.

1. CATEGORIES

Thus, there are four types of apprehended-apprehender concepts:
(1) Thorough affliction, (2) complete purification, (3) substantial, and (4) imputed.

The three types of concepts of the three spheres
Are definitely cognitive obscurations:
(1) Concepts of true existence, (2) concepts of reified signs, and
(3) Concepts that are merely dualistic appearances.

Thus, in general among apprehended-apprehender concepts,[188] there are four: two apprehended-concepts, which are of the apprehended phenomena of (1) thorough affliction or (2) complete purification; and two apprehender-concepts, which are of an apprehending person that is (3) substantial or (4) imputed. Divided by means of the degree of subtly, among these there are three concepts, which are concepts of the three spheres, that apprehend the phenomena of thorough affliction and complete purification: (1) concepts of true existence, (2) concepts of reified signs, and (3) concepts that are merely dualistic appearances. All three are definitely just cognitive obscurations.

2. STAGES

The first is manifest for ordinary beings;
The second is manifest at the time of the seven impure [grounds];
The third at times is even manifest
In the postmeditation of those on the pure grounds.

The first, manifest apprehensions of true existence, are like an ordinary being apprehending a pot as truly existent. The second [concepts of reified signs] are like a magician reifying (*mtshan mar 'dzin*) the shape, etc., of an illusory woman. Although not acknowledged to truly exist, a slight reification is sometimes manifestly present even at the time of the seven impure grounds. As for the third [concepts that are merely dualistic appearances], as it is said, "Due to being unperturbed by the two perceptions. . . . ,"[189] there are no perceptions that reify what exists or does not exist on the three pure grounds. However, in the postmeditation of those on the pure grounds, a slight, subtle pollution of dualistic appearance is at times even manifestly present.

3. *Supplementary Topics*

When these are manifest,
It is called a Sublime One's "lax postmeditation";
The six transcendent perfections, etc., that are polluted by these
Are just "worldly transcendent perfections."

When these concepts—reified signs and mere dualistic appearances—are manifest on the grounds and in the postmeditations of those on the grounds, it is called "lax postmeditation" in some of the doctrinal language of Mantra. However, the sūtras and *śāstras* express the six transcendent perfections, etc., polluted by reified signs and concepts that are dualistic appearances, as just worldly transcendent perfections. As is stated in the *Madhyamakāvatāra:*

> When the three are observed, the Blessed One
> Described them as "worldly transcendent perfections."[190]

3. Way of Abandonment

This section has three parts: (1) distinguishing the gross and subtle ways of abandonment and the objects of abandonment, (2) the stages of abandonment, and (3) supplementary topics: investigating the genuine and nominal [obscurations].

1. *Distinguishing the Gross and Subtle Ways of Abandonment and the Objects of Abandonment*

Concerning the way of abandonment, for both of the obscurations
There is a twofold division: the imputed and the innate [aspects].
Also for the innate [aspects], there is (1) what is potential
And (2) its extremely subtle latency.

Concerning the way of abandoning these objects to be abandoned in general, the great sūtras and *śāstras* explain that for both the afflictive and cognitive obscurations to be abandoned, there is a division into the imputed (*kun btags*) and innate (*lhan skyes*) [aspects]. And also for the innate [aspects], there is a division into the potential aspect (*sa bon gyi cha*) and its extremely subtle latency (*de'i bag nyal ches phra ba*).

2. Stages of Abandonment

This section has two parts: (1) the way of abandoning the imputed [aspects] and (2) the way of abandoning the innate [aspects].

1. WAY OF ABANDONING THE IMPUTED [ASPECTS]

This section has two parts: (1) the actual way of abandoning the imputed aspects and (2) dispelling objections.

1. THE ACTUAL WAY OF ABANDONING THE IMPUTED ASPECTS

Therefore, the imputed [aspects] of both obscurations
Are held to be only discards of the Path of Seeing.
The sublime spiritual community of bodhisattvas who have abandoned these
Are endowed with the eight qualities of awareness and freedom.

Due to that reason, the imputed aspects of both the afflictive and cognitive obscurations to be abandoned are held to be discards of just the Path of Seeing in [Mipam's] commentaries on the Wisdom [Chapter of the *Bodhicaryāvatāra*][191] and the *Madhyamakālaṃkāra*.[192] In this way, as is intended in the *Uttaratantra*—the great scripture of the Prāsaṅgika Mahāyāna—the entirety of the sublime spiritual community of bodhisattvas abiding on the ten grounds are also endowed with the eight qualities of awareness and freedom.[193]

2. DISPELLING OBJECTIONS

If someone says: "This assertion that cognitive obscurations are discards of the Path of Seeing
Is not the tradition of Candrakīrti.

It is the Svātantrika tradition, such as [said in] the
Abhisamayālaṃkāra;
*It is not the consummate hidden meaning."**

A hidden meaning [like theirs] does not account for:
The distinctive features of the Mahāyāna Path of Joining,
The discards of the Path of Seeing, the accomplishment of the accumulations of antidotes,
The summit of the uninterrupted Path of Seeing, and so on.

The distinctive feature of a Prāsaṅgika like theirs
Is a consummate hidden meaning of the Mother [Perfection of Wisdom]
That has not been renowned previously in Tuṣita Heaven,
Nor to scholars of India or Tibet!

If someone says: "This assertion that cognitive obscurations are discards of the Path of Seeing is not the tradition of Candrakīrti. Even though this is said in the *Abhisamayālaṃkāra*, etc., that is the Svātantrika tradition; it is not the consummate hidden meaning of the [Perfection of Wisdom] Sūtras."

However, a hidden meaning [like theirs] does not account for the explanations in the *Abhisamayālaṃkāra* such as: in the first section, the section on omniscience, the distinctive conceptual object of abandonment among the five distinctive features of the Mahāyāna Path of Joining[194]; likewise, the accomplishment of the accumulations of antidotes on the Path of Seeing by means of abandoning the cognitive obscurations to be abandoned; and in the fifth section, the peaking[195] of the uninterrupted Path of Seeing, and so on.[196]

It is reasonable to describe the distinctive feature of a Prāsaṅgika like theirs as a consummate hidden meaning of the Mother [Perfection of Wisdom] that has not been renowned at all previously in Tuṣita Heaven, nor to any scholars of India and Tibet!

---

*This view is attributed to the Geluk by Bötrül's student, Khenpo Chökhyap. In his commentary on Candrakīrti's *Madhyamakāvatāra*, Tsongkhapa states that cognitive obscurations are relinquished exclusively on the three pure grounds, after all the afflictive obscurations are relinquished. Tsongkhapa, *Thoroughly Illuminating the Viewpoint*, 59a.

2. Way of Abandoning the Innate [Aspects]

Regarding the way of abandoning the innate potentials,
The discards, such as the great of the great discards,
Are abandoned by the nine antidotes,
Such as the lesser of the lesser Path of Meditation.

Their extremely subtle latencies
Are difficult to demolish by an ordinary path of training;
They are abandoned by the uninterrupted path's summit—
The supreme uninterrupted [path] of only a Buddha.

In this, we assert the potentials for afflictive emotions
As what are discarded by the path on the seven impure grounds, and
The cognitive obscurations that are their latencies
As discards of the pure grounds.

Therefore, there are two types of cognitive obscurations—
Those that are latencies for afflictive emotions and those that are not.
Without knowing the division of these,
It is difficult to explain the great scriptural tradition.

Regarding the way of abandoning the innate potentials of cognitive obscurations, there is a division of nine classes, such as the great of the great objects to be abandoned. We accept these to be abandoned by their nine antidotes—such as the lesser of the lesser Path of Meditation (the wisdom of the second ground), etc.[197] Their very subtle latencies are extremely difficult to demolish by an ordinary path of training, as the *Abhisamayālaṃkāra* states:

> The uninterrupted [path] of only a Buddha,
> The uninterrupted meditative stabilization.[198]

We assert that they are abandoned by the uninterrupted path's summit—the identity of the supreme uninterrupted path of only a Buddha.

In general, the way of abandoning afflictive obscurations is as follows. There are two: (1) the aspects of potential afflictive emotions and (2) the aspects of their latencies. We accept the aspects of potential afflictive emotions to be discards of the path on the seven impure grounds, and the cognitive obscurations that are their latencies to be discards of the three pure grounds. Due to this reason, in accord with the viewpoint of the great sūtras and *śāstras,* in general there are two types of cognitive obscurations: those that are latencies for afflictive emotions and those that are not. Without knowing this, and the subtleties of these divisions, it is extremely difficult to explain the great scriptural tradition.

3. Supplementary Topics: Investigating the Genuine and Nominal [Obscurations]

Some scriptural traditions of the great chariot assert,
"Some obscurations with the name 'afflictive emotions'
Are discards of the pure grounds."
Nevertheless, they are not potentials for the obscurations that are afflictive emotions.

Rather, the latencies for afflictive emotions
Are merely designated with the name "afflictive emotions."
It widely appears as such
In the great Mahāyāna sūtras and śāstras.

If this meaning is understood,
Then the hardships of abandoning jointly
The nine types of cognitive obscurations on the impure grounds
Will be easily removed.

Therefore, in presentations of the abandonment of the two obscurations,
The lord of the doctrine, Mipam,
Holds the position that all the scriptural traditions of the great chariots
"Have a viewpoint that only accords."

Some scriptural traditions of the great chariot assert: "Some obscurations with the name 'afflictive emotions' are discards of the three pure grounds." Nevertheless, they are not potentials for afflictive emotions. Rather, they are latencies for afflictive emotions that are merely designated with the name "afflictive emotions." Such a presentation widely appears in the great sūtras such as the *Śrīmāl-*

ādevīsiṃhanādasūtra[199] and in great *śāstras* such as the expositions of Vimuktasena and Haribhadra.

If these meanings are understood as they are, then one easily removes the hardships of abandoning jointly—such as some masterly scholars who divide the cognitive obscurations into nine classes, and assert that the three of the great class are progressively discarded from the second to the fourth ground on the Path of Meditation; and that the three of the middling class and the three of the lesser class are both abandoned jointly on the fifth, sixth, and seventh grounds.

Due to this reason, in the general presentations of the abandonment of the two obscurations, the lord of the doctrine, Mipam, establishes that the great chariots—the commentaries on the view of the single Perfection of Wisdom Sūtras of the Middle Word—"have a viewpoint that only accords." He establishes this position in his explanation of both the Wisdom Chapter of the *Bodhicaryāvatāra* and the *Madhyamakālaṃkāra*.

3. Advice to Know Elsewhere Also

The intended meaning of the great chariots such as this
Was explained by the lord of the doctrine, Mipam.
Therefore, know the immense scriptural traditions
From his elegant discourses.

The apprehensions of thorough affliction and complete purification, which are the apprehended-concepts, and
The apprehensions of a substantial or imputed person, which are the apprehending concepts,
Are, in short, themselves the root
Of all afflictive and cognitive obscurations to be abandoned.

The root of the antidote is the clear realization of the selflessness of persons
And the complete selflessness of phenomena.
In short, the antidote to the darkness
Of the afflictive emotions and cognitive obscurations is selfless emptiness.

These are clarifying stanzas at the interlude.

As was just explained, the lord of the doctrine, Mipam, commented upon the intended meaning of these great chariots as it is, without distortion. For this reason, know the entirety of the immense scriptural traditions from his elegant discourses.

The following is a summary of this section: In accord with the intended meaning of the *Abhisamayālaṃkāra*, there are apprehended-concepts, which are apprehensions of the phenomena of thorough affliction and complete purification; and there are apprehending-concepts, which are apprehensions of both a substantial and an imputed person. In short, when the afflictive emotions to be abandoned are divided, there are immeasurable categories—those which are views and those which are not views; and within cognitive obscurations, there are the objects to be abandoned that are subtle and gross, etc.—immeasurable categories of time, place, and character. The root of all the afflictive and cognitive obscurations is just these apprehended-apprehender concepts that conceive phenomena and persons.

Likewise, for the path of the antidote there are also divisions into immeasurable categories of time, place, and character for the path to liberation and omniscience. Nevertheless, the root is the clear realization of (1) the selflessness of persons as taught in the first Word, the wheel of doctrine of the four truths, and (2) the complete selflessness of phenomena as taught in the Perfection of Wisdom Sūtras of the middle Word. In short, as the great bodhisattva, Śāntideva, said:

> Emptiness is the antidote to the darkness
> Of the afflictive emotions and cognitive obscurations.[200]

The wisdom that realizes selfless emptiness is established to be the antidote that destroys all the darkness of the afflictive emotions and cognitive obscurations to be abandoned. These are clarifying statements.

2. Distinguishing the Nature of the Path—The Antidote

This section has two parts: (1) a concise demonstration and (2) an extensive explanation.

1. Concise Demonstration

> *In this way, as for the antidote—the truth of the path,*
> *Which is the perfection of the types of realization of*
> *selflessness—*
> *I will briefly explain the divisions*
> *Of the ways of the antidote and clear realizations.*

As was just stated, concerning the antidote—the truth of the path, which is the perfection of the types of realization of selflessness—I will briefly explain the divisions of (1) the ways of identifying the essence of the antidote and (2) the ways of asserting the clear realizations, etc., of the three Sublime Ones.

2. Extensive Explanation

This section has four parts: (1) the way of the antidote, (2) the nature of the antidote, (3) the distinctive clear realizations, and (4) the ways of perfecting the types of realization.

1. Way of the Antidote

This section has two parts: (1) refuting other traditions and (2) presenting our tradition.

1. Refuting Other Traditions

Some people say: "The intelligence that realizes
The mere nonentity that is the lack of true existence—
A type of realization shared with the Auditors and Self-Realized Ones—
Cannot accomplish the destruction of cognitive obscurations.

Therefore, the clear realization, [like a] firefly,
That realizes the mere nonentity that is the lack of true existence
Still needs an accompaniment to accomplish
*The destruction of the great darkness of cognitive obscurations."**

The type of realization that knows a nonentity
Has no power by itself to destroy cognitive obscurations.
It is impossible for it to be accompanied by the assistance of another power—
Even if it were, what would it do?

---

*The position portrayed here is that of the Geluk forefather, Tsongkhapa, as stated by Khenpo Chökhyap. For Tsongkhapa's own words on this point, see Tsongkhapa, *Great Stages of Mantra,* 10–11; translated in Jeffrey Hopkins, *Tantra in Tibet,* 98–99. For more on this Geluk position, see José Cabezón, *A Dose of Emptiness: An Annotated Translation of the sTong thun chen mo of mKhas grub dGe legs dpal bzang,* 482n706.

Here concerning the distinctive essence of clear realization, which is the antidote, some masterly scholars explain as follows: "The wisdom antidote is the intelligence that realizes the mere nonentity that is the lack of true existence—a non-implicative negation. It is just a type of realization shared with the Sublime Auditors and Self-Realized Ones; it cannot accomplish the destruction of cognitive obscurations. Therefore, the distinctive antidote, the clear realization that realizes a mere nonentity—which is a non-implicative negation that is the lack of true existence—is like a firefly. As an accompaniment to destroy the great darkness of the cognitive obscurations, which is the distinctive abandonment, it still needs to be ornamented by limitless accumulations."

In this way, the type of realization that knows a mere nonentity, a lack of true existence, is established by both [their] assertion and by valid cognition to lack the ability to destroy cognitive obscurations by its own power. It is impossible for it to be accompanied by the assistance of another power; even if it were, from its own side, what sort of action—discarding what is to be abandoned, etc.—would it do? Other masterly scholars have stated how it is difficult [for this position] to be tenable.

2. Presenting Our Tradition

Even the realization of the common, mere categorized emptiness
Is not the direct antidote for cognitive obscurations.
The unique direct antidote for cognitive obscurations
Is the clear realization of the uncategorized.

When there dawns a clear realization [like] the Sun King,
Born from churning the ocean of the unified accumulations,
That itself destroys the darkness of ignorance,
Without needing to depend on another accompaniment.

Thus, in our tradition, even if there is realization of the most subtle, mere categorized selflessness—like the selflessness of persons common to the Auditors and Self-Realized Ones—other than [being an antidote for] only afflictive obscurations, it is not the direct antidote that relinquishes cognitive obscurations. The direct antidote that relinquishes cognitive obscurations—that which is the nature of the unique object of abandonment for the Mahāyāna—is the clear realization that realizes the most subtle selflessness, which is the uncategorized emptiness.

Such a distinctive clear realization is as follows: Realization, like that of the Path of Seeing on the first ground, is fully born from completely churning the oceanic unity of the two accumulations for the first incalculable [aeon] on both the [Paths of] Accumulation and Joining. When this distinctive clear realization, like the Sun King, dawns in the mental continuum of a sublime bodhisattva, all the darkness of ignorance corresponding to that particular ground can be destroyed from the root, without depending upon another newfound accompaniment that is other than that [realization].

2. Nature of the Antidote

This section has two parts: (1) a concise demonstration and (2) an extensive explanation.

1. Concise Demonstration

> *In this way, in the stages of clear realization*
> *Of the truth of the path, which is the antidote,*
> *There is a twofold division:*
> *The sublime path of meditative equipoise and postmeditation.*

There is a twofold division within the stages of clear realization for such an antidote, which is comprised within the truth of the path: (1) the nature of the sublime path of meditative equipoise and (2) its postmeditation.

2. Extensive Explanation

This section has three parts: (1) an overview: delineating meditative equipoise and postmeditation, (2) the topic of this section: an extensive explanation of the nature of meditative equipoise, and (3) supplementary topics: distinguishing with/without appearance.

1. An Overview: Delineating Meditative Equipoise and Postmeditation

> *There are also two types of meditative equipoise:*
> *Meditative stabilization with appearance and without appearance.*
> *Likewise, there are two types of postmeditation:*
> *Worldly postmeditation and transcendent postmeditation.*

In general, as it appears in the great sūtras and *śāstras*, there are two distinctive sublime paths of meditative equipoise: (1) the meditative stabilization of yogic direct perception with appearance and (2) the meditative stabilization of yogic direct perception without appearance. Likewise, there are also two types of postmeditation: (1) worldly postmeditation and (2) transcendent postmeditation.

2. The Topic of This Section: An Extensive Explanation of the Nature of Meditative Equipoise

This section has three parts: (1) a concise demonstration, (2) an extensive explanation, and (3) a summary.

1. *Concise Demonstration*

Others say regarding the nature of meditative equipoise:
"The object is a nonentity that is an emptiness of true existence.
The subject, which is the entity of mind,
*Meditates with a mode of apprehension ('dzin stangs).**

Such is the understood meaning
Of a valid cognition of confined perception; however,
It is not even a fraction of the profound nonconceptual wisdom
Of the meditative equipoise of a great Sublime One.

Our tradition asserts that from the perspective of the wisdom of meditative equipoise,
There is no appearance and no cognition;
The appearance of wisdom is inconceivable.
The essence of luminous clarity—profound, peaceful, and free from constructs—

Is the supreme, ultimate wisdom,
Which is the unity of the great expanse and wisdom.
In this, the difference between subject and object
Is just mental imputation.

---

*This view is attributed to those in the Geluk tradition, such as Pari Rapsel, by Bötrül's student, Khenpo Chökhyap. For Pari Rapsel's argument for the importance of meditating with an apprehension of the absence of true existence, see Pari Rapsel, *Ornament of Mañjughoṣa's Viewpoint,* 384–86. Also, such a view is found to in the works of the Geluk scholar, Gyeltsapjé. See, for instance, Gyeltsapjé, *Gateway to the Bodhisattvas,* 371. See also Karma Phuntsho, *Mipham's Dialectics and the Debates on Emptiness,* 121.

Concerning the nature of the sublime path of meditative equipoise, some other masterly scholars say: "The distinctive object is a mere nonentity that is the emptiness of true existence. The subject, which is the entity of mind, meditates with a mode of apprehension on the ultimate emptiness."

Such a meditative equipoise—the manner of meditating on the ultimate emptiness in this way—is the understood meaning of merely the way of meditation on selflessness in the manner of a valid cognition of confined perception. However, it is not even a fraction of the profound nonconceptual wisdom of a sublime bodhisattva abiding on the great grounds—as is stated in [Mipam's] "Rejoinders," etc.

Our tradition asserts as follows: From the perspective of the great wisdom of meditative equipoise on emptiness, there are no appearances of apprehended objects such as forms, and no cognitions of apprehending subjects such as eye-consciousnesses—as a sūtra states:

> No appearance and no cognition;
> The appearance of wisdom is inconceivable.

However, since the profound abiding reality of the ultimate great emptiness is seen as it is, the appearance of wisdom has an inconceivable identity. It is the abiding reality in one-pointed meditative equipoise on the viewpoint of the supreme ultimate wisdom, the essence of luminous clarity—profound, peaceful, and free from constructs—which is the great indivisibility of (1) the expanse of phenomena, which is the great expanse of emptiness, and (2) the wisdom of luminous clarity, which is its [the expanse of phenomena's] self-lucidity.

Regarding this, "the domain of the wisdom of reflexive awareness" shows, as a mere ancillary, symbolic knowledge, that such a difference between subject and object is mentally imputed.[201]

2. Extensive Explanation

This section has four parts: (1) distinguishing the object, (2) distinguishing the subject, (3) what is absent, and (4) the representational mode of apprehension (*rnam pa'i 'dzin stangs*).

1. Distinguishing the Object

> *Regarding the distinctive object, others say,*
> *"The object of meditative equipoise is a mere emptiness of true existence."*

Other than a categorized lack of true existence, which is [an object of] consciousness,
This is not the object of profound wisdom.

The domain of the wisdom of reflexive awareness
Is the unique ultimate, the nature of great purity.
It is the supreme mother of the Victorious Ones—
Unspeakable, inconceivable, and inexpressible.

To elaborate a little on the manner of these: Concerning the distinctive object at the time of meditative equipoise on the ultimate emptiness, some others say: "There must be meditation that takes a mere nonentity—an emptiness of true existence—as an object of the sublime path of meditative equipoise. If it is not like this, it is meditation on the view of Hvashang."*

As for this, other than what is merely an object of consciousness temporarily, this object—a lack of true existence that is the categorized ultimate—is not the distinctive object of the profound wisdom in a sublime bodhisattva's meditative equipoise. For example, it is said that just as a beggar has no opportunity to remain on the throne of a universal emperor, the mere categorized ultimate has no opportunity to roam in the domain of a Sublime One's wisdom.[202]

Therefore, our tradition [asserts that] the profound domain of the wisdom of reflexive awareness is the ultimate that is not shared with the Auditors and Self-Realized Ones. It is the great natural purity, the uncategorized ultimate, which is the supreme mother of the Victorious Ones of the three times—unspeakable, inconceivable, and inexpressible.

2. DISTINGUISHING THE SUBJECT

Others say: "The subject,
Which is a dualistic mind, is wisdom itself."†
They know merely basic logic primers [that say]
"Mind (blo), awareness (rig), and cognition (shes) are equivalents."

---

*This view is attributed to those in the Geluk tradition, such as Pari Rapsel, by Bötrül's student, Khenpo Chökhyap. For Pari Rapsel accusing Mipam of holding Hvashang's view, see Pari Rapsel, *Ornament of Mañjughoṣa's Viewpoint*, 385–86; 392–93; English translation in Karma Phuntsho, *Mipham's Dialectics and the Debates on Emptiness*, 110.

†This view is attributed to the Geluk by Bötrül's student, Khenpo Chökhyap.

Our tradition asserts the wisdom of the Sublime Ones
As the wisdom of reflexive awareness;
The mind is devoid of mind, but
Its nature is the great luminous clarity.

The mind (sems) is the dualistic mind of perceived-perceiver;
As such, it is only a valid cognition of confined perception.
Wisdom (ye shes) is nondual, the great luminous clarity;
It is the valid cognition of pure vision.

"The ultimate is not the domain of mind;
It is the domain of the wisdom of reflexive awareness."
In accord with the meaning of the words of sūtra,
The scholars' tradition distinguishes mind (sems) and awareness (rig).

Likewise regarding the distinctive subject, some other masterly scholars, in accord with the way of asserting in the philosophies of the lower vehicles, say: "The identity of consciousness—the mind of a separated subject and object together with perceived-perceiver—is wisdom itself without the appearance of the duality of perceived-perceiver."

Through such a way, they just understand merely the range of meanings of the basic logic primers, which state, "Mind, awareness, and cognition are equivalents."

Our tradition asserts the profound wisdom of a Sublime One's meditative equipoise as follows: As is said in the context of the knowledge of the path (*lam shes*) in the Perfection of Wisdom Sūtras:

> The mind is devoid of mind;
> The nature of mind is luminous clarity.

The expanse of phenomena is the great emptiness, which is the mind devoid of mind. Its self-lucidity is the identity of the mind's nature of luminous clarity—the wisdom of reflexive awareness.

Concerning this, *mind* refers to the dualistic mind of perceived-perceiver, or the aggregate of consciousness. No matter what name a mind like this is designated, such as *wisdom*, etc., it is still only a valid cognition of confined perception. The profound wisdom of reflexive awareness is the identity without the duality of perceived-perceiver; it is the nature of the great luminous clarity—the essence of the valid cognition of pure vision. It is taught that the profound emptiness is not the domain of mind, but the domain of wisdom. In this way:

> Unspeakable, inconceivable, and inexpressible—the transcendent perfection of wisdom. . . .

And:

> The domain of the wisdom of reflexive awareness.[203]

The *Madhyamakaśāstra* states:

> It turns back what can be expressed;
> It averts the domain of mind.[204]

Śāntideva states:

> The ultimate is not the domain of mind.[205]

Also, from the [*Abhisamaya-*]*alaṃkāra*:

> Since it averts what can be seen, etc.
> It is said to be difficult to realize.
> Since is cannot be known like a form, etc.
> It is asserted to be inconceivable. . . .[206]

These show that it is not the domain of mind. And, the following demonstrates it to be the domain of wisdom:

> That which is the object of authentic seeing is the ultimate. . . .[207]

Precisely in accord with the words and meanings of the great sūtras and *śāstras*, one is able to directly explain by means of distinguishing mind and awareness without needing to make any qualifications. This is the tradition of the scholars of the early generation—those who are clearly not confused with regards to the words and symbols of the great treatises.

3. WHAT IS ABSENT

> *Others explain the essence [of nonconceptual wisdom] as follows: "It is only free from concepts*
> *That apprehend words and objects as mixed."*

Such nonconceptuality is a property of all [direct perception] cognitions;
It is not unique.

The nonconceptual wisdom of meditative equipoise
Is explained in sūtras to have the character
Of a unique nonconceptuality
That is not mixed with the five kinds of common nonconceptuality.

Concerning the distinctive concepts that are absent in nonconceptual wisdom—which is the essence of the sublime path of meditative equipoise—some masterly scholars explain that a Sublime One's wisdom is free from concepts by means of merely being free from concepts that apprehend words and objects as mixed.

However, such a distinctive characterization of nonconceptuality—as merely being free from concepts that apprehend words and objects as mixed—is a property of all nonconceptual cognitions that are direct perceptions, such as an eye-consciousness. It is not the unique feature of a Sublime One's nonconceptual wisdom. Therefore, the profound nonconceptual wisdom of meditative equipoise is a unique nonconceptuality by way of being unmixed with the five types of common conceptuality, including the nonconceptuality that is free from apprehending words and objects as mixed. This character of a Sublime One's nonconceptual wisdom is stated in the Mahāyāna Sūtras. In accord with the viewpoint of the sūtras, the lord of doctrine, the undefeated regent [Maitreya], also stated:

> [Nonconceptual wisdom] has the character of being free from the five types: (1) mental nonengagement, (2) complete transcendence, (3) quietism, (4) essential meaning, and (5) premeditated signs.[208]

It is taught to be superior to these five nonconceptualities: (1) the mere nonconceptuality that is not mentally engaging (*yid la mi byed*) concepts that apprehend words and objects as mixed; and (2) the nonconceptuality that is a complete transcendence of the concepts of determination (*rtog pa, vitarka*) and discernment (*dpyod pa, vicāra*), as in the second concentration; (3) the nonconceptuality that is a temporary, quietist pacification of the concepts that are mind and mental states, like when one falls asleep or faints, (4) the nonconceptuality that is free from merely the essential conceptuality (*ngo bo nyid rtog*); and (5) the nonconceptuality that is a premeditated sign of "not thinking anything at all."

4. THE REPRESENTATIONAL MODE OF APPREHENSION

Concerning the meaning of whether or not there is a
representational mode of apprehension,
Others say: "[Meditative equipoise] definitely has a mode of
apprehension.
All perceived-perceiver duality dissolves
*While there is a mode of apprehension of nonexistence."**

Our tradition asserts that the mind that meditates on the mere
categorized ultimate
Has a mode of apprehension; [however,]
In the great clear realization of the uncategorized
It is free from all modes of apprehension.

Moreover, concerning whether or not there is a mode of apprehension for the wisdom of the sublime path of meditative equipoise, other masterly scholars assert that it definitely has a mode of apprehension. Furthermore, they say: "The object of the wisdom of meditative equipoise on emptiness is the emptiness that is a lack of true existence. Due to apprehending nonexistence, all perceived-perceiver duality dissolves while there is a mode of apprehension of nonexistence; thereby, it is meditative equipoise without appearance."

Our tradition asserts that a novice's mind is not suited to meditate in any other way than with a mode of apprehension on merely the categorized, concordant ultimate. However, in the clear realization of meditation on the uncategorized ultimate, it is taught to be free from all modes of apprehension.

3. Summary

Regarding the way of being free from the dualistic appearances
of perceived-perceiver,

*This view is attributed to those in the Geluk tradition, such as Pari Rapsel, by Bötrül's student, Khenpo Chökhyap. For Pari Rapsel's argument for the importance of apprehending a lack of true existence and not relinquishing all apprehensions, see Pari Rapsel, *Ornament of Mañjughoṣa's Viewpoint*, 384–86. Also, such a view is found in the works of the Geluk scholar, Gyeltsapjé. See, for instance, Gyeltsapjé, *Gateway to the Bodhisattvas*, 371. See also Karma Phuntsho, *Mipham's Dialectics and the Debates on Emptiness*, 121.

Others explain: "Subjects and objects exist, but
Are merely not apprehended by the mind;
This is the meaning of the absence of dualistic appearances."

Still they say: "The subject and object are indivisible,
[Like] water poured into water."
Such a meditative equipoise that is mistaken cognition—
With appearance and reality in discord—is a disgrace!

Therefore, from the perspective of the wisdom of meditative equipoise,
The entirety of perceived-perceiver duality dissolves into the expanse.
The expanse that transcends the constructed phenomena of the relative
Abides as the ultimate—the great luminous clarity.

As postmeditation's dualistic appearances
And cognitions dissolve into the expanse,
Luminous clarity—the self-lucidity of the mind devoid of mind—
Manifests.

Although it is beyond appearances and cognitions,
It is not like the time of being unconscious;
The wisdom appearances of luminous clarity—profound, peaceful, and stainless—
Are inconceivable.

The following is a summary: Concerning the distinctive way of asserting the freedom from dualistic appearances as the essence of the sublime path's wisdom of meditative equipoise, some masterly scholars explain, "In all domains there exists both a subject and an object. Even so, the subjective mind merely not apprehending duality is the meaning of the lack of dualistic appearances." And still they state, "From the perspective of meditative equipoise without appearance, the subject and object are indivisible, like water poured into water."

The unreasonable manner of a meditative equipoise like that, which is a mistaken cognition—the mode of reality of the object and the mode of appearance of the subject in discord—is stated in [Mipam's] *Rapsel Rejoinder*, etc.[209] Due to such reasons, from the perspective of the great wisdom of meditative equipoise, which directly perceives the ultimate truth of emptiness, the entirety of the constructed signs of perceived-perceiver duality dissolves into the expanse. The expanse beyond all constructed phenomena of the relative—the self-lucidity of the ultimate abiding reality free from extremes—abides as the essence of the manifest viewpoint of the great luminous clarity.

At that time, as is stated in the great sūtras and *śāstras*, the postmeditational perceived-perceiver duality comprising (1) distorted appearances of the six classes of beings, the nature of apprehended objects, and (2) distorted cognitions, the collections of thoughts that are the nature of the apprehending mind, dissolves into the expanse. As this happens, the self-lucidity of the great empty expanse of phenomena—the mind devoid of mind—manifests the nature of mind: the great luminous clarity, the wisdom of reflexive awareness.

Although it is beyond all appearances and cognitions in this way, it is also not like the time of being unconscious, such as when fainting or in deep sleep. From the side of the subjectivity (*yul can*), it is the profound abiding reality that is extremely difficult to realize, as is said:

> Since it averts what can be seen, etc.
> It is said to be difficult to realize. . . .[210]

And from the side of the object:

> Since it cannot be known like a form, etc.
> It is asserted to be inconceivable.[211]

As is said, from the aspect of the empty essence, it is the great stainlessness—the complete pacification of all constructed extremes of referent signs; and from the aspect of the nature of luminous clarity, it is the manifest, great identity of the inner wisdom of reflexive awareness's inconceivable appearances.

3. Supplementary Topics: Distinguishing With/Without Appearance

This section has three parts: (1) a general demonstration of the delineation of supplementary topics, (2) distinguishing the ways philosophies assert these, and (3) an extensive explanation of the natures of: (a) with appearance and (b) without appearance.

1. General Demonstration of the Delineation of Supplementary Topics

Regarding this, we assert that the sublime path of meditative equipoise is twofold:
Meditative stabilization with and without appearance.
Yogic direct perception that is a meditative equipoise with appearance
Is asserted as postmeditation's meditative stabilization with appearance.

Concerning the nature of the sublime path's meditative equipoise in general, in the great sūtras and *śāstras* there are said to be two: (1) meditative stabilizations with appearance, which are meditative equipoises comprised within illusory meditative stabilizations, and (2) meditative stabilizations without appearance, which are meditative equipoises comprised within *vajra*-like meditative stabilizations. From the aspect of making the relative its object, meditative equipoises with appearance are also asserted as postmeditation's meditative stabilizations with appearance.

2. Distinguishing the Ways Philosophies Assert These

Regarding this, some people say without reason:
"The Svātantrika-Madhyamakas accept the sublime path
Of meditative equipoise with appearance;
The Prāsaṅgikas accept without appearance."

In the scriptural tradition of the scholars of the early generation,
It is said that both the Svātantrika-Madhyamakas and the Prāsaṅgika-Madhyamakas
Accept both meditative stabilizations—
With and without appearance.

Concerning whether or not meditative equipoise is with or without appearance, others say without reason, "The sublime path of meditative equipoise in the Svātantrika-Madhyamaka tradition is accepted as with appearance, and the Prāsaṅgika tradition accepts without appearance."

However, in the scriptural tradition of the scholars of the early generation, in both traditions of the Great Prāsaṅgika-Madhyamaka and Svātantrika, both meditative stabilizations are accepted—postmeditation with appearance and meditative equipoise without appearance. In just this, there is evidently no distinction [between Svātantrika and Prāsaṅgika].

3. Extensive Explanation of the Natures of: (a) With Appearance and (b) Without Appearance

This section has two parts: (1) defining character and (2) illustration.

1. DEFINING CHARACTER

Some people say: "The meaning of with appearance and without appearance
Is the presence or absence of dualistic appearances."
Is this tenable for a tradition that asserts
That the wisdom that knows whatever there is has appearances?

A meditative stabilization that manifests whatever there is in the relative
Is with appearance;
A meditative stabilization that actualizes the ultimate as it is
Is without appearance.

Regarding the distinction between meditative equipoises with and without appearance in general, some Tibetans say: "The meaning of a Sublime One's meditative equipoise with and without appearance is as follows: With appearance is the presence of dualistic appearances and without appearance is the absence of dualistic appearances."

However, is this tenable for a tradition that accepts that the wisdom of the Buddha—that knows whatever there is—is with appearances? Therefore, (1) yogic direct perception with appearance is posited as a meditative stabilization that manifests whatever appearances there are of the relative, and (2) yogic direct perception without appearance is posited as a meditative stabilization that actualizes the ultimate as it is. Otherwise, although one may seem to proclaim a lot of chatter regarding the meaning of with appearance/without appearance, not even a fraction of the viewpoint of the great scriptures is known.

2. ILLUSTRATION

This section has three parts: (1) a concise demonstration, (2) an extensive explanation, and (3) a summary.

1. CONCISE EXPLANATION

Therefore, in a simultaneous way of the two truths,
No Sublime One on a ground of training
Can know the appearance of whatever there is
While in meditative equipoise on the meaning of what is.

In a manner of alternating between meditative equipoise and postmeditation—
From churning the ocean of the unified accumulations—
The great darkness of the two obscurations is utterly dispelled and
The maṇḍala of the unified two exalted bodies is perfected.

Due to this reason, in a simultaneous way of the two truths that does not rely on alternating between meditative equipoise and postmeditation, other than solely the Sublime Buddha, no Sublime One on a ground of training can know whatever appearances of the relative there are while in meditative equipoise on the ultimate emptiness as it is.

However, for the time being, in a manner of alternating between meditative equipoise and postmeditation, one traverses the grounds and progressively abandons the obscurations through completely churning the oceanic water-treasury of the two accumulations:

1. the accumulation of wisdom without appearance in meditative equipoise—by means of resting in meditative equipoise on the meaning of the profound abiding reality, the ultimate emptiness in which the are no appearances of constructed phenomena, and

2. the accumulation of merit with appearance in postmeditation—by means of manifesting the illusory meditative stabilizations, the dependently-arisen appearances of relative phenomena

Though the power of this, at one point the entirety of the great darkness of the two obscurations will be utterly dispelled:

> The Form Bodies of the Buddhas
> Arise here from the accumulation of merit;
> The Truth Body, in brief, O King,
> Is born from the accumulation of wisdom.[212]

As is said, the consummate fruition is the complete perfection of the great maṇḍala—the unity of the two exalted bodies.

2. EXTENSIVE EXPLANATION

> *Meditative stabilization that is meditative equipoise without appearance*
> *Engages the meaning of the ultimate as it is;*
> *Meditative stabilization that is postmeditation with appearance*
> *Engages the meaning of whatever there is in the relative.*
>
> *The profound* vajra-*like meditative stabilizations, such as [the meditations on]*
> *Selflessness, the sixteen emptinesses,*
> *And the sequence of the nature of nonentities,*
> *Are meditative equipoises without appearance.*
>
> *All illusory meditative stabilizations, such as [the meditations on]*
> *Retention and courageous eloquence, the thorough trainings, the qualities of the grounds,*
> *And the sequence of the six transcendent perfections,*
> *Are postmeditations with appearance.*

Regarding this, the sublime path of meditative equipoise—which is meditative stabilization without appearance—engages the meaning of profound emptiness, the ultimate as it is. Meditative stabilizations with appearance, which are its postmeditation—such as the precious seal meditative stabilization (*rin chen phyag rgya'i ting nge 'dzin*) and the inexhaustible space-treasury meditative stabilization[213]—engage the meaning of whatever there is in the relative.

Due to this, meditative equipoises that are profound *vajra*-like meditative stabilizations are meditative equipoises such as:

- meditations on the twofold selflessness of persons and phenomena
- meditations on the sixteen emptinesses such as the emptiness of the external,[214] and
- profound meditative equipoises that are meditations on the sequence of the nature of nonentities[215]

In short, these are asserted as meditative equipoises that are meditative stabilizations without appearance. This is because the great scriptures posit illustrations of yogic direct perception without appearance as: the meditative realization of the selflessness of persons in the continuum of an Auditor, the meditative stabilization in the continuum of a Self-Realized One that realizes one and a half of the two selflessnesses,[216] and the realization that knows the twofold selflessness in the continuum of a bodhisattva.

Likewise, there are contexts of postmeditation such as:

- the four gates of retention[217]
- the eight great treasuries of courageous eloquence[218]
- the thorough trainings taught in the Perfection of Wisdom Sūtras[219]
- the meditative stabilizations that actualize the twelve hundred qualities of the grounds,[220] as taught in the *Daśabhūmikasūtra*, and
- the certain enumeration of 173 features,[221] and the sequence of meditating in a certain progression, by means of the vast postmeditation endowed with the six transcendent perfections

In short, all postmeditations that are vast, illusory meditative stabilizations are asserted as postmeditation's meditative stabilizations with appearance. This is because the great scriptures posit as illustrations of yogic direct perception with appearance all the meditative stabilizations that take the appearances of the relative as an object:

> The Arhats, the Rhinoceros[-like] Self-Realized Ones, and the [Buddha] teachers
> [Respectively] see two, three, and countless thousand[fold world systems].[222]

3. *SUMMARY*

This section has two parts: (1) the actual summary and (2) supplementary topics.

1. Actual Summary

The mother of the Victorious Ones—the nondual,
Nonconceptual meditative equipoise—
Is the ultimate mind of awakening.
It is expressed as "the accumulation of wisdom without appearance."

Meditative stabilizations of postmeditation that are
Without concepts of the three spheres, such as magical acts of generosity,
Are transcendent perfections that transcend the world.
They are expressed as "the accumulation of merit with appearance."

In short, what is expressed as "the accumulation of wisdom without appearance" is meditation on emptiness with the essential nature of compassion—the mother of the Victorious Ones, the Perfection of Wisdom, the precious ultimate mind of awakening—which is the nature of the profound, nonconceptual wisdom in meditative equipoise without the duality of perceived-perceiver. What is expressed as "the accumulation of merit with appearance" is the vast wisdom without concepts of the three spheres in its postmeditation, engaging in the oceanic transcendent perfections that transcend the world—such as magical acts of generosity in illusory meditative stabilizations like the space-treasury meditative stabilization.

2. Supplementary Topics

In postmeditation, acts of generosity, etc., with reference—
Constricted by reified signs of the three spheres and
Manifest concepts that apprehend duality—
Are "worldly transcendent perfections."

Due to a Sublime One's postmeditation lacking the meditative stabilization without concepts of the three spheres, there are reified signs of the three spheres on the seven impure grounds, and manifest concepts of the mere apprehension of duality on the three pure grounds. Constrained by these, acts of generosity, etc., with reference are called "worldly transcendent perfections in postmeditation." It is stated in the *Madhyamakāvatāra*:

> When the three are observed, the Blessed One
> Described them as "worldly transcendent perfections."[223]

3. Distinctive Clear Realizations

This section has two parts: (1) refuting other traditions and (2) presenting our tradition.

1. Refuting Other Traditions

This section has two parts: (1) refuting the assertion that the types of realization are the same and (2) refuting other traditions that assert that although it is the same [realization], it is different.

1. Refuting the Assertion that the Types of Realization are the Same

> *Concerning the distinctive types of realization, most of the later generation say,*
> *"The three Sublime Ones have the same type of realization."**
> *The type of realization that is a non-implicative negation is the same, [but]*
> *What does the trouble of proving that do?*
>
> *The Mahāyāna's unique type of realization—*
> *Giving rise to the nonconceptual wisdom of phenomena—[comes from]*
> *Completely pleasing virtuous spiritual friends and*
> *Completely gathering the accumulations of merit and wisdom.*
>
> *It would be very amazing if*
> *All of a sudden, an Auditor abruptly perfects*
> *The Mahāyāna's unique type of realization,*
> *Without the causes and conditions preceding it!*

*This is a Geluk position. See, for instance, Tsongkhapa, *Thoroughly Illuminating the Viewpoint*, 7. See also Tsongkhapa, *Great Stages of Mantra*, 10–11; translated in Jeffrey Hopkins, *Tantra in Tibet*, 98.

Concerning the distinctive types of realization among the three Sublime Ones, most masterly scholars of the later generation say: "The three Sublime Ones have the same type of realization because there is no difference among the realizations of emptiness by the three Sublime Ones—Auditors, Self-Realized Ones, and bodhisattvas—as is stated in the Prāsaṅgika-Madhyamaka scriptures."

However, if they establish the same type of realization for the three Sublime Ones due to their realization of a mere non-implicative negation that is the absence of true existence, then what does the trouble of proving that do? Merely that is not the consummate emptiness.

Therefore, the unique clear realization of the Mahāyāna is the type of realization that knows the uncategorized ultimate. As is said in the *Sūtrālaṃkāra:*

> Completely serving the perfect Buddhas and
> Thoroughly gathering the accumulations of merit and wisdom,
> Nonconceptual wisdom of phenomena is born;
> Therefore, it is asserted as ultimate.[224]

It is stated that the sacred realization on the first ground, the nonconceptual wisdom of phenomena, initially arises from the power of: (1) serving the sacred teachers, the virtuous spiritual friends who are the conditions, such as the hundred Supreme Emanation Bodies of the Buddha, and (2) being preceded by the nature of the sacred causal accumulations in postmeditation, the gathering of accumulations subsumed within the first incalculable [aeon], and (3) meditation that is a semblance of the sacred realization—the essence of nonconceptual wisdom.

Therefore, in the continuum of an Auditor, all of the sudden an abrupt presence of the complete type of realization that is unique to Mahāyāna, without such preceding causes and conditions, seems to be very amazing!

2. Refuting Other Traditions that Assert that Although It is the Same [Realization], It is Different

> *Others say: "Even the irreducibles, which are difficult to realize,*
> *Are realized [by Auditors and Self-Realized Ones];*
> *However, their types of realization are distinguished by some [phenomena] that are easy to realize."*

They have a tradition proclaiming that there is no liberation in the Abhidharma scriptures!

Other all-seeing masterly scholars distinguish the types of realization, saying: "Even the irreducibles, which are extremely difficult to realize, are realized as empty of true existence by both Auditors and Self-Realized Ones. However, there are differences among the types of realization of the three Sublime Ones due to Auditors and Self-Realized Ones not realizing some [phenomena] that are easy to realize as empty of true existence, like unconditioned phenomena."

However, if one must realize the lack of true existence of the irreducibles in order to attain merely the liberation of an Auditor and Self-Realized One, then this becomes a tradition proclaiming that there is no liberation in the Abhidharma scriptures! This follows because the Abhidharma scriptures teach that the irreducibles are truly established, but do not speak of a path to ascertain their lack of true existence.

2. *Presenting Our Tradition*

This section has three parts: (1) a concise demonstration, (2) an extensive explanation, and (3) dispelling objections.

1. Concise Demonstration

In general, selfless emptiness is the nondual door of pacification;
It is the mother of the four Sublime Ones.[225]
Therefore, in order to liberate beings,
Its twofold division is stated.

In general, selfless emptiness is the mother of her children, the four Sublime Ones, as it is said in the *Perfection of Wisdom Sūtra:*

> Whoever wants to attain the awakening of an Auditor should train in this transcendent perfection of wisdom. Whoever wants to attain the awakening of a Self-Realized One should train in this transcendent perfection of wisdom. Whoever wants to attain unexcelled awakening should train in this transcendent perfection of wisdom.

[For] the three awakenings comprising liberation and omniscience, there is no path observed that relies upon the realization of a selfless emptiness other than the sole realization of the selfless emptiness that is the nondual door of pacification. Therefore, the explicit teaching of emptiness—the objective emptiness of the "Collection of Reasonings" by the great chariot, the sublime Nāgārjuna—demonstrates the abiding reality of the nondual door of pacification. And the hidden teaching of clear realization—the subjective clear realization of the transcendent perfection of wisdom in the *Abhisamayālaṃkāra* by the great chariot, the regent Maitreyanātha—also demonstrates the path of the nondual door of pacification. Due to this, Āryadeva says: "Since the door of pacification is nondual. . . ."[226] Also, Śāntideva says:

> Nirvāṇa is difficult for a mind
> That is together with reference.[227]

And:

> . . . Because scriptures say that
> There is no liberation without this path.[228]

Candrakīrti also states three consequences in the first chapter of the *Madhyamakāvatāra*, the meaning-commentary, that if the Auditors and Self-Realized Ones also did not realize selfless emptiness in general, then there would be no difference between [their realization and that of] non-Buddhists' freedom from attachment.

Therefore, with many distinctive reasonings and scriptures that establish that the Auditors and Self-Realized Ones must realize emptiness, the clear realization that is knowledge of emptiness is established as the path of the nondual door of pacification. This is the single viewpoint of the chariots, fathers and sons, which are the commentaries on the viewpoint of the Perfection of Wisdom.

In this way, all sūtras and *śāstras* teach in general that the entirety of Auditors, Self-Realized Ones, and bodhisattvas must realize emptiness. When distinguished specifically, the *Perfection of Wisdom Sūtra* states:

> Knowledge of the ground (*gzhi shes pa*) is posited in the Auditors and Self-Realized Ones. Knowledge of the path is posited in bodhisattvas. . . .

Both the Auditors and the Self-Realized Ones are shown to have merely knowledge of the ground—a specific instance of selfless emptiness. In the context of the knowledge of the ground in the [Perfection of Wisdom] Sūtras, it is widely stated that apart from the specific instances of the knowledge of the ground—merely knowledge of the distant ground (*ring ba'i gzhi shes*)[229] and knowledge of the ground of what is to be abandoned—the knowledge of the ground of the antidote is not completely realized. Also, the great chariot, Nāgārjuna, demonstrated that there is a distinction between the types of realization:

> The Mahāyāna teaches non-arising;
> The other's extinction is emptiness.[230]

And:

> Therefore, you taught it completely
> In the Mahāyāna.[231]

Likewise, the great chariot, Maitreyanātha, also stated the way that there is a distinction between the types of realization. Moreover, Āryadeva said that both the Auditors and Self-Realized Ones, who are middling beings, must realize the mere selflessness of persons, which is a specific instance of selfless emptiness:

> Malevolence is averted in the beginning;
> In the middle, the self should be averted.[232]

Śāntideva also stated:

> If by abandoning afflictive emotions there is liberation, then
> Immediately following that [abandonment], they should become that [complete nirvāṇa]. . . .[233]

He stated the distinction between the types of realization by saying that Auditors and Self-Realized Ones, who have partial abandonment and realization, at one time need to attain omniscience by means of consummately perfecting abandonment and realization.

In particular, Candrakīrti stated in the sixth chapter of the *Madhyamakāvatāra*, the meaning-commentary:

> For the sake of liberation, this selflessness
> Is said to be twofold; it is divided into persons and phenomena.[234]

In the root text and [auto]commentary, he showed that there are differences among the types of realization of the three Sublime Ones.

In short, all the chariots, fathers and sons—which are the commentaries on the viewpoint of the Perfection of Wisdom—teach through making specific distinctions among the types of realization of selfless emptiness by the three Sublime Ones. Since the single essential viewpoint is that there are distinctions among the types of realization, two types of selflessness, of persons and phenomena, are taught for the sake of liberating beings (who are comprised within the three types) into the domains of liberation and omniscience.

2. Extensive Explanation

The partial selflessness, which is merely categorized,
Is the type of realization of the Sublime Auditors and Self-Realized Ones;
Merely that is a type of realization shared with
The Sublime Ones of the Mahāyāna.

The type of realization unique to the Mahāyāna
Is the great uncategorized ultimate.
The distinctive type of realization of selflessness is unexcelled—
Clearly, extensively, and completely.

Due to this reason, all the sūtras and *śāstras* accept the type of realization of the Sublime Auditors and Self-Realized Ones as the path of the nondual door of pacification:

- the distinctive observed object, which is the ascertainment of merely a categorized emptiness, is a specific instance of selfless emptiness. It is a realization that the nature of the self of persons lacks true existence, by means of realizing the nonexistent nature of the apprehension of the aggregates as truly existent as one; and
- the distinctive meditation, which is the realization of the manner of the four truths and the sixteen [aspects such as] impermanence

Merely this is a type of realization that is also the knowledge of the ground shared with the Sublime Ones of the Mahāyāna.

The type of realization that is unique to the Mahāyāna is the selfless emptiness that is the great uncategorized ultimate. This is established as the unexcelled type of realization distinguished from the clear realizations of the Auditors and Self-Realized Ones by means of clarity, extensiveness, and completeness.

There is a distinction of *clarity* because, for the sake of Auditors and Self-Realized Ones realizing the mere gross ground of the aggregates as lacking intrinsic nature, there is nothing taught other than mere metaphors, such as "forms are like a mass of foam. . . ."[235] Yet the Mahāyāna is distinguished by clearly teaching by means of the *Four Applications of Emptiness*—from form until omniscience—for the sake of realizing all subtle and gross phenomena of the threefold ground, path, and fruition as lacking intrinsic nature.

Similarly, there is a distinction of *extensiveness* because the Auditors and Self-Realized Ones—by means of the methods for realizing merely the gross ground of the aggregates as lacking intrinsic nature—only realize the knowledge of the ground comprised within the selflessness of persons. Yet the Mahāyāna is distinguished by the extensive realization of the selflessness of phenomena in the manner of the three knowledges[236] by means of the twenty emptinesses[237] of all phenomena of the ground, path, and fruition.

Also, there is a distinction of *completeness* because the Auditors do not meditate [on emptiness] other than a meditation upon the four truths and the sixteen [aspects such as] impermanence, which is characterized by the selflessness of persons. The Mahāyāna is distinguished by the complete meditation free from the thirty-two superimpositions,[238] which is characterized by the great emptiness of all phenomena.

3. Dispelling Objections

If someone says: "This distinction among types of realization
Is that of the Svātantrika tradition, such as the
Abhisamayālaṃkāra.
This is not a unique feature
Of the Prāsaṅgika Mahāyāna."

Go ahead and explain a hidden meaning that does not account for
The distinctive features of the Mahāyāna Path of Joining,
The greatness of the unique knowledge of the path, and
The distinctive knowledge of the ground, such as the distinctive signs!

Go ahead and profess a Prāsaṅgika tradition
That was not previously explained by the supreme regent [Maitreya]
Nor even was Candrakīrti's viewpoint of
The hidden meaning of sūtras!

If someone says: "The claim that there are distinctions among the three Sublime Ones' types of realization is explained in texts such as the *Abhisamayālaṃkāra*. However, this is the Svātantrika tradition. Such a distinction among the types of realization is not a unique feature of the Prāsaṅgika Mahāyāna because in this tradition, the types of realization of the three Sublime Ones must be asserted as the same."

However, if all these following explanations of distinctions among the types of realization are the Svātantrika tradition:

- the distinctive observation, among the five distinctions of the Mahāyāna Path of Joining taught in the first section of the *Abhisamayālaṃkāra*[239]
- the greatness of the knowledge of the path, which is exclusively a clear realization unique to the Mahāyāna, in the second section[240]
- the distinction of the knowledge of the ground in the third section,[241] and
- the distinctive signs of the sixteen knowledges of forbearance in the fourth section[242]

Then go ahead and profess a Prāsaṅgika tradition with a hidden meaning of the Perfection of Wisdom that does not account for these distinctions! Its distinguishing feature would be a hidden meaning that was previously not at all renowned in India or Tibet, nor commented upon by the supreme regent [Maitreya], the great chariot of clear realization; it would be a previously nonexistent hidden meaning of the Perfection of Wisdom Sūtras that was not the viewpoint of Candrakīrti, the great chariot of Prāsaṅgika reasoning, either!

4. Ways of Perfecting the Types of Realization

This section has two parts: (1) refuting other traditions and (2) presenting our tradition.

1. Refuting Other Traditions

This section has two parts: (1) refuting error regarding the lower limit of the Mahāyāna type of realization and (2) refuting error regarding the upper limit of the Hīnayāna type of realization.

1. Refuting Error Regarding the Lower Limit of the Mahāyāna Type of Realization

Concerning the ways of perfecting the types of realization,
Others say: "The Mahāyāna type of realization
Has the distinctive feature of being perfected in the continuum
*Of those who have not entered the Mahāyāna path."**

Concerning the distinctive ways of perfecting the types of realization, other masterly scholars say: "The type of realization unique to the Mahāyāna is perfected in the continuum of Auditors and Self-Realized Ones who have not entered the Mahāyāna path. This is a distinctive feature of the Great Prāsaṅgika-Madhyamaka."

2. Refuting Error Regarding the Upper Limit of the Hīnayāna Type of Realization

Some people claim: "A bodhisattva on the first ground
Has perfected the type of realization of the Auditors and Self-Realized Ones."†
Such elegant discourses as these, which do not accord with either
The Middle Way or Mind-Only, are a disgrace!

---

*This view is attributed to Geluk scholars such as Tsongkhapa, Pari Rapsel, and Drakar Trülku (*brag dkar dpal ldan bstan 'dzin snyan grags*, 1866–1928) by Bötrül's student, Khenpo Chökhyap. Such a claim is an implication of the position that, according to the Geluk presentation of Prāsaṅgika, the three Sublime Ones—Auditors, Self-Realized Ones, and bodhisattvas—have the same type of realization. For Drakar Trülku's argument against Mipam's position that Auditors and Self-Realized Ones do not fully realize the selflessness of phenomena, see Drakar Trülku, *Profound Discourse* (*'jam dbyangs rnam rgyal gyi 'dod tshul la klan ka bgyis pa zab mo'i gtam*), in *Collected Works*, vol. 12, 438.5–445.1.

†This view is attributed to the Sakya scholar, Gorampa, by Bötrül's student, Khenpo Chökhyap. In his commentary on the *Abhisamayālaṃkāra*, Gorampa asserts that bodhisattvas on the first ground have completely abandoned and realized what Auditors and Self-Realized Ones have. See Gorampa, *Open Treasury of the Profound Hidden Meaning*, 40.1–40.3.

Some great all-seeing ones assert: "At the time when bodhisattvas are on the first ground, they have completely perfected a type of realization to the extent of the realization of the Auditors and Self-Realized Ones."

However, such a tradition appears to be in accord with neither the Middle Way nor Mind-Only; elegant discourses such as these are just a disgrace!

2. *Presenting Our Tradition*

This section has two parts: (1) a concise demonstration and (2) an extensive explanation.

1. Concise Demonstration

The illustrious tradition of the Lion of the Śākyas,
From the scriptural tradition of scholars of the school of early translations,
Explains the delineation of the grounds and paths, and
The ways of perfecting abandonment and realization, as follows.

The school of early translations has the meaning of the name *Nyingma* (old school)—the old scriptural tradition of the illustrious tradition of the Victorious One, the Lion of the Śākyas—from which the delineation of the three vehicles' ways of perfecting abandonment and realization on the paths and grounds of the great bodhisattvas is explained as follows.

2. Extensive Explanation

This section has three parts: (1) a concise demonstration of the distinctive essences, (2) the way of dividing the distinctive abandonments and realizations from those, and (3) through this, the delineation of the ways of perfecting abandonment and realization.

1. Concise Demonstration of the Distinctive Essences

This section has two parts: (1) a concise demonstration of the two ways of abandonment and realization and (2) through this, the actual presentation of abandonment—the truth of cessation.

1. CONCISE DEMONSTRATION OF THE TWO WAYS OF ABANDONMENT AND REALIZATION

Regarding this, abandonment and realization is twofold:
The truth of the path and the truth of cessation.

The essence of abandonment and realization is as follows: Abandonment is destroying the seeds of whatever obscurations there are to be abandoned. Realization is seeing selflessness, the antidote by means of which they are abandoned. These two are (1) the truth of cessation and (2) the truth of the path.

2. ACTUAL PRESENTATION OF ABANDONMENT—THE TRUTH OF CESSATION

Nāgārjuna asserted that the truth of cessation, emptiness, and the ultimate
Have the same meaning;
Therefore, selflessness, emptiness, and the authentic limit
Are just the same meaning.

Thus, in the Great Middle Way tradition, the master Nāgārjuna in the "Collection of Reasonings" asserted that, in general, the truth of cessation, emptiness, and the ultimate truth have the same meaning. For this reason, selflessness, emptiness, and the authentic limit of cessation are just the same meaning.

2. *Way of Dividing the Distinctive Abandonments and Realizations*

This section has two parts: (1) a concise demonstration of the two purities and (2) through this, the actual way of dividing the distinctive abandonments and realizations.

1. CONCISE DEMONSTRATION OF THE TWO PURITIES

Regarding this, there are two:
(1) Natural purity and (2) purity that is free from the adventitious [obscurations].

Thus, when the truth of cessation, which is the nature of emptiness, is divided by means of contradistinctions, there are two:

(1) the distinction of the primordially pure essence—the naturally pure cessation in which the obscurations to be abandoned do not abide in the foundational nature, and (2) the distinction of being free from the adventitious [obscurations]—the cessation freed of the adventitious in which the adventitious obscurations to be abandoned are relinquished by the path.

2. ACTUAL WAY OF DIVIDING THE DISTINCTIVE ABANDONMENTS AND REALIZATIONS

Within the natural purity of selflessness,
There is the twofold selflessness: of phenomena and persons.
From the ways of clearly realizing these,
There are two truths of the path: Mahāyāna and Hīnayāna.

Within abandonment, the purity that is free from the adventitious,
There are two cessations: the abandonment of the afflictive and cognitive [obscurations].
From the ways of manifestly attaining these,
There are two nirvāṇas: Mahāyāna and Hīnayāna.

Thus, when emptiness, which is the essence of the natural purity of selflessness, is divided by means of quality-bearers (*chos can*), there are two: the selflessness of phenomena and the selflessness of persons. As such, the ways of the direct, clear realizations of these are posited as twofold: (1) the direct realization of the selflessness of phenomena, the abiding reality, which is the truth of the path that is unique to the Mahāyāna, and (2) the direct realization of the selflessness of persons, which is the truth of the path of the Hīnayāna type of realization.

Likewise, [when] abandonment, which is the truth of cessation—the purity free from the adventitious [obscurations]—[is divided] by means of what is abandoned, there are two: (1) the cessation that is the abandonment of afflictive obscurations and (2) the cessation that is the abandonment of cognitive obscurations. Through the ways of manifest attainment by relinquishing the afflictive and cognitive obscurations to be abandoned, cessation is posited as twofold: (1) Mahāyāna nirvāṇa, which is the truth of cessation that has exhaustively relinquished the cognitive obscurations to be abandoned, and (2) Hīnayāna nirvāṇa, which is the truth of cessation that has exhaustively relinquished the afflictive obscurations to be abandoned.

3. *Delineation of the Ways of Perfecting the Distinctive Abandonments and Realizations*

This section has two parts: (1) a concise demonstration of the two ways of clear realization and (2) through this, the actual delineation of the ways of perfecting the abandonments and realizations.

1. CONCISE DEMONSTRATION OF THE TWO WAYS OF CLEAR REALIZATION

This meaning is twofold: (1) the way of realization temporarily and
(2) The way of perfecting abandonment and realization consummately.

Thus, concerning the distinctive meanings of these abandonments and realizations, they should be ascertained as twofold: (1) the way of realization temporarily—on which ground, and in what way, and (2) the way of perfecting abandonment and realization consummately—on which ground, and in what way.

2. ACTUAL DELINEATION OF THE WAYS OF PERFECTING THE ABANDONMENTS AND REALIZATIONS

This section has two parts: (1) the way of realizing natural purity and (2) the way of perfecting abandonment and realization—the purity free from the adventitious [obscurations].

1. *WAY OF REALIZING NATURAL PURITY*

Regarding this, natural purity is seen
On the Path of Seeing, from the [first] ground of Sublime Joy.

The abiding reality and authentic limit—which is the emptiness that is the natural purity of the selflessness of persons and phenomena—is directly seen on the Mahāyāna Path of Seeing from the first ground, the ground of Sublime Joy. From the side of the object, the twofold selflessness characterized by natural purity is seen perfectly. From the side of the subject, it is the identity of the path that comprises the types of realization of the three vehicles.

However, [bodhisattvas on the first ground] not only [have not yet perfected abandonment and realization] in the Mahāyāna, but the perfection of abandonment and realization of the Hīnayāna is not yet complete. Hence, as in the viewpoint of scriptures such as the *Daśabhūmikasūtra*,[243] these bodhisattvas still do not outshine the Auditors and Self-Realized Ones who have completed the activities of the four truths: knowledge, abandonment, actualization, and reliance.

2. Way of Perfecting Abandonment and Realization—The Purity Free from the Adventitious [Obscurations]

This section has two parts: (1) the way of the Hīnayāna perfection of abandonment and realization and (2) the distinctive Mahāyāna perfection of abandonment and realization.

1. Way of the Hīnayāna Perfection of Abandonment and Realization

At [the seventh ground,] Gone Afar,
Abandonment and realization is shared with the Auditors and Self-Realized Ones:
The cessation is the abandonment of afflictive obscurations and
The perfection of the truth of the path is the selflessness of persons.

Thus, at the time of the seventh ground, Gone Afar, the abandonments and realizations shared with both the Auditors and Self-Realized Ones are completely perfected. There is the exhaustive attainment of the truth of cessation that is the complete abandonment of whatever the Auditors and the Self-Realized Ones have abandoned—the afflictive obscurations. Also, there is the complete perfection of the truth of the path that is the realization of whatever the Auditors and Self-Realized Ones have realized—the meaning of selflessness.

Therefore, the great bodhisattvas on the seventh ground have not only completed the perfection of the abandonment and realization of the Auditors and Self-Realized Ones, but they have gone far beyond all the activities of the Auditors and Self-Realized Ones who have completed the activities of the four truths—knowledge, abandonment, actualization, and reliance. These bodhisattvas have gone far beyond by means of abiding in the greatness of wisdom, which is the absorption in their unique domain of the authentic limit—the expanse of phenomena, the clear essential nature of all entities—in a way that is not conditioned moment by moment.[244]

Without trying to force one's lineage with hardheaded attachment, one should seek out where the viewpoint of the great sūtras and *śāstras* lies with an honest, discerning mind.

2. Distinctive Mahāyāna Perfection of Abandonment and Realization

However, since the consummate cessation and path—
The selflessness of phenomena and abandonment freed from cognitive obscurations—
Have not been perfected,
The Victorious Ones rouse them from cessation.

When perfecting, ripening, and training have been completed,
There is the consummate great freedom from the adventitious;
Abandonment free from cognitive obscurations and
The antidote, the selflessness of phenomena, are perfected.

The truth of cessation that is the perfection of abandonment
Is the nature of the Essential Body;
The great truth of the path of perfect realization
Is the discovery of the consummate Wisdom Truth Body.

This is a quintessential instruction
From the matchless spiritual friend—
A lineage from the mouth to the ears not propagated to others.
We are fortunate!

As was just explained, due to the power of bodhisattvas abiding on the seventh ground having completely perfected the abandonments and realizations of the Auditors and Self-Realized Ones, on the eighth ground, the *Madhyamakāvatāra* states:

> They have exhausted afflictive emotions and have become teachers of the three worlds;
> However, they are not able to attain all of the space-like qualities of a Buddha, free from extremes.[245]

Like the Auditors and Self-Realized Ones, they have completely transcended the three realms, and have become teachers of the three worlds. However, they have not perfected the consummate cessation and path that are unique to the Mahāyāna, namely, (1) the realization of the antidote, the complete selflessness of phenomena, and (2) the abandonment free from the cognitive obscurations. Hence, as is said, "However, due to compassion they are joined to existence until awakening," due to the power of great compassion, which is the inner teacher—the outer teachers, who are the victorious and perfect Buddhas, rouse them from cessation. The way of this is stated in sūtra:

> Very good! Very good! This thorough realization of the Buddha's doctrine is also the forbearance of the ultimate. However, noble child, you do not have the perfect, unshared qualities of a Buddha—my ten powers, four fearlessnesses, and so forth. In order to seek out the perfect qualities of the Buddhas, practice! Be diligent! With forbearance, do not give this up! Noble child, although you have attained the abode of peaceful liberation as such, think of the immature beings, the ordinary beings, those who are not at peace, those who are not at all tranquil, those for whom a variety of afflictive emotions completely wells up, those whose minds are distracted by manifold concepts. . . .

As is stated in the *Daśabhūmikasūtra*, they are roused from cessation.

Through such a means—through being embraced by their special inner and outer teachers—the bodhisattvas, the great beings abiding on the three pure grounds, do not fall to the extreme of peace. Through the accumulations of the third incalculable [aeon], when perfecting, ripening, and training are completed, they completely perfect the realization of selflessness—the consummate abandonment and realization:

- the great purity that is free of the adventitious [obscurations]—abandonment that is the complete freedom from the entirety of cognitive obscurations, and
- the completely perfect realization of the selflessness of phenomena, the antidote

This is the consummate truth of cessation, which is the perfection of abandonment, the nature of the Essential Body; and the consummate truth of the path, which is the perfection of realization, the discovery of the Wisdom Truth Body.

The cessation at this time should be known as stated in the [auto]commentary on the *Madhyamakāvatāra*:

> The absorption of cessation is the absorption in the authentic limit. Therefore, it is called "cessation within thusness"; here, the entirety of constructs has ceased.[246]

In this, as was demonstrated previously, (1) the cessation that is free from afflictive obscurations is the nirvāṇa that is shared with the Auditors and Self-Realized Ones, and (2) the cessation that is free from cognitive obscurations is the unique Mahāyāna nirvāṇa. Even though the first of these is attained, one does not fall to the extreme of peace by merely actualizing it. Having the inner teacher, which is great compassion, and being thoroughly exhorted by the outer teachers, the Buddhas, the consummate great nirvāṇa is accomplished through training in the oceanic threefold perfecting, ripening, and training.

Therefore, since the Auditors and Self-Realized Ones lack the method of the inner teacher of great compassion, they actualize merely a nirvāṇa that is a perfection of the realization and abandonment of the selflessness of persons. For ten thousand aeons, they fall to the extreme of peace and even the hand of the Buddha cannot rouse them.

However, having completely perfected the abandonments and realizations shared with the Auditors and Self-Realized Ones, those who are the great beings, the bodhisattvas, are liberated from existence. Even so, it is impossible for them to actualize only that [Hīnayāna nirvāṇa] because they accomplish nirvāṇa that does not abide in the extreme of peace; they are exhorted again and again by the outer teachers—the victorious, perfect Buddhas—through the power of being endowed with the inner teacher, great compassion. Otherwise, [mere] peace would be taught as nirvāṇa. A sūtra says:

> If the Blessed Ones did not cause the bodhisattvas to enter the door to manifestly accomplish omniscient wisdom, then at that time itself there would be complete nirvāṇa.

Therefore, at the time of explaining the fault of actualizing the authentic limit without performing the three practices,[247] the great commentary on the *Eight Thousand*[*-Stanza Perfection of Wisdom Sūtra*] states:

> "Actualizing the authentic limit. . . ." is actualizing the nirvāṇa of the Auditors and Self-Realized Ones.

Also, from the [auto]commentary of the *Madhyamakāvatāra:*

> By abandoning those [afflictive emotions], although they have become teachers of the three realms, at that time the

> bodhisattvas cannot attain the endowments of the Blessed Buddhas; in order to attain them, they must strive. How is that? Because it is said, ". . . at that time, they would attain complete nirvāṇa."[248]

Also, the *Bṛhṭṭīkā* states:

> The domain of omniscience is the authentic limit of the nirvāṇa of the Auditors and Self-Realized Ones.

Regarding this, some people say, "The nirvāṇa at that time is neither the Hīnayāna nor Mahāyāna nirvāṇa because (1) it is not possible to actualize the former [Hīnayāna nirvāṇa] and (2) the later [Mahāyāna nirvāṇa] is not able to be actualized."

However, formulating such statements of [absurd] consequence disregards the meaning of the impossibility to actualize mere peace, the reason that the former is impossible to actualize—namely, due to being embraced by the distinctive outer and inner teachers. It appears to be similar to the manner of the following: "It [absurdly] follows that the subject, the last existence of a bodhisattva, would not need to be exhorted by the gods of the pure domain for the purpose of definitive emergence because it would be impossible for the bodhisattva not to definitively emerge. This follows because it is the bodhisattva's last existence." Also, some people say: "It follows that the subject, a bodhisattva on the eighth ground, actualizes the authentic limit at an inappropriate time because of attaining the nirvāṇa of cessation."

However, if [the nirvāṇa of cessation] were attained, who is able to establish the necessity of its actualization? This is just arbitrary speech.

Also, some people evidently speak various irrelevant statements such as, "It [absurdly] follows that at the end of manifesting the three practices, the Hīnayāna nirvāṇa is actualized." However, they do not understand the essential point.

In short, although the naturally pure nirvāṇa is realized from the first ground, "the attainment of cessation" is not expressed by merely that—that is, a cessation shared with the Hīnayāna. As is stated in sūtras and in the root text and [auto]commentary of the *Madhyamakāvatāra*, it is obvious that many distinctions need to be made, such as:

- on the sixth ground, the manifest attainment through an exalted transcendent perfection of wisdom

- on the seventh ground, entering and emerging in an unconditioned way through perfecting the abandonments and realizations
- on the eighth ground, being liberated from existence through perfecting the strength, but not actualizing the extreme of peace, and
- at the stage of the Buddha, actualizing great awakening through performing the three practices, but not in a manner that is the extreme of peace

Thus:

> This is a quintessential instruction
> From the matchless spiritual friend—
> A lineage from the mouth to the ears not propagated to others.
> We are fortunate!

This is a stanza at the interlude between sections

3. Consummate Fruition—
Distinguishing the Two Exalted Bodies

This section has two parts: (1) the way that the fruition is attained and (2) distinguishing the fruition that is attained.

1. Way that the Fruition is Attained

This section has two parts: (1) refuting other traditions and (2) presenting our tradition.

1. Refuting Other Traditions

> *Concerning the way of attaining the fruition,*
> *Those of the later generation explain a presentation of the path and fruition; however,*
> *They do not account for the profound meaning of [the modes of] reality and appearance—*
> *Abiding purity and transformation.**

*This view is attributed to the Geluk, and Sakya scholars such as Rongtön, by Bötrül's student, Khenpo Chökhyap. The reason for this attribution is apparently because the mainstream within these traditions do not accept the qualities of the Buddha, such as the powers and so forth, to exist when one is a sentient being.

Thus, concerning the way in which there is attainment of the fruition—the completion of path—the masterly scholars of the later generation extensively explain a presentation of the path and fruition in general. However, they do not account for the presentations of the profound meaning of the modes of reality and appearance: (1) the abiding purity of the actualized fruition by means of the abiding purity of the obscurations to be abandoned and (2) the transformation of the two causal accumulations. Although they establish a slight meaning of transformation within the essence of fruition, since it is not conventionally established, these presentations are not explained.

2. Presenting Our Tradition

This section has three parts: (1) a concise demonstration, (2) an extensive explanation, and (3) a summary.

1. Concise Demonstration

Our tradition, the tradition of the scholars of the early generation,
Asserts by means of the modes of (1) reality and (2) appearance:
(1) Abiding purity, which is a freed effect, and
(2) Transformation, which is a ripened effect.

Our tradition, the tradition of the scholars of the early generation, asserts that by means of (1) the mode of reality and (2) the mode of appearance, there is:

1. abiding purity, which is the actualization of the fruition of the mode of reality's natural purity due to being free from the adventitious defilements to be abandoned, and
2. transformation, which is the ripened effect within the essence of the nature of the two causal accumulations

2. Extensive Explanation

In the explanation of the unique mode of reality
By the conventional valid cognition of purity,
The consummate fruition is the naturally abiding purity—

The abiding purity that is the effect freed from the
adventitious [defilements].

In the common explanation of the mode of appearance
By the conventional valid cognition of confined perception,
The causal phenomena are completely transformed in time
(gnas skabs)—
The effect is asserted as a transformation into a ripened effect.

Moreover, like the intended meaning of texts such as the *Mahāyāna-Uttaratantra,* in the explanation according to the unique nature of the mode of reality by means of the conventional valid cognition of purity, the consummate freed effect of the Truth Body's qualities naturally abide in the manner of purity from the beginning—like the maṇḍalas of the sun and moon freed from clouds. Due to being freed from the adventitious defilements, there is abiding purity in the actualization of this as it is.

In the explanation according to the common mode of appearance by means of the valid cognition of confined perception, the causal phenomena are completely transformed in time, and the identity of the effect that is attained is asserted to be a transformation into a ripened effect—like a seed transforming into a sprout.

3. Summary

Due to [the modes of] reality and appearance—
Freed and ripened from the natures of the two causal
accumulations—
We assert the Truth Body's qualities as a freed effect and
The accomplishment of the Form Bodies as a ripened effect.

This way, in short, is the distinction between the freed and ripened [effects] by means of the modes of reality and appearance:

The Form Bodies of the Buddhas
Arise here from the accumulation of merit;
The Truth Body, in brief, O King,
Is born from the accumulation of wisdom.[249]

As is said, from the nature of the two accumulations of merit and wisdom, which are the causal phenomena of the path, (1) the freed effect, the qualities of the Truth Body, depends upon the accumulation of wisdom; and (2) the complete establishment of the ripened effect, the Form Bodies, depends upon the accumulation of merit. This is widely accepted according to the teachings from the Word and the great *śāstras*.

2. Distinguishing the Fruition that is Attained

This section has three parts: (1) a general demonstration of the nature of the fruition, (2) a particular demonstration differentiating the array of the three mysteries, and (3) a summary of the accomplished meaning—the great, inconceivable transformation.

1. General Demonstration of the Nature of the Fruition

This section has two parts: (1) refuting other traditions and (2) presenting our tradition.

1. Refuting Other Traditions

Concerning the nature of the fruition, others say,
"The identity of the three exalted bodies of the Buddha
Is an object of a mind of confined perception—
Limited to matter, cognition, and non-concurrent
*[formations]."**

Such a common locus of sentient beings and Buddhas,
Which is not beyond the phenomena of aggregates and
constituents, and
Has not relinquished the activity of mental feeling (sems tshor),
Is a disgrace!

Concerning the nature of the attainment of fruition, other masterly scholars say that the great, consummate awakening—the identity of the three exalted bodies—is an object of a mind of confined perception, limited to merely:

- the essence of a Buddha's Form Bodies that is the identity of the aggregate of form—the nature of matter composed of particles

*This view is attributed to the Geluk and Sakya by Bötrül's student, Khenpo Chökhyap. Such a claim is an implication of the lack of the valid cognition of pure vision in these traditions; their conventional valid cognition is limited to confined perception.

- the essence of an omniscient Truth Body that is the nature of cognition subsumed within the aggregate of consciousness, and
- the identity of these as impermanent, etc.—the nature of a non-concurrent formation

However, when analyzed, the nature of a consummate fruition of great awakening that is not beyond the phenomena of aggregates, constituents, and sense-fields, nor has thoroughly relinquished the activity of mental feeling, is designating the name "Buddha" upon that which has the quality of a sentient being. The way that such a common locus of sentient beings and Buddhas is unreasonable is extensively taught in texts such as the *Rapsel Rejoinder.*

2. *Presenting Our Tradition*

The nature of the three exalted bodies
Stated in the profound, definitive meaning sūtras
Is free from the aggregates and
Transcends the constituents and sense-fields.

Therefore, it is said that anyone who regards [the nature of the Buddha]
As a form or as a sound
Has entered into the mistaken path of conceptuality;
That one does not know this nature.

Therefore, the nature of the three mysteries
Is the display of great wisdom;
The omniscience of a perfect Buddha
Is solely the nature of the Truth Body.

The displays of the Guides' Form Bodies
Are appearances that are like forms, [but]
Are not material phenomena composed of particles.
View them as the self-lucidity of the expanse of phenomena.

In this way, profound suchness
Is not what is known by logicians.
A mind of confined perception
Is not able to fully know these.

In this way, the consummate fruition of great awakening, which is the nature of the three exalted bodies, is stated in the profound, definitive meaning sūtras as the identity that:

- is free from the aggregates, which are the objects of confined perception
- not endowed with the constituents, and
- transcends the phenomena of sense-fields

Due to this reason, concerning the identity of the three exalted bodies, anyone who—through a mind of confined perception—sees the profound mystery of the Buddha's body as an individual form, or regards the identity of exalted speech as particular sounds and words, is a person who has entered the negative, mistaken path of conceptuality. That one does not know the nature of the three mysteries.

Therefore, the nature of the three mysteries, which is the consummate fruition of great awakening, is the display of only great wisdom. Moreover, the complete abandonment and realization that is the omniscience of the perfect Buddhas is solely the nature of the exalted mind, the Truth Body. Appearances that are the displays of Form Bodies, such as the Guide's Body of Perfect Rapture, are not material phenomena that are composed of particles. View them as the self-lucidity of the suchness expanse—the identity that arises as major and minor marks.

In this way, the suchness of the profound mysteries of the fruition—the Buddha's body, speech, and mind—is not known by means of a logician's valid cognition. Even if a mind of confined perception's valid cognition contemplated for a hundred aeons, it would not be able to fully know the profound mysteries of the Buddha. As is said:

> Those who see me as form [and]
> Those who hear me as sound
> Have entered the wrong path;
> They do not see me.
>
> The Buddhas, the Truth Body, and
> The Guides are seen as suchness.
> Suchness is not an object of knowledge;
> Hence, it cannot be known at all.[250]

2. Particular Demonstration Differentiating the Array of the Three Mysteries

This section has two parts: (1) the array of the three mysteries in general and (2) distinguishing the qualities of omniscience specifically.

1. Array of the Three Mysteries in General

> *Others' perceptions are*
> *A limitless array of a variety of exalted bodies*
> *Simultaneously appearing in each part of every particle;*
> *[A Buddha's] own perception is the changeless wisdom body.*
>
> *Others' perceptions are*
> *A manifold array of as many languages as there are in the six classes of beings,*
> *Simultaneously resounding.*
> *[A Buddha's] own perception is the unobstructed wisdom speech.*
>
> *Others' perceptions are*
> *An array of a mind that knows everything instantly—*
> *Simultaneously seeing objects of knowledge.*
> *[A Buddha's] own perception is the unwavering wisdom mind.*

The consummate fruition of supreme awakening's profound mystery of the exalted body is as follows: Although a Buddha's own perception transcends particles and momentary phenomena, from the perspective of others to be trained, on each part of every smallest particle, there are simultaneously all the appearances of the vastly immeasurable and limitless arrays of a variety of exalted bodies and [Buddha-]fields. However, [a Buddha's] own perception is the wisdom body with the nature of the major and minor marks—abiding as the identity of the simultaneous knowledge of all objects of knowledge without exception through each and every pore.

Likewise, the profound mystery of the exalted speech is as follows: Although a Buddha's own perception transcends the phenomena of particular sounds and words, from the perspective of others to be trained, there are simultaneously all the resonances of a limitless array of whatever variety of languages are spoken in each of the six classes of beings. However, [a Buddha's] own perception is the unobstructed wisdom speech—the identity with the nature of the sixty qualities endowed with the totality of all aspects.[251]

The profound mystery of the exalted mind is as follows: Although a Buddha's own perception transcends momentary, conditioned phenomena, from the perspective of others to be trained, there is the complete, simultaneous vision of all the vast extent of objects of knowledge—the wisdom of the omniscient mind that is an array of a mind that fully knows, directly and instantly, all aspects of knowledge comprising what is and whatever there is. However, [a Buddha's] own perception is the unwavering wisdom mind—abiding as the essence of the understanding of all aspects of knowledge, with the nature of the eighteen unshared qualities.[252]

2. *Distinguishing the Qualities of Omniscience Specifically*

This section has two parts: (1) omniscience in the tradition of confined perception and (2) omniscience in the tradition of the valid cognition of pure vision.

1. Omniscience in the Tradition of Confined Perception

When a valid cognition of confined perception
Investigates the nature of the omniscient subject,
Due to knowing entities,
Omniscience is asserted as conditioned in the mere mode of appearance.

In general, when the essence of omniscience, the nature of the subject, is investigated by merely a valid cognition of confined perception, it is asserted as conditioned in the mere mode of appearance. This is because it is a valid cognition that realizes existent entities—the distinctive objects known are conditioned, impermanent phenomena. As is said:

There is no permanent valid cognition
Because the realization of the existence of entities is valid.[253]

2. Omniscience in the Tradition of the Valid Cognition of Pure Vision

This section has two parts: (1) the essence of the omniscient Truth Body and (2) distinguishing omniscience's domain of knowledge.

1. Essence of the Omniscient Truth Body

However, wisdom's self-appearance is the great luminous clarity,
Profound, peaceful, and free from constructs.
It is self-existing, unconditioned, and spontaneously present—
The great freedom from the extremes of purity, bliss, self, and permanence.

However, the omniscience that is the object of the conventional valid cognition of pure vision is as follows: The identity of the Truth Body, which is the essence of wisdom's self-appearance, transcends the domain of an immature mind's confined perception. Hence, it is the profound, consummate fruition endowed with the twofold purity—the great emptiness free from constructs—which is the identity of the Essential Body that has completely pacified the frames of mind comprised by mind and mental states. The identity of the Wisdom Truth Body is the great nature of luminous clarity endowed with knowledge, love, and powers. It is self-existing, unconditioned, and spontaneously present; it is the nature of the great wisdom that is free from the extremes such as purity, bliss, self, and permanence posited by a valid cognition of confined perception.

2. Distinguishing Omniscience's Domain of Knowledge

Regarding omniscience's domain, the assertions:
"Omniscience itself does not perceive impure phenomena of delusion," and
"Omniscience does perceive—a Buddha's own perception also has deluded perceptions,"
Are confusion at the core.

[Deluded perceptions are seen] in the way that someone with superknowledge
Sees the phenomena of deluded perceptions in another's dream.
However, they are not his own perceptions;
His own perceptions are his waking perceptions.

Likewise, omniscience itself sees and knows
All the impure fields of others' perceptions.
However, they are not [a Buddha's] own perception;
A Buddha's own perception is the pure field.

Concerning the way that omniscient wisdom knows its domain, some people say: "A Buddha's omniscience itself does not perceive the impure phenomena that are the deluded perceptions of the six classes of beings." Also, some people assert: "The Buddha does perceive all the impure, deluded perceptions; the Buddha's own perception also has deluded perceptions." Both of these are confusion at the core.

Therefore, the way in which a Buddha knows the impure, deluded perceptions is as is shown in the great sūtras and *śāstras* by means of analogy: When one person fell asleep inside a bejeweled palace, another person living there with superknowledge saw, as they were, the various deluded perceptions of the dream by means of his superknowledge. However, the deluded perceptions of the dream were not the own perceptions of the one with superknowledge; his own perception was the sight of only his waking perception of the bejeweled palace. Likewise, a Buddha knows and perceives all the appearances of the impure fields that appear in the perspectives of others—individually unmixed to omniscient wisdom. However, these are not a Buddha's own perception; a Buddha's own perception is only the pure realm of all environments and inhabitants.

3. Summary of the Accomplished Meaning—The Great, Inconceivable Transformation

This section has three parts: (1) demonstrating the limitless qualities of transformation, (2) through this, establishing the infinite way of knowing, and (3) advice to know the essential mystery, the profound meaning illustrated by this.

1. Demonstrating the Limitless Qualities of Transformation

When perfecting, ripening, and training have been completed,
And when the three realms are a manifest, perfect Buddha,
The three exalted bodies are perfected in the field of the Victorious Ones, and
The viewpoints of Sūtra and Mantra are integrated indivisibly.

The mode of appearance is the impurity of others' perceptions and
All the phenomena of appearance, resonance, and cognition;
The mode of reality is the pure field of [the Buddha's] own perception and
The perfect array of exalted body, speech, and mind.

Objects, faculties, and awareness abide as pure and,
The qualities of transformation know no end.
Although it may not taste good in the perceptions of others,
It appears in [the Buddha's] own perception as the supreme taste of purity.

In short, when perfecting, ripening, and training have been completed, there is the great maṇḍala of the three realms as a manifest, perfect Buddha. The three exalted bodies are perfected in the field of the Victorious Ones, and all the paths of Sūtra and Mantra are indivisibly integrated within one stream of the viewpoint.

The mode of appearance is the impurity of others' perceptions, those of the six classes of beings, and all the phenomena of appearance, resonance, and cognition. However, the mode of reality is the great pure realm of the Buddha's own perception—completely perfected in the great array of appearances as the maṇḍala of exalted body, resonances as the maṇḍala of exalted speech, and cognitions as the maṇḍala of exalted mind.

By means of objects, faculties, and awareness [naturally] abiding as pure, and through their transformation, there is the endowment of qualities—such as mastery over the twelve hundred qualities of the faculties[254]—that know no end. Through this, although it may not taste good in the perceptions of others, like a horse's rotten saddlebags, it appears in the Buddha's own perception as the supreme taste of purity, like food of the gods.

2. Establishing The Infinite Way of Knowing

The way of knowing that sees appearance and emptiness as equality
Knows the pure and impure simultaneously.
The one taste of knower and known
Is inconceivable and inexpressible by a mind of confined perception.

In short, the profound, definitive mystery of the distinctive way that omniscient wisdom knows the immense extent of objects of knowledge is as follows:

- objects of knowledge comprised within the two truths of appearance and emptiness are seen as equality

- all the pure and impure appearances of *saṃsāra* and nirvāṇa are known simultaneously
- the knower and known, which is the nature of subject and object, are seen as one taste

The attributes of this great identity are inconceivable and inexpressible by a mind of confined perception.

3. Advice to Know the Essential Mystery, the Profound Meaning

There are two objects of knowledge: (1) what is and (2) whatever there is.
Within the appearing phenomena of whatever there is, there are two:
(1) [A Buddha's] own perception, which is the pure mode of reality, and
(2) The perceptions of others, which are the modes of appearance of the six classes of beings.

Although there are five wisdoms that know,
There are two: (1) the wisdom of what is and (2) the wisdom of whatever there is.
Through this, know the infinite definitive mystery of
The way in which wisdom knows the objects of knowledge.

In general, there are two types of known phenomena: (1) emptiness, which is the abiding reality of what is, and (2) relative phenomena, which are the modes of appearance of whatever there is. There are also two types of relative phenomena—the modes of appearance of whatever there is: (1) the own perception of a Buddha, which is the pure mode of reality, and (2) the perceptions of others, which are the impure modes of appearance of the six classes of beings. Although there is a way of abiding as the five wisdoms, which see and know these as they are, they are complete in two when condensed: (1) the wisdom that knows what is and (2) the wisdom that knows whatever there is. Through this, know completely what is difficult to realize—the infinite definitive mystery of the way that the extent of objects of knowledge are known.

4. Concluding Meaning of the Completed Composition

This section has two parts: (1) the way in which this was composed and (2) completely dedicating the roots of virtue.

1. The Way in Which This was Composed

In this way, without pollution of the poisons of attachment and aggression,
This was a concise lamp that elucidates the mode of reality—
The distinctive essential meanings, without mixing them—
Distinguishing the early and later traditions of masterly scholars in the Land of Snow.

In the dominion of the kingdom of the school of early translations' doctrine of the great secret—
Which is the supreme, illustrious tradition of the Victorious One, the Lion of the Śākyas—
With the pretense of staying a long time, I held a begging bowl of the three faiths
At the threshold of the vast and profound feast of doctrine.

Due to this, the fortune that this inquisitive youth attained well is
This fortune of food from the feast of doctrine.
In order to repay the kindness of my glorious teachers,
And in order to benefit some honest people with discerning minds,

Sākya[muni]'s monk from the eastern region of Dakpo,
The one called "Dongak Tenpé Nyima,"[255]
Wrote clearly from the path of authentic reasoning,
In accordance with the scriptures of sūtra and tantra, and the quintessential instructions of my teacher.

In just the way that was demonstrated before, without pollution in my mind from the poisoned waters of negative conceptuality—intolerable attachment and aggression—I have shown a concise lamp that elucidates the mode of reality distinguishing the early and later traditions of the masterly scholars in the Land of Snow—without mixing the important distinctions of the essential meanings of the ground, path, and fruition.

Moreover, in the dominion of the school of early translations' doctrine of the great secret—which is the supreme, illustrious tradition of the Victorious One, the Lion of the Śākyas—the spiritual friends who reign over the kingdom of the doctrine gave a delightful, great feast of the immensely vast and profound doctrine to the ocean of fortunate disciples gathered. With the pretense of staying a long time, this lowly, inferior student, who was just about to cast off even the name of "one of the Nyingma school of Secret Mantra," passed his life standing at the threshold of the door holding a huge begging bowl of the three faiths—pretending to have inspired faith, aspiring faith, and confident faith.

Due to this, my cherishing mind does not want to waste the fortune that this inquisitive youth attained well—this slight morsel of food that is the fortune of the feast of the doctrine. So in order to repay the kindness of my glorious teachers in general, and to benefit the one or two people there may be who are honest and have discerning minds, Śākya[muni]'s monk called "Dongak Tenpé Nyima" from the eastern direction, the region of Dakpo, clearly wrote these few words through the path of authentic reasoning—in accordance with the valid scriptures of sūtra and tantra, and the valid quintessential instructions of my teacher.

2. *Completely Dedicating the Roots of Virtue*

By this virtue, may all beings that exist, equal to [the extent of] space,
Enjoy the splendor of the seven qualities of high birth.
Having completely entered the path of the three beings,
May they all attain unexcelled awakening!

May I also, from now until the extent of existence,
Enter the realms of beings in a variety of forms
And play in the sacred light, without parting from the sole refuge,
The infallible youth with the top-knot [Mañjughoṣa]!

May the light of the wheels of explanation and practice of the Victorious Ones' teaching
Pervade all the kingdoms of the vast territories and regions!

May we abide in discipline and perfect study, contemplation, and meditation,
Beautifying the Capable One's teaching with exposition, debate, and composition!

By the virtue of this completed composition, may it be a cause of benefit and happiness for the welfare of others: May all beings that exist, equal to [the extent of] space, enjoy the splendor of the seven qualities of high birth,[256] which is the support of the path; and for the time being completely enter into the path of the three beings, which is the essence of the path. May all beings comprising the three types of beings[257] quickly accomplish the consummate fruition—the great, unexcelled awakening!

Moreover, may it be a cause of delighting the exalted deity for the welfare of myself: May I, from now until the extent of existence, enter the realms of the six classes of beings in the manner of the four modes of birth,[258] by means of a variety of forms such as birds, wild animals, and village beggar women. Without parting from the venerable Mañjughoṣa, the youth with the fivefold top-knot—the infallible, sole guide and refuge—may I behold the signs and marks of his face, the viewpoint of his loving mind, and completely play in the sacred light of his Brahma speech!

Likewise, may it be a cause of perpetuating the teachings for the welfare of both [myself and others]: May the light of the wheels of the integrated sun and moon of explanation and practice of the Victorious One's precious teachings pervade all the kingdoms of the vast territories and regions. May all assemblies of the spiritual community in the four directions abide in pure discipline, which is the foundation of the trainings. May we fulfill our own welfare: study, contemplation, and meditation; and for the welfare of others: by means of exposition, debate, and composition, may the precious teachings of the Capable One—the nonsectarian old and new [schools of translations]—be beautified by expanding, developing, and lasting a long time!

In this way, the meaning of the words of this text, *Distinguishing the Views and Philosophies*, was set forth as a concise exposition. Yet in general, most of the monastic textbooks of other factions do not state any distinctive claims of the scriptural tradition of the early translations other than merely the understood meanings of an old grandfather. Also, it is evident that even among those with the pretense of upholding our own position, many do not know any of the distinctive claims of the scriptural meanings, and there is a lot of carelessness—accomplishing the causes of perpetuating attachment and aggression, et cetera. Based on this, with a mind without attachment or aggression, I had the pretension to disseminate merely a concise summary in the short composition. I did not at all want to write a commentary, as it would seem to be a cause of perpetuating pointless attachment and aggression.

However, [I wrote it] based on the request of many sacred beings that recently came to the crown of my head with the divine substances of auspiciousness—such as Gyelsé Rinpoché, who is the lord of doctrine of Minling; the all-seeing Jamyang Chödrak (*'jam dbyangs chos grags*); the glorious Yönten Gyatsodé (*yon tan rgya mtsho sde*); the master of accomplishment and precious scholar of the supreme Dzokchen [monastery] with the name Padma; the renunciate and great upholder of the scriptural collection with the name Chöjor (*chos 'byor*); the supreme emanation of Gojo Khalék (*go 'jo kha legs*) with the name Padma; and Tsültrim Tendzin (*tshul khrims bstan 'dzin*), the cousin of the supreme Tupten,[259] the precious, great scholar.

By the merit of this dissemination by Śākya[muni]'s monk called "Dongak Tenpé Nyima" from the eastern direction, the region of Dakpo, may it be a cause for the precious teachings of the Victorious One—the nonsectarian old and new [schools of translations]—to develop and spread in all directions, lasting a long time!

> May the precious teachings of the Victorious One, impartial (*phyogs*) and nonsectarian,
> Completely pacify the *duḥkha* of strife and factionalism (*phyogs*).
> May the Sage's teachings, victorious in all directions (*phyogs*),
> Beautify all the kingdoms of the vast territories and regions (*phyogs*)!

May it be virtuous! *sarva mangalaṃ*.

Outline

Notes

Translator's Introduction

1. Bötrül, *Ornament of Mañjughoṣa's Viewpoint: An Explanation of the Words and Meanings of "Distinguishing the Views and Philosophies: A Lamp of Essential Points" (lta grub shan 'byed gnad kyi sgron me'i tshig don rnam bshad 'jam dbyangs dgongs rgyan)*, 63. For a study and translation of Mipam's text, see John Pettit, *Mipham's Beacon of Certainty*.

2. In particular, I have in mind here Georges Dreyfus's *Recognizing Reality*, which contrasts Sakya and Geluk traditions of epistemology; and his more recent *The Sound of Two Hands Clapping: The Education of a Tibetan Buddhist Monk*, in which he contrasts Geluk and Nyingma approaches to monastic education. Jeffrey Hopkins's recent works, including *Reflections on Reality*, compare Jonang and Geluk interpretations of the Middle Way. Also, José Cabezón's recent translation of Gorampa's (*go rams pa bsod nams seng ge*, 1429–1489) *Distinguishing the Views*—which notably has a similar title as Bötrül's present work—situates a Sakya interpretation of the Middle Way in contrast to Geluk and Jonang interpretations. See José Cabezón and Geshe Lobsang Dargyay, *Freedom from Extremes: Gorampa's "Distinguishing the Views" and the Polemics of Emptiness*.

3. Bötrül, *Ornament of Mañjughoṣa's Viewpoint*, 299.

4. Ibid., 299.

5. Tupten Tsültrim Namdak (*thub bstan tshul khrim rnam dag*), *Nourishment for Faith: A Short Hagiography of Bötrül (rje kun gzigs bod sprul bstan pa'i nyi ma'i rnam thar bsdus pa dad pa'i gsos sman)*, in Bötrül, *Collected Works*, vol. 1, 24.

6. Khenpo Tsültrim Lodrö told me that Bötrül wrote the commentary on a trip doing village rituals (*grong chog*) and that this is the reason why there are not many citations in the text (Bötrül did not have his books with him).

7. Tupten Tsültrim Namdak, *Nourishment for Faith*, 23.

8. The Perfection of Wisdom Sūtras, for example, is an example of an early "treasure text" that was believed to have been hidden and later revealed when the time was right.

9. Bötrül, *Words of Maitreya: An Explanation of the Meaning of the Words of the Abhisamayālaṃkāra (sher phyin mngon par rtogs pa'i rgyan gyi tshig don rnam par bshad pa ma pham zhal lung)*, in Bötrül, *Collected Works*, vol. 2.

10. *Words of Candrakīrti* (*zla ba'i zhal lung*) and *Ornament of Candrakīrti* (*zla ba'i dgongs rgyan*).

11. Bötrül, *Ornament of Master Nāgārjuna"s Viewpoint* (*klu dbang dgongs rgyan*), Bötrül, *Collected Works*, vol. 3, 3–229.

12. Bötrül, *The Fast Path to Great Bliss: An Instruction Manual on the Prayer for the Pure Field of Sukhāvatī* (*rnam dag bde chen zhing smon gyi khrid yig bde chen myur lam*), in Bötrül, *Collected Works*, vol. 3, 232–84.

13. Mipam, *Lion's Roar: Exposition of Buddha-Nature* (*bde gshegs snying po'i stong thun chen mo seng ge'i nga ro*), in *Collected Works*, vol. 4 (*pa*), 563–607; English translation in Douglas Duckworth, *Mipam on Buddha-Nature*, 147–80.

14. Bötrül, *Notes on the Essential Points of [Mipam's] Exposition [of Buddha-Nature]* (*stong thun gnad kyi zin thun*), in Bötrül, Collected Works, vol. 1, 261–74; English translation in Duckworth, *Mipam on Buddha-Nature*, 181–89.

15. Bötrül, *Rousing Swift Blessings: A Guru Yoga for the Glorious Teacher Rigzin Chödrak* (*dpal ldan bla ma chos kyi grags pa'i bla ma'i rnal 'byor byin rlabs myur 'jug*), in Bötrül, *Collected Works*, vol. 3, 297–300.

16. Bötrül, *Collected Works* (*bod sprul mdo sngags bstan pa'i nyi ma'i gsung 'bum*), vols. 1–3.

17. Nyoshül Khenpo (*smyo shul mkhan po 'jam dbyangs rdo rje*, 1931–1999), *Garland of Lapis: History of the Great Perfection* (*rang bzhin rdzogs pa chen po'i chos 'byung rig 'dzin brgyud pa'i rnam thar ngo mtshar nor bu baidurya'i phreng ba*), vol. 2, 356.2–357.5.

18. Tarthang Tulku also wrote a very brief biographical sketch of Bötrül (misspelled as *sPos-pa sPrul-sku*) in his *Lineage of Diamond Light: Crystal Mirror*, vol. 5, 305–306.

19. Nyoshül Khenpo, *Garland of Lapis*, vol. 2, 359.6–360.4.

20. When I stayed at Larung Gar in the summer of 2006, the population there was around ten thousand. For further information on Khenpo Jikmé Püntsok and Larung Gar, see David Germano, "Re-membering the Dismembered Body of Tibet," in *Buddhism in Contemporary Tibet*, ed. Melvyn Goldstein and Matthew Kapstein, 53–94.

21. For a brief sketch of Tarthang Tulku's activities in the United States, see Charles Prebish, *Luminous Passage: The Practice and Study of Buddhism in America*, 43.

22. I mainly draw from Tupten Tsültrim Namdak's *Nourishment for Faith*. Other sources for Bötrül's life can be found in Khenpo Petsé (*padma tshe dbang lhun grub*, 1931–2002), *A Short Biography of Bötrül* (*bod sprul sku'i rnam thar nyung bsdus*), published in *lta grub shan 'byed rtsa 'grel* (Sichuan: Nationalities Press, 1996); Nyoshül Khenpo, *Garland of Lapis*, vol. 2, 354.4–357.5; Tenzin Lungtok Nyima (*bstan 'dzin lung rtogs nyi ma*), *The Great History of Dzokchen* (*snga 'gyur rdzogs chen chos 'byung chen mo*), 715–18.

23. *dwags po*. Presently known as the district of Gyatsa (*rgya tshwa*) in the region of Lhokha (*lho kha*).

24. Tupten Tsültrim Namdak, *Nourishment for Faith*, 3–5.

25. Ibid., 5–6.
26. Ibid., 7.
27. Ibid., 7–8.
28. Ibid., 8–9.
29. Khenpo Petsé, *A Short Biography of Bötrül*, 1.
30. Tupten Tsültrim Namdak, *Nourishment for Faith*, 9.
31. Ibid., 41.
32. Ibid., 9–11.
33. Khenpo Petsé, *A Short Biography of Bötrül*, 2.
34. Tupten Tsültrim Namdak, *Nourishment for Faith*, 12.
35. Ibid., 13–14.
36. Ibid., 14.
37. Ibid., 15–16. For a short biography of Chöying Rangdröl, written by someone who met him, see Tulku Thondup, *Masters of Meditation and Miracles*, 260–65.
38. Mipam, *Overview: Essential Nature of Luminous Clarity* (*spyi don 'od gsal snying po*), 381–605; English translation in Dharmachakra Translation Committee, trans., *Luminous Essence: A Guide to the Guhyagarbhatantra*.
39. Tupten Tsültrim Namdak, *Nourishment for Faith*, 17–19.
40. Ibid., 19–21.
41. Ibid., 21–22.
42. Ibid., 25.
43. Ibid., 26–27.
44. This text apparently is no longer extant; it is not in his *Collected Works*.
45. Ibid., 27.
46. Ibid., 28–29.
47. Ibid., 30–31.
48. I borrow this term from Geoffrey Samuel's book *Civilized Shamans* (Washington, D.C.: Smithsonian Institution Press, 1993).
49. Candrakīrti, *Madhyamakāvatāra* VI.23: "That which is the object of authentic seeing is thusness; false seeings are relative truths" (*yang dag mthong yul gang de de nyid de/ mthong ba rdzun pa kun rdzob bden par gsung*). Published with autocommentary in *Autocommentary of the Madhyamakāvatāra* (*dbu ma la 'jug pa'i rang 'grel*), 104.
50. Candrakīrti, *Madhyamakāvatāra* VI.97.
51. Kongtrül (*kong sprul blo gros mtha' yas*, 1813–1899) identifies the four Mind-Only Sūtras as: the *Laṅkāvatārasūtra*, *Saṃdhinirmocanasūtra*, *Avataṃsakasūtra*, and *Gaṇḍavyūha*. Kongtrül says that these are renowned as four "Mind-Only Sūtras," but also are definitive meaning sūtras. See Kongtrül, *Roar of the Non-Returning Lion: Commentary on the Uttaratantra* (*theg pa chen po rgyud bla ma'i bstan bcos snying po'i don mngon sum lam gyi bshad srol dang sbyar ba'i rnam par 'grel pa phyir mi ldog pa seng ge'i nga ro*), 6; see also Shenpen Hookham, *The Buddha Within*, 266–67.
52. In his *Granting Request*, Dölpopa lists the ten Buddha-Nature Sūtras as follows: the *Tathāgatagarbhasūtra*, the *Avikalpapraveśadhāraṇī*, the *Śrīmālādevīsiṃhanādasūtra*, the *Mahābherīhārakaparivartasūtra*, the *Aṅgulimālīyasūtra*,

the *Mahāśūnyatāsūtra*, the *Tathāgataguṇajñānācintyaviṣayāvatārasūtra*, the *Mahāmeghasūtra*, the *Tathāgatamahākaruṇānirdeśasūtra* (*Dhāraṇīśvararājasūtra*), and the *Mahāparinirvāṇasūtra*. Dölpopa, *Granting Request* (*zhu don gnang ba*), in *Collected Works*, vol. 6, 285.

53. Maitreya, *Uttaratantra* I.155.

54. Candrakīrti, under *Madhyamakāvatāra* VI.95, in *Autocommentary of the Madhyamakāvatāra*, 196. See also D.T. Suzuki, trans., *The Laṅkāvatāra Sūtra*, 68–69; Jeffrey Hopkins, *Meditation on Emptiness*, 615–16.

55. One version of this famous verse is found in the *Prajñāpāramitā Sūtra* in *Eight-Thousand Lines* (*Aṣṭasāhasrikāprajñāpāramitā*, *'phags pa shes rab kyi pha rol tu phyin pa brgyad stong pa*), D.10, vol. 33, 5.3. English translation in Edward Conze, *The Perfection of Wisdom in Eight Thousand Lines & Its Verse Summary*, 84.

56. See Gorampa, *Distinguishing the Views* (*lta ba'i shan 'byed*), 3; English translation in José Cabezón and Geshe Lobsang Dargyay, *Freedom from Extremes*.

57. Tsongkhapa's eight unique assertions of Prāsaṅgika can be found in his *Thoroughly Illuminating the Viewpoint* (*dgongs pa rab gsal*), 226. The eight listed there are: the unique manners of (1) refuting a universal ground distinct from the six consciousnesses, (2) refuting reflexive awareness, (3) not asserting that autonomous arguments (*rang rgyud kyi sbyor ba, svatantraprayoga*) generate the view of thusness in the continuum of an opponent, (4) the necessity of asserting external objects as one asserts cognitions, (5) the assertion that Auditors and Self-Realized Ones realize the selflessness of phenomena, (6) the assertion that grasping to the self of phenomena is an afflictive emotion, (7) the assertion that disintegration is an entity, and (8) the consequent unique presentation of the three times. Tsongkhapa also lists a different set of unique assertions in his *Notes on the Eight Difficult Points* (*bka' gnas brgyad kyi zin bris*). See David Ruegg, *Two Prolegomena to Madhyamaka Philosophy*, 144–47. For a discussion of the unique assertions of Prāsaṅgika according to the Geluk tradition, see Dan Cozort, *Unique Tenets of the Middle Way Consequence School*.

58. For instance, Kongtrül states: "Prāsaṅgikas negate the assemblages of constructs by means of many kinds of reasoning; however, they do not establish a freedom from constructs." Kongtrül, *Encyclopedia of Knowledge* (*shes bya kun khyab*), 715. Bötrül's language here similarly contrasts with the words of his Nyingma predecessor, Longchenpa, in his *Precious Treasury of Philosophies*, 812: "The Prāsaṅgika's way of eliminating constructs . . . is not like the Svātantrikas, who establish the relative as false through negating its truth, and establish a lack of constructs through negating constructs regarding the ultimate. Rather, [Prāsaṅgikas] explicitly negate whatever is held onto while not implicitly establishing anything at all; thus, they avert the misconceptions of others."

59. According to Mipam, the two truths as authentic/inauthentic experience is the two-truth scheme of "other-emptiness": "The manner of establishing the ultimate of other-emptiness is by means of whether or not appearance accords with reality." Mipam, *Difficult Points of Scriptures in General* (*dbu ma sogs gzhung spyi'i dka' gnad skor gyi gsung sgros sna tshogs phyogs gcig*

tu bsdus pa rin po che'i za ma tog), in *Collected Works*, vol. 22, 450.3–450.4.

60. The significance of this placement was brought to my attention by Charlie Orzech.

61. Maitreya, *Dharmadharmatāvibhāga* v. 42.

62. Bötrül, *lta grub shan 'byed rtsa 'grel* (Sichuan, China: Nationalities Press, 1996).

63. Bötrül, *Collected Works* (*bod sprul mdo sngags bstan pa'i nyi ma'i gsung 'bum*), vols. 1–3 (Sichhuan, China: Nationalities Press, 2004).

64. Bötrül, *lta grub shan 'byed gnyad kyi sgron me* (Varanasi, India: Tarthang Tulku, 1963), and *nges shes sgron med / lta grub shan 'byed rtsa 'grel*, published in series: *dpal snga 'gyur rnying ma'i gzhung lugs chen mo'i skor* (Berkeley, Calif.: Dharma Publishing, 2004).

Ornament of Mañjughoṣa's Viewpoint

1. The eight bodhisattvas are: Mañjughoṣa, Vajrapāṇi, Avalokiteśvara, Kṣitigarbha, Sarvanivarṇaviṣkambhin, Ākāśagarbha, Maitreya, and Samantabhadra.

2. The six ornaments are: Nāgārjuna and Āryadeva (the two ornaments of the Middle Way), Vasubandhu and Asaṅga (the two ornaments of Abhidharma), and Dignāga and Dharmakīrti (the two ornaments of valid cognition).

3. The two supreme ones are the two Vinaya scholars: Śākyaprabha and Guṇaprabha.

4. The three Mañjughoṣas of Tibet are Sakya Paṇdita, Longchenpa, and Tsongkhapa, according to the *Tibetan-Chinese Dictionary* (*bod rgya tshig mdzod chen mo*).

5. The four philosophies are Vaibhāṣika, Sautrāntika, Mind-Only, and Middle Way.

6. The four Vinaya traditions are Sthavira, Sarvāstivāda, Mahāsaṃmata, and Mahāsaṃghika.

7. The three sections of the Tripiṭaka: Sūtra (discourses), Vinaya (code of discipline), and Abhidharma (philosophy/cosmology).

8. The three "inner-tantras" (*nang rgyud*) are Mahāyoga, Anuyoga, and Atiyoga.

9. This is a prayer composed by Mipam, *snga 'gyur bstan pa rgyas pa'i smon lam chos rgyal dgyes pa'i zhal lung*, in *Collected Works*, vol. 27, 685–91.

10. The Boudha stūpa in Kathmandu, Nepal.

11. Mipam's overview (*spyi don*) of the *Madhyamakālaṃkāra* is found in his *Words That Delight Guru Mañjughoṣa: Commentary on the Madhyamakālaṃkāra* (*dbu ma rgyan gyi rnam bshad 'jam byangs bla ma dgyes pa'i zhal lung*), 17–117. English translation in Thomas Doctor, trans., *Speech of Delight: Mipham's Commentary on Śāntarakṣita's* Ornament of the Middle Way, 9–145.

12. The rituals for the three foundations of the Vinaya (*gdul ba'i gzhi gsum*) are: the biweekly ritual of the vows for individual liberation (*gso sbyong*), summer retreat (*dbyar gnas*), and the ritual for summer retreat recess (*dgag dbye*).

13. The five degenerations are: (1) degenerate lifespan, (2) degenerate afflictive emotions, (3) degenerate sentient beings, (4) degenerate time, and (5) degenerate view.

14. The four seals are: (1) all contaminated phenomena are suffering, (2) all conditioned phenomena are impermanent, (3) all phenomena are selfless and empty, and (4) nirvāṇa is peace.

15. The three trainings are: (1) the training in discipline, (2) the training in meditative stabilization, and (3) the training in insight.

16. Atīśa (982–1054), *Bodhipathapradīpa* (*byang chub lam gyi sgron ma*), P.5343, vol. 103. This quote is not in Atīśa's *Bodhipathapradīpa*.

17. "Excluding properties that are not endowed" is a technical phrase that distinguishes what is a necessary (but not sufficient) condition for a defining character to suitably apply to a defined term. It contrasts with "excluding the endowment of other properties" (*gzhan ldan rnam gcod*), which pertains to what is a sufficient condition.

18. See Longchenpa, *White Lotus: Autocommentary of the Precious Wish-Fulfilling Treasury* (*theg pa chen po'i man ngag gi bstan bcos yid bzhin rin po che'i mdzod kyi 'grel pa padma dkar po*), 922.2–926.3.

19. See note 17.

20. Gyurme Dorje and Matthew Kapstein cite this text as a section of the *Heart Essence of Vimalamitra* (*bi ma snying thig*). See Dudjom Rinpoche, *The Nyingma School of Tibetan Buddhism*, 233.

21. Tsongkhapa speaks of these four qualities in *The Great Exposition of the Stages of the Path* (*lam rim chen mo*), 134.

22. *Dhvajāgrasūtra* (*rgyal mtshan dam pa*). P.959, vol. 38, p. 285, 293a.1–293a.2.

23. The five Mahāsaṃmata schools are among the eighteen Vaibhāṣika schools. The five are: the Tāmrāśaṭīyas, the Avanatakas, the Kurukullas, the Bahuśrutīyas, and the Vatsīputryīyas. For more on the eighteen Vaibhāṣika schools, see Jeffrey Hopkins, *Meditation on Emptiness*, 340; 713–19; and Jeffrey Hopkins, *Maps of the Profound*, 210–18.

24. A proponent of a Buddhist philosophy that is not the Middle Way (i.e., Mind-Only, Sautrāntika, and Vaibhāṣika).

25. The two irreducibles are irreducible particles and irreducible moments of consciousness.

26. Kongtrül cites this prophecy in his *Encyclopedia of Knowledge*, 534. See English translation in Elizabeth Callahan, trans., *Treasury of Knowledge: Frameworks of Buddhist Philosophy*, 139. The prophecy is from the *Svapnanirdeśasūtra* (*rmi lam bstan pa'i mdo*), D. vol. 39, 406.1–473.7.

27. They may assert this, but they do not realize the complete selflessness of phenomena.

28. In his *Gateway to Scholarship* (*mkhas pa'i tshul la 'jug pa'i sgo*), Mipam states: "The minimal distinction between a Buddhist and a non-Buddhist is made through whether or not one authentically accepts the source of refuge, the three jewels," 144.

29. Mipam, *Concise Summary of the Philosophies from the Wish-Fulfilling Treasury* (*yid bzhin mdzod kyi grub mtha' bsdus pa*), in *Collected Works*, vol. 21, 439–500.

30. The seven greatnesses of the Mahāyāna, drawn from the *Mahāyāna-sūtrālaṃkāra* XX.59–60, are: (1) great observation, (2) great practice, (3) great wisdom, (4) great diligent endeavor, (5) great skillful means, (6) great authentic accomplishment, and (7) great enlightened activity. See Longchenpa, *White Lotus*, 1054.2–1057.1; see also Mipam, *Concise Summary of the Philosophies from the Wish-Fulfilling Treasury*, 470.6–471.3.

31. The Perfection of Wisdom Sūtras enumerate different numbers of emptiness, such as sixteen, eighteen, and twenty. See note 214.

32. The thirty-seven factors are: (1–4) the four mindfulnesses, (5–8) the four correct exertions, (9–12) the four bases of miraculous power, (13–17) the five powers, (18–22) the five strengths, (23–29) the seven branches of awakening, and (30–37) the noble eightfold path.

33. The six transcendent perfections are: (1) generosity, (2) discipline, (3) patience, (4) diligence, (5) concentration, and (6) insight.

34. Longchenpa, *Precious Wish-Fulfilling Treasury*, 104.3–104.4.

35. The three Sublime Ones are: (1) the Sublime Auditors, (2) the Sublime Self-Realized Ones, and (3) the Sublime bodhisattvas.

36. "Gone Afar" (*ring song*) is the seventh bodhisattva ground.

37. Mipam wrote an important commentary on the Wisdom Chapter of the *Bodhicaryāvatāra* (*spyod 'jug sher 'grel ke ta ka*). Mipam's two rejoinders to criticisms of his commentary on the Wisdom Chapter are: *Light of the Sun* (*brgal lan nyin byed snang ba*) and *Shedding Light on Thusness* (*gzhan gyis brtsad pa'i lan mdor bsdus pa rigs lam rab gsal de nyid snang byed*).

38. The four tantra sets are Action Tantra (*bya rgyud, kriyātantra*), Performance Tantra (*spyod rgyud, caryatantra*), Yoga Tantra (*rnal 'byor rgyud, yogatantra*), and Unexcelled Yoga Tantra (*rnal 'byor bla na med pa'i rgyud, anuttaratantra*). The Nyingma tradition also speaks of six classes of tantras, which include three outer-tantras and three inner-tantras. The outer-tantras are the first three mentioned above and the inner-tantras (Mahāyoga, Anuyoga, and Atiyoga) are subdivisions of the fourth, Unexcelled Yoga Tantra.

39. Mipam, *Beacon of Certainty* (*nges shes sgron me*), 5.

40. This quote, worded in a slightly different way, is found in Mipam, *Beacon of Certainty*, 50.

41. See Mipam, *Overview: Essential Nature of Luminous Clarity*, 437–38; English translation in Dharmachakra Translation Committee, trans., *Luminous Essence*, 41.

42. The full stanza of Sakya Paṇḍita's famous statement reads as follows: "If there were a view superior to the freedom from constructs of the Perfection [Vehicle], then that view would possess constructs; if free from constructs, then there is no difference [in view between Mantra and the Perfection Vehicle]." Sakya Paṇḍita, *Clear Differentiation of the Three Vows* (*sdom gsum rab dbye*), III.255: "*pha rol phyin pa'i spros bral las/ /lhag pa'i lta ba yod na ni/ /lta de spros*

pa can du 'gyur/ /spros bral yin na khyad par med." Published in Jared Douglas Rhoton, trans., *A Clear Differentiation of the Three Codes*, 308.

43. The three seats (*gtan gsum*) in general are the aggregates and constituents (*phung khams*), which are the seats of the male and female Tathāgatas; the faculties and their objects (*dbang yul*), which are the seats of the male and female bodhisattvas; and the body's limbs (*yan lag*), which are the seats of the male and female wrathful deities.

44. See, for instance, Mipam, *Overview: Essential Nature of Luminous Clarity*, 437–43; English translation in Dharmachakra Translation Committee, trans., *Luminous Essence*, 41–45.

45. See Mipam, *Overview: Essential Nature of Luminous Clarity*, 413–14; English translation in Dharmachakra Translation Committee, trans., *Luminous Essence*, 23–24.

46. The "five previous actualities" (*sngon byung dngos lnga*) refer to the manner by which the meaning of suchness has been directly ascertained by the five exalted bodies, five retinues, and five types of speech. The "five subsequent analogies" (*rjes 'jug tshul lnga*) refer to (1) the ocean, (2) a reflection in a mirror, (3) the sun, (4) an echo, and (5) Brahma's melody; these five "reasons" are analogies for the speech of the five exalted bodies (Truth Body, Body of Perfect Rapture, Body of Manifest Awakening, Vajra Body, and Emanation Body). See Lochen Dharmaśrī, *The Lord of Secrets' Words* (*gsang bdag zhal lung*), in *Collected Works*, vol. 7, 424.1–426.5.

47. For instance, Kongtrül (*kong sprul blo gros mtha' yas*, 1813–1899) states that proponents of self-emptiness claim that the only difference in Mantra is the subjectivity, and not the object that is free from conceptual constructs; on the other hand, proponents of other-emptiness claim that there is a difference in the object as well: "Mantra distinguished by the subjectivity, [through] the method of bliss, and not the object, which is the freedom from constructs, is the tradition of self-emptiness. Proponents of other-emptiness assert that the object also is not merely the freedom from constructs, but is endowed with all the supreme aspects, [appearing] like [reflections in a] divination mirror (*pra phab*)." Kongtrül, *Encyclopedia of Knowledge*, 716.

48. Maitreya, *Uttaratantra* I.5.

49. *drang nges lde'u mig*. Unfortunately, this text by Bötrül is apparently no longer extant; it was not published in his *Collected Works*.

50. See note 51 in translator's introduction.

51. See note 52 in translator's introduction.

52. The four covert intentions are: the covert intention of entry (*gzhugs pa ldem por dgongs pa*), the covert intention of the [three] natures (*mtshan nyid ldem por dgongs pa*), the covert intention of an antidote (*gnyen po ldem por dgongs pa*), the covert intention of a transformation (*bsgyur ba ldem por dgongs pa*); the four intentions are those which are: intended for equality (*mnyam pa nyid la dgongs pa*), intended for another meaning (*don gzhan la dgongs pa*), intended for another time (*dus gzhan la dgongs pa*), intended for a person's mind state (*gang zag gi bsam pa la dgongs*). For examples of these, see Jeffrey Hopkins, *Maps of the Profound*, 319–21.

53. Mipam, *Sword of Insight*, v. 73–74, *Collected Works*, vol. 4, 808.4–808.6. See Khenpo Pelden Sherap (*dpal ldan shes rab*, 1941–2010), *Lamp of the Blazing Sun and Moon: A Commentary on [Mipam's] Sword of Insight* (*don rnam nges 'grel pa shes rab ral gri'i 'grel pa shes rab nyi zla 'bar ba'i sgron me*), 142.

54. The *Akṣayamatisūtra* states: "Sūtras that teach an owner where there is no owner for instance, and describe objects with various words [such as] self, sentient being, living being, sustainer, being, person, human being, individual, agent, and experiencer are 'the provisional meaning.' Sūtras that teach the gates of liberation, the emptiness of entities, signlessness, wishlessness, no composition, no arising, no sentient beings, no living beings, no persons, and no owners are 'the definitive meaning.' " P.842, vol. 34, p.64, 156a.4–156a.7.

55. The *Dhāraṇīśvararāja* states: "Noble child, observe this: a person skilled in gemstones, for instance, knowing well the manner of refining gems, takes an unrefined gemstone from the class of valuable jewels. After washing it in a strong astringent fluid, he scrubs it with a black haircloth. However, he does not cease his efforts with just this; after that, he washes it in a strong solution containing mercury and rubs it with wood and wool. However, he does not cease his efforts with just this; after that, he washes it in a great medicinal serum and then rubs it with a fine cloth. Having polished it, the jewel is free from the various defilements and is called a *'vaiḍūrya'* (star-gem). Noble child, likewise a Tathāgata, knowing the constituents of thoroughly impure sentient beings, by means of the disquieting discourse of impermanence, suffering, selflessness, and unpleasantness, makes sentient beings who delight in *saṃsāra* give rise to disillusionment, causing them to enter into the disciplinary doctrine of Sublime Ones. However, a Tathāgata does not cease his efforts by just this; after that, by means of the discourse of emptiness, signlessness, and wishlessness, he causes them to realize the manner of the Tathāgatas. However, a Tathāgata does not cease his efforts by just this; after that, by means of the discourse on the wheel of the irreversible doctrine and the discourse on the complete lack of the threefold conceptualization (*'khor gsum*), he causes those sentient beings to enter the realm of the Tathāgatas. Those sentient beings of various predispositions and natures, having entered equality, realize the suchness of the Tathāgatas; thus, they are known as 'the unexcelled place of offering.' " *Dhāraṇīśvararāja (Tathāgatamahākaruṇānirdeśasūtra)*, P.814, vol. 32, 300–301, 176b.4–177a.3.

56. Lochen Dharmaśrī states: "Although there are a lot of discordant assertions regarding what are the definitive or provisional [meanings] of the middle and last [wheels], since there is no scripture of sūtra that clearly states that the middle [wheel] is the definitive meaning and the last [wheel] is a provisional meaning, and [this] also would contradict the intended meaning of the metaphors of the patient's medicine and learning to read, my tradition asserts that the middle [wheel] is half-definitive and half-provisional, or definitive for the time being, and the last [wheel] itself is the definitive meaning because it is clearly explained in sūtras such as the *Saṃdhinirmocanasūtra*, the *Mahāparinirvāṇasūtra*, and the *Aṅgulimālīyasūtra*." Lochen Dharmaśrī (*lo chen dharmaśrī*, 1654–1717), *Cluster of Supreme Intentions: Commentary on "Ascertaining*

the Three Vows" (*sdom pa gsum rnam par nges pa'i 'grel pa legs bshad ngo mtshar dpag bsam gyi snye ma*), 290.5–291.2. Lochen's text is a commentary on *Ascertaining the Three Vows* (*sdom gsum rnam nges*) written by Ngari Paṇchen (*mnga' ris paṇ chen padma dbang rgyal*, 1487–1542).

57. Mipam states: "The emptiness taught in the middle wheel and the exalted body and wisdom taught in the last wheel should be integrated as a unity of emptiness and appearance. Without dividing or excluding the definitive meaning subject matters of the middle and last wheels, both should be held to be the definitive meaning in the way of just this assertion by the omniscient Longchen Rapjam." Mipam, *Lion's Roar: Exposition of Buddha-Nature*, 586.2–586.4; see also *Mipam on Buddha-Nature*, 164. Nearly the same text is also found in Mipam's *Uttaratantra* commentary compiled by his students, *Words of Mipam: Interlinear Commentary on the Uttaratantra* (*theg pa chen po rgyud bla ma'i bstan bcos kyi mchan 'grel mi pham zhal lung*), in *Collected Works*, vol. 4, 382.1–382.2.

58. The four reliances are: (1) reliance on the doctrine, not individuals, (2) reliance on the meaning, not words, (3) reliance on the definitive meaning, not provisional meanings, and (4) reliance on wisdom, not consciousness.

59. The "Five Treatises of Maitreya" are: (1) *Abhisamayālaṃkāra*, (2) *Mahāyānasūtrālaṃkāra*, (3) *Madhyāntavibhāga*, (4) *Dharmadharmatāvibhāga*, and (5) *Uttaratantra*.

60. Nirgrantha, which Bötrül refers to as the Sky-clad Ones (*nam mkha' gos can*), are also known as "the Nudists" (*gcer bu pa*). The Nirgrantha refers to the Jain tradition. Mipam also references the Nirgrantha in distinguishing Buddha-nature from a mere absence in a citation from the *Mahāparinirvāṇasūtra*. He states: "Merely the aspect of a non-implicative negation (*med dgag*) is not suitable as nirvāṇa, again from the scripture [*Mahāparinirvāṇasūtra*]: " 'Emptiness, emptiness'—at the time you search, you find nothing at all. The Nirgrantha also have 'nothing at all,' but liberation is not like that." Mipam, *Lion's Roar: Exposition of Buddha-Nature*, 573.5–573.6; English translation in Duckworth, *Mipam on Buddha-Nature*, 154.

61. The three gates of liberation are the empty essence, signless cause, and wishless effect.

62. In his autocommentary on the *Madhyamakāvatāra*, Candrakīrti states: "Mahāmati, my Buddha-nature teaching is not similar to the non-Buddhists' declaration of Self. Mahāmati, the Tathāgatas, Arhats, and completely perfect Buddhas teach Buddha-nature as the meaning of the words: emptiness, the authentic limit, nirvāṇa, non-arising, wishlessness, etc. For the sake of immature beings who are frightened by selflessness, they teach by means of Buddha-nature." Candrakīrti, under *Madhyamakāvatāra* VI.95, in *Autocommentary of the Madhyamakāvatāra*, 196. See also D.T. Suzuki, trans., *The Laṅkāvatāra Sūtra*, 68–69; Jeffrey Hopkins, *Meditation on Emptiness*, 615–16.

63. See Mipam, *Shedding Light on Thusness* (*gzhan gyis brtsad pa'i lan mdor bsdus pa rigs lam rab gsal de nyid snang byed*), 298.

64. See Mipam, *Eliminating Doubts* (*dam chos dogs sel*), in *Collected Works*, vol. 13, 394; also published in *dbu ma rgyan rtsa 'grel*, 539–40.

65. See Mipam, *Light of Wisdom: Commentary on the Dharmadharmatāvibhāga (chos dang chos nyid rnam 'byed 'grel pa ye shes snang ba)*, in *Collected Works*, vol. 4 (*pa*), 611.3–613.1; English translation in Jim Scott, trans., *Distinguishing Maitreya's Phenomena and Pure Being*, 59–65.

66. Khenpo Zhenga (*mkhan po gzhan dga'*, 1871–1927), for instance, says that the *Abhisamayālaṃkāra* is a Svātantrika scripture in his *Interlinear Commentaries on the Thirteen Great Scriptures (gzhung chen bcu gsum gyi mchen 'grel)*, vol. 1, 72.4.

67. See Mipam, *Words That Delight Guru Mañjughoṣa*, 68–69; English translation in Doctor, trans., *Speech of Delight*, 75.

68. The eight qualities are: (1) inconceivable, (2) nondual, (3) nonconceptual, (4) pure, (5) clear, (6) antidotal, (7) freed from attachments (cessation), and (8) freeing from attachments (path). From the *Uttaratantra* I.10: "Since it is inconceivable, nondual, nonconceptual, pure, clear, and antidotal, it is freed from attachments and frees from attachment; that with the character of the two truths is the dharma."

69. The eight qualities are: (1) awareness and (2) freedom; which are subdivided into three qualities of awareness: (3) wisdom that knows what is, (4) wisdom that knows whatever there is, and (5) inner wisdom; and three qualities of freedom: (6) freedom from attachment, (7) freedom from obscuration, and (8) unsurpassabilty. See under *Uttaratantra* I.14, Kongtrül, *Roar of the Non-Returning Lion*, 50–51; English translation in Rosemary Fuchs, *Buddha Nature: The Mahayana Uttaratantra Shastra*, 109–10.

70. Maitreya, *Uttaratantra* I.21.

71. The eight qualities are: (1) unconditioned, (2) spontaneously present, (3) not realized by an extrinsic condition; possessing (4) knowledge, (5) love, and (6) powers; and endowed with the twofold benefit of (7) self and (8) other. From the *Uttaratantra* I.5: "The Buddha is unconditioned, spontaneously present, not realized by an extrinsic condition; possessing knowledge, love, and powers; and the twofold benefit."

72. Maitreya, *Uttaratantra* I.21: "In the ultimate meaning, the refuge of beings is solely the Buddha—due to the sage possessing the Truth Body and being the consummated assembly, too."

73. Maitreya, *Uttaratantra* I.21.

74. The three attitudes are as follows: (1) like a shepherd leads all the sheep first, and follows behind, one wishes to bring all beings to become Buddhas before oneself; (2) like a ferryman rides along with his passengers, one wishes to become a Buddha at the same time as everyone else; and (3) like a king, who saves himself first before his subjects, one wishes to first become a Buddha oneself, and then bring others to become Buddhas.

75. Mipam, *Sword of Insight (don rnam par nges pa shes rab ral gri mchan bcas)*, *Collected Works*, vol. 4 (*pa*), 789.3–790.1.

76. *Lalitavistarasūtra* XXV. P.763, vol. 27, p. 238, 211b.6.

77. Mipam, *Difficult Points of Scriptures in General*, 427–710.

78. The five aggregates are: forms, feelings, perceptions, formations, and consciousnesses; and the five Buddha families are: Tathāgata, Vajra, Padma,

Ratna, and Karma. The five elements are: earth, water, fire, wind, and space; and the five goddesses are: Buddhalocanā, Māmakī, Pāṇḍaravāsinī, Samayatārā, and Ākāśadhātvīśvarī.

79. *Guhyagarbhatantra* XI.1. For this quote and its explanation, see Mipam, *Overview: Essential Nature of Luminous Clarity*, 434, 465–66; English translation in Dharmachakra Translation Committee, trans., *Luminous Essence*, 38, 61–62. For the five previous actualities and the five subsequent analogies, see note 46 above.

80. Candrakīrti mentions these four valid cognitions in his *Prasannapadā (tshigs gsal)*, 25b.

81. Candrakīrti, *Madhyamakāvatāra* VI.27.

82. Candrakīrti, *Madhyamakāvatāra* under VI.27, in *Autocommentary of the Madhyamakāvatāra*, 108.

83. *Samādhirājasūtra* IX.23. P.795, vol. 31, p. 283, 29a.1.

84. Candrakīrti, *Madhyamakāvatāra* VI.30.

85. Candrakīrti, *Madhyamakāvatāra* under VI.29, in *Autocommentary of the Madhyamakāvatāra*, 114.

86. The seven treatises on valid cognition are: *Pramāṇavārttika* (*tshad ma rnam 'grel*), *Pramāṇaviniścaya* (*tshad ma rnam nges*), *Nyāyabindu* (*tshad ma rigs thigs*), *Hetubindu* (*gtan tshigs thigs pa*), *Sambandhaparīkṣa* (*'brel ba brtags pa*), *Saṃtānāntarasiddhi* (*rgyud gzhan sgrub pa*), and *Vādanyāyaḥ* (*rtsod pa'i rigs pa*).

87. Nāgārjuna, *Mūlamadhyamakakārikā* XXIV.8.

88. The sixteen aspects of the four truths are as follows: for the truth of suffering, there are the four aspects of (1) impermanence, (2) suffering, (3) emptiness, and (4) selflessness; for the truth of origin, there are the four aspects of (5) cause, (6) origin, (7) complete production, and (8) condition; for the truth of cessation, there are the four aspects of (9) cessation, (10) peace, (11) perfection, and (12) definitive emergence; and for the truth of the path, there are the four aspects of (13) path, (14) suitability, (15) accomplishment, and (16) deliverance.

89. Mipam, *Eliminating Doubts*, 499.

90. The Geluk scholar, Pari Lozang Rapsel, wrote a refutation of Mipam's commentary on the ninth chapter of Śāntideva's *Bodhicaryāvatāra*, called *Ornament of Mañjughoṣa's Viewpoint ('jam dpal dbyangs kyi dgongs rgyan rigs pa'i gzi 'bar gdong lnga'i sgra dbyangs)*, in *Collected Works*, 354–412. Mipam subsequently wrote a rejoinder to his critique. For a study of the issues at stake in the exchange between these two scholars, see Karma Phuntsho, *Mipham's Dialectics and the Debates on Emptiness*.

91. This refers to a statement made by Pari Rapsel in his *Ornament of Mañjughoṣa's Viewpoint*, 387. See also Karma Phuntsho, *Mipham's Dialectics and the Debates on Emptiness*, 156.

92. Mipam, *Shedding Light on Thusness*, 295–96.

93. See Mipam, *Eliminating Doubts*, 499.

94. See Mipam, *Words That Delight Guru Mañjughoṣa*, 55–56; English translation in Doctor, trans., *Speech of Delight*, 57.

95. The "meaning-commentary" is Candrakīrti's *Madhyamakāvatāra;* the "word commentary" is Candrakīrti's *Prasannapadā.*

96. Candrakīrti, *Madhyamakāvatāra* VI.23. In the second verse, the *Madhyamakāvatāra* reads "thusness" (*de nyid*) rather than "ultimate" (*don dam*) as in Bötrül's citation. See *Autocommentary of the Madhyamakāvatāra,* 104. See also Guy Newland, *The Two Truths,* 95.

97. The "Collection of Reasonings" (*rigs tshogs*) refers to six texts of Nāgārjuna: *Prajñāmūlamadhyamakakārikā* (*dbu ma rtsa ba'i shes rab*), *Ratnāvalī* (*rin chen phreng ba*), *Vigrahavyāvartanī* (*rtsod zlog*), *Śūnyatāsaptati* (*stong nyid bdun cu pa*), *Vaidalyaśūtra* (*zhib mo rnam 'thag*), and *Yuktiṣaṣṭikā* (*rigs pa drug cu pa*).

98. See Mipam, *Words That Delight Guru Mañjughoṣa,* 56; English translation in Doctor, trans., *Speech of Delight,* 57.

99. The seven ultimate treasures (*don dam dkor bdun*) are: exalted body (*sku*), exalted speech (*gsung*), exalted mind (*thugs*), qualities (*yon tan*), enlightened activities (*phrin las*), expanse (*dbyings*), and wisdom (*ye shes*).

100. Maitreya, *Uttaratantra* I.155.

101. Maitreya, *Uttaratantra* I.155.

102. Glossing this verse from the *Uttaratantra* I.28, Mipam explains these three reasons—of efficacy, dependency, and the nature of things—to support the existence of Buddha-nature in his *Lion's Roar: Exposition of Buddha-Nature.* See English translation in Duckworth, *Mipam on Buddha-Nature,* 149–67.

103. See Mipam, *Words That Delight Guru Mañjughoṣa,* 56; English translation in Doctor, trans., *Speech of Delight,* 57.

104. Sakya Paṇḍita, *Elegant Sayings of the Sakya* (*sa skya legs bshad*), III.7, 19.

105. It is not possible to define the uncategorized ultimate by stating what it is through inclusion (*yongs gcod*); yet it can be characterized by stating what it is not through exclusion (*rnam gcod*). See Mipam, *Commentary on the Wisdom Chapter of the Bodhicaryāvatāra,* 13.

106. Candrakīrti, *Madhyamakāvatāra* VI.23: "That which is the object of authentic seeing is thusness. . . ."

107. Śāntideva, *Bodhicaryāvatāra* IX.2: "The ultimate is not the domain of mind. . . ."

108. Candrakīrti, *Madhyamakāvatāra* VI.23: ". . . false seeings are relative truths"; Śāntideva, *Bodhicaryāvatāra* IX.2: ". . . the [domain of] mind is relative."

109. Candrakīrti, *Madhyamakāvatāra* VI.36.

110. Candrakīrti, *Madhyamakāvatāra* VI.81.

111. Candrakīrti, *Madhyamakāvatāra* VI.25.

112. I am using two sets of English terms *categorized/nominal* and *uncategorized/actual* to translate the same Tibetan terms here. I do so because Bötrül is showing a difference between the way his tradition represents the uncategorized ultimate (as free from all conceptual constructs) and the way his opponent represents the actual ultimate (as a non-implicative negation). I feel that *uncategorized* is a translation that reflects Bötrül's own representation

of such an ultimate—that is beyond the mind—whereas the quality of being uncategorized (or unschematized) by thought does not represent the way his opponent conceives such an ultimate. Hence, given that I use *uncategorized* to convey the meaning in the distinctive way that is understood in Bötrül's tradition, the context here calls for two terms.

113. See Mipam, *Shedding Light on Thusness*, 303–304.

114. Toh. 3881, *dbu ma, sa*, ff.1–3. The text is also printed in Tibetan and translated into English in Malcolm David Eckel, *Jñānagarbha's Commentary on the Distinction Between the Two Truths*.

115. Mipam, *Commentary on the Wisdom Chapter of the Bodhicaryāvatāra*, 9.

116. Nāgārjuna, *Bodhicittavivaraṇa (byang chub sems gyi rnam par bshad pa)*, P.5470, vol.103, pp. 274, 244b.2.

117. The four faults of each are stated in chapter III of the *Saṃdhinirmocanasūtra*. If the relative and ultimate truths were not different, then (1) ordinary beings would realize the ultimate and attain nirvāṇa just like Sublime Ones, (2) the ultimate would be characterized by the afflictions just like the relative, (3) the relative would be undifferentiated just like the ultimate, and (4) yogis would not seek the ultimate truth because there would be no ultimate other than ordinary beings' perceptions of the relative. If the relative and ultimate truths were different, then (1) realizing the ultimate would not suffice for liberation, (2) the ultimate would not be the universal character of relative things, (3) the ultimate would not be the empty nature of relative things, and (4) affliction and complete purification would be simultaneous within one mind. John Powers, trans., *Wisdom of the Buddha: The Saṃdhinirmocana Mahāyāna Sūtra*, 36–45. See also Donald Lopez, *A Study of Svātantrika*, 213–15.

118. *Saṃdhinirmocanasūtra*, chapter III: "The character of the conditioned realm and the ultimate is a character free from being the same or different; thus, those who conceive [them] as the same or different have entered into an improper view." See John Powers, trans., *Wisdom of the Buddha*, 48–49.

119. The prologue to Nāgārjuna's *Madhyamakakārikā* states: "I pay homage to the best of teachers, the perfectly awakened one who taught dependent arising—the pacification of conceptual constructs—without ceasing or arising, not annihilated nor eternal, neither coming nor going, and neither different nor the same." P.5224, vol. 95, pp. 1, 1a.4–1b.2.

120. See, for instance, Mipam, *Lion's Roar: Exposition of Buddha-Nature*, 585; English translation in Duckworth, *Mipam on Buddha-Nature*, 164.

121. On the four stages of the Middle Way view, see Mipam, *Essential Nature of Luminous Clarity*, 461–62; see also Duckworth, *Mipam on Buddha-Nature*, 40–42.

122. Mipam, *Difficult Points of Scriptures in General*, 427–710.

123. In the famous eighth-century debate at Samyé, Hvashang was the Chinese monk who advocated a sudden path to enlightenment that rejects all analysis and mental engagement. In Tibetan historical accounts, he lost the debate to the Indian scholar, Kamalaśīla.

124. *Prasannapadā* under I.1. See English translation and comments on this passage in David Ruegg, *Two Prolegomena to Madhyamaka Philosophy*, 18–24.

125. The complete verse, from Śāntarakṣita's *Madhyamakālaṃkāra* v. 71, reads: "Since there is no arising, etc., then non-arising, etc., is impossible. . . ." (*skye la sogs pa med pa'i phyir/ skye ba med la sogs mi srid*). Bötrül uses "negate" (*bkag*) in his citation, instead of the negative existential verb (*med*) in the *Madhyamakālaṃkāra*.

126. The complete verse, from Śāntarakṣita's *Madhyamakālaṃkāra* v. 70, reads: "Since it accords with the ultimate meaning, this is called 'ultimate'; [yet] actually, it is free from all assemblages of constructs."

127. *red mda' bar phul pa'i shog dril*. Rendawa (*red mda' ba*, 1349–1412) was one of Tsongkhapa's teachers.

128. The complete verse, from Nāgārjuna's *Madhyamakakārikā* XXV.13, reads: "Entities and nonentities are conditioned; nirvāṇa is unconditioned."

129. Nāgārjuna, *Madhyamakakārikā* XXIV.11.

130. See Candrakīrti, *Madhyamakāvatāra* VI.36 for the three reasonings: (1) ultimate production would not be negated, (2) conventional truth would withstand analysis, and (3) the meditative equipoise of Sublime Ones would be a cause for the destruction of entities.

131. Candrakīrti, *Madhyamakāvatāra* VI.141.

132. See, for instance, Mipam, *Difficult Points of Scriptures in General*, 471, 487, 529.

133. See edition of Changkya's text with Mipam's commentary in Mipam, *[Commentary on Changkya's] "Song of the View" (lta ba'i mgur ma)*, in *Collected Works*, vol. 4 (*pa*), 821–67. For the passage referenced here, see ff. 838.6–839.1; English translation of Changkya's text with Mipam's commentary in Karl Brunnhözl, *Straight from the Heart: Buddhist Pith Instructions*, 409–10.

134. Candrakīrti, *Madhyamakāvatāra* VI.36.

135. Nāgārjuna, *Mūlamadhyamakakārikā* XXIV.14.

136. Five arguments common to Prāsaṅgika and Svātantrika are: (1) the argument of lacking singularity or plurality (*gcig du bral gyi gtan tshigs*), which analyzes the essence (*ngo bo la dpyod pa*), (2) the argument of the diamond shards (*rdo rje gzegs ma'i gtan tshigs*), which analyzes the cause (*rgyu la dpyod pa*), (3) the argument refuting the four alternatives of production (*mu bzhi skye 'gog pa'i gtan tshigs*), which analyzes the effect (*'bras bu la dpyod pa*), (4) the argument refuting the production of what is existent or nonexistent (*yod med skye 'gog pa'i gtan tshigs*), which analyzes both the cause and the effect (*rgyu 'bras gnyis ka la dpyod pa*), and (5) the argument of dependent arising (*rten 'brel gyi gtan tshigs*), which analyzes everything (*thams cad la dpyod pa*). For references to these arguments accepted by both Prāsaṅgika and Svātantrika, see José Cabezón and Geshe Lobsang Dargyay, *Freedom from Extremes*, 213, 331n380.

137. Four arguments said to be "reasons unique to the Prāsaṅgika" are: (1) a consequence expressing contradiction (*'gal ba brjod pa'i thal 'gyur*), (2) a parallel [absurd consequence following] from the same reasoning (*rgyu

mtshan mtshungs pa'i mgo snyoms), (3) [pointing out that evidence is] not established due to the proof not being distinct from what has yet to be proven (*sgrub byed bsgrub bya dang mtshungs pa'i ma grub pa*), and (4) inference that is renowned to others (*gzhan la grags pa'i rjes dpag*). See Kongtrül, *Encyclopedia of Knowledge*, 559.

138. A Tibetan expression of wonderment.

139. "Father and sons" in this context refers to Tsongkhapa (the father) and his two main disciples, Gyeltsapjé and Khedrupjé.

140. This refers to Saraha, as stated by Khenpo Chökhyap.

141. "Heruka" in this context refers to a practitioner of yoga who has generated the view and conduct of Mantra within his or her continuum. This was stated to me by Khenpo Tsültrim Namdak.

142. According to Gö Lotsāwa, the three monks were Mar Śākyamuni (*dmar ban shākyamune*), Yo Gejung (*g.yo dge 'byung*), and Tsang Rapsel (*gtangs rab gsal*). See Gö Lotsāwa (*'gos lo tsā ba gzhon nu dpal*, 1392–1481), *Blue Annals* (*deb ther sngon po*), vol. 1, 89; English translation in George Roerich, trans., *Blue Annals*, 63.

143. Lachen Gongpa Rapsel (*bla chen dgongs pa rab gsal*, 892–975) played an influential role in the transmission of the Vinaya in Tibet. For Lachen Gongpa Rapsel's ordination history referenced here, see Butön (*bu ston rin chen grub*, 1290–1364), *History of Buddhism* (*bde bar gshegs pa'i bstan pa'i gsal byed chos kyi 'byung gnas gsung rab rin po che'i mdzod*), 193–94; English translation in Eugene Obermiller, *The History of Buddhism in India and Tibet*, 203–205.

144. *Laṅkāvatārasūtra*, 265a.

145. *Guhyagarbhatantra* II.2.

146. *Samādhirājasūtra* IX.23. P.795, vol. 31, p. 283, 29a.1.

147. See Mipam, *Light of the Sun* (*brgal lan nyin byed snang ba*), 465–79.

148. See Longchenpa, *Precious Wish-Fulfilling Treasury*, 7.3–8.4.

149. Candrakīrti, *Madhyamakāvatāra* VI.89.

150. The eight examples of illusion are: (1) a dream (*rmi lam*), (2) an echo (*brag ca*), (3) a city of scent-eaters (*dri za'i grong khyer*), (4) an apparition (*mig yor*), (5) a mirage (*smig rgyu*), (6) an illusion (*sgyu ma*), (7) a reflected image (*gzugs brnyan gyi snang ba*), and (8) an emanated city (*sprul pa'i grong khyer*).

151. Longchenpa, *Precious Wish-Fulfilling Treasury*, 8.1–8.2.

152. Longchenpa, *Precious Wish-Fulfilling Treasury*, 8.2–8.4.

153. See Longchenpa, *White Lotus*, 162–65.

154. See Mipam, *Words That Delight Guru Mañjughoṣa*, 208. Here Mipam states that in the end, inference (*rjes dpag*) comes down to direct perception (*mngon sum*), and direct perception to reflexive awareness; hence, reflexive awareness is indispensable when asserting a presentation of valid cognition of confined perception; English translation in Doctor, trans., *Speech of Delight*, 273. In the same text, Mipam states that the universal ground is indispensible when appearances are accepted as mind. See Mipam, *Words That Delight Guru Mañjughoṣa*, 266; English translation in Doctor, trans., *Speech of Delight*, 357.

155. See Mipam, *Commentary on the Wisdom Chapter of the Bodhicaryāvatāra*, 31.

156. Nāgārjuna, *Madhyamakakārikā* XXV.13.

157. Candrakīrti, *Madhyamakāvatāra* VI.39.

158. *Karmaśataka* (*mdo sde las brgya pa*). P.1007, vol. 39.

159. One enumeration of four inconceivable phenomena is as follows: (1) the ripening of karma, (2) the different domains of sentient beings, (3) the liberation of Buddhas, and (4) the completely pure births of bodhisattvas. See the *Dictionary of Internal Knowledge* (*nang rig pa'i tshig mdzod*), ed. Purbu Tsering (*phur bu tshe ring*), 268.

160. Candrakīrti, *Madhyamakāvatāra*, VI.42.

161. See Longchenpa, *White Lotus*, 1166.4–1168.3

162. See Mipam, *Words That Delight Guru Mañjughoṣa*, 69–70; English translation in Doctor, trans., *Speech of Delight*, 77.

163. Candrakīrti, *Madhyamakāvatāra* VI.81.

164. Rather, in his eight unique features of Prāsaṅgika, Tsongkhapa asserts that external objects *exist* as do cognitions.

165. Unfortunately, this text by Bötrül is no longer extant; it is not published in his *Collected Works*.

166. See Mipam, *Lion's Roar: Exposition of Buddha-Nature*, 589.4–591.4; English translation in Duckworth, *Mipam on Buddha-Nature*, 167–68.

167. See Mipam, *Lion's Roar: Exposition of Buddha-Nature*, 591.4–593.4; English translation in Duckworth, *Mipam on Buddha-Nature*, 168–70.

168. See Mipam, *Lion's Roar: Exposition of Buddha-Nature*, 569.6–571.2; 593.4–597.2; English translation in Duckworth, *Mipam on Buddha-Nature*, 151–52; 170–73.

169. In the phrase "Longchenpa, father and son," the "son" of Longchenpa (the father) commonly refers to Jikmé Lingpa (*'jigs med gling pa*, 1729/30–1798). The lord of doctrine at Minling, father and son, apparently refers to Terdak Lingpa (*gter bdag gling pa 'gyur med rdo rje*, 1646–1714) and his student and younger brother, Lochen Dharmaśrī.

170. *Lalitavistarasūtra* XXV. P.763, vol. 27, p. 238, 211b.6.

171. This is a paraphrase of *Uttaratantra* I.47: "According to the progression of impure, impure/pure, and extremely pure, they are called 'sentient beings,' 'bodhisattvas,' and 'Tathāgatas.' "

172. See Mipam, *Lion's Roar: Exposition of Buddha-Nature*, 589.4–591.4; English translation in Duckworth, *Mipam on Buddha-Nature*, 167–68.

173. See Mipam, *Lion's Roar: Exposition of Buddha-Nature*, 591.4–593.4; English translation in Duckworth, *Mipam on Buddha-Nature*, 168–70.

174. In his commentary on the three vows, Lochen Dharmaśrī states: "Regarding the view of what is to be experienced in meditation, according to the explicit teaching of the middle wheel explained in the way of [Nāgārjuna's] 'Collection of Reasonings' (*rigs tshogs*), since the definitive meaning is accepted as a non-implicative negation, meditating on nothing whatsoever is said to be meditation on emptiness, and seeing nothing at all is said to be the realization of thusness. According to the viewpoint of the last wheel explained in the

way of the texts of Maitreya, Asaṅga and [half-]brother [Vasubandhu], as well in Nāgārjuna's 'Collection of Praises' (*bstod tshogs*), meditating on just the wisdom which is free from duality is what is to be experienced, and this also accords with the viewpoint of the profound tantras of Secret Mantra." Lochen Dharmaśrī, *Cluster of Supreme Intentions*, 377.1–377.4.

175. Again in his commentary on the three vows, Lochen Dharmaśrī states: "In the traditions of the Middle Way that ascertain other-emptiness, due to the difference of asserting all objects of knowledge within the three natures or condensing objects of knowledge into the imagined and thoroughly established natures, there are two ways of identifying the subject (*chos can*): (1) in Yogācāra texts, the empty-ground is the dependent nature, the imagined nature is the object of negation, and the emptiness of the imagined nature in the dependent nature is the thoroughly established nature; (2) in texts such as the *Uttaratantra*, suchness, the thoroughly established nature, is empty of the imagined nature. Therefore, in the essence of the thoroughly established nature—which is the ultimate expanse and the suchness of mind—there are no defilements to remove, nor previously absent qualities to newly establish, because it is primordially pure by nature and has qualities that are spontaneously present." Lochen Dharmaśrī, *Cluster of Supreme Intentions*, 374.1–374.5.

176. Maitreya, *Uttaratantra* I.155.

177. Lochen Dharmaśrī, *The Lord of Secrets' Words* (*gsang bdag zhal lung*), *Collected Works*, vol. 7.

178. In a text summarizing the four philosophies, Getsé Paṇchen (*dge rtse paṇ chen, 'gyur med tshe dbang mchog grub*, 1761–1829) says that the viewpoint free from assertions that is stated by Prāsaṅgikas accords with the essence of primordial purity's mode of abiding. He goes on to say that the aspect of spontaneous presence lies in the viewpoint of the last wheel and the doctrines of Maitreya. Getsé Paṇchen, *Elucidating the Definitive Meaning Viewpoint: A Short Explanation of the Four Great Philosophies* (*grub mtha' chen po bzhi'i rnam par gzhag pa mdo tsam phye ba nges don dgongs pa gsal byed*), *Collected Works*, vol. 1, 70.7–71.2.

179. This is a reference to the ten powers of a Buddha, which are: (1) the power of knowing what is and is not correct (*gnas dang gnas ma yin*), (2) the power of knowing the ripenings of karma, (3) the power of knowing various inclinations (*mos pa*), (4) the power of knowing thorough affliction and complete purification, (5) the power of knowing faculties that are supreme and those that are not, (6) the power of knowing the path of all transmigrations (*thams cad 'gro ba'i lam*), (7) the power of knowing various dispositions (*khams sna tshogs*), (8) the power of remembering previous existences (*sngon gyi gnas*), (9) the power of knowing death, transference, and birth, and (10) the power of knowing the exhaustion of contamination (*zag pa*)." *The Dictionary of Internal Knowledge* (*nang rig pa'i tshig mdzod*), ed. Purbu Tsering, 671.

180. This refers to the process of determining the validity of a scripture. The three analyses are: (1) that the demonstration of what is evident (*mngon gyur*) is not invalidated by direct perception (*mngon sum*), (2) that the

demonstration of what is hidden (*lkog gyur*) is not invalidated by inference (*rjes dpag*), and (3) that the demonstration of what is extremely hidden (*shin tu lkog gyur*) is not contradicted (internally) by previous or later statements.

181. *lta grub chen mo* apparently refers to Changkya Rolpé Dorjé's *Presentation of Philosophical Systems*.

182. Maitreya, *Uttaratantra* V.14.

183. See *Saṃdhinirmocanasūtra*, chapter IX, where the twenty-two thorough stupidities (*kun tu rmongs ba*) and eleven negative states are mentioned. See John Powers, trans., *Wisdom of the Buddha*, 228–33.

184. Candrakīrti, *Madhyamakāvatāra* VIII.2.

185. See Mipam, *Words That Delight Guru Mañjughoṣa*, 424–25; English translation in Doctor, trans., *Speech of Delight*, 587–89.

186. Maitreya, *Uttaratantra* V.14.

187. See Maitreya, *Madhyāntavibhāga* II.17; English translation in Dharmachakra Translation Committee, trans., *Middle Beyond Extremes: Maitreya's Madhyāntavibhāga with Commentaries by Khenpo Shenga and Ju Mipham*, 67.

188. For more on these two types of concepts, see José Cabezón and Geshe Lobsang Dargyay, *Freedom from Extremes*, 315n239, 316nn242–3.

189. Maitreya, *Mahāyānasūtrālaṃkāra* XXI.37: "Due to being unperturbed by the two perceptions, [the eighth bodhisattva ground] is called 'immovable.' " Mipam explains the two perceptions as (1) the perceptions of signs up to the sixth ground, and (2) the effortful signless perception on the seventh ground. See Mipam, *A Feast on the Nectar of the Supreme Vehicle: Commentary on the Mahāyānasūtrālaṃkāra* (*theg pa chen po mdo sde'i rgyan gyi dgongs don rnam par bshad pa theg mchog bdud rtsi'i dga' ston*), in *Collected Works*, vol. 2 (*a*), 745.2–745.3.

190. Candrakīrti, *Madhyamakāvatāra* I.16.

191. See Mipam, *Commentary on the Wisdom Chapter of the Bodhicaryāvatāra*, 55.

192. See Mipam, *Words That Delight Guru Mañjughoṣa*, 427; English translation in Doctor, trans., *Speech of Delight*, 592–93.

193. For the eight qualities of awareness and freedom, see note 69 above.

194. For the distinctive features of the Mahāyāna Path of Joining (*sbyor lam*), see Bötrül, *Words of Maitreya*, 42–47.

195. Within the "eight topics of the Perfection of Wisdom" (*sher phyin dngos po brgyad*), "peaking" is one of "the four joinings of practice" (*mnyam su len pa'i sbyor ba gzhi*): (1) joining with all the clear and perfect aspects (*rnam kun mngon rdzogs sbyor ba*), (2) peaking (*rtse mor sbyor ba*), (3) sequential joining (*mthar gyis pa'i sbyor ba*), and (4) instantaneous joining (*skad cig ma'i sbyor ba*).

196. For the distinctive features of the uninterrupted Path of Seeing, see Bötrül, *Words of Maitreya*, 232–37.

197. The great of the great discards is abandoned on the second ground, the middling of the great on the third ground, the lesser of the great on the fourth ground, the great of the middling on the fifth ground, the middling of

the middling on the sixth ground, the lesser of the middling on the seventh ground, the great of the lesser on the eight ground, the middling of the lesser on the ninth ground, and the lesser of the lesser on the tenth ground. For references regarding these nine discards of the nine bodhisattva grounds, see José Cabezón and Geshe Lobsang Dargyay, *Freedom from Extremes*, 321n288.

198. Maitreya, *Abhisamayālaṃkāra*, 10b. For Bötrül's comments on these lines, see Bötrül, *Words of Maitreya*, 251–52.

199. *Śrīmālādevīsiṃhanādasūtra*, P.760.48.

200. Śāntideva, *Bodhicaryāvatāra* IX.54.

201. That is, the object, or domain (*spyod yul*), is expressed as if it were distinct from the subject, the wisdom of reflexive awareness (*so so rang rig ye shes*), but it is not.

202. Mipam states in *Light of the Sun*, 544: "The categorized ultimate is in the context of a novice progressively engaging in emptiness from merely a conceptual perspective. As such, it cannot roam in the territory of a mind like the nonconceptual meditative wisdom of a Sublime One, for which duality has subsided, like a beggar that has no power to sit on the universal emperor's throne."

203. The full quote, which Mipam attributes to Rāhulabhadra's *Praise to the Mother*, is: "Unspeakable, inconceivable, and inexpressible—the transcendent perfection of wisdom—I pay homage to the mother of the Victorious Ones of the three times, the domain of the wisdom of reflexive awareness that is unborn and unceasing, with the nature of space." See Mipam, *Light of the Sun*, 547.

204. Nāgārjuna, *Madhyamakakārikā* XVIII.7.

205. Śāntideva, *Bodhicaryāvatāra* IX.2.

206. Maitreya, *Abhisamayālaṃkāra*, 6a. For Bötrül's comments on these lines, see Bötrül, *Words of Maitreya*, 135–36.

207. Candrakīrti, *Madhyamakāvatāra* VI.23. The wording here deviates slightly from Candrakīrti's statement: "That which is the object of authentic seeing is *thusness*." Bötrül says "ultimate" where Candrakīrti said "thusness." Candrakīrti, *Autocommentary of the Madhyamakāvatāra*, 104.

208. Maitreya, *Dharmadharmatāvibhāga* v. 42.

209. See, for instance, Mipam, *Shedding Light on Thusness*, 293–94.

210. Maitreya, *Abhisamayālaṃkāra*, 6a.

211. Maitreya, *Abhisamayālaṃkāra*, 6a. For Bötrül's comments on this stanza, see Bötrül, *Words of Maitreya*, 135–36.

212. Nāgārjuna, *Ratnāvalī*, III.12.

213. The "space-treasury meditative stabilization" (*nam mkha' mdzod kyi ting nge 'dzin*) is the ability to make whatever you want manifest out of space. For more on this, see Mipam, *A Feast on the Nectar of the Supreme Vehicle*, 166.4–166.5

214. Sixteen types of emptiness are found in the Perfection of Wisdom Sūtras, referenced in the *Madhyāntavibhāga*. The sixteen are: (1) the emptiness of the internal, (2) the emptiness of the external, (3) the emptiness of the external and internal, (4) the emptiness of the great, (5) the emptiness of emptiness,

(6) the emptiness of the ultimate, (7) the emptiness of the conditioned, (8) the emptiness of the unconditioned, (9) the emptiness of the limitless, (10) the emptiness of the beginningless and endless, (11) the emptiness of the non-discarded, (12) the emptiness of intrinsic nature, (13) the emptiness of own characteristics, (14) the emptiness of all phenomena, (15) the emptiness of nonentities, and (16) the emptiness that is the nature of nonentities. There is a variation in the enumeration of sixteen emptinesses cited by Candrakīrti in *Madhyamakāvatāra* VI.180–223; see *Autocommentary of the Madhyamakāvatāra*, 301–36. Candrakīrti cites "the emptiness of the unobserved" (*mi dmigs pa stong pa nyid*) for the fifteenth instead of "the emptiness of nonentities" as in the *Madhyāntavibhāga*. Although Candrakīrti uses the same term as the *Madhyāntavibhāga* for the sixteenth, "the emptiness that is the nature of nonentities," a better translation to reflect his explanation of it would be "the emptiness of the nature of nonentities." These two interpretations of the sixteenth, reflected in the translations as "the emptiness *of* . . ." (Candrakīrti) or "the emptiness *that is* . . ." (*Madhyāntavibhāga*), reveal the crucial distinction between emptiness interpreted as a quality (in the former) or a substrate (in the latter); the distinction here prefigures the "self-emptiness versus other-emptiness" controversy in Tibet.

215. The sequence of the nature of nonentities (*dngos med ngo bo nyid kyi mthar gyis pa*) is that which perfects the accumulations in meditative equipoise without appearance. On the sequence of the nature of nonentities, see Bötrül, *Words of Maitreya*, 258.

216. A Self-Realized One realizes the selflessness of persons, but only half of the selflessness of phenomena (the emptiness of objects, not of subjects). This was stated to me by Khenpo Tsültrim Namdak.

217. The four gates of retention (*gzungs kyi sgo bzhi*) are: (1) patient retention (*bzod pa'i gzungs*), (2) mantra retention (*sngags kyi gzungs*), (3) word retention (*tshig gi gzungs*), and (4) meaning retention (*don gyi gzungs*).

218. The eight great treasuries of courageous eloquence (*spobs pa'i gter chen brgyad*) are: (1) the treasury of memory (*dran pa'i gter*), (2) the treasury of intelligence (*blo gros kyi gter*), (3) the treasury of realization (*rtogs pa'i gter*), (4) the treasury of retention (*gzungs kyi gter*), (5) the treasury of courage (*spobs pa'i gter*), (6) the treasury of doctrine (*chos kyi gter*), (7) the treasury of the mind of awakening (*byang chub sems kyi gter*), and (8) the treasury of accomplishment (*sgrub pa'i gter*).

219. For a discussion of the thorough trainings (*yongs sbyong*) on the bodhisattva grounds, see Bötrül, *Words of Maitreya*, 67–86.

220. Citing Könchok Jikmé Wangpo (*dkon mchog 'jigs med dbang po*, 1728–1791), Jeffrey Hopkins enumerates the twelve hundred qualities of the bodhisattva grounds as follows: "The twelve sets of a hundred qualities during one instant on the first ground after a Bodhisattva has risen from meditative equipoise are: (1) seeing a hundred Buddhas in one instant, (2) receiving the blessings of a hundred Buddhas, (3) going to a hundred Buddha Lands, (4) illuminating a hundred lands, (5) vibrating a hundred worldly realms, (6) living for a hundred aeons, (7) seeing with true wisdom the past

and future of a hundred aeons, (8) entering into and rising from a hundred meditative stabilizations, (9) opening a hundred different doors of doctrine, (10) ripening a hundred sentient beings, (11) emanating a hundred versions of one's own body, (12) surrounding each of the hundred bodies with a hundred Bodhisattvas."

"The number increases with each ground:

1st 100

2nd 1000

3rd 100,000

4th 100 ten million

5th 1000 ten million

6th 100,000 ten million

7th 100,000 ten trillion

8th a number equal to the particles of a billion worlds

9th a number equal to the particles in ten million billion worlds

10th a number equal to the particles of an inexpressible number of an inexpressible number of Buddha Lands."

Jeffrey Hopkins, *Maps of the Profound*, 975–76.

221. For a discussion of the 173 features, see Bötrül, *Words of Maitreya*, 146–59.

222. Vasubandhu, *Abhidharmakośa*, 23b.

223. Candrakīrti, *Madhyamakāvatāra* I.16.

224. Maitreya, *Mahāyānasūtrālaṃkāra* V.8.

225. The four Sublime Ones are: (1) the Sublime Auditors, (2) the Sublime Self-Realized Ones, (3) the Sublime bodhisattvas, and (4) the Sublime Buddhas.

226. Āryadeva, *Catuḥśataka* XII.13.

227. Śāntideva, *Bodhicaryāvatāra* IX.44.

228. Śāntideva, *Bodhicaryāvatāra* IX.40.

229. Knowledge of the distant ground is a clear realization that is lacking the distinctive method. For more on knowledge of the distant ground, see Bötrül, *Words of Maitreya*, 131–32.

230. Nāgārjuna, *Ratnāvalī* III.86.

231. Nāgārjuna, *Lokātītastava* v. 27.

232. Āryadeva, *Catuḥśataka* VIII.15.

233. Śāntideva, *Bodhicaryāvatāra* IX.45.

234. Candrakīrti, *Madhyamakāvatāra* VI.179.

235. The whole verse reads: "Forms are like a mass of foam, feelings are like bubbles, perceptions resemble mirages, formations are like the trunks of banana trees, consciousnesses resemble magical illusions." See *Saṃyutta Nikāya III*, ed. Leon Feer, 141–42. Reference cited from Donald Lopez, *A Study of Svātantrika*, 451n4.

236. The three knowledges are the first three among the "eight topics of the Perfection of Wisdom" (*sher phyin dngos po brgyad*): (1) knowledge of the ground (*gzhi shes*), (2) knowledge of the path (*lam shes*), and (3) omniscience (*rnam mkhyen*).

237. Citing the Perfection of Wisdom Sūtras, Candrakīrti enumerates twenty emptinesses in *Madhyamakāvatāra* VI.180–223. In addition to the enumeration of sixteen emptinesses (see note 214 above), there are four, which summarize the sixteen: (1) emptiness of entity, (2) emptiness of nonentity, (3) emptiness of nature, and (4) emptiness of another entity. See also Edward Conze, trans., *The Large Sutra on Perfect Wisdom*, 144–48.

238. There are two superimpositions, of existence and nonexistence, for each of the sixteen aspects of the four noble truths (see note 88).

239. For the distinctions of the Mahāyāna Path of Joining, see Bötrül, *Words of Maitreya*, 42–47.

240. For a discussion of the greatness of the Mahāyāna knowledge of the path, see Bötrül, *Words of Maitreya*, 106–107.

241. For a discussion of the knowledge of the ground, see Bötrül, *Words of Maitreya*, 128–46.

242. For a discussion of the sixteen signs of the knowledges of forbearance (*bzod shes*), see Bötrül, *Words of Maitreya*, 198–201.

243. *mdo sde sa bcu pa*. Toh. 44, *phal chen, kha,* chapter XXXI. P.761, *li*.

244. On this, Candrakīrti's autocommentary on the *Madhyamakāvatāra* states under I.8: "Since the bodhisattvas on the seventh ground abide in the greatness of wisdom, they go far beyond the Auditors and the Self-Realized Ones." *Autocommentary of the Madhyamakāvatāra*, 19.

245. Candrakīrti, *Madhyamakāvatāra* VIII.2. Bötrül cites the text using the word "qualities" (*yon tan*) where the *Madhyamakāvatāra* states "endowments" (*'byor ba*).

246. Candrakīrti, autocommentary under *Madhyamakāvatāra* VII.1, in *Autocommentary of the Madhyamakāvatāra*, 340.

247. The three practices are: perfecting (*rdzogs*), ripening (*smin*), and training (*sbyangs*).

248. Candrakīrti, autocommentary under *Madhyamakāvatāra* VIII.2, in *Autocommentary of the Madhyamakāvatāra*, 345. Bötrül adds the gloss "How is that?" (*ji ltar na*) in his citation.

249. Nāgārjuna, *Ratnāvalī*, III.12.

250. *Vajracchedikā* (*rdo rje gcod pa*), P.739, vol. 21, p. 255, 74a.4–74a.5. Bötrul cites a slightly modified version of this passage.

251. For the sixty qualities of the Buddha's speech, see Mipam, *Gateway to Scholarship*, 330–34; English translation with Tibetan edition in Erik Pema Kunzang, trans., *Gateway to Knowledge*, vol. III, 246–49.

252. The eighteen unshared qualities are enumerated as follows. There are six non-endowments (*mi mnga' ba drug*): (1) bodily delusion (*sku la 'khrul ba*), (2) cacophonous speech (*gsung la ca co*), (3) forgetful mind (*thugs la dran pa nyams pa*), (4) non-meditative equipoise (*mnyam par ma bzhag pa*), (5) attitude of separatedness (*tha dad pa'i 'du shes*), and (6) undiscerning indifference (*so sor ma brtags pa'i btang snyoms*); there are six endowments (*mnga' ba drug*): (7) aspiration (*'dun pa*), (8) diligence (*brtson 'grus*), (9) mindfulness (*dran pa*), (10) meditative stabilization (*ting nge 'dzin*), (11) insight (*shes rab*), and (12) freedom (*rnam par 'grol ba*); wisdom precedes and follows after the activities

of the (13) body, (14) speech, and (15) mind; and wisdom is not attached to, nor obstructed by, events of the (16) past, (17) future, and (18) present. See also Mipam, *Gateway to Scholarship*, 318–20; English translation with Tibetan edition in Erik Pema Kunzang, trans., *Gateway to Knowledge* vol. III, 236–37.

253. Dharmakīrti, *Pramāṇavārttika* II.8.

254. The twelve hundred qualities of the transformed faculties can be found in the *Mahāyānasūtrālaṃkāra* X.41. Mipam explains these twelve hundred qualities—how in the six directions, each of the five sense faculties can perceive the objects of the other four sense faculties in ten directions (6 x 5 x 4 x 10 = 1,200)—in his commentary on the *Mahāyānasūtrālaṃkāra*: "By dividing into the six directions, and through the five objects divided again into the ten directions, it is as follows—as illustrated by the eye: through apprehending sounds, scents, tastes, and textures, the eye has two hundred forty qualities—seeing forms is not counted because it is not a special quality. When adding together all five [faculties], there are one thousand two hundred." Mipam, *A Feast on the Nectar of the Supreme Vehicle,* 164.1–164.2.

255. Dongak Tenpé Nyima (*mdo sngags bstan pa'i nyi ma*) is one of Bötrül's names.

256. The seven qualities of high birth (*mtho ris yon tan bdun*) are: (1) long life, (2) good health, (3) beauty, (4) good fortune, (5) high class, (6) great wealth, and (7) great intelligence. Mipam, *Gateway to Scholarship,* 176.

257. The three types of beings are: lesser beings (who seek their happiness in *saṃsāra*), mediocre beings (who seek their personal liberation), and great beings (who seek Buddhahood for everyone).

258. The four modes of birth are: (1) birth from an egg, (2) birth from a womb, (3) birth from warmth, and (4) miraculous birth.

259. The Fifth Dzokchen Rinpoché, Tupten Chödor (*thub bstan chos kyi rdo rje,* 1872–1935).

Bibliography

(D.) *sde dge mtshal par bka' 'gyur: a facsimile edition of the 18th century redaction of Situ chos kyi 'byung gnas prepared under the direction of H.H. the 16th rgyal dbang karma pa.* Delhi, India: Delhi Karmapae Chodhey Gyalwae Sungrab Partun Khang, 1977.

(P.) The Tibetan Tripitika, *Peking edition*. Edited by Daitetz T. Suzuki. Tokyo, Japan: Tibetan Tripitika Research Institute, 1957.

(Toh.) *A Catalogue of the Tohoku University Collection of Tibetan Works on Buddhism*. Edited by Prof. Yensho Kanakura et al. Sendai, Japan, 1953.

Translated Word (*bka' 'gyur*):

Akṣayamatisūtra (blo gros mi zad pas bstan pa). P.842, vol. 34.

Aṣṭasāhasrikāprajñāpāramitā (shes rab gyi pha rol tu phyin pa brgyad stong pa). P.734, vol. 21; D.10, vol. 33.

Dhāraṇīśvararāja (gzungs kyi dbang phyug rgyal pos zhus pa'i mdo)/Tathāgatamahākaruṇānirdeśasūtra (de bzhin gshegs pa'i snying rje chen po nges par bstan pa'i mdo). P.814, vol. 32.

Dhvajāgrasūtra (rgyal mtshan dam pa). P.959, vol. 38.

Lalitavistarasūtra (rgya cher rol pa). P.763, vol. 27.

Laṅkāvatārasūtra (lang kar gshegs pa'i mdo). P.775, vol. 29. Asian Classics Input Project, Release IV, KL0107.

Samādhirājasūtra (ting nge 'dzin gyi rgyal po'i mdo). P.795, vols. 31–32.

Saṃdhinirmocanasūtra (dgongs pa nges 'grel). P.774, vol. 29.

Śrīmālādevīsiṃhanādasūtra (dpal phreng gi mdo). P.760.48.

Svapnanirdeśasūtra (rmi lam bstan pa'i mdo). D. vol. 39.

Other Tibetan Sources

Āryadeva. *Catuḥśataka* (*bzhi brgya pa*). P.5246, vol. 95.

Atīśa. *Bodhipathapradīpa* (*byang chub lam gyi sgron ma*). P.5343, vol. 103.

Bötrül (*bod sprul mdo sngags bstan pa'i nyi ma*, 1898–1959). *Collected Works* (*bod sprul mdo sngags bstan pa'i nyi ma'i gsung 'bum*). 3 vols. Sichuan, China: Nationalities Press, 2004.

———. *Distinguishing the Views and Philosophies: A Lamp of Essential Points* (*lta grub shan 'byed gnad kyi sgron me*). *Collected Works*, vol. 1, 1–51; also in *lta grub shan 'byed gnad kyi sgron me'i rtsa 'grel*. Sichuan, China: Nationalities Press, 1996; also in edition published by Mewa Khenpo Tupten, 1981?; also in *nges shes sgron med / lta grub shan 'byed rtsa 'grel*. Published in series: *dpal snga 'gyur rnying ma'i gzhung lugs chen mo'i skor*. Berkeley, Calif.: Dharma Publishing, 2004; also in *lta grub shan 'byed gnyad kyi sgron me*. Varanasi, India: Tarthang Tulku, 1963.

———. *The Fast Path to Great Bliss: An Instruction Manual on the Prayer for the Pure Field of Sukhāvatī* (*rnam dag bde chen zhing smon gyi khrid yig bde chen myur lam*). *Collected Works*, vol. 3, 232–84. Sichuan, China: Nationalities Press, 2004.

———. *Ornament of Master Nāgārjuna's Viewpoint* (*klu dbang dgongs rgyan*). *Collected Works*, vol. 3, 3–229. Sichuan, China: Nationalities Press, 2004.

———. *Rousing Swift Blessings: A Guru Yoga for the Glorious Teacher Rigzin Chödrak* (*dpal ldan bla ma chos kyi grags pa'i bla ma'i rnal 'byor byin rlabs myur 'jug*). *Collected Works*, vol. 3, 297–300. Sichuan, China: Nationalities Press, 2004.

———. *Ornament of Mañjughoṣa's Viewpoint: An Explanation of the Words and Meanings of "Distinguishing the Views and Philosophies: A Lamp of Essential Points"* (*lta grub shan 'byed gnad kyi sgron me'i tshig don rnam bshad 'jam dbyangs dgongs rgyan*). *Collected Works*, vol. 1, 53–259; the same title is also published in Varanasi, India: Nyingma Students' Welfare Committee, 2006.

———. *Notes on the Essential Points of [Mipam's] Exposition [of Buddha-Nature]* (*stong thun gnad kyi zin thun*). *Collected Works*, vol. 1, 261–74. Sichuan, China: Nationalities Press, 2004.

———. *Words of Maitreya: An Explanation of the Meaning of the Words of the Abhisamayālaṃkāra* (*sher phyin mngon par rtogs pa'i rgyan gyi tshig don rnam par bshad pa ma pham zhal lung*). *Collected Works*, vol. 2. Sichuan, China: Nationalities Press, 2004.

Butön (*bu ston rin chen grub*, 1290–1364). *History of Buddhism* (*bde bar gshegs pa'i bstan pa'i gsal byed chos kyi 'byung gnas gsung rab rin po che'i mdzod*). Qinghai, China: Nationalities Press, 1988.

Candrakīrti. *Autocommentary of the Madhyamakāvatāra* (*dbu ma la 'jug pa'i rang 'grel*). P.5263, vol. 98; also in *dbu ma la 'jug pa'i rang 'grel*. Sarnath, India: Sakya Students' Union, 1999.

———. *Madhyamakāvatāra* (*dbu ma la 'jug pa*). P.5261, P.5262, vol. 98.

———. *Prasannapadā* (*tshig gsal*). P.5260, vol. 98. Asian Classics Input Project, Release IV, TD3860.

Chandra, Lokesh. *Tibetan-Sanskrit Dictionary*. Delhi, India: International Academy of Indian Culture, 2000/1961.

Changkya Rolpé Dorjé (*lcang skya rol pa'i rdo rje*, 1717–1786). *Presentation of Philosophical Systems* (*grub pa'i mtha' rnam par bzhag pa gsal bar bshad pa thub bstan lhun po'i mdzes rgyan*). Qinghai, China: Nationalities Press, 1998/1989.

Dharmakīrti. *Pramāṇavarttika* (*tshad ma rnam 'grel*). P.5709, vol. 130.

Dölpopa (*dol po pa shes rab rgyal mtshan*, 1292–1361). *Granting Request* (*zhu don gnang ba*). *Collected Works* (*'dzam thang* ed.), vol. 6, 284–86.

Drakar Trülku (*brag dkar dpal ldan bstan 'dzin snyan grags*, 1866–1928). *Profound Discourse* (*'jam dbyangs rnam rgyal gyi 'dod tshul la klan ka bgyis pa zab mo'i gtam*). *Collected Works* (Chengdu ed.), vol. 12, 433–48.

Getsé Paṇchen (*dge rtse paṇ chen, 'gyur med tshe dbang mchog grub*, 1761–1829). *Elucidating the Definitive Meaning Viewpoint: A Short Explanation of the Four Great Philosophies* (*grub mtha' chen po bzhi'i rnam par gzhag pa mdo tsam phye ba nges don dgongs pa gsal byed*). *Collected Works* (Sichuan ed.), vol. 1, 13–74.

Gö Lotsāwa (*'gos lo tsā ba gzhon nu dpal*, 1392–1481). *Blue Annals* (*deb ther sngon po*) vols. 1–2. Varanasi, India: Vajra Vidhya Institute, 2003.

Gorampa (*go rams pa bsod nams seng ge*, 1429–1489). *Completely Elucidating the Definitive Meaning* (*rgyal ba thams cad kyi thugs kyi dgongs pa zab mo dbu ma'i de kho na nyid spyi'i ngag gis ston pa nges don rab gsal*). *Collected Works*, vol. 5, 1–415. Dehra Dun, India: Sakya College, 1979.

———. *Distinguishing the Views* (*lta ba'i shan 'byed*). Sarnath, India: Sakya Students' Union, 1988.

———. *Open Treasury of the Profound Hidden Meaning* (*shes rab kyi pha rol tu phyin pa'i man ngag gi bstan bcos mngon rtogs rgyan gyi gzhung snga phyi'i 'brel dang dka' ba'i gnas la dbyad pa spas don zab mo gter gyi kha 'byed*). *Collected Works*, vol. 7, 1–453. Dehra Dun, India: Sakya College, 1979.

Gyeltsapjé (*rgyal tshab rje dar ma rin chen*, 1364–1432). *Commentary on the Uttaratantra* (*theg pa chen po rgyud bla ma'i ṭīka*). *Collected Works* (*lha sa* ed.), vol. 3. Asian Classics Input Project, Release IV, S5434.

———. *Gateway to the Bodhisattvas* (*rgyal sras 'jug sngogs*). Published in *spyod 'jug rtsa 'grel*. Qinghai, China: Nationalities Press, 2006.

Jamyang Zhepa (*'jam dbyangs bshad pa ngag dbang brtson 'grus*, 1648–1722). *Philosophical Systems: Lion's Song Abandoning Delusion* (*grub mtha' rnam par bzhag pa 'khrul spong gdong lnga'i sgra dbyangs kun mkhyen lam bzang gsal ba'i rin chen sgron me*). Gansu, China: Nationalities Press, 1994.

Khedrupjé (*mkhas grub rje dge legs dpal bzang*, 1385–1438). *rgyud sde spyi'i rnam par bzhag pa rgyas par bshad pa*. Published in Ferdinand Lessing and Alex Wayman, trans., *Mkhas grub rje's Fundamentals of the Buddhist Tantras*. The Hague, The Netherlands: Mouton, 1968.

Khenpo Pelden Sherap (*dpal ldan shes rab*, 1941–2010). *Lamp of the Blazing Sun and Moon: A Commentary on [Mipam's] Sword of Insight* (*don rnam nges 'grel pa shes rab ral gri'i 'grel pa shes rab nyi zla 'bar ba'i sgron me*). Varanasi, India: Nyingmapa Students' Welfare Committee, 2000.

Khenpo Petsé (*padma tshe dbang lhun grub*, 1931–2002). *A Short Biography of Bötrül* (*bod sprul sku'i rnam thar nyung bsdus*). Published in *lta grub shan 'byed rtsa 'grel*. Sichuan, China: Nationalities Press, 1996.

Khenpo Zhenga (*mkhan po gzhan dga'*, 1871–1927). *Interlinear Commentaries on the Thirteen Great Scriptures* (*gzhung chen bcu gsum gyi mchen 'grel*). Dehra Dun, India: D. G. Khocchen Tulku, 1978.

Kongtrül (*kong sprul blo gros mtha' yas*, 1813–1899). *Encyclopedia of Knowledge* (*shes bya kun khyab*). Beijing, China: Nationalities Press, 2002.

———. *Roar of the Non-Returning Lion: Commentary on the Uttaratantra* (*theg pa chen po rgyud bla ma'i bstan bcos snying po'i don mngon sum lam gyi bshad srol dang sbyar ba'i rnam par 'grel pa phyir mi ldog pa seng ge'i nga ro*). Varanasi, India: Kagyud Relief & Protection Committee, 2002/1999.

krang dbyi sun, ed. *Tibetan-Chinese Dictionary* (*bod rgya tshig mdzod chen mo*). Beijing, China: Nationalities Press, 1998/1993.

Lochen Dharmaśrī (*lo chen dharmaśrī*, 1654–1717). *Cluster of Supreme Intentions: Commentary on "Ascertaining the Three Vows"* (*sdom pa gsum rnam par nges pa'i 'grel pa legs bshad ngo mtshar dpag bsam gyi snye ma*). Bylakuppe, India: Ngagyur Nyingma Institute, n.d.

———. *The Lord of Secrets' Words* (*gsang bdag zhal lung*). *Collected Works*, vol. 7. Dehra Dun, India: D. G. Khocchen Tulku, 1977.

Longchenpa (*klong chen rab 'byams*, 1308–1364). *Great Chariot: Autocommentary of Resting in the Nature of Mind* (*sems nyid ngal so'i 'grel pa shing rta chen po*). Published in *rdzog pa chen po ngal gso skor gsum dang rang grol skor gsum* (reproduction of *a 'dzom* xylographic edition). Gangtok, India, 1999.

———. *Precious Treasury of Philosophies* (*theg pa mtha' dag gi don gsal bar byed pa grub pa'i mtha' rin po che'i mdzod*). Published in *Seven Treasuries* (*mdzod bdun*), vol. 2.

———. *Precious Wish-Fulfilling Treasury* (*theg pa chen po'i man ngag gi bstan bcos yid bzhin rin po che'i mdzod*). Published in *Seven Treasuries* (*mdzod bdun*), vol. 7, 1–137.

———. *Seven Treasuries* (*mdzod bdun*). 7 vols. Edited by Tarthang Tulku.

———. *White Lotus: Autocommentary of the Precious Wish-Fulfilling Treasury* (*theg pa chen po'i man ngag gi bstan bcos yid bzhin rin po che'i mdzod kyi 'grel pa padma dkar po*). Published in *Seven Treasuries* (*mdzod bdun*), vol. 7, 139–1544.

Maitreya. *Abhisamayālaṃkāra* (*mngon rtogs rgyan*). P.5184, vol. 88. Asian Classics Input Project, Release IV, TD3786.

———. *Dharmadharmatāvibhāga* (*chos dang chos nyid rnam par 'byed pa*). P.5523, vol. 108.

———. *Mahāyānasūtrālaṃkāra* (*theg pa chen po'i mdo sde rgyan gyi tshig le'ur byas pa*). P.5521, vol. 108.

———. *Uttaratantra* (*theg pa chen po rgyud bla ma'i bstan bcos*). P.5525, vol. 108; also in *theg pa chen po rgyud bla ma'i rtsa 'grel*. Sichuan, China: Nationalities Press, 1997.

Mipam (*'ju mi pham rgya mtsho*, 1846–1912). *Beacon of Certainty* (*nges shes sgron me*). Sichuan, China: Nationalities Press, 1997.

———. *Collected Works* (Dilgo Khyentsé's expanded redaction of *sde dge* edition). Kathmandu, Nepal: Zhechen Monastery, 1987.

———. *[Commentary on Changkya's] "Song of the View"* (*lta ba'i mgur ma*). In *Collected Works*, vol. 4 (*pa*), 821–67.

———. *Commentary on the Wisdom Chapter of the Bodhicaryāvatāra (spyod 'jug sher 'grel ke ta ka)*. Sichuan, China: Nationalities Press, 1993.

———. *Concise Summary of the Philosophies from the Wish-Fulfilling Treasury (yid bzhin mdzod kyi grub mtha' bsdus pa)*. *Collected Works*, vol. 21, 439–500.

———. *Difficult Points of Scriptures in General (dbu ma sogs gzhung spyi'i dka' gnad skor gyi gsung sgros sna tshogs phyogs gcig tu bsdus pa rin po che'i za ma tog)*. In *Collected Works*, vol. 22, 427–710.

———. *Eliminating Doubts (dam chos dogs sel)*. Published in *dbu ma rgyan rtsa 'grel*. Sichuan, China: Nationalities Press, 1990.

———. *A Feast on the Nectar of the Supreme Vehicle: Commentary on the Mahāyānasūtrālaṃkāra (theg pa chen po mdo sde'i rgyan gyi dgongs don rnam par bshad pa theg mchog bdud rtsi'i dga' ston)*. In *Collected Works*, vol. 2 (*a*), 1–760.

———. *Gateway to Scholarship (mkhas pa'i tshul la 'jug pa'i sgo)*. Published in *mkhas 'jug*. Qinghai, China: Nationalities Press, 1994.

———. *Light of the Sun (brgal lan nyin byed snang ba)*. Published in *spyod 'jug sher 'grel ke ṭa ka*, 465–579. Sichuan, China: Nationalities Press, 1993.

———. *Light of Wisdom: Commentary on the Dharmadharmatāvibhāga (chos dang chos nyid rnam 'byed 'grel pa ye shes snang ba)*. In *Collected Works*, vol. 4 (*pa*), 609–58.

———. *Lion's Roar: Exposition of Buddha-Nature (bde gshegs snying po'i stong thun chen mo seng ge'i nga ro)*. In *Collected Works*, vol. 4 (*pa*), 563–607.

———. *Overview: Essential Nature of Luminous Clarity (spyi don 'od gsal snying po)*. Published in *bka' brgyad rnam bshad dang spyi don 'od gsal snying po yang dag grub pa'i tshig 'grel bcas bzhugs*, 381–605. Sichuan, China: Nationalities Press, 2000.

———. *Shedding Light on Thusness (gzhan gyis brtsad pa'i lan mdor bsdus pa rigs lam rab gsal de nyid snang byed)*. Published in *spyod 'jug sher 'grel ke ta ka*, 133–463. Sichuan, China: Nationalities Press, 1993.

———. *Sword of Insight (don rnam par nges pa shes rab ral gri mchan bcas)*. In *Collected Works*, vol. 4 (*pa*), 787–820.

———. *Words of Mipam: Commentary on the Uttaratantra (theg pa chen po rgyud bla ma'i bstan bcos kyi mchan 'grel mi pham zhal lung)*. In *Collected Works*, vol. 4 (*pa*), 349–61.

———. *Words That Delight Guru Mañjughoṣa: Commentary on the Madhyamakālaṃkāra (dbu ma rgyan gyi rnam bshad 'jam byangs bla ma dgyes pa'i zhal lung)*. Published in *dbu ma rgyan rtsa 'grel*. Sichuan, China: Nationalities Press, 1990.

Nāgārjuna. *Bodhicittavivaraṇa (byang chub sems gyi rnam par bshad pa)*. P.5470, vol. 103.

———. *Lokātītastava ('jig rten las 'das par bstod pa)*. P.2012, vol. 46.

———. *Mūlamadhyamakakārikā (dbu ma rtsa ba)*. P.5224, vol. 95.

———. *Ratnāvalī* (*rin chen phreng ba*). P.5658, vol. 95.

Nyoshül Khenpo (*smyo shul mkhan po 'jam dbyangs rdo rje*, 1931–1999). *Garland of Lapis: History of the Great Perfection (rang bzhin rdzogs pa chen po'i chos 'byung rig 'dzin brgyud pa'i rnam thar ngo mtshar nor bu baidurya'i phreng ba)*, vols. 1–2. Thimphu, Bhutan: Indraprastha Press, 1996.

Paṇchen Sonam Drakpa (*paṇ chen bsod nams grags pa*, 1478–1554). *Clear Lamp (rnam bshad snying po rgyan gyi don rigs lam bzhin du gsal bar 'chad pa'i yum don yang gsal sgron me). Collected Works*, vol. 4. Mundgod, India: Drepung Loseling Library Society, 1985.

Pari Lozang Rapsel (*dpa' ris blo bzang rab gsal*, 1840–1910). *Ornament of Mañjughoṣa's Viewpoint ('jam dpal dbyangs kyi dgongs rgyan rigs pa'i gzi 'bar gdong lnga'i sgra dbyangs)*. In *Collected Works*, 354–412. Xining, China: Nationalities Press, 1998.

Purbu Tsering (*phur bu tshe ring*), ed. *The Dictionary of Internal Knowledge (nang rig pa'i tshig mdzod)*. Beijing, China: Nationalities Press, 1994.

Rongtön Sheja Kunrik (*rong ston shes bya kun rig*, 1367–1449). *Commentary on the Uttaratantra (rgyud bla ma'i 'grel pa)*. Published in *bde gshegs snying po rigs kyi chos skor*, 89–206. Dharamsala, India: Institute of Tibetan Classics, 2007.

Sakya Paṇḍita (*sa skya paṇḍita*, 1182–1251). *Clear Differentiation of the Three Vows (sdom gsum rab dbye)*. Published in Jared Douglas Rhoton, trans. *A Clear Differentiation of the Three Codes*. Albany, N.Y.: SUNY Press, 2002.

———. *Elegant Sayings of the Sakya (sa skya legs bshad)*. Qinghai, China: Nationalities Press, 2006.

Śāntarakṣita. *Madhyamakālaṃkāra (dbu ma rgyan)*. P.5284, vol. 101; also in *dbu ma rgyan rtsa 'grel*. Sichuan, China: Nationalities Press, 1990.

Śāntideva. *Bodhicaryāvatāra (byang chub sems dpa'i spyod pa la 'jug pa)*. P.5272, vol. 99; also in *byang chub sems dpa'i spyod pa la 'jug pa rtsa ba dang 'grel ba*. Sichuan, China: Nationalities Press, 1990.

Tāranātha (*jo nang rje btsun tā ra nā tha*, 1575–1634). *Essence of Other-Emptiness (gzhan stong snying po). Collected Works ('dzam thang* ed.), vol. 18, 171–93.

Tenzin Lungtok Nyima (*bstan 'dzin lung rtogs nyi ma*). *The Great History of Dzokchen (snga 'gyur rdzogs chen chos 'byung chen mo)*. Beijing, China: Nationalities Press, 2004.

Tsongkhapa (*tsong kha pa blo bzang grags pa*, 1357–1419). *Essence of Eloquence (drang nges legs bshad snying po). Collected Works*, vol. 14. Lhasa, Tibet: Zhol spar khang. Asian Classics Input Project, Release IV, S5396.

———. *The Great Exposition of the Stages of the Path (lam rim chen mo)*. Qinghai, China: Nationalities Press, 2000/1985.

———. *Great Stages of Mantra (sngags rim chen mo)*. Qinghai, China: Nationalities Press, 1995.

———. *The Lesser Exposition of the Stages of the Path (lam rim chung ba). Collected Works*, vol. 21, 1–438. New Delhi, India: Ngawang Gelek Demo, 1979.

———. *Thoroughly Illuminating the Viewpoint (dgongs pa rab gsal)*. Sarnath, India: Central Institute of Higher Tibetan Studies, 1998. Asian Classics Input Project, Release IV, S5408.

Tupten Tsültrim Namdak (*thub bstan tshul khrim rnam dag*). *Nourishment for Faith: A Short Hagiography of Bötrül (rje kun gzigs bod sprul bstan pa'i nyi ma'i rnam thar bsdus pa dad pa'i gsos sman)*. In Bötrül, *Collected Works*, vol. 1, 1–46. Sichuan, China: Nationalities Press, 2004.

Vasubandhu. *Abhidharmakośa (chos mngon pa'i mdzod)*. P.5509, vol. 115. Asian Classics Input Project, Release IV, TD4089.

Non-Tibetan Sources

Brunnhözl, Karl. *Straight from the Heart: Buddhist Pith Instructions*. Ithaca, N.Y.: Snow Lion Publications, 2007.

Cabezón, José. *A Dose of Emptiness: An Annotated Translation of the sTong thun chen mo of mKhas grub dGe legs dpal bzang*. Albany, N.Y.: SUNY Press, 1992.

Cabezón, José and Geshe Lobsang Dargyay. *Freedom from Extremes: Gorampa's "Distinguishing the Views" and the Polemics of Emptiness*. Boston: Wisdom Publications, 2007.

Callahan, Elizabeth, trans. *Treasury of Knowledge: Frameworks of Buddhist Philosophy*. Ithaca, N. Y.: Snow Lion Publications, 2007.

Conze, Edward. *The Large Sutra on Perfect Wisdom*. Berkeley, Calif.: University of California Press, 1975.

———. *The Perfection of Wisdom in Eight Thousand Lines & Its Verse Summary*. Bolinas, Calif.: Four Seasons Foundation, 1973.

Cozort, Dan. *Unique Tenets of the Middle Way Consequence School*. Ithaca, N.Y.: Snow Lion Publications, 1998.

Dharmachakra Translation Committee, trans. *Middle Beyond Extremes: Maitreya's Madhyāntavibhāga with Commentaries by Khenpo Shenga and Ju Mipham*. Ithaca, N.Y.: Snow Lion Publications, 2006.

———. *Luminous Essence: A Guide to the Guhyagarbhatantra*. Ithaca, N.Y.: Snow Lion Publications, 2009.

Doctor, Thomas, trans. *Speech of Delight: Mipham's Commentary on Śāntarakṣita's* Ornament of the Middle Way. Ithaca, N.Y.: Snow Lion Publicatons, 2004.

Dreyfus, Georges. *The Sound of Two Hands Clapping: The Education of a Tibetan Buddhist Monk*. Berkeley, Calif.: University of California Press, 2003.

———. *Recognizing Reality*. Albany, N.Y.: SUNY Press, 1997.

Duckworth, Douglas. *Mipam on Buddha-Nature*. Albany, N.Y.: SUNY Press, 2008.

Dudjom Rinpoche. *The Nyingma School of Tibetan Buddhism*, vol. 1. Translated and edited by Gyurme Dorje and Matthew Kapstein. Boston: Wisdom Publications, 1991.

Eckel, Malcolm David. *Jñānagarbha's Commentary on the Distinction Between the Two Truths*. Albany, N.Y.: SUNY Press, 1987.

Fuchs, Rosemary, trans. *Buddha Nature: The Mahayana Uttaratantra Shastra*. Ithaca, N.Y.: Snow Lion Publications, 2000.

Germano, David. "Re-membering the Dismembered Body of Tibet." In *Buddhism in Contemporary Tibet*, edited by Melvyn Goldstein and Matthew Kapstein, 53–94. Berkeley, Calif.: University of California Press, 2003.

Hookham, Shenpen. *The Buddha Within*. Albany, N.Y.: SUNY Press, 1991.

Hopkins, Jeffrey. *Emptiness in the Mind-Only School*. Berkeley, Calif.: University of California Press, 1999.

———. *Maps of the Profound*. Ithaca, N.Y.: Snow Lion Publications, 2003.

———. *Meditation on Emptiness*. London: Wisdom Publications, 1983.

———. *Reflections on Reality*. Berkeley, Calif.: University of California Press, 2002.

Lopez, Donald. *A Study of Svātantrika*. Ithaca, N.Y.: Snow Lion Publications, 1987.

Mipham, Jamgön Rinpoche. *Gateway to Knowledge*, vol. 3. Translated by Erik Pema Kunsang. Hong Kong, China: Rangjung Yeshe Publications, 2002.

Napper, Elizabeth. *Dependent Arising and Emptiness*. Boston: Wisdom Publications, 2003/1989.

Ngawang Jorden. "Buddha-nature: Through the Eyes of Go rams pa bsod rnams seng ge in Fifteenth-Century Tibet." Ph.D. thesis, Harvard University, 2003.

Newland, Guy. *The Two Truths*. Ithaca, N.Y.: Snow Lion Publications, 1992.

Obermiller, Eugene. *The History of Buddhism in India and Tibet*. Delhi, India: Paljor Publications, 1999; originally published as *History of Buddhism*, vol. 2. Heidelberg, Germany: In kommission bei O. Harrassowitz, 1931–32.

Phuntsho, Karma. *Mipham's Dialectics and the Debates on Emptiness*. London: RoutledgeCurzon, 2005.

Powers, John, trans. *Wisdom of the Buddha: The Saṃdhinirmocana Mahāyāna Sūtra*. Berkeley, Calif.: Dharma Publishing, 1995.

Prebish, Charles. *Luminous Passage: The Practice and Study of Buddhism in America*. Berkeley, Calif.: University of California Press, 1999.

Roerich, George, trans. *Blue Annals*. Delhi, India: Motilal Banarsidass, 1988.

Ruegg, David Seyfort. "On the dGe lugs pa Theory of the *tathāgathagarbha*." In *Pratidānam*, edited by J.C. Heesterman. The Hague, The Netherlands: Mouton, 1968: 500–509.

———. *Two Prolegomena to Madhyamaka Philosophy*. Wien, Austria: Arbeitskreis für Tibetische und Buddhistische Studien, 2002.

———. *Three Studies in the History of Indian and Tibetan Madhyamaka Philosophy*. Wien, Austria: Arbeitskreis für Tibetische und Buddhistische Studien, 2000.

Samuel, Geoffrey. *Civilized Shamans*. Washington, D.C.: Smithsonian Institution Press, 1993.

Scott, Jim, trans. *Maitreya's Distinguishing Phenomena and Pure Being*. Ithaca, N.Y.: Snow Lion Publications, 2004.

Stearns, Cyrus. *The Buddha from Dolpo: A Study of the Life and Thought of the Tibetan Master Sherab Gyaltsen*. Albany, N.Y.: SUNY Press, 1999.

Suzuki, D. T., trans. *The Laṅkāvatāra Sūtra*. London, U. K.: Routledge, 1968.

Tarthang Tulku. *Crystal Mirror*, vol. 5. Emeryville, Calif.: Dharma Publishing, 1971.

Tsong-ka-pa. *Tantra in Tibet: The Great Exposition of Secret Mantra.* Introduced by the Dalai Lama, translated and edited by Jeffrey Hopkins. London, U. K.: George Allen & Unwin, 1977.

Tulku Thondup. *Buddha Mind: An Anthology of Longchen Rabjam's Writings on Dzogpa Chenpo.* Ithaca, N.Y.: Snow Lion Publications, 1989.

———. *Masters of Meditation and Miracles.* Boston: Shambhala, 1996.

Index